Band Director's Complete Handbook

Donald E. Bollinger

Parker Publishing Company, Inc.
West Nyack, New York

Library of Congress Cataloging in Publication Data

Bollinger, Donald E.
    Band director's complete handbook.

    Bibliography: p.
    Includes index.
    1. Bands (Music) I. Title.
MT733.B64   785'.06'7   78-20844
ISBN 0-13-055442-1

Printed in the United States of America

DEDICATION

To all of my students, past and present. Without their willing participation, the teaching methods presented in this book would not have been developed and proven to be valid.

ACKNOWLEDGMENTS

The author is indebted to the following individuals for their expert assistance:

Henry W. Tamutis for his excellent photographs;

Thomas P. Browne for his expertise in creating the artwork;

Larry Wilson for various marching band ideas;

All my colleagues who have influenced the development of the teaching methods found in this book;

And all those who gave permission to use excerpts from published materials.

ABOUT THE AUTHOR

Donald E. Bollinger has been Director of Bands and teacher of the Music Sequence in the Gowanda Central Schools, Gowanda, New York, for 22 years. He received two B.M. degrees from the Eastman School of Music of the University of Rochester, one in Applied Music and another in Public School Music Supervision. He received his M.M. from the Eastman School of Music, majoring in Music Literature and Pedagogy of Theory.

His military experience includes service with the Second Army Band, Advanced Bandsman training at the Naval School of Music, and eight years with the Fostoria, Ohio, National Champion V.F.W. Band.

Mr. Bollinger's high school bands have attained 26 "A" ratings in the past 18 years in New York State School Music Association competitions, competing in the highest categories of difficulty.

Among his writings are two works found in the Sibley Music Library of the Eastman School of Music, *The Use of the Trumpet in the Bach Church Cantatas* and *Pedagogy of the Trumpet*. While at the Naval School of Music, he did a research project entitled *Analysis of Four Major Theory Texts*, which is in the Naval School of Music reference library. He has been recently published in *The Instrumentalist*.

Mr. Bollinger is active in NYSSMA as an adjudicator, guest conductor, and Conference chaperone. He has been an advisor in the development of new music sequence materials for New York State. His school was one of the pilot schools for a new New York State offering, Comprehensive Foundations of Music, a course now used in the Gowanda Central Music Sequence.

WHAT THIS BOOK
WILL DO FOR YOU

This book gives you one in-depth source covering all aspects of teaching the complete band program. With this book as a master guide, you can develop a comprehensive, first-class band program without consulting other sources. The book indicates clearly and precisely how to expand your knowledge in every area of instrumental teaching. Dozens of resources are listed, covering every problem the band director will probably face. The book contains hundreds of tips for improving your teaching. These have been assimilated through years of formal education, taking part in daily problem-solving, and developing a stimulus-response approach to the teaching of each student.

This book is the result of my own 22 years of experience as a successful high school band director and, in addition, includes many ideas from other resources. The writing of this manual was initiated by the many formal and informal conferences that experienced band directors have with members of their profession. We all seem to encounter similar problems, which can be documented, with possible solutions, in one volume. The second factor leading to the writing of this book was the realization of the overwhelming complexity of the school band program when the author was working with student teachers who were about to enter the field of music education. Each year we discover new solutions to many of the problems we encounter in our profession; thus, the number of years of experience and the number of problem-solving mechanisms developed are directly proportional. Sharing this experience with you is the primary function of this book.

Quality performance is only one part of a successful program. Organization of the entire program into a cohesive and workable whole is the key to your success. This book deals equally with *performance* and *organization*, enabling you to organize each day's work efficiently and to solve everyday problems quickly and effectively. It offers advice and assistance on every aspect of your program and leads to more effective and efficient handling of your work by saving time, preventing errors, and improving performance.

The daily psychological set of lessons and rehearsals, as presented in this book, is based upon three principles. The *first* is the realization by the students and the teacher that *each session* together *must be* a *learning experience*; each lesson or rehearsal must be carefully and efficiently planned. If nothing is learned that will improve performance or musical comprehension, the experience has been unsuccessful. The *second* is the "Prove-it" theorum, the realization that *practice* is necessary to become proficient on an instrument; knowledge alone is not sufficient to assure successful performance. When we not only comprehend the musical problem at hand but also conquer it through quality practice and performance, we begin to develop a superior program. The *third* principle is the *acceptance of music as a language*. This automatically dictates the treatment of an instrumental music program as an academic subject, indicating that emphasis must be placed upon the development of intellectual and reading skills. "Rote" teaching should be used only when the intellectual approach fails or for specific reasons of teaching interpretation. You will gain a working knowledge of these principles and their successful application through use of this book.

   • **Chapter 1 shows you how to develop valid behavioral, philosophical, and psychological objectives for your band program.** Included are in-depth studies of how to evaluate your educational environment; how to develop positive relationships with the Board of Education, Administration, teachers, community, parents, and your students; and how to develop effective methods of motivation through solos, ensembles, academic grading of performance and practice time, friendships, praise, variation of curriculum, classroom atmosphere, and discipline. A detailed explanation of how to use behavioral objectives in music is a special feature of this chapter.

   • **Chapter 2 shows you how to organize and develop the prerequisites to a fine school band program.** Included are detailed plans for preband preparation, the beginner program, the elementary band, and the junior high band. Several preband methods are investigated, including Orff, Kodaly, Suzuki, tonette, flutophone, recorder, and percussion classes. Thorough explanations of the use of the foot to count and rhythmic flash cards are given. How to form a successful beginner program is covered in detail: when to start beginners, testing and choosing beginners, and using musical aptitude tests. A special feature of this chapter is a unique plan for evaluating and recruiting your beginner candidates, a plan that assures getting the best possible students for your program. Details are given on post-testing procedures: how to create proper balance in your beginning program, how to secure satisfactory beginner instruments, and how to select effective beginner materials. Comprehensive plans for developing successful performing elementary and junior high bands are presented, including their function in the overall program, their size and physical organization, how to rehearse these groups, what materials and repertoire to use, and plans for rehearsal routines and scheduling.

• **Chapter 3 shows you how to develop and maintain the physical aspects of your program.** These include personnel considerations, size of groups, feeder system, instrumentation, and band seating charts. Symphonic band, concert band, and the wind ensemble are discussed in detail. Included are their relative sizes, scheduling, and instrumentation. Comments by Dr. Frederick Fennell, founder of the wind ensemble concept, and Dr. Donald Hunsberger, present conductor of the Eastman Wind Ensemble, are included. Solutions to physical problems of rehearsal and performing areas, using risers, handling reverberation problems, using the Leonard Smith directional brass concept, and so on are discussed in detail. A special feature of this chapter is the diagramming of several seating plans to help you to choose the best seating arrangements for your concert groups under various indoor and outdoor conditions.

• **Chapter 4 is a detailed study of how to develop successful programming and repertoire for your bands.** Many suggestions are given for symphonic band, concert band, and wind ensemble repertoires, including specific selections for each group. Motivating through popular music and band competitions is discussed. Representative repertoire is given for all types of band music. Specific steps are given for effective programming, concert content, and program variation. Special features of this chapter are charted methods of programming several groups throughout the entire school year and sample concert programs.

• **Developing tone, intonation, technique, and rhythm through the band medium is presented in Chapter 5.** Detailed warmup routines for rehearsals are given, including exercises to develop tone, intonation, tonguing, fingering, and counting techniques. How to use warmup routines, warmup chorales, hymns, and warmup numbers is discussed in detail. Examples are given to help you to create effective lesson plans for rehearsals. A special feature of this chapter is a detailed plan to involve your percussion section in band warmups.

• **You will find Chapter 6 valuable in your teaching of style and interpretation through band literature.** Objective and subjective interpretation are discussed in detail. You will learn how to choose materials to be used in the teaching of style. Specific devices and musical examples show you how to teach interpretation through marches of various styles, Broadway musicals, popular music, and jazz. You can learn how to use original recordings and media presentations as interpretive guides and how to use students to help interpret contemporary popular music. Various methods of interpreting Latin rhythms, orchestral and keyboard transcriptions, original band compositions, and contemporary and avant-garde music are discussed in detail.

• **Chapter 7 shows you how to develop an effective summer program.** It includes detailed plans for starting beginners in the summer, scheduling beginners, materials to use, evaluating your beginners, and setting up your complete summer lesson schedule. Comprehensive outlines are given for the development of a specific curriculum for each summer session and for keeping summer attendance records.

• **Chapter 8 covers every aspect of the stage band program, how to start the stage band, and how to develop all of the musical aspects of the stage band, including tone quality, intonation, range, volume, technique, rhythmic concepts, phrasing, and interpretation.** Lists of books, articles, and recordings pertaining to the stage band are included. Improvisation is discussed in detail; lists of books and articles on improvisation are included. The use of transposition as a valuable technique for the stage band musician is discussed. Choosing proper literature, developing a combo, and finding sources for stage band materials and information are also included. Of special interest is a selected bibliography of articles from *The Instrumentalist*.

• **Chapter 9 shows you how to develop an effective marching band program.** Detailed explanations are given of how to evaluate your marching band resources (personnel, equipment, and so on), the advantages of a large marching band, and how to develop the elementary and junior high bands. The traditional marching band is compared in detail with the "corps" approach, including a contrast of parade marching and football shows. A unique plan for a concert band to march in seven days of outside rehearsal is presented for the band director who must march once a year but does not have a marching band program. Detailed plans are presented for developing the marching fundamentals for a corps-type marching program, planning corps-type shows, and scheduling the marching band. Tips are given on how to develop a marching percussion section, how to improve brass playing on the march, and how to develop a majorette corps, a flag line, and a color guard. Suggestions are made for selecting and arranging marching music and for finding detailed information on marching band techniques. A selected bibliography of articles from *The Instrumentalist* and sources for marching band texts round out this valuable chapter.

• **Chapter 10 shows you how to develop a comprehensive syllabus for all band instruments and includes a year-by-year program, outlined in detail for each instrument.** A general syllabus for elementary, junior high, and senior high bands is presented, which designates tone and intonation requirements, technical goals, and objectives for all instruments and general musical knowledge to be taught. Comprehensive lists of solo, ensemble, and method book materials are given for each instrument, and methods are presented for expanding study of literature through clef reading, transposition, and adapting various literature to all instruments.

• **Chapters 11 and 12 show you how to develop effective woodwind and brass syllabi.** A comprehensive plan for the teaching of each band instrument is presented from the first lesson until graduation. This includes lists of literature to be used, recordings, solos, ensembles, method books, and so on covering all levels of difficulty. A selected bibliography is found at the end of each instrument's presentation. The teaching of each instrument is approached through embouchure, tonguing, fingering, breathing, musical symbols, and materials to be used (listed according to level of difficulty).

• **Chapter 13 is an extremely important and valuable chapter for the band director who is not a percussion major.** A detailed and comprehensive plan is given for teaching snare drum rudiments, a method that will work for the teacher who is not a percussionist. A detailed syllabus is included for snare drum that includes a syllabic approach to the teaching of all types of rolls, a method that works musically and rhythmically, especially with younger students. Sticking and rhythmic syllables for all rudiments are charted concisely and can be duplicated for classroom teaching. Both simple (divisions of two) and compound (divisions of three) time are considered in teaching rolls musically to the younger student. Method books are listed for all levels of teaching tympani and mallet instruments. A selected bibliography of percussion articles and books is found at the end of the chapter.

• **Chapter 14 shows you how to teach general band skills in lessons and small ensembles.** Comprehensive outlines for warmup, practice, and lesson routines are given. Diagrams of the proper way to breathe on a wind instrument are found in this chapter. The chapter also includes detailed practice routines, giving the amount of time to be spent on each aspect, and specific routines and exercises for each instrument. Every band instrument is covered in detail, including embouchure exercises for brasses, an embouchure placement drill for clarinets, and a harmonic drill for flutes. Of particular value is the section on teaching rhythm through small ensembles and lessons and a special approach to teaching the four main types of rhythmic notation (the beat equals the eighth note, the quarter note, the half note, or the dotted-quarter note).

• **Chapter 15 shows you how to develop an outstanding band through solo and ensemble competitions, using solos and ensembles at all levels as motivating tools.** Recitals and concerto programs are discussed, and a sample program is given. Comprehensive information is given on how to choose effective literature for soloists and ensembles and how to prepare your students for solo and ensemble competitions. The chapter includes a detailed explanation of preparation, including specific suggestions on every musical aspect to be graded.

• **Chapter 16 covers every aspect of planning concert programs and preparing budgets, including publicity, program content, use of program notes, and the printed program.** Examples are given for each page of the printed program. Posters, press releases, and audio visual communication are discussed. This chapter tells you how to make effective use of the talents and abilities of individuals at your disposal, including performers, the audience, and individuals who help with the business aspects of your program (ushers, lighting crew, program typists, stage crew, and so on). A special seating chart diagrams how to set up an efficient stage crew. Detailed information is given on how to prepare requisitions and budgets. Sample requisitions are given for textbooks (method books), library materials, instructional supplies, equipment, maintenance and repair, audio-visual materials, building improvements, transportation requests, conference expenses, student registration fees, awards, and periodicals. A special section on how to set up an effective boosters organization completes the chapter.

• **Chapter 17 shows you how to efficiently organize the internal business of your band program.** This includes how to organize and file all aspects of your music library (band music, solos, ensembles, method books, and so on). A detailed library filing system is presented, a system that allows for unlimited expansion. Pictures of filing cabinets and folder filing racks are supplied. Detailed plans are given for organizing field trips and assembly programs; a sample itinerary is given. This chapter shows you how to use a rotating schedule to best advantage; detailed plans are presented and a sample schedule is given. Details are presented on how to objectively grade lessons and develop an effective evaluation and grading system. Evaluation tests are presented for all levels, and requirements are spelled out in detail for realistic evaluation of each level.

• **Chapter 18 shows you how to operate instrument maintenance and repair programs.** Details are given on simple repairs that can be done by the band director. Pictures are shown for built-in instrument storage lockers and a percussion center to provide proper instrument storage. Details are presented for setting up a repair department, building your own work bench, and developing your repair inventory. Information is given on the purchase of private instruments and mouthpieces, the pros and cons of reeds, and working with double reeds. Developing relationships with maintenance men, industrial arts teachers, and music dealers is discussed in detail. A selected bibliography is given for repair articles and books, plus resource materials for making and adjusting reeds.

• **Chapter 19 shows you how to give vocational guidance to band members and how to train practice teachers.** Detailed information is given on how to inform your students about career opportunities in music. Included is a detailed chart of music careers. How to develop an academic music sequence and a syllabus for each course is explained in detail. Outlines are given for Theory I and II and Comprehensive Foundations of Music offerings. This chapter also tells you how to write effective recommendations for your students. Detailed information is given on how to train and use practice teachers, which includes a practice teacher evaluation form. A selected bibliography of music career information books and articles is given at the end of the chapter.

• **Chapter 20 is full of useful aids and guidelines for the instrumental teacher, including conducting tips, score study, and reading tips.** A special approach to score study is explained. The use of audio-visual equipment, professional publications, and records in your teaching is discussed. Valuable publications are listed. A selected list of recording resources and a list of recordings for each instrument are given. Band, woodwind quintet, and brass ensemble recordings are included.

• **The five Appendices of this book may be its most valuable resource.** Appendix A contains comprehensive lists of method books, études, and supplementary materials for each band instrument, covering the entire program from beginners through high school. Appendix B lists selected solos for all band instruments graded according to difficulty. Appendix C contains selected small ensemble materials graded according to difficulty. Appendix D contains a comprehensive list of band music, including all types of music graded according to difficulty. Appendix E lists selected stage band charts and sources graded according to difficulty.

This is a large book physically and in terms of content. It contains a comprehensive treatment of hundreds of important daily details facing the band director. It is complete in its coverage of all aspects of the band program, from selecting beginners to performing at the highest levels of proficiency with advanced bands, ensembles, and soloists. I sincerely hope that it will bring as much success to your program as it has to mine.

Donald E. Bollinger

TABLE OF CONTENTS

HOW TO DEVELOP
VALID OBJECTIVES
FOR YOUR BAND PROGRAM

1

There are two types of objectives to consider when you establish goals for your program:

1) *Behavioral objectives*, which may be evaluated by measuring the tangible results of your teaching. These include various material goals that you set for evaluating your students' progress. Such goals are based upon *physical* and *musical skills* that the student is expected to perfect within a given time limit.

2) *Philosophical* and *psychological objectives*, which must be evaluated in a much less tangible manner, since they measure *relationships* and *attitudes* and do not usually set materially measurable goals.

Behavioral objectives should be considered specific objectives for music education. Philosophical and psychological goals should include general educational objectives, which deal with human relationships that must be developed within the context of the entire educational program. The latter goals are just as essential to the successful program as are the easily measurable behavioral objectives. The in-depth development of both categories will result in the ultimate success of your band program.

DEVELOPING A BASIC TEACHING APPROACH
THROUGH ESTABLISHED OBJECTIVES

Evaluating Your Educational Environment

Your objectives should be based upon a realistic appraisal of your teaching and learning situations. This includes evaluation of every aspect of your educational environment, such as:

1) physical plant

2) equipment

3) music staff availability and proficiency

4) available student personnel

5) administrative and general staff attitude toward music education

6) ethnic background of your community

7) attitude of your community toward music education

8) rural or urban values of your community in relation to their effect upon your students' attitudes toward the music program

Establishing Philosophical Teaching Goals

Consider the following philosophical goals that may be achieved through your work with your students:

1) Evaluate the learning potential of each of your students; establish a goal to *develop each student to the extent of his potential*, both intellectually and musically.

2) *Consider the importance of the individual*; work toward a goal of developing the individual in relation to his personal potential, background, and motivation.

3) *Stress* should be placed upon *the uninhibited nature of each student*; develop this musically *within* each *classroom situation*. Though discipline is maintained, the student's musical progress and freedom of musical expression should not be inhibited by an extreme control situation. An apprehensive student will not do his best work musically under very strict classroom conditions.

4) *Creating good motivation* at all times should be another primary goal and should be developed and expanded on a continuing basis.

5) *Develop a student-centered program of objectives.* Education should be student-centered, and all decisions should be based upon the welfare of the student, leading to the development of his talents and the completion of his preparation for a healthy mental, physical, and emotional life. Every student, regardless of the depth of his talents, should be developed to the extent of his potential. A student who believes in his individuality and his importance to your program will develop a pride and a self-discipline that cannot be developed by mass regimentation. A student-centered program is developed by consideration of the welfare of the individual student when you form objectives and make decisions affecting your students' roles in your program.

6) *Develop objectives based upon the student's complete life*, not just upon the time he spends with music. Consideration of the whole or complete student dictates that you be aware when developing objectives and

goals that the subject you are teaching is only a small part of what the student is to learn in public schools. It is a good teaching technique to develop relationships with other subjects when presenting your subject. Therefore, you should attempt to be a well-read and well-informed individual, and you should constantly update your knowledge and understanding in fields outside of your own certified area. Being reasonably knowledgeable in other subject areas helps you to insure that the overall education of each student may be properly correlated.

The whole student can be represented by a complete circle, the area of which is divided into pie-shaped wedges, each wedge representing a part of the student's education and outside interests. One wedge may represent music, another sports, another mathematics, and so on. His complete existence results from the understanding of and exposure to many educational stimuli. A circle that is not complete indicates a lack of some element or elements in that person's development which should be pursued in order to develop a well-rounded individual.

Your student has many fields of endeavor, and each may be equally important to him. Develop your share of his life as deeply and as broadly as possible, without infringing upon any of the other subject areas or interests contained in his circle. It is difficult to establish musical objectives realistically without serious consideration of these other activities and studies that make daily demands on your student's time. Ignoring any aspects of any individual's life may lead to loss of some of your better students, who are involved in many activities and who may respond negatively to excessive pressure to perform at a higher level musically. This can result in the student's having to spend more time with music than he is willing or able to give. You should consider whether any goal that puts a student into this situation is worth the possible loss of the student.

Goals 7 and 8 are based upon two *democratic principles: equal opportunity to learn* and *equal right to participate*.

7) *Each student should have equal opportunity to learn* and to excel on his instrument. Your teaching effort and teaching time should be given equally to each student, regardless of his innate musical talent. The less talented student is often neglected because of lack of ability; the most talented student is also sometimes neglected because he has the ability to "learn on his own."

8) *Every student* in your school system *has* the innate *right to take part* in any aspect *of the music program*. His continuance should be based upon satisfactory progress. "Select" groups should not exist unless a large group is available for the participation of those students who may be less talented, but desire to share in your music education offerings. Both participation and quality performance may be served if your band objectives are developed along valid music education guidelines.

General Objectives for Senior Band

1) To develop an *understanding for* and *appreciation of music* of all types in as many students as our program can possibly reach. Each student must maintain a set minimum standard of instrumental proficiency to remain in the program.

2) To develop the most talented students to the highest degree of *instrumental proficiency* possible while in our program, and to provide the opportunity for any who choose music as a career to obtain excellent pre-college preparation.

3) To develop within each student a *desire to support music and its related arts* upon graduation from our program.

As you consider this group of objectives, it becomes quite clear that all objectives and goals cannot be merely behavioral in nature. Valid goals leading to a successful program are usually broader and deeper than the measurement of obvious material objectives. Many of your objectives would grow from these goals, but your ultimate objectives will be unique to you personally since you will choose the components and the degree of emphasis. Ideas of your own will be included in your finalized objectives, resulting in a list of goals that can be modified many times during your teaching career.

DEVELOPING OBJECTIVES
IN RELATIONSHIPS WITH OTHERS

You are faced with the "Learning" or "Success" Triangle (See Figure 1) in your everyday teaching activities. It forms the basis for establishing your primary objectives in relationships with others. You must relate properly to the other two-thirds of the triangle, the parents and the stu-

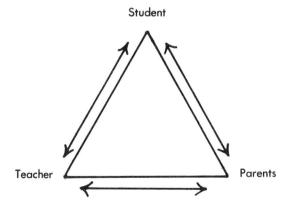

Figure 1. The "Learning" Triangle

dent. The important goals to set in this triangular relationship are the *establishing of good communication with parents* and the *gaining* of *their full support for your program* in general and for your work with their child in particular. Your objectives and goals should be based upon consideration of the student, the parents, and the teacher and their relative functions within the interrelationships of the "Learning" Triangle.

You should also develop professional relationships with other teachers and with your administration and school board. Goals in these areas include successful establishment of the following interrelationships:

1) Teacher/Administration and Board of Education
2) Teacher/Community
3) Teacher/Other Teachers in your school system
4) Teacher/Other Teachers within the Fine Arts Departments
5) Teacher/Business and Maintenance Staff
6) Teacher/Parents
7) Teacher/Student

Developing Positive Relationships with Administration and Board of Education

Your objective in developing and refining these relationships should be to *create a professional rapport* that possesses as little friction as possible and as much active support for your program as you can muster. This may be done by giving careful attention to the following:

1) Follow all school rules, regulations, and procedures.
2) Use proper channels of communication at all times.
3) Don't "rock the boat," though you may disagree with some school policies.
4) Be willing to use your talents and those of your students for functional school events.
5) Be willing to use these same talents for community events that may strengthen public relations.

Developing Community Support for Your Program

One of your objectives should be to develop community support for your program since it is a very valuable and powerful motivating force when you are dealing with Boards of Education and Administration. This support is an absolute necessity for the ultimate success of your program. Some important factors in establishing and maintaining community support are:

1) Your program's educational worth

2) Your willingness to use your personal resources and those of your instrumental program in community activities

3) Your personal relationships with your students, their parents, and other members of the community

Refining Teacher/Teacher Relationships
Outside the Fine Arts Departments

Many of your objectives should be based upon teacher/teacher relationships. These include the following:

1) Collective teaching of the whole student

This necessitates *developing flexibility and cooperation* in professional relationships *with other teachers.* You share each student with many other teachers, and each teacher has the right to reserve a part of the student's time for study of a particular subject. You should develop objectives of flexibility and cooperation in regard to sharing the student's time. Your direct relationship with other teachers is exemplified when students come to you for lessons having been released from other teachers' classes as a result of your rotating instrumental music lesson schedule. Occasionally, for example, a teacher may ask you to excuse a student from his lesson so that he may attend a very important class, a class that for some reason cannot be made up later. You also share students with other teachers in relation to after-school or evening activities. If you have developed a good relationship with each of the teachers in your school system, almost any conflict in relation to the student's time can be worked out to everyone's satisfaction. Never place a student in the middle, demanding that he choose between two conflicting educational opportunities. The student must sacrifice 50% of his educational experiences in this manner. It is also possible that you or the other teacher will lose the student permanently.

2) Establishing Equality of Importance
of Each Subject

If each teacher realizes that you consider his subject equal in importance to any other subject the student is taking, he is very likely to consider your subject, instrumental music, as equally important to the one he teaches. Equality of importance will work for the instrumental teacher only if he has earned this distinction through the educational value of his program. Instrumental music should therefore be taught as an academic subject, following as closely as possible the plan book and grading procedures of other subject areas. Education, not entertainment, should be stressed. When this approach is observed by other teachers, the educational impact upon them should be a very positive one. In addition, each student should consider all subjects he studies to be of equal importance if you are to succeed in developing the whole student.

3) Assisting Other Teachers in the Teaching of Their Subject Areas

Whenever the opportunity arises to assist other teachers, whether academically in the classroom (humanities approach) or through the musical resources of your band program, you should always respond positively. This is good not only for your establishment of a positive working relationship with other teachers, it also affords your student the opportunity to experience the interrelationships between the subjects he is studying. For example, in the presentation of Wagner's "Ring Cycle" to a mythology class, I was able to bridge the gap between the study of this epic work of art musically and study of the work within the context of mythological literature. The impact upon the students involved was a very positive one.

4) Supplying Musical Groups for Other Teachers' Activities

Employment of your musical groups to assist teachers in other academic areas in presenting programs of varying content (assembly programs, and so on) is an obvious use of the cross-relationship between the disciplines that should be established in a public school system. Taking advantage of these opportunities also gives your students many opportunities to perform functionally for their school.

Developing Objectives Within the Fine Arts Departments

Your objectives and goals in relationships with the Fine Arts departments should include the following:

1) Sharing of Talented Students

Sharing of talented students with the other members of the Fine Arts Staff of your school system is extremely important. Most moderately sized school systems have a limited number of talented students at the disposal of the music, art, and drama teachers. If all of these teachers are not willing to share students, they not only weaken their own ultimate talent resources, they also ignore the development of the whole student. If scheduling is properly worked out, there is no reason why a student cannot have experience in several of the arts. All of the arts programs will be strengthened when this procedure is adopted. Since methods of scheduling vary greatly from one school system to another, only one definite suggestion is given. *Schedule all arts-related programs at different times*;

never schedule them against one another, a situation that creates an either/or choice.

If you are in a moderately sized school, the cooperation among the choral, orchestral, and band instructors in the sharing of talented students is absolutely necessary for the highest possible degree of success for each group. It is always best to avoid scheduling conflicts before embarking upon development of cooperation and reinforcement of each other's programs.

2) Developing Goals and Objectives
Together as a Department

This refers to the Music Department if no Fine Arts Department is formally established. The program of a music department should be developed and maintained through the joint effort of all members of the music staff. At no time should major decisions be made unilaterally by the department chairman. The best professional and educational atmosphere for joint production of a fine music department must be developed through a team effort. For example, a syllabus for the instrumental program should be developed jointly by all instrumental teachers.

3) Establishing Each Teacher's Freedom
to Use His Individual Teaching Methods
to Reach the Department's Goals and Objectives

The department should establish ultimate goals for each subject area, but the individual teacher should have the freedom of reaching these goals by his own means. This is very important to the success of the individual teacher since most departments include teachers of varying formal educational background.

Developing Positive Relationships with Your Business and Maintenance Staff

Your main objective here is to create and maintain good rapport with the business and maintenance staff of your school system. Many times circumstances arise where their willingness to help will rescue you from a difficult situation. It is of utmost importance that you develop a relationship with these individuals that is not only cordial but that also creates a feeling of mutual respect and understanding. Never treat any of these individuals as anything but first-class citizens of the school and community. They can become the most valued friends you have within the school system. Their immediate assistance when unexpected problems arise can mean the difference between success and failure.

Establishing Objectives in
Relationships with Parents

Your relationships with parents should be treated with considerable care. The following objectives will help create positive results that grow from a strong teacher/parent relationship.

1) Develop Good Rapport

Establish yourself as a human being, well-rounded, and genuinely interested in the personal nonmusical interests of parents. Most parents expect a music teacher to be completely immersed in music, perhaps to the exclusion of other areas of human endeavor. When they find that you are interested in many things in addition to music, including things that are important to them in their everyday lives, it becomes increasingly easy to establish and maintain a condition of mutual trust and understanding.

2) Establish Good Communication Links
Between Your Program and Parents

The major problem in your teacher/parent relationships is communication. It is ultimately easier for a band director and his program to become known by the public than it is for most classroom teachers to communicate in a similar manner. Telling parents of the educational value of your program at "open houses" or similar events may be the only way most classroom teachers can communicate the content of their programs to parents, but you have the added advantage of demonstrating the educational value of your program every time you present a public performance. The more successful the performances you give before the public, the more support you should receive from them in return. If you communicate at these performances with some informative narration related to the numbers being presented, you have even more opportunity to influence your band parents and your community favorably in relation to the objectives of your band program. You must maintain a professional image, but at the same time you must exude a personal warmth that helps parents to identify with you as a part of the team that is developing the minds and esthetic values of their children.

3) Attempt to Solve Student Problems
Before Parents Become Directly Involved

You will have many opportunities to meet informally with parents outside of school hours. These opportunities should not be spent discussing school problems. If problems do arise with particular students, the parents are to be contacted only when all other means of solving the problem have failed. The mutual relationship and trust that you must establish with each of your students can be destroyed if you take a problem to the parents before you have attempted to solve it with the student. If your relationship with your students is one of high rapport, very few problems cannot be solved between you and the student involved. Both parents and students are very appreciative of this approach.

4) Do Not Alienate Parents When a Parent/Teacher Conference Becomes Necessary

If you finally are forced to contact a parent, approach the situation as one of mutual concern to the parent and the teacher, with the ultimate result of your conversation being to positively benefit the student in question. Do not alienate the parents, no matter how difficult the situation may be. Without their consent and assistance, you cannot effect a satisfactory conclusion to the problem. It is always best to attempt to solve these problems in a meeting with the parents, where eye contact makes possible immediate assessment of the progress you are making toward a satisfactory solution to the problem. Talking on the telephone or corresponding by letter are seldom as successful and can easily lead to misunderstandings and possible negative resolution of the problem.

5) Use Your Administration and Guidance Department to Assist in Teacher/Parent Relationships

Sometimes it is a better procedure to work through your principal or guidance counselor if the problem with the student is a serious one. They are more familiar with the handling of difficult student/teacher/parent situations and have been trained formally to handle them in the best way possible for the good of the student's overall education.

6) Create a Direct Approach to Parents for Assistance Through Their Support of Your Program and Its Goals and Objectives

The direct approach to parents, asking for support of your program and explaining very candidly how they may help you, can bring about favorable results. An "Open Letter to Senior Band Parents" is an example of this approach to parental motivation. Objectives and goals involved in the use of this type of letter include the following:

a) Securing parental support for your program by parent attendance at performances

b) Having the parents supply their child with a satisfactory instrument

c) Securing the parents' help in encouraging proper practice habits

    d) Securing parental assistance in getting students to all performances

    e) Securing parental encouragement directed toward the student's developing of his talents to the best of his ability

Developing Objectives in Teacher/Student Relationships

Teacher/student relationships are extremely complex, no two of these ever being quite the same. You see your students daily under all circumstances, and you work with human stimulus-response patterns that can become very sensitive and complicated. You should be aware of your students' oscillating emotional patterns and calmly understanding and patient when a student is upset. However, you should seek to motivate your students, regardless of their psychological set when they enter your classroom. You should be able to change that set within a few moments to a psychological set conducive to creating fine music together.

Your objectives in teacher/student relationships should include the following:

1) Cultivation of Individual Student Interests, Creating a Bond of Mutual Interests Between the Teacher and the Student

Your first step is the development of good rapport with each of your students, which not only includes showing understanding and patience in times of stress but also demonstrates a genuine regard for each student's personal interests outside the field of music. Again, being a well-rounded individual is not only important, but absolutely necessary. If a student is interested in basketball, discuss the subject with him whenever the opportunity presents itself. If he is interested in art, draw him into discussions of various phases of art that interest him. If he enjoys Civil War history, discuss this subject with him whenever it is opportune. Use various audio-visual materials to cultivate these mutual interests; these may include books, slides, and magazine and newspaper articles that relate to subjects of student interest. Always show a genuine interest in your student's activities; "faking" this interest will most certainly bring negative results to your relationship.

2) Development of a "Professional Personality"

Your second step is the development of a "professional personality" that always has a healthy psychological set toward the musical job to be done, regardless of the problems you may be facing personally outside the classroom. This means creating a personality that on the surface is pleasant and unchanging day after day. You must strive to develop this pure teaching personality, even though you realize as a human being that you will weaken at times and show anger and impatience.

3) Development of Goals Based upon Stimulus-Response Situations Occuring Within a Pleasant and Relaxed Classroom

You are now ready to work within a relatively pure learning atmosphere, devoid of your own personal problems and prejudices. The pleasant and relaxed atmosphere of your classroom begins immediately to affect the psychological set of your students. By applying stimulus-response mechanisms, you set forth to discover how far and how deeply you may proceed with the students during a given class period, always being cognizant of the students' reactions to your stimuli and making immediate adjustments in your presentation if you feel you are failing to bring all members of the class with you to the lesson's ultimate conclusion.

DEVELOPING EFFECTIVE METHODS OF MOTIVATION

Motivation is a very important objective in teacher/student relationships. Methods of student motivation fall into both categories of objectives; some are tangible behavioral objectives, but many are less measurable psychological objectives. The following are methods of motivation that will bring considerable success to your program on a daily basis. Each should be established as an objective.

1) Using the "Challenge" System

This system of motivation is familiar to all instrumental teachers. Its advantages in motivating better performing proficiency are quite obvious, but the harm such a system does may outweigh its advantages. It may motivate the student to practice more diligently, but it certainly transforms what should be a pleasant experience into one of apprehension and even distaste. It is an advantage for the serious, the exceptionally talented, and the aggressive student; but it can become a nightmare for the average student. The great majority of your groups are made up of what may be considered average students, not only in ability but also in dedication. Your program will fail without these individuals, and many of them may be lost through a pure challenge system. A modified system that recognizes the individuality of the student in addition to performance criteria can be workable and advantageous. Evaluations may be made at regular intervals, and seating adjusted by the director, without the traumatic experience of a pure everyday challenge system. Your band should trust your judgment in making seating decisions by the evaluation of each student privately at previously announced times and on previously announced material. You should avoid "head-to-head combat," especially when it is done in front of the students' peers.

2) Developing Motivation Through Solos, Ensembles, and Special Performances

Motivating through solos, ensembles, and special performances is a very positive method of creating a good psychological set toward fine musical performances. There is no substitute for the pressure of a coming public performance in motivating the student to study diligently. It is much more difficult to motivate a student to study étude material than it is to motivate him to properly prepare performance material. The obvious value of any ensemble material lies in the fact that it is more fun and more challenging to play different parts together than it is to play them in unison. Solos, however, remain the strongest motivating factor since the success of the performance is entirely dependent upon the preparation of the individual student.

3) Using Academic Grading and Grades for Practice Time as Motivation

The academic grading of the student's musical progress will have a strong influence on motivation, considering that most of your band members are strong academic students. If a student believes he is being graded objectively, based upon his actual musical performance in lessons and rehearsals, he is likely to be well-prepared because he has developed a pride in being the recipient of good academic grades. Giving a grade for outside practice time, a grade that is averaged into the student's final band mark, is another method of achieving proper motivation.

4) Using Student Friendships as a Motivation Tool

Not only the students' friendships for each other should be considered, but also the friendship that can be nurtured between the student and his teacher. Your students are young adults, and there is no reason to believe that valid friendships, based upon common interests and mutual concerns that grow from working closely together, cannot be effected. You should depend upon the students' maturity in the development of these friendships, always being careful to assure that they stay within the confines of a professionally controlled relationship.

Students' friendships for each other many times determine your success in recruiting, and in keeping, individuals in your program. If you have the misfortune of losing an individual who has many friends in your organization and is influential with his peers, you may well lose several band members before the situation resolves itself. You also can insure harmony and good musical results by carefully using student friendships in the form of peer pressure to solve minor motivation and discipline problems.

Combining close friends in lesson and ensemble situations whenever possible helps to create a good working atmosphere in your classroom. Know each of your students individually, not only through your class contact with him, but also through study of his home environment and his record in school and the community.

5) Using Praise as a Motivating Factor

Praise, along with necessary constructive criticism, is very important in properly motivating the individual student. Be sure praise is given uniformly throughout the group, even though some individuals may be outstanding and deserving of more praise than others. You should always avoid any possibility of "teacher's pets" being established, whether unknowingly by the teacher or in the minds of the students.

6) Motivating Through Variation

The curriculum you use in rehearsals and lessons can have a strong effect upon the positive psychological set of your students. Varying the literature and teaching approach will create fresh interest, where lack of variation will cause stagnation. Routines are valuable tools, but they may begin to work negatively if they are slavishly adhered to without variation.

7) Creating Proper Classroom Atmosphere

Your classroom atmosphere should be pleasant and should exhibit a degree of relaxation so that the student may work up to his potential without inhibition. I have told my students on many occasions to feel relaxed physically and emotionally during lessons and rehearsals but to be extremely alert mentally. If you can effect this atmosphere in your rehearsals and lessons, your students will play musically; "up-tight" rehearsals tend to produce the right notes but little musical warmth.

8) Motivating Through Discipline

I believe in developing personal discipline, both in lessons and in rehearsals, stressing that the student must care enough for what he is doing and for the welfare of his fellow musicians to discipline his actions accordingly. Of course, you should be in control at all times, but once the majority of your group understands personal discipline the students tend to solve discipline problems for you through peer pressure. This approach requires equal parts of wisdom, patience, and courage, but once it is established your discipline problems are minimal.

9) Using Teacher Participation
in Performance as a Motivating Tool

Your participation as a performer can have a very positive effect in motivating your students. You may appear as a soloist with your band in a concert, or you may join some members of your band in presenting an ensemble performance. Using a guest or student conductor upon occasion frees the director to play with the band in some capacity. Playing with your students during lessons is also an excellent motivation tool, assuming that you play well and motivate the students to improve by imitation. Any method you use to become actively involved in the musical development of your students will work to your advantage, especially if it happens to include popular music. You should establish yourself in the minds of your students not only as a fine musician but also as a human being. This leads to the creation of a "team" atmosphere in rehearsals and performances instead of a "lord-serf" relationship between the conductor and his students. This procedure should result in an increase in your band's respect for you, even though the authoritative image may not be as obvious in your approach.

10) Developing the "Prove-It" Game

The "Prove-It" game can be very helpful in creating self-motivation and self-discipline. If you convince your group to live by the "Prove-It" theorum, you will find they will be properly prepared for performances, lessons, and evaluations. The theorum simply states that actions, not words, indicate whether you are capable of doing a particular act, an act that may be proper performance of a composition or proper behavior in a rehearsal. This is a behavioral objective since the performance and the behavior of a student can be tangibly measured. You should be willing to enter into the "Prove-It" game also, which dictates that you should be able to do, within reason, the things you ask your students to do. You should not only be a fine innate musician, but you should also be able to perform on each instrument to at least an intermediate level. This procedure is an advantage for a strong teacher if you must teach all the band instruments yourself and are not able to rely upon private experts on each instrument to help train your students. The "Prove-It" game quickly exposes the student or the teacher who is not well prepared in the performance idiom.

11) Motivating by Proper Preparation

Proper preparation in all aspects of your program has a strong impact upon the psychological set of your students. A simple thing, such as not having the rehearsal area properly set up when a rehearsal is scheduled to begin, can destroy the psychological set of your band before a note is played. If you do not have a definite plan for each rehearsal and each lesson, you may destroy the optimum learning atmosphere for your students. Always be prepared, whether your lesson plans are in your head or written. If you appear to be confused or struggling during a rehearsal or a lesson, your students may soon lose confidence in your leadership ability.

Any weakness on your part when you are on the podium may undermine your band's confidence in you and in your group's ability to succeed. If you do make mistakes, as we all do occasionally, admit your mistakes honestly and openly. Do not attempt to cover up your errors; most well-trained students will catch the errors and your cover-up.

BEHAVIORAL OBJECTIVES IN MUSIC

In recent years behavioral objectives have become extremely important in planning public school curriculum syllabi. Educators believe that specific educational goals will be reached more successfully if students work within the context of this method. Many schools have adopted plans of behavioral objectives for their academic programs, and progressive music departments have developed similar methods of evaluation so that they may be prepared for the day when they are asked to justify their programs on the basis of behavioral objectives.

Behavioral objectives are not new to music educators; as in the case of many "new" concepts in education, we have been using this method for many years. All tangible goals that are based upon student achievement are behavioral objectives. These are measured by both individual and group performance. When you develop a syllabus for your instrumental program, your evaluation of each student's progress is based upon what you believe the student should be able to play technically and understand musically at certain points in his development. If your goals have been specific ones, not generalities, you have been working with behavioral objectives.

An excellent source for development of behavioral objectives is *A Taxonomy for Behavioral Objectives in Music* by Lloyd Schmidt, Music Consultant, Connecticut State Department of Education, Bureau of Elementary and Secondary Education, Hartford, Conn. A free copy can be obtained upon request. Mr. Schmidt's definition of behavioral objectives in music will give you valid guidelines for developing this procedure:

> Behavioral objectives simply provide a procedure for stating the musical behavior which is expected to result from a learning experience. A good objective states in clearest possible terms what the learner will do under what *conditions* and to what *extent*.
>
> The objective specifies:
> 1. The desired performance.
> 2. The situations and conditions in which the outcome is expected to occur.
> 3. The extent to which the performance must be accomplished.

> 4. The implied measuring device to determine the success in achieving the objective should be apparent.[1]

Under these conditions, which of the following is an acceptable behavioral objective?

1) At the end of two years of study a cornet student should be able to play the first seven major scales.

2) At the end of two years of study a cornet student should be able to play the major scales of C, F, G, B-flat, D, E-flat, and A through one octave ascending and descending in 16th notes at m.m.= 60.

The first statement is a generality, not dictating the number of octaves nor the tempo involved in the evaluation of the goal stated. The second statement is specific, stating a definite behavioral objective to be evaluated.

Two types of behavioral objectives may be used, those used in measuring individual performance and those used in measuring ensemble performance. You may be very specific in the measurement of individual achievement; the specific measurement of ensemble performance is a bit more difficult.

Here are two additional samples of behavioral objectives that can be used in the development of individual instrumental syllabi. The first example of each objective is unsatisfactory since it lacks the specificity required for an effective behavioral objective.

Example 1. Subject—flute vibrato

A. The flutist will be able to play with vibrato at the end of two years of study.

B. The flutist will begin formal development of vibrato at the end of the first year of study, and he will be able to produce controlled vibrato at two, three, and four pulsations to a beat (m.m.= 60) by the end of the second year of study.

Example 2. Subject—clarinet tonguing

A. The clarinetist will be able to tongue sixteenth notes by the end of two years of study.

B. The clarinetist will be able to tongue consecutive sixteenth notes on a repeated pitch (m.m. = 72) to the duration of nine beats by the end of his second year of study. (The ninth beat shall be a quarter note.)

Behavioral objectives used in evaluation of ensemble performance are

---

[1]Lloyd Schmidt, *A Taxonomy for Behavioral Objectives in Music*, August, 1971, p. 1.

similar but may not be as specific in some cases. The first example given below is unsatisfactory because it lacks sufficient specificity.

Example. Subject—band technique

A. The band will be able to play the B-flat concert scale in sixteenth notes at the end of the second week of rehearsals.

B. At the end of the second week of rehearsals the full band will be able to play the B-flat concert scale with acceptable precision in sixteenth notes at m.m. = 96, three consecutive times of one octave ascending and descending. (There is a lack of definition involved in evaluating acceptable precision; this is determined by your standard of good precision.)

Band technique may be evaluated in this manner, but such musical elements as intonation, balance, dynamic nuances, tone quality, and musical feeling cannot be measured in specific terms. Their evaluation results from the individual opinion or judgment of the conductor. Therefore, we must conclude that not all musical objectives can be purely behavioral objectives.

The following facts should be contained in a satisfactory behavioral objective for instrumental music:

1. Exact definition of the specific act to be performed
   Example—G Major scale; two octaves, ascending and descending

2) Tempo and rhythm pattern to be used
   Example—m.m. = 96; sixteenth notes

3) Duration involved in specific performance
   Example—two consecutive times, a total of 16 beats

4) Point in study at which objective should be reached
   Example—at the end of two years of study

There is a genuine concern in relation to measuring objectives that are not purely physical or tangible in nature. I have explained various ways by which intellectual, psychological, or philosophical objectives may be developed. Whether these objectives are called behavioral or not is a matter of semantics. Only an approximate measurement of these may be made by substituting a material objective; however, this may be the best method we have of measuring the intangible. Many elements that are purely musical cannot be measured by exact material evaluation. We must conclude that if a goal is not purely material, its measurement cannot be purely material.

This chapter has presented several types of goals and objectives. Behavioral objectives alone are not sufficient to cover all objectives you should set for your program. Music is not just technique, but its subtleties and its dependence upon the intangible elements of human behavior and esthetic feeling dictate an establishment of other types of objectives. The successful program will be the result of the blending of these different types of objectives into a strong, cohesive program. The evaluation of the ultimate performance of a student, an ensemble, or your entire band is the most accurate measurement of your program's success. This measurement should always include both the tangible and the intangible aspects of that performance; to ignore the intangible would be to turn the musician into a machine and to relegate the production of music to a predictable mechanical act.

HOW TO ORGANIZE
PRE-BAND, BEGINNER,
AND YOUNGER BAND PROGRAMS

2

The success of your high school band program is very dependent upon the foundation a student receives in the lower grades, beginning with his formal background in kindergarten general music classes. When a student enters high school, he should have developed a deep and varied background in music as an art form and as a language and should have developed an interest in and an enjoyment of music as a part of his everyday life. You may help mold this background by becoming involved in the planning of the music education of the younger student.

DEVELOPING INTEREST IN THE PROGRAM
THROUGH PRE-BAND PREPARATION

Early general music classes are extremely important; they not only influence the student's attitude toward future participation in the band program, they also affect his learning to read music as a language. The well-established *general music program should develop esthetic experiences and* elemental *reading skills.*

Three Important Plans of
Pre-Band General Music Preparation

Three programs that have had a strong influence upon elementary school music education are:

1) *The Orff Method*—This is an excellent method for developing the potential instrumentalist, since it actively uses various types of instruments and stresses elemental reading of music. Orff stresses the involvement of the student. The child actively participates in the making of music; motivation and interest are created through games and songs, with each of the elements of music (rhythm, melody, harmony, musical form, and improvi-

sation) being introduced in this manner. Many of Orff's methods of teaching may be used by the band director on any level of instruction.

2) *The Kodaly Method*—The curriculum of this method includes reading and writing of music, ear training, rhythmic movement, choral singing, and listening. The main objective of the program is to develop a musician with a trained ear, trained musical feeling, a trained intellect, and trained hands. The human voice is the primary instrument of instruction. A development of pitch recognition through the use of solfeggio is a primary objective.

3) *The Suzuki Method*—The Suzuki method is not practical for the American band instructor. It is based upon "rote" teaching and *very* active parent involvement, beginning with a controlled musical environment from birth. The child's learning of his native language and the language of music should follow parallel courses. The complexity of parent involvement is unrealistic when applied to the average American public school.

These programs are representative of what is being taught in the lower grades in many strong music departments. A method similar to Orff's program is best for pre-band preparation since it is strongly oriented to instrumental music. An excellent source for detailed explanations of the Orff, Kodaly, and Suzuki methods is *Major New Movements in Elementary School Music Education*, (Albany: The State Education Department, Bureau of Music Education, 1969). This comprehensive pamphlet also includes sources for purchasing Orff instruments.

Using Supplemental Pre-Band Programs

General music classes supply most of the pre-band experiences for your students. These additional pre-band programs can be used to supplement instrumental background:

1) The Tonette, Flutophone, or Recorder Programs

Flutophones and tonettes have been used as pre-band instruments with great success for many years. Recorders, however, because of their cost and their relative difficulty in tone production and control, should not be used for pre-band programs. Because of scheduling difficulties, the general music teacher should teach this element of pre-band training. If this is not possible, the instrumental teacher may reserve time during general music classes to teach the program himself.

At the completion of this type of program, each student can be evaluated according to his musical ability and his attitude toward music and the playing of a band instrument.

2) The Pre-Band Percussion Program

Some music departments have established the study of percussion instruments as a pre-band program. Each student in the music class has his own snare drum sticks and pad and is taught how to hold the sticks, how to strike the pad, and how to gradually read and play progressively more complex rhythm patterns. Since rhythm is the most difficult aspect of music to read accurately, this program has great validity as pre-band preparation. Its value is limited, however, as a general music approach because the study is so specifically rhythmic and does not develop concepts of melody and harmony.

3) Using Rhythmic Flash Cards

It is possible when teaching rhythm to pre-band students to use rhythmic flash cards similar to those used in teaching multiplication and division tables to elementary school students. These cards may begin with the identification of a single note value, progress to simple rhythmic patterns using like note values (four quarter notes, and so on), and ultimately combine different note values and rests into advanced rhythmic patterns. Rhythms are clapped at sight by the class, which ultimately progresses to team clapping, where several different patterns are clapped at the same time. Rhythmic flash cards have been published under the title *Music Rhythm Teaching Series*, which comes in two sets of approximately 160 cards each. These cards, first published in 1962, are called *Select-O-Cards*. You may obtain the cards or information pertaining to them by writing to: William D. Lockwood, Cafferty Hill Road, Endicott, New York 13760.

Using the Foot to Count Rhythm

I have found that keeping the pulse with the foot is the most accurate method of teaching rhythm to the wind player. The approximate interpretation of rhythms by many students and teachers who reject the use of the foot-beat is a serious musical problem. Ensemble playing is absolutely dependent upon the exact interpretation of both durations and subdivisions, plus a controlled feeling for the pulse. My students have developed mathematically accurate subdivisions of the beat, conquered superimposed rhythms, and kept a metronomically even beat through use of the foot-beat. However, they do realize that the foot is a tool that will be replaced in band rehearsals and ensemble performances by the conductor's beat. As soon as a student has complete control over and understanding of the foot as a metronomic device, he no longer needs to use it. This normally occurs after several years of study. Your goal when teaching rhythm should be the development of the ability of the student to read at sight all material placed before him with correct rhythmic divisions and a steady, controlled beat.

Beginning at their first lesson, all of my students use a controlled foot-beat to count. Every note they produce is based upon the foot-tapping of an absolutely even and controlled beat, and all notes are held to their exact values. This approach seems very mechanical at first, but it results in rhythmic understanding, control, and absolute accuracy. All subsequent rhythms and their subdivisions are based upon the continued use of the foot-beat.

Since the student can neither produce a conductor's beat nor verbalize when playing his horn, the foot-beat becomes extremely important to his accuracy and musical results when he practices alone. If his correct rhythm in lessons or rehearsals has been the result of imitation or rote response, the student may be unable to solve musical and rhythmic problems by himself when learning new material.

Each down-beat of the foot represents the beat or pulse of the music and is equivalent to the conductor's beat used in lessons, rehearsals, and performances. The up-beat, or the "and" of a two-part beat, is played exactly at the highest point of the foot arc. Any simple beat situation (background divisions of two) can be taught in this manner. If you analyze your conductor's beat, you will find similar up-beat placement in most of your beat patterns. The examples found below use arrows to indicate where the down-beats and up-beats occur in certain simple rhythm patterns.

Examples:

Compound rhythm patterns can be handled in a similar manner. In this case you do have to develop within the student an ability to feel three background pulsations to a foot-tap. The first note comes on the tap, and the other two notes are placed within an evenly divided beat and before the next foot-tap. When you conduct, you produce a similar beat. There is a definite down-beat, but your divisions of three are contained within your beat, just as they are within the foot-beat. Below are examples of the foot-beat as applied to compound time.

Examples:

Percussionists do not need to develop a foot-beat, but my best percussion students do add this to their learning tools. Percussionists, as in the case of keyboard and string students, can verbalize rhythmic patterns. Very young students can learn to use two syllable systems, one for simple rhythmic patterns, 1-e-&-a, and another for compound patterns, 1-la-lee. Because of the verbal possibilities of counting that are available to string, keyboard, and percussion students, it may be difficult at times to justify the use of the foot to other music teachers and to students who double on keyboard or string instruments. If the verbalization potential for counting is eliminated, you should have little difficulty in defending foot-tapping in teaching the wind player. Challenge your opponents with the question: "What do you use as an *objective substitute* for the conductor's beat or verbalization?"

The importance of establishing an effective method of teaching rhythm is introduced at this point because rhythmic weaknesses are often the most serious problems you face as a band director. Rhythm should be taught properly when the student is very young; it is extremely difficult to solve rhythmic problems in "midstream."

HOW TO FORM A SUCCESSFUL BEGINNER PROGRAM

When to Start Your Beginner Program

The most satisfactory time to start your beginners is during the summer months after they have completed the fourth grade. At this point the young student has developed a maturity, both physically and mentally, that will insure the best possible results for your program. The only valid objectives in starting a student earlier are the development of an interest for playing an instrument at some later date and the creation of an activity for the exceptionally talented child.

The Testing and Choosing of Beginners

Your first step in setting up a beginner program is the testing of all students. This is done most often at the end of the fourth grade. Test students during their regular general music classes, if possible. This procedure causes the least disruption of classes and is the easiest to set up. General music classes are usually 25 to 30 minutes long, which is the minimum time you need to administer a standard musical aptitude test.

You may administer the test personally or have it given by tape or record. If the test is recorded, the administration of the test and the supervision of the testing area are much easier, and the test will be presented in exactly the same manner to all classes. If the test is given "live," there is always the chance that slight variations in your presentation could affect the outcome of the testing. My test (verbal instructions and musical examples) was recorded on reel-to-reel tape and was presented to each class in this manner.

Have the general music teacher assist you during each testing period. Materials must be passed out for each class, and a certain amount of proctoring must be done to assure the validity of the testing. This is very difficult to do without some assistance in a 30-minute period.

How to Choose a Musical Aptitude Test

A musical aptitude test should evaluate a student's innate rhythmic ability, sense of pitch, and tonal memory. Various published tests are available, ranging from the *Seashore Measures of Musical Talent* to the *McCreery Elementary Rhythm and Pitch Test*. I have not used the *Seashore* because of the relative difficulty of evaluating the results and the difficulty of administering it to the average elementary student. The *McCreery* has produced excellent results for my beginning program. It is presented in the following manner:

1) The first ten examples measure rhythmic tonal memory. Two rhythmic examples are played, and the student identifies whether these examples are exactly the same (S) or are different *in any way* (D).

2) In the next eight examples the student is asked to compare two melodic motifs. These examples may be from two to five notes in length; the student designates whether the motifs in each pair of examples are the same (S) or different (D).

3) The third part of the test compares eight pairs of examples according to their relative pitch levels. You ask, "Is the second 'short melody' higher (H) or lower (L) than the first?"

4) The next eight examples present two melodies of moderate length to be defined as the same (S) or different (D). These examples test true tonal memory.

5) In the next eight examples, triads are played. The student indicates whether the sonorities heard are exactly the same (S) or different (D).

6) In the final eight pairs of triad examples, the student designates whether the second triad is higher (H) or lower (L) than the first.

Include the following information at the bottom of your test answer sheet: Name, Phone, Address, Piano Background (years), Home Room. Note the inclusion of piano background (lessons from a *qualified piano teacher*), an important consideration when choosing your beginners.

Making a Complete Evaluation of Your Beginning Candidates

Musical aptitude is only one part of your evaluation of each student. His final composite score is based upon the following materials:

1) *Musical Aptitude Score*

2) *Academic Average*, based upon English, Science, Social Studies, and Mathematics marks. Note if the student has repeated a grade.

3) *Intelligence Quotients* give you an approximate potential for each student; they may vary as much as ten points upward or downward.

4) *Class Rank* gives you an immediate indication of a student's academic achievement in comparison to others in his class.

5) *Attitude* is determined from comments made by academic teachers, music teachers, and the building principal in relation to the student's attitude academically, musically, and socially. The student whose attitude is positive toward *all aspects* of his school experience is the best risk as a beginning candidate.

This evaluation works in the following manner: MA = Musical Aptitude; AA = Academic Average; IQ = Intelligence Quotient; CR = Class Rank.

	MA	AA	IQ	CR	Attitude
Student A	86	B+	116	8	Good worker; no discipline problems; likes music class
Student B	98	A	132	1	Excellent student; good music potential
Student C	66	D	96	24	Weak academically; also a discipline problem; not interested in music class
Student D	76	A+	137	1	Gifted academically; tries in music class, non-singer, pitch problem
Student E	94	C	126	18	Under-achiever academically; poor work habits; does not show interest in music class, but does disturb class at times
Student F	88	A	106	4	Very hard worker; over-achiever; fine attitude; good student in music class

How to Evaluate Your Information

I have developed a composite score for each student in the following manner:

1) The musical aptitude score is converted into a decimal. Example: 92 becomes .92

2) The academic average is converted into a decimal, using the following conversion chart:

A+	= 1.00	C+	= .78
A	= .95	C	= .75
A−	= .92	C−	= .72
B+	= .88	D+	= .68
B	= .85	D	= .65
B−	= .82	F	= .60

3) The intelligence quotient is converted into a decimal according to the following conversion chart:

$$
\begin{aligned}
130 - 130+ &= 1.00\\
120 - 129 &= .90\\
110 - 119 &= .80\\
100 - 109 &= .70\\
90 - 99 &= .60\\
80 - 89 &= .50\\
70 - 79 &= .40
\end{aligned}
$$

etc.

4) Class rank is converted into a decimal according to the following table of adjusted reciprocals:

Individual Class of 25	*Entire Class of 250*
Class rank 1 = .25	Class rank 1 = 2.50
2 = .24	2 = 2.49
3 = .23	3 = 2.48
4 = .22	4 = 2.47
5 = .21	5 = 2.46
etc.	etc.

5) Attitude comments are used only subjectively and therefore are not shown in the composite score of the student.

By this system of evaluation, the composite scores of the students given above are:

Student A = MA	.86		Student B = MA	.98
AA	.88		AA	.95
IQ	.80		IQ	1.00
CR	.18 (based upon 25)		CR	.25
Total	2.72		Total	3.18

Students: C = 1.93; D = 3.01; E = 2.67; F = 2.75

Your Post-Testing Procedure

Place the entire class in order of these composite scores; your number one candidate will be the person with the highest composite score. Determine how many students you will accept for your immediate beginner program. Send home letters of invitation to join the instrumental music program. Each letter should be accompanied by an information blank to be returned by a given date. This blank will tell you who has accepted candidacy in your program. I have received positive replies from 90% of the students selected in this manner; very rarely does a student in the top ten possible candidates reject this invitation. It has become a matter of pride to be selected through this evaluation system.

The Beginner Questionnaire:

Please return this questionnaire immediately.

I am interested in having my child join the band program . . .

YES_____   NO_____

My child is interested in playing: _____

(instrument—1st choice)

_____

(instrument—2nd choice)

Pupil's Name _____   Parents' Name _____

School _____   Home Address _____

Grade _____   Phone Number _____

An excellent text on organizing beginning instrumental programs, which includes the *McCreery Elementary Rhythm and Pitch Test* and a letter to parents of beginning candidates, is *Recruiting the School Band and Orchestra* by Howard R. Lyons (Chicago, Illinois: Lyons Band Instrument Company, 1956). Information pertaining to this test and text may be obtained from Lyons Band, 530 Riverview Avenue, Elkhart, Indiana 46514.

Supplemental Testing of Beginning Candidates

Follow-up testing and individual interviews should be done after your beginning candidates have returned their questionnaires. During a five to ten minute interview, you may check the student's jaw and lip structure, teeth, and fingers to find any physical problems that might cause the student to be unable to succeed on the instrument he has chosen. Retest each student's sense of pitch by a short vocal examination. Have him sing back to you single pitches and short melodies as you play them on the piano. Brass and double-reed candidates should respond positively to this test. Play all examples on the piano within the voice range of each student. Inform any student of a pitch handicap so that he may be prepared to switch to another instrument in the future. Since some students are not able at this age to use the human voice as an instrument, you are never absolutely sure that a serious pitch problem exists until you find that the student's progress on the instrument he is studying is impaired because of a lack of pitch recognition.

Creating Balanced Instrumentation
by Placing a Student on the Proper Instrument

A student should have the opportunity to choose his own instrument whenever possible. This should insure that he will have a positive attitude toward serious study of his instrument. If a student is placed on an instrument he does not like, his chances of success and of continuing in your program are minimal. The letter that the candidate takes home should ask him to choose his own instrument and to indicate his second choice in case his first choice is not recommended. Include a chart of desired instrumentation with your beginner letter to help the student make his choices. After all beginners' questionnaires have been returned and all supplemental testing has been completed, tabulate the first choices of the students and compare the totals with your planned beginning instrumentation. Usually a few changes will be required for balance. Those students who indicate that they are less definite in their choices or are willing to play any instrument you choose for them should be switched to create proper balance.

Securing Satisfactory Beginning Instruments

All woodwind and brass students must start on *easy blowing* instruments that are in good mechanical condition. A struggling student's problems may be the result of a defective horn, or his problems may be related to his own physical application. If the instrument is unsatisfactory, a beginner can become discouraged very quickly and want to change instruments or possibly drop from your program. I check every beginner's instrument by playing it before he takes it home to practice. I also regularly check the reeds on my beginners' horns during the first few weeks of study since their reeds will undoubtedly be mistreated.

Develop a good working relationship with a music dealer who has satisfactory beginner instruments available for rental and who can be depended upon to keep these instruments in fine working condition.

Assign school-owned instruments carefully. If a promising beginner cannot afford to rent or eventually buy an instrument, talk to him and his parents about starting on a school instrument. Many fine oboe, bassoon, bass clarinet, French horn, baritone horn, and so on students are started in this manner.

How to Select Effective Beginning Materials

Chapters 11 through 13 contain a detailed syllabus for each instrument, including the method books and supplementary materials to be used for elementary classes. Materials are selected that allow the student to progress as rapidly as possible and to avoid any degree of boredom. Most of the students secured through my beginning evaluation plan are above-average academically and must be challenged with rapidly progressing materials to keep their interest at a high level.

Starting Your Beginning Program in the Summer

I have found it very advantageous to start my beginners during the summer instrumental program. Any student who is not able to start in the summer may be started in September. Many beginners may be ready for elementary band participation by the beginning of the school year. This not only gives you a larger elementary band, it also gets the student actively involved in a meaningful group activity before his interest begins to diminish. Students started in September should be prepared for band participation before the end of the first semester.

At the end of the summer session, each beginner is evaluated, and a report is sent to the parents. An outline of that report follows:

Instrumental Music Department
Beginner Report—1977
Summer Program

Student _____ Instrument _____

Attendance _____ Grade _____

Comments: Recommendation:

DEVELOPING A SUCCESSFUL PERFORMING ELEMENTARY SCHOOL BAND

After six or eight one-hour lessons, the good beginning student should be prepared to start band training. He should have developed range and rhythmic background to handle second and third parts in your elementary band. Most lower parts in elementary band music are composed so that the relatively inexperienced player can technically play in a band ensemble. For example, the third clarinet parts are usually written entirely below the "break."

The Function of the Elementary Band

The elementary band has two major functions:

1) To be a *training organization* and *feeder source* for your junior high band. The elementary band experience should teach the student the beginning principles of the following: a) Tone quality; b) Intonation; c) Precision, rhythmical and technical; d) Balance; e) Interpretation, including dynamics; f) Adaptation to following a conductor's beat.

2) To be a *functional performing organization* for your elementary school. The elementary band should present as many public per-

formances as possible and should be a functional ensemble for grade school assemblies and special programs.

The Size and Physical Organization of the Elementary Band

The following are specifications for the elementary band. They are based upon a program that has one elementary school; grades 5 and 6 are used for band participation. They should be adjusted accordingly for multiple grade schools.

1) *Size:* 85–95, which should correspond with the sizes of the junior and senior bands
2) *Instrumentation:* as close as possible to that of the older bands
3) *Seating:* Similar to senior band seating; this is dependent upon the facilities available for the elementary band rehearsals
4) *Concert programming:* similar to content and variety of senior band programs; two formal concerts per year

If the structure of your elementary program closely resembles your high school program, the transition of your students will be smoothly accomplished from one level to the next.

Rehearsing the Elementary Band

The elementary band rehearsal should begin with some type of warm-up material. The content and the methods used to train your elementary students should be similar to those used in junior and senior band rehearsals. The following is a possible rehearsal lesson plan:

1) Play the Concert B-flat scale in one octave, ascending and descending, in whole notes. Have each student carefully feel the beat with you so that all changes may be made together. (Warmup of tone and preliminary check of intonation.)
2) Play a simple rhythmic pattern on each pitch of the B-flat scale, ascending and descending; use legato tongue ascending and staccato tongue descending. (Warmup of tongue attack and subdivision of beat into twos.)
3) Using a simple rhythmic pattern involving quarter and eighth notes, play the Concert B-flat scale up and down three consecutive times at m.m. = 80. (Warmup of fingers and tongue coordination.) Various articulations may be introduced to vary this exercise.
4) Always spot-tune before going on with your rehearsal; all obvious intonation problems should be pointed out and improved at this time.
5) Band composition "A": A warmup march here is good motivation.

6) Band composition "B": A contrasting piece to "A," perhaps a legato folk song.

7) Band composition "C": A contrasting piece to "A" and "B." By using pieces of contrasting style, you may teach varied interpretations during each rehearsal and also keep the interest and attention of your band members.

Selecting Elementary Band Materials

Many acceptable elementary band books and hundreds of original and transcribed compositions scored especially for elementary students are being published. Seek materials that are representative of good music literature. Choose your musical content with varied repertoire in mind; you can teach style at this age level through different types of music. The level of difficulty of the music is limited only by the talent you have available.

DEVELOPING A
SUCCESSFUL PERFORMING JUNIOR BAND

The formation of a successful junior high band should be only a matter of maintaining a proper feeder system from the elementary band. Each student should move smoothly from the elementary level to the junior high level, with a logical connection taking place in his lesson progress and in band procedure. The major difference between the levels will be the difficulty of the music being studied.

The Function of the Junior High Band

The junior high band has two major functions, which are very similar to those of the elementary band:

1) To be a *training organization* and *feeder source* for your senior high band.

To be a successful training band, the junior high band should continue to teach and improve the six elementary band principles listed above.

2) To be a *functional performing organization* for your junior high school.

The junior band should present three or four concerts per year. This is very possible if the junior band presents a short program of three or four numbers on one or two of the senior band programs. The junior band should also be the functional ensemble for junior high school assemblies and special programs. If the senior band attends a competition festival each year, the junior band should also take part in a similar festival. In preparing younger players for senior band, you must be sure that they receive the most complete background possible. Competition preparation should be the same as that given to the senior band, with the exception that the music being prepared will not be as difficult. Marching experience should also be given at this level if the senior band has marching obligations.

Recruiting at the Junior High Level

A strong potential band member can be started on an instrument at any level. I have started innately talented students in the 7th, 8th, and 9th grades who have become some of the most proficient musicians in my senior band. To dogmatically set one grade level at which a student may begin the study of a band instrument is not conducive to producing your best possible program.

Since the number of students you may start at the junior high level is limited, you should select your candidates very carefully, using the following steps:

1) *Determine* what *additional personnel* is *needed* to strengthen your present junior and senior bands.

2) *Seek fine academic students* who were not started in your elementary program.

3) *Seek students who have* had several years of *formal keyboard or vocal background.*

4) *Use* present *band members as recruiters.* Explain to them the needs of the band and your standards for beginning candidates. They will seldom fail to bring fine potential band members to you.

5) *Interview* possible *candidates personally.*

6) From this point onward, *use* your own *judgment in assessing* the candidates' *innate* musical *ability* and their potential to succeed in your program. Have candidates fill out a questionnaire similar to that used in your beginning program.

The Size and Physical Organization of the Junior Band

The junior band size, instrumentation, seating, and concert programming should be planned to correspond with the feeder from the elementary band and the requirements of the senior band.

Rehearsing the Junior High Band

Rehearsal procedure for the junior band is similar to that of the elementary band and is developed in such a way as to assure a smooth transition of the students to the senior band. A possible rehearsal lesson plan for junior band follows:

1) Play the Concert E-flat Major scale, ascending and descending, in half notes at m.m. = 80. (Tone and intonation warmup.)
2) Play a rhythmic pattern of eighth and sixteenth notes to a duration of four beats on each pitch of the Concert E-flat scale, both ascending and descending, at m.m. = 96. (Tongue and rhythm warmup.)
3) Play the Concert E-flat scale, sixteenth notes ascending and descending, eighth notes for the E-flats, three consecutive times at m.m. = 108.
4) Rehearse the *Washington Post March* of Sousa (not too difficult for most strong junior bands).
5) Work in detail on a contrasting number; i.e., *Allerseelen*; R. Strauss-Davis.
6) Work in detail on a contrasting number; i.e., *Court Festival*; Latham.

The rehearsal repertoire should be varied stylistically. This rehearsal is planned for a period of not less than 40 minutes. All procedures used with the senior band may be applied to the junior band.

Scheduling Junior Band Rehearsals

Daily rehearsals are ideal, if possible. If not, rehearsing on alternate days, opposite the junior high chorus, will work very well in moderately sized school systems. The most important consideration is avoiding conflict between band and chorus programs so that the students can participate in both. The elementary band and chorus may be scheduled in the same manner.

Sharing Equipment

If the junior and senior bands share a rehearsal area, it is possible to use the same drum equipment and color instruments. Students sharing color instruments should be provided with their own mouthpieces and should do their practicing at school or practice on smaller instruments at home. For example, a baritone saxophonist may continue to study alto saxophone and to technically practice on this instrument at home.

Selecting Junior High Band Materials

Materials used at the junior high level will depend upon the instrumentation and the proficiency of your band. There is actually no "junior high level" since some junior high programs are developed only to an elementary level, and others are developed to a very high degree, both musically and technically. Most of your material should come from the intermediate levels of difficulty. The level your junior band will attain is dependent upon the talent of your group and upon your goals and objectives.

There are many fine original band compositions and exceptional transcriptions that are playable by a good junior band. Whenever possible, avoid materials that do not have a direct bearing upon good music literature. The Appendices of this book contain selected lists of solo, ensemble, and band literature that can be used for your junior high instrumental program.

HOW TO DEVELOP AND MAINTAIN THE PHYSICAL ASPECTS OF YOUR PROGRAM

3

The physical setup of your band includes personnel-oriented problems, such as the sizes of your groups, the "feeder" system you have established, and your bands' instrumentation considerations. The most advantageous setups for your groups should be selected, based upon the quality of players available, the physical plant available for your rehearsals and performances, the basic acoustics of the rehearsal and performance areas, and the use or non-use of risers.

HOW TO USE YOUR PERSONNEL POOL

As you contemplate what group or groups should be established, consider the following three general plans for dividing your personnel.

Plan A—Two separate performing groups

Plan B—One large performing group, from which a select group is chosen

Plan C—One performing group

Plan A considers establishment of separate groups by division of your personnel pool. (The personnel pool may be defined as an objective assessment of the number of students in your program, their individual musical abilities, and the instrumentation resulting from their participation.) This plan would usually apply to large school systems with ample equipment, staff, facilities, and band personnel.

Plan B presents the feasibility of establishing one large performing group, including all of your personnel pool, and drawing from this group a select group to play more advanced compositions. This method best applies to schools of average size, where moderate limitations make this a better plan of organization than Plan A.

Plan C is the establishment of one performing group, formed by the use of your entire personnel pool and necessitated by the limitations of a small school system.

Establishing the Symphonic Band, the Concert Band, and the Wind Ensemble

The size of a group usually determines the category into which a band falls. In general terms, a Symphonic Band will have from 80 to 120 members, a Concert Band could number from 45 to 80 members, and a Wind Ensemble usually has 45 or fewer members. The names given to bands indicate much more than size, but the size ultimately determines the other characteristics of a group. The number of students you have available for your bands, students who meet your minimum standards of proficiency, will determine your primary establishment of one or more of these groups.

Hypothetically, if 120 players are available, the director has several options. You can establish a Symphonic Band using all 120 players for one organization (Plan C). Or you may choose to use your best 40 for a Wind Ensemble and group the other 80 as a Concert Band or Symphonic Band (Plan A). The adoption of Plan A is dependent upon several factors: 1) Is the instrumentation available adequate for such a plan? 2) Is rehearsal time available for two groups, and is their scheduling during the school day possible? 3) Are facilities and staff adequate for two separate groups? 4) Is enough talent available so that both groups can rehearse at the same time? 5) Are there enough "color" instruments available so that both groups can rehearse at the same time? 6) Can you accomplish the musical and functional goals you have set for your organization in this manner?

Plan B is also possible with 120 available musicians and entails the establishment of a large symphonic band including all players and the establishment of a quality concert band or wind ensemble using the best players from the large group. This plan has several advantages: 1) Your best musicians can be utilized for leadership in both groups; 2) One rehearsal area, one set of "color" instruments, and one conductor will be adequate to run the program; 3) Your less experienced musicians will be able to perform music of greater difficulty, thereby gaining a better musical experience. Most importantly, this plan succeeds in attaining the two main goals in music education that are of equal importance: 1) participation in the band of all students who are able to meet the minimum standards for membership, a very important credo of overall music education philosophy; 2) the establishment of a smaller group that will challenge the best students intellectually and musically through performance of music of advanced difficulty and musical worth.

If you choose Plan B, your rehearsal should be set up on alternate days. Since your large group is the training ground for your advanced group, its rehearsals should be on Mondays, Wednesdays, and Fridays.

Your advanced group will then rehearse on Tuesdays and Thursdays. Your select players will be rehearsing every day. Your less experienced musicians, although playing only on alternate days, may have their lessons placed on Tuesdays or Thursdays, thus assuring that they are playing under ensemble conditions and your guidance at least four days of the school week. Use the following rehearsal schedule:

Scheduling for Plan B

Monday	Tuesday	Wednesday	Thursday	Friday
Full Band	Select Band	Full Band	Select Band	Full Band

When you are rehearsing your select group, you should arrange to have your students who are not in your smaller band assigned to a study hall or occupied objectively with a faculty member in charge. If members not in the select band are assigned to study halls on Tuesdays and Thursdays, a flexible plan should be set up with your Guidance Director so that you may use all of your musicians when needed. In the fall and in the spring, your obligations to football games and marching can be handled most successfully when you have all 120 of your musicians at your disposal each day. The select band can go into operation as soon as your football program is prepared musically and needs no more mass rehearsal. If marching is done in the spring (Memorial Day, for example), your entire group must be at your disposal again. Your "best friend" can be your Guidance Director since he sets up your students' schedules. Without his help, your program cannot succeed.

You should evaluate your particular situation before making the decisions for your bands. Small schools or departments may only be able to establish one group. Average-sized schools may be able to utilize Plan B to great advantage. Large schools will probably use Plan A since their personnel pool is much greater, and they could establish several performing groups without duplication of personnel or difficulties in scheduling.

A healthy high school band program should attract at least 10 to 15 percent of the gross high school population to the personnel pool. Therefore, a high school of 1,000 students should have a band personnel pool of 100 to 150 students. Many programs exceed this percentage and may be considered to be doing a fine job in music education if their standards are reasonably high. Many other schools are not reaching this percentage and therefore may not be reaching their minimum music education goals if these goals are both realistic and educationally oriented.

The "Feeder" System

The "feeder" system is absolutely necessary for the continued success of your program. The first step in developing a workable "feeder" system is your assessment of the instrumentation needed per year to establish and maintain the high school band sound you desire. Instrumentation in this case not only implies the specific instrument but also the proportionate number of each instrument to be used in your full band sound. Since this is a personal decision to be made by the band director based upon the needs of your specific band situation and the musical tastes you desire to pursue, the following is suggested as a possible solution to this problem.

In the establishment of instrumentation needs, balance that will result in the band tonal quality desired is the major consideration. Let us consider, hypothetically, the following symphonic band, based upon 100 members, and the possible "feeder" system needed each year to maintain this band.

Band Instrumentation			*"Feeder" per year*		
12 flutes (piccolo)	8	french horns	3-4 flutes	2-3	French horns
4 oboes	14	cornets/trumpets	1 oboe	3-4	cornets/trumpets
4 bassoons	9	trombones	1 bassoon	2-3	trombones
20 clarinets	4	baritones	5-6 clarinets	1	baritone
4 alto clarinets	4	tubas	1 alto clarinet	1	tuba
4 bass clarinets	6	percussion	1 bass clarinet	1-2	percussion
4 alto saxophones		Total 100	1-2 alto saxophones		
2 tenor saxophones			1 tenor saxophone		
1 baritone saxophone					

The "feeder" system shown at the right will establish and maintain a band as described at the left. Porportionately, any size band or instrumentation desired could be established and maintained by dividing your full band instrumentation by four or by three, depending upon whether you have a 9 through 12 band or a 10 through 12 band. The above chart is based upon a high school band membership that includes freshmen.

The final "feeder" system adopted should take into consideration losses and additions to instrumentation that do happen occasionally; this indicates that a flexible "feeder" system is absolutely necessary. An excess of good performers in some areas may be handled by switching willing players to other areas of instrumentation where help is needed. This should be done carefully for musical and psychological reasons; it is a very important part of instrumentation balance control. Of utmost importance is assurance at all times that your best musicians are playing in positions that will lead to the success of the desired overall band sound.

HOW TO ESTABLISH PROPER INSTRUMENTATION FOR YOUR BANDS

The basic instrumentation of an ensemble remains the same, regardless of whether it is a symphonic band, concert band, or wind ensemble.

The symphonic band and the concert band differ only in size and should be proportionately the same in percentage of instrumentation, based upon the previously discussed band instrumentation chart for 100 members. This may be expanded by addition of "color" instruments, such as contra bass clarinet and English horn. However, these parts are usually doubled by a bass clarinetist or an oboist since these "color" instruments are seldom called for in the score.

The E-flat soprano clarinet does have a written part in most compositions. The difficulty in utilizing this instrument effectively is that it must be played by a fine clarinetist to assure any degree of acceptable intonation. Because of the critical intonation problem, many directors do not use the E-flat soprano clarinet when its part is doubled by other instruments of the ensemble. Some choose to never use it and transcribe undoubled parts for B-flat clarinet or flute. An E-flat soprano flute became popular a few years ago and was used to cover the E-flat clarinet part since it had no part of its own in modern band instrumentation. Even though it had few intonation problems and added a new and pleasant sound to our rapidly growing flute sections, it fell into disuse soon after its inception.

Wind Ensemble Instrumentation

The wind ensemble is unique in size and instrumentation. Dr. Frederick Fennell, founder of the wind ensemble concept, states the following in regard to its creation:

> It had long been my conviction that matters of instrumentation have always been the province of composers rather than committees; the music to be played would be the only factor to govern the choice of instruments that would be assembled. At the outset it listed 25 reeds, 18 brass, 8 percussion, harp, etc., an instrumental force permitting performance of the exemplary music written for the wind band; these forces, when reduced or expanded to those required for music which in no way lay within the band medium offered a group capable of performing a rich and neglected music literature.
>
> Our instrumental fabric could, therefore, be flexible and minimum, it being our further desire to eliminate the multiple doubling of players on a part—a practice that had become so consistent a liability to the large wind band.[1]

You should not attempt to set up a genuine wind ensemble situation unless most of your musicians are qualified soloists. Each member of the wind ensemble may be responsible for a part by himself; he must not only be able to play the technique required, he must also be a first-class performer in regard to intonation and tone quality.

---

[1]Frederick Fennell, "Inception—From Long Distilled Thoughts." Reprinted from *The Instrumentalist* (February 1972, p. 17), © The Instrumentalist Co. 1972. Used by permission of The Instrumentalist Co.

Instrumentation of the Contemporary Wind Ensemble

Dr. Donald Hunsberger, present conductor of the Eastman Wind Ensemble, states the following in regard to instrumentation of the "symphonic wind ensemble":

> Many attempts have been made by various professional organizations to establish standardized instrumentations. In spite of these sincere efforts the instrumentation question remains a "local option" situation; this is primarily due to the fact that although published band music lists the number of parts, it seldom, if ever, indicates the number of players to each part.
>
> The symphonic wind ensemble concept places the responsibility for instrumentation and performer requirements upon the individual best qualified to establish the vertical, horizontal and linear weights and balances desired—the composer. This concept firmly establishes the primary importance of the relationship necessary between conductor and composer. (Since first-hand contact between composers and each individual wind conductor is a physical impossibility, a great need exists for quality definitive recordings to be made—under the composer's supervision.) . . .
>
> I feel that a composer has the right to stipulate his exact wishes in establishing musical conditions such as dynamic registrations, vertical sonority weights and balances, individual and doubled tone colors, and independence of inner voices, and should not have his wishes thrown asunder by random doubling of parts by the conductor. [2]

One may conclude that contemporary compositions written for the wind ensemble idiom should be carefully marked by the composer so that his concept of sound for a particular composition is accurately reproduced. This requires that the conductor follow the composer's instructions explicitly. When playing older literature that has been transcribed for wind ensemble performance, you should return to the "local option" concept and make a personal decision regarding instrumentation and the resulting tonal interpretation.

The following is a possible wind ensemble instrumentation:

1	piccolo	2	alto saxophones
1	1st flute	1	tenor saxophone
1	2nd flute	1	baritone saxophone
2	oboes	4-5	French horns
1	English horn (optional)	3	cornets
2	bassoons	2	trumpets
1	E-flat soprano clarinet	3	trombones

---

[2]Donald Hunsberger, "The Symphonic Wind Ensemble—An Overview for the 1970's." Reprinted from *The Instrumentalist* (February 1972, p. 18), © The Instrumentalist Co. 1972. Used by permission of The Instrumentalist Co.

6	clarinets (divide equally)	1-2	baritones
1	alto clarinet	1	string bass (optional)
1	bass clarinet	1-2	tubas
1	contra alto clarinet (optional)	1	harp (optional)
1	contra bass clarinet (optional)	4	percussion

This instrumentation should be flexible, depending upon the instrumentation and tonal quality desired in the specific music being performed and upon the quality of your personnel. Doubling of a principal part, such as solo cornet, can be done if necessary.

Tonal Quality of the Wind Ensemble

The tonal quality produced by a wind ensemble should be clean, bright, and in most cases light. Because of these qualities, most wind ensemble music has been written specifically for this instrumentation and demands these tonal qualities for proper interpretation. Therefore, a larger band ensemble will have limited success in performing wind ensemble repertoire. Orchestral transcriptions taken from works written for small orchestra, such as Mozart serenades and overtures and Gluck overtures, may be very successfully performed by the wind ensemble. Such compositions performed by large groups fall short of acceptable sound interpretation because the resulting texture is too heavy. Conversely, heavy numbers, such as Wagner overtures, are best adapted to a large group sound and result in less than a successful musical performance by a wind ensemble.

Technical Advantage of the Wind Ensemble

Another musical decision that should be made when you are choosing a performing group for a particular composition is the speed and technical facility needed to effect a successful performance of a given work. A smaller ensemble has greater success with a difficult work, especially in regard to speed and technique. A slow or relatively uncomplex composition technically may be performed successfully by a larger group, considering the texture of the composition is not extremely light.

CHOOSING THE PROPER SETUPS
FOR YOUR GROUPS

Setups for any of these groups are dependent upon the facilities available for rehearsal and performance and the acoustical properties found within each of these facilities. Before selecting a particular setup for your group, you should study the following considerations in depth.

Space and Geometric Design

The size and shape of each individual setup is dependent upon the size and shape of the performing and rehearsing areas. If ample space and geometric design are available, the plans diagrammed later in this chapter may be used. If the rehearsal or performing area is not adequate for these plans, you should improvise a setup that will work in your particular situation.

Solving Problems of Rehearsal and Performance Areas

Let us first consider a stage rehearsal or performance area, where the following problems may exist:

1) A stage is used that is open in the wings (no shell is available): Don't place any instrument in a position where much of its sound may be lost in these wings. This is especially critical to the French horn section; since they actually "blow backwards," their sound must be reflected to the audience.

2) A solid back wall constructed of a highly reflective substance (metal or cement block) exists in your playing area: Drape this back wall with a less reflective material, such as a heavy curtain, so that harshness and balance problems are tempered. This can be a very difficult problem, especially if your percussion section is against this wall.

3) An overhang exists over the skirt of the stage, which produces poor balance by accentuating the sound of instruments in front of this area, while deadening the sound of instruments placed farther back on the stage: Constructing a band shell for your stage, or flying 4' by 8' flats above your playing area can solve the problem but may be an expensive solution. Risers are most helpful in this situation, placing your trumpets, trombones, baritones, and tubas on elevated areas with their bells pointed directly toward the audience. This enables the brass to blow over the woodwind sound instead of into it and utilizes the natural directional advantage of a bell-front instrument. I prefer my brass to be blowing forward, orchestral style, in all band situations. This seems to lead to better balance within each brass section. Other setups, such as placing first trumpet or first trombone on the outside or front of the stage, may produce poor balance within those sections. A stage with a complete shell neutralizes most of the directional advantages of brass bells, thereby giving the director a much more flexible setup possibility.

Directional Brass Concept

Leonard Smith states the concept of directional brass sound very well:

> If our primary concern is to provide for the possibility of a balanced tone of the band . . . then the seating of the brass players must

be taken into account for the obvious fact that their instruments are directional in sound. By contrast, the sound of the woodwinds emanates from the tone holes; thus the sound of these instruments is non-directional.

Placing cornets, trumpets, and trombones so that their tones are directed across the band, to the opposite side of the stage, simply means that a large portion of the audience will be hearing a deflected and/or muffled tone from these instruments.[3]

Use of Risers

4) Risers are advantageous under any condition. They not only permit brasses in the center and back of the band setup to utilize their natural directional bell sound, they also increase the player's view of the director and improve his aural comprehension of the entire sonority. The director's view of his individual players is enhanced and his musical and disciplinary control of the group is increased.

How to Handle "Dead" and "Live"
Reverberation Problems

5) Various auditoriums have different reverberation times; some performing areas may be "dead," while others are "live." "Live" areas can be controlled by drapes, carpets, or other absorbent materials. "Dead" areas can be improved by removal of absorbent materials or by addition of reflective materials. Shells and various flats added to the stage area fall into the category of reflective materials. Various kinds of reflective acoustical paint can also be used.

The effect of acoustics upon the success of a band cannot be overestimated. To perform well together all players must be able to hear all other parts being played, especially in reference to balance and intonation. The director must be able to hear all individual sounds being produced in relation to the total context of ensemble sound desired.

Rehearsal rooms may have many acoustical problems also, including being too "live" or too "dead." These problems may be adjusted in the same manner as similar problems found in auditorium areas. However, rehearsal rooms do have acoustical problems unique to a closed room. If a rehearsal room is not built with a high ceiling, acoustical problems may result that cannot be overcome. The same is true if a rehearsal room is too small for the group using it. Such problems, when extreme, can make a "band room" practically useless.

Ventilation must be considered in a closed-room situation. The more people there are in a group the more ventilation is needed for their comfort and for the sound produced to be acceptable. A stuffy room leads to intonation problems that may be insurmountable.

---

[3]Leonard Smith, "Seating the Band Out-of-Doors." Reprinted from *The Instrumentalist* (June 1968, p. 46), © The Instrumentalist Co. 1968. Used by permission of The Instrumentalist Co.

Under all rehearsal room conditions it is absolutely essential that one hear exactly what is being produced in band sound. If this is not possible, intelligent rehearsal is impossible.

If you have acoustical problems to solve, seek advice from your dramatics, art, and industrial arts teachers. Their training should have included work with the construction medium involved.

CHOOSING THE BEST SEATING ARRANGEMENTS FOR YOUR GROUPS

After you have considered the problems that may be involved in choosing a setup for your group, you should study the following tentative seating plans for symphonic bands, concert bands, and wind ensembles. Seven plans are presented, including these specific situations: playing out-of-doors; the stage setup for large band with risers; the wind ensemble setup as normally used and as expanded for concert band; the setup used in an auditorium pit; performing from bleachers.

The Changing Concepts of Seating Arrangements

Bands, such as the Sousa Band, derived their setups from the following considerations:

1) Risers were not used in early setups.

2) Early bands were small and had very limited rehearsal time. The most common seating arrangement, the clarinets sitting to the left and the cornets to the right of the podium, was derived from the desire to have the major melodic parts close to the conductor. This enabled the conductor to give verbal instructions during performances and to control the group through conducting techniques specifically aimed at the individuals playing the principal melodic lines.

3) Cornet and trombone sections were seated to the right of the podium. Cornet and trombone soloists were featured at most performances and could be heard and seen better if they were seated on the front of the stage.

4) It became a tradition to line up the cornets and trombones across the front of the stage for the finale to "Stars and Stripes Forever." It was, therefore, more convenient to march these sections out to the edge of the stage if they were seated near the front of the ensemble.

5) Double rows of brasses were sometimes used in the seating of larger groups.

Contemporary seating arrangements are quite different from those used by Sousa. For example, the cornet section is rarely placed on the front of the stage facing the clarinets today, except in some service and professional bands. Occasionally the trombone section is placed in the last row to the conductor's right, the first trombone sitting at the front edge of the stage and blowing across the ensemble instead of directly toward the audience. Considering the obvious directional characteristics of bell-front brasses, most contemporary directors would agree that such setups have little to offer to the composite sound of the modern high school band.

Outdoor Setups for Concert Bands

Leonard Smith's seating plan for the Detroit Concert Band (Plan 1A), although an outdoor plan, shows much study and a common sense application to the seating of concert and symphonic bands. (See Figure 1.)

A study of Mr. Smith's plan reveals the following seating considerations:

1) Woodwinds are nondirectional and are seated toward the front of the setup and across the entire width of the seating plan.

2) The oboes are placed at the front and center to assure that their sound is properly balanced within the ensemble.

3) Flutes face the audience. This makes it possible to blend the entire flute section more successfully with the full ensemble.

4) Although the French horn is a brass instrument, it is nondirectional when compared to bell-front brasses. It should be treated as a woodwind instrument in seating arrangements.

5) Saxophones and horns are placed adjacent to each other and in the middle of the ensemble. They produce the middle range of the total sound and should be well balanced in this position. These sections frequently perform parts together and can perform with more precision in this setup.

6) Directional brass are facing the audience in slightly curved rows and are placed behind (and above, if risers are used) the woodwinds. This creates an excellent blend and balance of the ensemble sound.

7) First-chair players are placed in positions where the leaders of the basic woodwind and brass quintets can easily hear each other (positions of first-chair players are indicated by solid black dots).

In expanding this setup for larger bands, I would never use double rows of homogeneous brasses. Directional-bell instruments of the same category, such as cornets or trombones, can create a difficult hearing problem for the individuals placed in front when double lines are used. For example, a cornetist will have difficulty assessing the tones he is producing

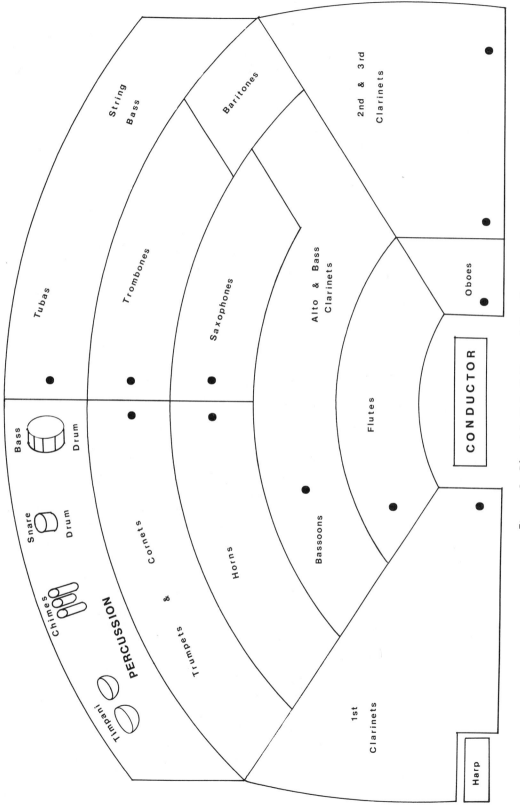

Figure 1. Plan 1A, Detroit Concert Band[4]

[4]Ibid. Reprinted from *The Instrumentalist* (June 1968, p. 47). © The Instrumentalist Co. 1968. Used by permission of The Instrumentalist Co.

when another cornetist is "blowing into his ear." This can be very discon-
certing, particularly to the young player, and should be avoided if at all
possible. A different seating plan may be needed.

The following questions can be used to evaluate seating plans for your
groups:

1) Does the plan place directional brass instruments with their bells
   facing the audience?

2) Are section leaders placed in proper positions in relation to the
   woodwind quintet or brass quintet concept?

3) Are sections that must perform the same melodic lines of the
   composition in a position where they can work musically together?

4) Can a complete ensemble balance be maintained with this setup?

5) Are the rhythmic aspects of the ensemble (percussion, horns, and
   tubas) in positions where good rhythmic precision can be maintained at all times?

6) Is the line of vision between the conductor and each performer
   unhindered?

7) How does your personnel pool fit the setup? Remember to
   evaluate the individual abilities of your personnel.

8) Will your facilities accept the setup with positive musical results?

Plan 1A is obviously a plan well adapted to an outdoor band shell with
risers, but it may not be as successful if no shell or risers exist. Plan 1B is an
outdoor plan I have used successfully for many years. (See Figure 2.)

Plan 1B can be utilized in an outdoor or an indoor situation where no
shell or risers are available. Note that the directional brass are given more
room in the setup than the woodwinds. This additional space in front of
their bells allows the sound to come through to the audience without being
severely muffled by the bodies and equipment of the woodwinds. Brass
players must be instructed to keep their bells at a horizontal position and to
seek out holes in the setup to blow through directly to the audience. They
should also be cautioned not to play into their own stands. The indented
brass setup will help the tone quality and balance, but it can only be a
somewhat inadequate substitute for risers.

Most of the section leaders are placed directly in front of the conductor or on the front of the playing area. The placement of the trumpet parts
in the cornet section is flexible. Oboes and bassoons may be reversed, if
this change is needed to effect tonal balance of the ensemble. It is also
possible to reverse the alto and bass clarinets with the horns if you feel that
there is an advantage to this change. Plan 1B is based upon an instrumentation of 100.

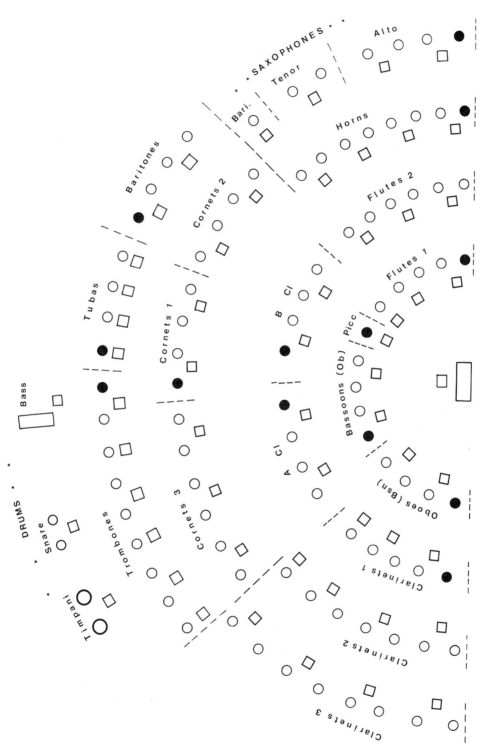

Figure 2. Plan 1B

71

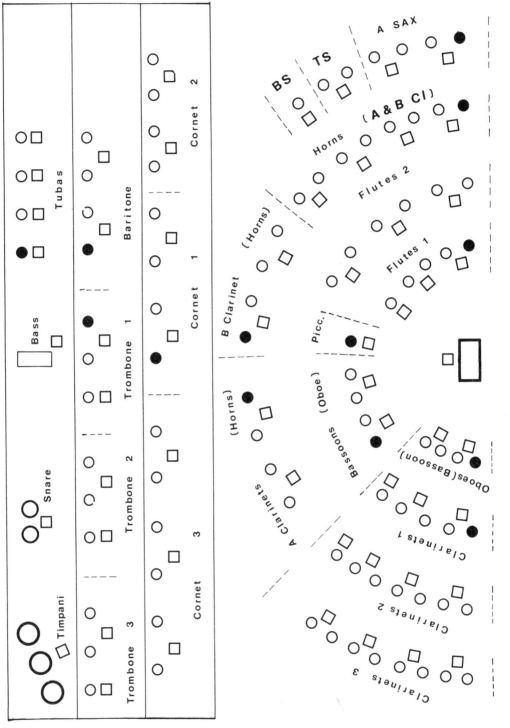

Figure 3. Plan 2

72

Indoor Setup for Concert or Symphonic Bands

Plan 2 is an indoor plan for concert or symphonic bands, using risers for the directional brass and percussion. This plan is quite similar to Plan 1B in its possible variations, as indicated by instrumentation in parentheses in Figure 3. Plan 2 is based upon an instrumentation of 100 but can be expanded or contracted with the current size of your personnel pool.

The Wind Ensemble Setup

Plan 3A is a wind ensemble setup as designed by Dr. Fennell for his first wind ensemble at the Eastman School of Music. Risers were used for

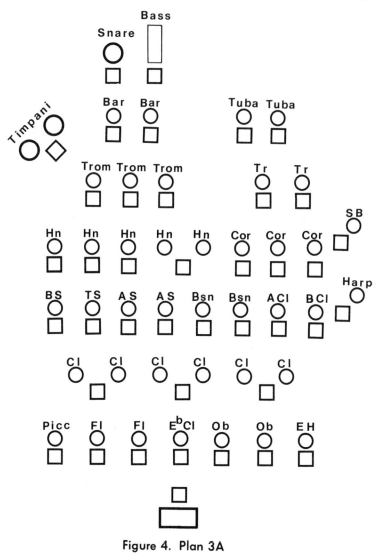

Figure 4. Plan 3A

each row at that time, but the plan can be used successfully without risers. (See Figure 4.)

This type of setup was unique because cut-down instrumentation was used and all performers faced the audience. The directional sound advantage is obvious, but the setup is limited to smaller groups because of the visual problems that occur between the musicians and the conductor when the lines of performers across the stage become too long. However, I have observed a similar setup being used for an All State band of over 100 members; the clarity and balance of sound were excellent.

Plan 3B is a variation of the traditional wind ensemble setup expanded for an 80 piece concert band. Note that the lines of instruments are broken by a slight angle at center stage, enabling the musicians to have better visual contact with the conductor. (See Figure 5.)

Band members who have become accustomed to traditional concert band setups will have some difficulty adjusting to the difference in what they hear of the total band sound. However, most will agree after a period of rehearsal within this kind of setup that the individual musician does hear the total context of the composition better and is able to improve his performance through this improved aural comprehension. The wind ensemble setup will expose the weaknesses of your group as well as accentuate its strengths, so approach its use with caution. I have used Plan 3B with considerable success but have found our stage area inadequate in depth for comfortable performance.

The wind ensemble setup, when used for a large band, demands a stage with a larger seating area than needed by a traditional setup. As the size of the setup increases, the conductor must be able to move his podium far enough away from the first row of his setup to enable band members on the extreme ends of that row to see him properly. The setup requires more depth of stage area than normally used in band setups.

If risers are used, certain types of risers will limit the types of setups you may consider. If your risers are simple, flexible 4' by 8' rectangles, you will have no problem using them for most of the plans shown here. Each riser level will normally increase by 8 inches.

The Pit Setup

When you are performing from an auditorium pit, the advantages and limitations of your stage are eliminated. All instruments should be heard equally well, but brass and percussion usually must lower their dynamic levels to balance the more fragile woodwind sound. Because of the oblong size of the pit area, problems in rhythmic precision may occur, caused mainly by the time lag when the extreme ends of the ensemble hear each other. This is a difficult problem to overcome; the only solution seems to be the performers' awareness that the problem does exist and must be

Figure 5. Plan 3B

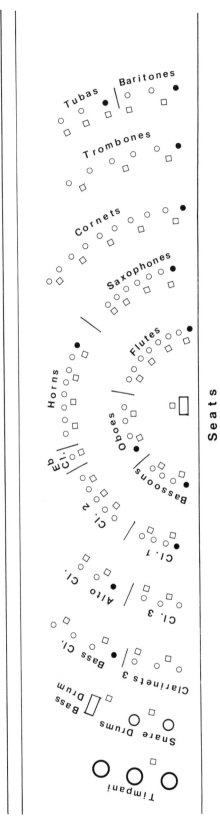

Figure 6. Plan 4, Pit Setup

76

corrected by watching the conductor more and listening to the other instruments less. It is certainly a wise decision to limit the size of the pit band whenever possible.

Plan 4 is a pit setup based upon an instrumentation of 80. Occasions do arise when a concert band may have to perform from a pit, and successful performance is difficult at these times but not impossible. (See Figure 6.)

I have used Plan 4 for many performances from a moderate pit area and on occasion have even added a large Baldwin organ to the setup; but I prefer to use a small band of 20 or 30 players for assemblies and less formal occasions. If you have such a small select group on call from your regular band, you can quickly and efficiently answer the last minute requests for assembly music, and so on. A similar, but smaller seating plan can be used on these occasions.

Seating on Bleachers

The concert or symphonic band will be called upon occasionally to perform from bleachers in the gym or at the athletic field. The band should be cut for such performances since use of some of the instrumentation is not practical under these conditions. Because of the fragile double reeds, the unwieldly bassoons and bass clarinets, and the ineffective tone of the alto clarinets in constant forte playing, these instruments can be eliminated without harming the functional effect of the band. Most of these instruments do not have provisions for music lyres, which must be used on these occasions.

Plan 5 is a suggested plan for seating your band on bleachers. Note that some of the bleachers are not used so that directional brasses and slide trombones will have the space necessary for successful performance. Percussion could be placed at the top of the setup very effectively.

Flutes
Clarinets
Saxophones   Horns
Cornets & Trumpets
(Skip row)
Trombones   Baritones
(Skip row)
Percussion   Tubas

Figure 7. Plan 5

The physical structure of your band program will determine the degree of success you will ultimately attain musically and educationally. The personnel pool, the type of ensembles established, the feeder system for these ensembles, the instrumentation of each ensemble, and the seating arrangements used are all integral parts of the successful whole. The plans I have presented to you in this chapter have been tested and found to deliver the end result we all desire, a first-class high school band that is both educational and functional for all concerned. Serious study and lengthy consideration of the problems presented here and their possible solutions will save you many hours of trial-and-error attempts in the resolution of your particular problems of structure.

HOW TO DEVELOP
SUCCESSFUL PROGRAMMING AND
REPERTOIRE FOR YOUR BANDS

4

The music you select for study and performance by your bands is extremely important to the development of a successful program. Your primary consideration should be the music education value of your selected repertoire. However, the various functional requirements of a public school program will determine a generous portion of the materials finally selected. Functional repertoire includes music for various athletic events, assemblies, and performances where content is determined by events or holiday observances on local, state, or national levels.

The size and proficiency of your groups will influence repertoire choice also. You must determine on a continuing basis what limitations these two facets place on your repertoire selection.

The types of compositions you choose will have a strong effect upon the motivation of your students. You must constantly appraise student reaction to the literature you present for study. Your consideration and recognition of "their music" is extremely important, as is the consistent use of an active stimulus-response mechanism that will measure your degree of success.

The tastes and needs of your potential audiences must be taken into consideration. If you ignore these in your planning, you will be faced with the extremely difficult task of trying to effect successful motivation and inspired performance without a large and responsive audience. The role your audience plays in the ultimate success of your group cannot be over-estimated.

SELECTING MUSIC FOR
SPECIFIC TYPES OF BAND ENSEMBLES

The symphonic band should perform music of heavy texture requiring the homogeneous sound of a full symphony orchestra. Music demanding an almost overpowering sound dynamically is more effective when this sound is "mass-produced" instead of performed by a smaller group, which may become overtaxed in its attempt to create a greater magnitude of sound. Bigness is not related only to decibels, however, but at times may be required in producing the heaviness or broadness needed to imitate a full symphony orchestra sound. Orchestral transcriptions from the Romantic Period and much of our contemporary symphonic literature may be included in this category. Wagner and Verdi transcriptions are excellent representative material of this type if the arrangements are not technically too difficult.

The symphonic band must avoid performance of compositions written specifically for small orchestral or wind ensemble sound unless the large group consists of very capable musicians. Such an exceptional group may be found in an All State or an All County band but rarely in the band of one school system. Even then, the resulting texture of the performance is usually much too heavy for proper interpretation.

Music of less technical difficulty, making possible clear and clean technique, is also fine symphonic band literature. Music of great or moderately great technical difficulty becomes increasingly more difficult in regard to performance precision as a group is increased in size. Richard Strauss's *Die Nacht*, J. S. Bach's "Gavotte" from the Third English Suite, Robert Washburn's *Ode for Band*, J. S. Bach's Prelude and Fugue in D Minor, and Mozart's *Trauermusik* are excellent examples of fine symphonic band literature of moderate difficulty.

The Instrumentation Flexibility Concept

The symphonic band may be utilized very successfully in some compositions that contain passages of light texture or great technical difficulty by "cutting down" the number of musicians playing at specific places in the compositions. The possibilities here are extensive but are dependent upon fine solo-chair players and upon the ability of the director to use his resources effectively. An excellent example of a composition that may become extremely effective musically when you are using the above method is Richard Wagner's "Elsa's Procession to the Cathedral" from the opera *Lohengrin*. This composition can be started with a few soloists, can be expanded gradually by the addition of a few section players at a time as the dynamic level increases, and then can break forth into a most impressive and thrilling musical conclusion by use of the entire band ensemble at the climax of the composition. Few compositions are as obvious in this application of band tonal resources, but this example certainly explains clearly the use of the symphonic band in this manner. The "Liebestod" from Wagner's *Tristan and Isolde* may be performed in a similar manner.

Listed below are a few examples of the compositions that can utilize the symphonic band very effectively. They include two categories, those that can utilize the instrumentation-flexibility concept of "Elsa's Procession to the Cathedral" and those that can use the entire ensemble throughout the composition.

A selected list of band compositions is found in the Appendices.

Bach-Moehlmann, Prelude and Fugue in D Minor, H. T. FitzSimons Co., Chicago.

Bach-Willhoite, Gavotte, Shawnee Press.

Dello Joio, *Scenes from the Louvre*, Marks Music Corp.

Erickson, Second Symphony (Finale), Bourne Inc.

Erickson, *Royal Armada*, Carl Fischer.

Erickson, *Golden Gate*, Bourne Inc.

Franck-Johnson, *Piece Heroique*, Carl Fischer.

Frescobaldi-Gray, *Preambulum and Canzona*, Mills Music Inc.

Frescobaldi-Slocum, Toccata, Mills Music Inc.

Holst, First Suite in E-flat, Boosey-Hawkes, Inc.

Hunsberger, *Folk Legend*, Sam Fox Pub. Co.

Luigini-Bennett, *Ballet Egyptian*, Mills Music Inc.

Mozart-Osterling, *Trauermusik*, Ludwig Music Pub.

Persichetti, *Pageant*, Carl Fischer.

Reid, *Festival Prelude*, Marks Music Corp.

Saint-Saens-DeRubertis, Symphony No. 1 in E-flat, Finale, Warner Brothers 7-Arts Music.

Strauss-Davis, *Die Nacht*, Ludwig Music Pub.

Wagner-Bainum, *Liebestod*, Neil A. Kjos Music Co.

Washburn, *Ode for Band*, Shawnee Press Inc.

Washburn, *Pageantry*, Boosey-Hawkes, Inc.

The "Tutti" Aspect

The brief list above does not include many compositions that are scored for continuous band sound ("tutti" or fully scored compositions) and may be effectively performed by the symphonic band. Many arrangements of musicals and popular songs are scored in this manner.

The Concert Band Repertoire

The concert band, falling between the symphonic band and the wind ensemble, is the most effective single organization to establish if only one band may be created from your personnel pool. It is sufficient in size to play heavy symphonic compositions but at the same time small enough to create an acceptable sound and effect in performing wind ensemble or small orchestra literature. The concert band is also small enough to effect the precision needed to play technically difficult compositions. Successful performance, of course, is dependent upon the overall proficiency of the group. The conclusion is drawn that a group that is not large enough to create the symphonic sound and not small enough to match a wind ensemble's lightness and precision must be called a concert band. The literature for such a group is without limitation if all of the members of the group are highly proficient musicians. Therefore, a list of repertoire will not be provided here for the concert band.

Wind Ensemble Repertoire

When the wind ensemble concept was developed by Dr. Frederick Fennell, he stated that its repertoire should be confined to original music for the wind medium. It was a unique concept—its foundation developed from earlier brass and woodwind ensemble repertoire and its future based upon an active program to stimulate the composition of new music for the wind ensemble. Its basic instrumentation premise was that a unique and extremely clear and clean wind sound could be effected by the use of various small ensembles, such as a woodwind quintet and brass quintet, combined into a quasi-band organization that would include only one player on each part scored. Exceptions to this rule were made in the B-flat clarinet and tuba parts, where each scored part was doubled. This instrumentation is flexible today in relation to the ensemble sound the director feels should be produced for a specific composition.

The conservative approach to programming for this medium, as formulated by Dr. Fennell, would appear to limit performance to compositions written specifically for wind ensemble and to various wind music for smaller ensembles as originally scored. Transcriptions would evidently not be performed.

The High School Wind Ensemble

After many years of experience, I prefer a liberal approach to wind ensemble repertoire when it is applied to high school groups since extreme limitation of the group's repertoire would be impractical in most high school situations. Any music written expressly for small orchestra or small band ensemble would be very effective musically in wind ensemble performance. Music of high technical difficulty, especially in regard to tempo, would also be more effectively performed with this select group. Music of exceptionally light texture should be performed with a small group, if possible. Conversely, music requiring a heavy or dynamically intense sound will not be effective musically with this limited instrumentation in most high school situations. The wind ensemble concept, as employed by high school music programs, is one of a select band rather than a special ensemble with restricted repertoire and tightly restricted instrumentation.

The wind ensemble is an excellent medium for accompaniment of a soloist or small ensemble because of the automatic advantage in balance offered between the soloist, or solo group, and the band ensemble. This medium is very effective musically in performing orchestral transcriptions written specifically for small orchestra. For example, Mozart's overture to the opera *The Marriage of Figaro* must be performed by a small group. Its light musical texture and its florid technique demand that the performing medium be small. Of course, compositions that are written specifically for wind ensemble, such as Frackenpol's *Allegro Giocoso*, should be performed with that fact in mind. Brass or woodwind ensemble music, expanded to the band medium, is also good literature for wind ensemble. Keyboard transcriptions of harpsichord and piano works are successfully recreated by a small group; heavy organ transcriptions are more successfully done by a large group. The "William Byrd Suite," transcribed from English virginal music by Gordon Jacob, is superior music for this ensemble.

Dr. Fennell's First Wind Ensemble Performance

The freedom and flexibility of the wind ensemble instrumentation is exemplified by Dr. Fennell's first performance with his new group. From this performance came the beginnings of a programming philosophy that ranged from the best of large instrumentation works to chamber music for winds. This initial program is found below:

Serenade No. 10 in B-flat Major, K. 361, Wolfgang Amadeus Mozart.

Nonet for Brass, Wallingford Riegger.

Symphony in B-flat, Paul Hindemith.

The first two compositions are woodwind and brass ensemble literature, performed with the original instrumentation; the Symphony in B-flat was scored for band instrumentation.

Dr. Fennell began a series of articles called "Basic Band Repertory" in the February, 1975, issue of *The Instrumentalist*. You can gain much valuable information through this series from one of the most knowledgeable wind conductors in the United States.

USING BAND PROGRAMMING
AND BAND COMPETITIONS FOR MOTIVATION

Motivating students to study instruments, to become a part of a band program, and to put forth the individual effort needed for ultimate success of the program has become increasingly difficult. Two motivation tools will work well, if properly utilized. The type of band programming the director chooses has a strong influence upon student motivation and morale. Band competitions, if properly used with music education goals in mind, can be great motivation tools, especially when an "esprit de corps" has been established and group pride is involved.

Motivating Through the Medium of Popular Music

The director should become familiar with the music that is popular with his students. If he neglects to program music that is constantly a part of the students' private lives, he not only alienates many of his students, but he misses the opportunity to motivate them through the medium of popular music. Not only must he program and teach such musical styles as "rock," "swing," and "ragtime," but he must make every effort to utilize somewhere in his program the good combo groups the students have formed themselves. Featuring one of these good student groups on a concert will not only increase the motivation of most band members and raise band morale, it will undoubtedly fill your auditorium for your concert and bring to your band the support of your student body. Full auditoriums and student body support can increase band motivation and "esprit de corps" tremendously in a short period of time. The director's position is greatly strengthened in the minds and hearts of his students and of the entire student body when students realize that he considers "their" music to be important and of musical worth. A word of caution here, however. Don't alienate your adult audience, and perhaps your school officials, by overdoing this aspect of the program. In gaining a student audience and the band's interest and confidence, you must not lose the adult audience that is responsible for community support of your program. If the popular element of your program is presented and taught as a part of a solid music education philosophy, it will add great strength to your band program without loss of any of the values and strengths the program may already possess. Remember, you must be willing to learn and sincerely appreciate your students' popular music first and then integrate it into your program as music education. In this guise, and united with your sincerity in the project, this method of motivation cannot fail.

Having a student "rock" group perform a number with your band and then add to your program by performing a 20-minute intermission segment by themselves is an excellent way to present this idea to the public during a "pops" concert. Programming in this manner allows the older segment of the audience the freedom of leaving their seats for a few minutes if the music is too loud for their tastes.

Motivation Through Band Competitions

Band competitions can be very valuable motivational tools if the band is prepared for these competitions as an integral part of a solid music education program. The band must not work on a few numbers for many months, perhaps even the entire school year, in order to score high or win a band competition. If this is done, many of your best students will certainly lose interest in your program, a negative result that can spell disaster for the motivation of your group. Modified perfection can be attained without destroying good curriculum and repertoire for the sake of "winning" or for the sake of "ego." No good music education goals are enhanced when one succumbs to these false values. The positive values of band competitions will be felt when the band moves through its year studying a large and varied repertoire, from which a few numbers can be chosen for considerably deeper study a few weeks before the competition. If good principles of study, perfection, and musicianship have been taught throughout the year, your band's internal pride will give it the sharp edge needed to produce a fine product in competition.

When the conductor is faced with a rural situation, where musical values are difficult to develop because of the lack of live professional groups to influence levels of performance, competitions once each year in which competent professional musicians are judges can be of great value in motivating standards of performance for your musicians. These standards become established after several of these adjudications so that your band members begin to strive for this type of perfection throughout the school year, whether in performance of serious music or popular music. A competition where a band is judged in relation to perfection instead of comparison with other bands is ultimately more valuable as a part of a music education curriculum. Many "band competitions" are arranged for public entertainment and are not based upon standards of musicianship or music education. These competitions can be more harmful than helpful and should be avoided as often as possible. They can teach many false values to young music students and to supporting members of your community who may become confused as to your goals in music education.

Developing the Proper Repertoire for Your Band

Repertoire should be limited only by what is available in your library and the ability of your musicians. A proper library can be developed in time by careful use of music requisition moneys and by knowledgeable planning in the expansion of your library resources. Simpler arrangements can be found for a band that is limited either technically or in instrumentation so that a solid music education repertoire can be developed.

A proper repertoire should include all kinds of musically acceptable compositions, such as many types of marches, Latin rhythm compositions, Broadway show selections, movie and TV selections, "pops" music of today ("rock" is only one of many kinds available), solos with band accompaniment (piano and organ included as solo instruments), ensembles with band accompaniment, novelty tunes, orchestral transcriptions of all types, original band compositions, Christmas music, keyboard transcriptions, processional or ceremonial music and so on. Popular music of yesterday should also be taught and performed. A balanced mixture of these categories of music on your programs and in your teaching will best serve the aims of music education since a band student should be exposed to and perform all kinds of worthwhile music as part of his band experience. If such a balanced repertoire is not offered by the director, he has fallen short of his responsibility to his students, his education system, and the community that employs him.

Three or four examples of each category of composition are given here:

MARCHES:

King	*Center Ring* (circus march)
Sousa	*Fairest of the Fair* (basic quickstep march)
Barber	*Commando March* (concert march)
Tarver	*El Conquistador* (Spanish march)

LATIN RHYTHM:

Benjamin	*Jamaican Rhumba*
Binge	*Red Sombrero*
Osterling	*Latinette*
Tucci-Hunsberger	*La Bamba de Vera Cruz*

BROADWAY SHOWS:

Rodgers-R. R. Bennett	*The King and I*
Styne-R. R. Bennett	*Funny Girl*
Sullivan-R. R. Bennett	*The Pirates of Penzance*
(Arrangements of Robert Russell Bennett are exceptional)	

MOVIES AND TV:

Arr. Hawkins	*How the West Was Won*
Jarre-A. Reed	*Lawrence of Arabia*
Rodgers-R. R. Bennett	*Victory at Sea*
Sherman-Kostal-Reed	*Mary Poppins*

"POPS" OF TODAY:

Holcombe (arr.)	*Get Together/Light My Fire*
Holcombe (arr.)	*Sounds of Sonny & Cher*
Hayes-Lowden	*Selections from Shaft*
Lowden	*Sounds of the Three Dog Night*

SOLOS-BAND ACC.:

Cavallini-Waln	*Adagio-Tarantella* (clarinet)
Rodgers-Lang	*Slaughter on Tenth Avenue* (piano)
Vivaldi-Reed	Concert in C Major for Piccolo and Band

ENSEMBLES-BAND ACC.:

Simeone	*Flute Cocktail* (trio)
Anderson	*Buglers' Holiday* (trumpet trio)
Simeone	*Slide Kicks* (trombone trio)

NOVELTY TUNES:

Walters	*Waggery for Woodwinds*
Walters	*Badinage for Brasses*
Schreiner-Osterling	*The Worried Drummer*

ORCHESTRAL TRANS.:

Hanson-Goldberg	Romantic Symphony No. 2 (2nd mvt.)
Rossini-Cailliet	*La Gazza Ladra*
Tchaikovsky-Safranek	*Symphonie Pathetique* (2nd and 4th mvts.)
Wagner-Winterbottom	*Tannhauser Overture*

ORIGINAL BAND COMPOSITIONS:

Bennett, R. R.	*Symphonic Songs for Band*
Dello Joio	*Scenes from the Louvre*
Jacob	Concerto for Band
Nelhybel	*Tritico*

CHRISTMAS:

Anderson	*A Christmas Festival*
Anderson	*Sleigh Ride*
Faith-Warrington	*Brazilian Sleigh Bells*

KEYBOARD TRANSCRIPTIONS:

Bach-Abert-Weiss	Chorale and Fugue in G Minor
Bach-Rhodes	Prelude and Fugue in E Minor
Prokofieff-Leidzen	*Summer Day Suite*

PROCESSIONAL/CEREMONIAL:

Washburn	*Pageantry*
Williams, Clifton	*Academic Procession*
Vaughan Williams-Houseknecht	*Sine Nomine*

PROGRAMMING FOR THE MAXIMUM EFFECT
IN RELATION TO MUSIC EDUCATION

As a music educator you should not only present all types of repertoire to your students as a part of their musical education, you should also enrich and nurture the musical understanding of audiences in your community. The high school music teacher is the only source of music education for many smaller communities, and his concert repertoire may be his community's main source of music exposure. Your power to do good or harm for music education is awesome and must be considered carefully at all times. Performing poor arrangements or "music" of very little musical merit can only reduce the positive impact of your program on its audiences and students. This fact alone certainly points out the importance of having fine musicians enter the field of music education and of assuring that they receive a fine music education at the college level. Poor teacher education can destroy the very core of a music education program, the knowledge and ability of the teacher.

Steps for Effective Programming

From a positive standpoint, programming for a maximum effect in relation to music education means choosing a varied repertoire, choosing arrangements and compositions of musical value, and teaching both your students and your public to be well-rounded musical listeners through excellent performance of this repertoire. The programming explained earlier in this chapter will do this job for you with maximum success. When you are programming for your audience, every attempt must be made to reach each listener with at least one number, regardless of his individual musical taste. To do this, you obviously must select varied programs, in addition to doing some musical "detective work" in relation to the various tastes represented in your audience. One must never be afraid to try something new, but always in moderate doses, keeping in mind at all times the safe programming ground that the majority of your audience will accept without difficulty.

Educating through programming will present different challenges in every geographical and ethnic situation. You should analyze these challenges and attempt to please your audience but at the same time continue to educate through broadening your audience's musical experiences. Whatever your course may be, you should always keep in mind the reason for your professional existence, music education, primarily of your students, but, just as importantly, of your community audience.

Concert Content and Program Variation

Concert content may be varied in four basic ways: 1) using various types of repertoire for each concert, 2) varying the combination of musical groups to be used (including choral groups), 3) featuring guest soloists, accomplished professionals on their instruments (guest conductors may be used also), and 4) performing combined concerts with groups from outside your school system.

Two methods of programming can be used to effect your music education goals. Each concert given could present a varied repertoire, or the repertoire to be covered could be presented within the context of the entire school year. The first method would include all kinds of compositions on each concert, a system of programming that would be repeated with different literature for each concert presented. If the second method is adopted, complete concerts could be varied in content, with each concert presenting a special segment of the repertoire. A variety of performing groups could also be utilized. A plan for this method, based upon four major concerts per year, is given below:

Concert	Date	Repertoire	Groups Used
1) Fall Concert	November	varied repertoire	Junior Band Senior Symphonic Band Senior Concert Band
2) Christmas Concert	December	Christmas music	Senior Concert Band Junior Chorus Senior Chorus
3) "Pops" Concert	March	Varied popular music	Junior Band Senior Symphonic Band Senior Concert Band
4) Spring Concert (High School)	May	Serious repertoire (competition literature)	Senior Chorus Senior Symphonic Band Senior Concert Band
Spring Concert (Junior High)	May	Serious repertoire (competition literature)	Junior Chorus Junior Band

I have adopted the second method of programming. A symphonic band of 120 is used, and the concert band is a select band of 75 drawn from the large group. Programs presented by these groups, demonstrating the use of a varied repertoire, are found below. Only literature performed by senior high bands is listed.

Fall Concert

Concert Band

Sea Songs	R. Vaughan Williams
La Bamba de Vera Cruz	Tucci-Hunsberger
First Movement of Piano Concerto in A Minor (piano soloist)	Grieg-Bain
An Original Suite	Gordon Jacob
Cabaret Selections	Kander-Leyden

Symphonic Band

The Liberty Bell March	John Philip Sousa
Prelude and Fugue in D Minor	Bach-Moehlmann
Jamaican Rumba	Arthur Benjamin
First Suite in E-flat	Gustav Holst
Oliver Selections	Bart-Leyden

This Fall Concert Program is presented with the varied-repertoire theory in mind. My bands have performed many concerts of this type with enthusiastic response from both band members and audience. The Christmas program presented below is another example of varied-repertoire programming. I attempt in this program to present one popular number (*Sleigh Ride*), one arrangement of traditional Christmas carols (*A Christmas Festival*), and at least one serious or classical selection. Only three or four numbers are performed since this is considered basically a choral concert. An organ prelude and brass and woodwind ensemble offerings have been added to most programs very effectively. I use my Concert or Select Band for this program.

Christmas Concert

Sleigh Ride	Leroy Anderson
Jesu, Joy of Man's Desiring (with organ soloist)	Bach-Leidzen
La Boutique Fantasque	Rossini-Respighi
A Christmas Festival	Leroy Anderson

Two "Pops" Concerts are presented here, one done with stylistic variations and one done as a completely contemporary presentation. The latter drew a standing-room-only audience. Although many students attended, it was well received by all age levels. The second program was studied as music education and presented in that manner.

"Pops" Concert

Concert Band

His Honor March	Henry Fillmore
How the West Was Won (A Western Fantasy)	Arr., Robert Hawkins
Concert Rhumba	Theodore Peterson
Suite of Old American Dances	R.R. Bennett
Sea Songs	R. Vaughan Williams
Night and Day	Porter-Krance

Symphonic Band

The Thunderer March	John Philip Sousa
Bolero Español	Ernesto Lecuona
A Foster Fantasy	Maurice Whitney
Tango Americano	Henry Mancini
Selections from the "Music Man"	Willson-Lang
Italian Festival	Glenn Osser

In the "pops" program given below all compositions are contemporary, except the "ragtime" demonstration and the Fillmore march. These were used as background for presentation of the Scott Joplin composition. The Concert and Symphonic Bands were assisted by guitar, bass guitar, and traps.

"Pops" Concert

1974

Concert Band

Marching Up Broadway "Cabaret" "Hey, Look Me Over" "Consider Yourself"	Arr. Robert Lowden
Sounds of Sonny and Cher "Gypsys, Tramps and Thieves" "A Cowboy's Work Is Never Done" "Living in a House Divided"	Arr. Bill Holcombe
Ragtime Piano Demonstration	
Lassus Trombone	Henry Fillmore
The Entertainer	Scott Joplin-Nowak
Theme from "The Men"	Isaac Hayes-Nowak
Selections from "Shaft"	Isaac Hayes-Lowden

Intermission

"Fantasy"
(student "rock" group)

Symphonic Band

New Sounds of the Carpenters   Arr. Robert Lowden
   "Goodbye to Love"
   "Top of the World"
   "I Won't Last a Day Without You"
Carly Simon   Arr. Robert Lowden
   "You're So Vain"
   "The Right Thing to Do"
Sounds of the Three Dog Night   Arr. Robert Lowden
   "Out in the Country"
   "Family of Man"
   "An Old Fashioned Love Song"

The Spring Concert Program shown here is an example of serious competition literature. Intensive study for this type of repertoire begins approximately six weeks prior to competition.

Spring Concert

Concert Band

The Man of the Hour March	Henry Fillmore
Preambulum and Canzona	Fescobaldi-Gray
William Byrd Suite	Byrd-Jacob
Les Biches	Poulenc-Cailliet

Symphonic Band

The Liberty Bell March	John Philip Sousa
Ode for Band	Robert Washburn
Elsa's Procession to the Cathedral	Wagner-Cailliet
Prelude and Fugue in D Minor	Bach-Moehlmann
Second Symphony for Band Finale	Frank Erickson

Soloists and ensembles were normally featured on most programs, though they do not appear in these examples.

If methods outlined in this chapter are used in conjunction with the repertoire found in the Appendices of this book, you may develop many fine and successful programs for your bands. It must be noted, however, that new compositions are constantly being written, especially in the field of popular music, and new arrangements of all types are being published on a continuing basis. It is your responsibility to keep your knowledge of repertoire up to date by using the varied resources available to a band director, many of which are found throughout this book. Music publishing companies will supply you with their latest catalogues, and publications such as *The Instrumentalist* review new music each month.

DEVELOPING TONE, INTONATION, TECHNIQUE, AND RHYTHM THROUGH THE HIGH SCHOOL BAND MEDIUM

Most of the principles of good musicianship are developed and refined over a period of years through lesson materials presented in class or individual lessons. Student intonation, however, must be learned in a group situation, starting with two or three individuals working together and expanding to a full ensemble. Tone, intonation, technique, and rhythm can be taught in the following ways in a full band, even though less effectively than through small group training.

Rehearsals should be planned to include study of all aspects of music, utilizing a stimulus-response situation. Lesson plans should be used for each rehearsal, plans that specifically include study of these individual elements of good musicianship. As rehearsal corrections are made in intonation, balance, and so on, the entire group learns through correction of individual's mistakes. Through these two methods, comprehensive lesson plans and continuous rehearsal corrections, good musicianship can be taught very effectively.

HOW TO DEVELOP A
WARMUP ROUTINE FOR REHEARSALS

The most effective time to devote to planned study of tone, intonation, technique, and rhythm is the beginning of a rehearsal, the warmup period. All of the above elements can be interpolated into a good warmup routine, a routine that must have many variations in order not to become a boring repetition of materials where the full attention of the students may be lost. Below is an example of a ten-minute warmup routine that has been used successfully. A tempo of approximately m.m. = 80 should be used; a gradually increasing metronomic rate should be employed for development of technique.

Warmup Routine

1) Scale in whole notes, ascending and descending (warmup of tone and intonation)

2) Rhythmic tonguing pattern, repeated on each scale degree, ascending and descending (warmup of tongue)

3) Rapid fingering exercise, ascending and descending scale (warmup of fingers)

4) Use of chorale (optional in this warmup routine)

1) **Begin rehearsal with a scale in whole notes, played at an "easy" mezzo-forte.** A "Concert" key is indicated by the director. All members of the band must understand this concept and be trained to find "their" key immediately. (See the chart of "Concert" keys below.) The director should have instantaneous understanding of each instrument's relationship to a "Concert" pitch so that he may assist any confused student. Warmup of each individual's tone will occur during this period, plus preliminary adjustments in intonation. An intonation level for the band has been established prior to this by methods used in small group lessons. This level should be as close to A = 440 as possible; most bands play very sharp. After the scale has been played up and down one octave, move on to the second aspect of warmup. This scale warmup may have many variations, including daily changes of key or mode (possible scales include major, three forms of minor, chromatic, whole-tone, modal, and so on), changes in dynamics or even dynamic nuances (crescendo and/or diminuendo), use of a pulsated vibrato warmup by those instruments that use vibrato in mature tone production, and so on. Not more than two to three minutes should be consumed during this opening warmup exercise.

Concert Pitch Chart

Concert Pitch	C Instruments	B-flat Instruments	E-flat Instruments	F Instruments
C	C	D	A	G
F	F	G	D	C
B-flat	B-flat	C	G	F
E-flat	E-flat	F	C	B-flat
A-flat	A-flat	B-flat	F	E-flat
D-flat (C$\sharp$)	D-flat (C$\sharp$)	E-flat (D$\sharp$)	B-flat (A$\sharp$)	A-flat (G$\sharp$)
G-flat (F$\sharp$)	G-flat (F$\sharp$)	A-flat (G$\sharp$)	E-flat (D$\sharp$)	D-flat (C$\sharp$)
C-flat (B)	C-flat (B)	D-flat (C$\sharp$)	A-flat (G$\sharp$)	G-flat (F$\sharp$)
G	G	A	E	D

Concert Pitch Chart (continued)

Concert Pitch	C Instruments	B-flat Instruments	E-flat Instruments	F Instruments
D	D	E	B	A
A	A	B	F♯	E
E	E	F♯	C♯	B

The chart above may be used for quick reference while seeking scales to be played when a specific "Concert" key is chosen. Instruments built in C play "Concert" pitch. Each of the instruments built in other keys requires transposition. The intervals of transposition are:

> B-flat instruments—a major second up from given "Concert" pitch
>
> E-flat instruments—a major sixth up from given "Concert" pitch
>
> F instruments—a perfect fifth up from "Concert" pitch
>
> E-flat clarinet—a minor third down from "Concert" pitch

Actual transposition may require addition of an octave in the case of some instruments, but the key of transposition can be arrived at using the basic interval given. A chart of band instruments and their keys follows:

Instruments Built in C	Instruments Built in B-flat	Instruments Built in E-flat	Instruments Built in F
Piccolo	Clarinet	E-flat clarinet	English horn
Flute	Bass clarinet	Alto clarinet	French horn
Oboe	Tenor saxophone	Alto saxophone	
Bassoon	Trumpet	Baritone saxophone	
Trombone, Baritone (bass clef) and Tuba read concert pitches, although they are built in B-flat.	Baritone-treble clef		

2) Use a rhythmic tonguing exercise employing various rhythm patterns. This will create a formal vehicle for warming up the tonguing attack and also will be a useful tool for the study of rhythm. Basic patterns might include the following, a quarter note being used at the end of the pattern for momentary relaxation of the tongue:

Use a four-beat pattern at the beginning; vary meter later as a part of interest-oriented variation. One pattern can be used, both ascending and descending; or pattern R-1 can be used ascending, the complete pattern being used before leaving a scale degree, followed by pattern R-2 descending, in the same manner. Any rhythm pattern, combination of rhythm patterns, or meter can be used for a given rehearsal. Any scale form, arpeggio, or scale by thirds can be used for a tonal medium in this exercise. Examples of intermediate rhythm patterns follow:

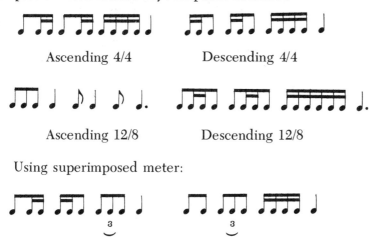

Ascending 4/4   Descending 4/4

Ascending 12/8   Descending 12/8

Using superimposed meter:

Ascending 4/4   Descending 4/4

Superimposed rhythms and unusual figures, such as five or seven notes to a beat, can be used in subsequent rehearsals. The rhythmic imagination of the conductor is the only limit to variation of this element of warmup. Not more than two to three minutes should be devoted to this exercise. Day-by-day use of this method will produce excellent results over a period of time.

This form of exercise may also be used to develop double and triple tonguing on those instruments that use such techniques. In all cases of rapid tonguing development, including double and triple tonguing, a legato approach should be employed. A continuous air stream and the use of the syllables "da" and "ga" will be most helpful, "ga" being used for the extra double and triple tonguing attacks.

3) **Having specifically studied tone, intonation, attack and rhythm in the first four to six minutes of the rehearsal, the band moves on to technique related to the fingers.** There are no limitations to the amount of variation that can be used. Two of the most important elements necessary for good technique are finger and tongue dexterity. The ultimate coordination at rapid speeds of fingers and tongue is an absolute necessity. Again, a legato style should be employed to develop this technique. The coordination of tongue and fingers can be accomplished quite successfully in this

manner. The speed of the exercise is rapid enough that proper separation will occur between the notes by simply using a "da" tongue attack.

Most of the work in technical development must be done outside of band rehearsals. A limited technique can be developed in this third band warmup exercise, which should not exceed two to three minutes. Any form of scale can be played for this exercise, perhaps in the following manner:

(Repeat three times without breath)

During use of this exercise we also begin to see application of breath control and basic phrasing, which at a moderate tempo usually require control of one breath to the duration of seven to nine beats. Arpeggios may be used for this part of the warmup in the following manner:

These may include major, minor, dominant seventh, or diminished seventh patterns (others are also possible).

The technical development of your individual player will determine whether these patterns must be written out for your group or whether they can be played spontaneously from memory. Undoubtedly, as the patterns and exercises become more complex, patterns will have to be written out by the director and duplicated for the group. I know of no existent method book for band that approaches a rehearsal in quite this manner. Such a method would greatly simplify the establishment of this method of warmup for your band, but variation would be limited. Three possible sources of materials related to scale study are: 1) various scale sheets for band, clarinet, flute, saxophone, and so on are available from Selmer Inc., Elkhart, Indiana; 2) *The Goldman Band System for Developing Tone, Intonation and Phrasing*, Edwin Franko Goldman, Mus. Doc., Erik W. Leidzen, Associate Editor, Carl Fischer, Inc., New York, New York; and 3) *Treasury of Scales*, Leonard B. Smith, J.W. Pepper & Son, Inc., Valley Forge, Pa.

Scales by thirds and chromatic scales should be utilized for this exercise also. The chromatic scale is especially useful since it contains 12 notes to the octave, a figure divisible by two or three (four or six). This three-part method of warmup will consume six to nine minutes of rehearsal time and can be expanded or contracted to fit any time period you wish to devote to your warmup period.

HOW TO USE CHORALES, HYMNS, AND
APPROPRIATE SONG MATERIAL
AS WARMUP LITERATURE

Using a Warmup Number

A warmup number should also be interpolated into the daily warmup routine. This may vary from a good chorale arrangement to a simple arrangement of a folk tune, which should be of a legato nature, with flowing lines if it is contrapuntal. Even a composition or portion of a composition that you might be planning to perform that seems appropriate as a warmup vehicle can be used. These warmup vehicles are discussed in detail below. The chorale will be used to explain application of these materials.

The Warmup Chorale

The chorale is an extremely valuable medium for band warmup. Its obvious uses are to develop ensemble tone quality and balance, to train the musician to hear intonation within the context of harmony, and to train individuals and sections to be rhythmically independent. This is especially true in the case of advanced Bach chorales, a resource for your band warmup that numbers several hundred. They may also be used as a training vehicle for conducting, bandstration, and various combinations of tonal colors within the full band ensemble. In addition, hundreds of hymns can be utilized in the same manner.

If you work with student conductors or student teachers, the chorale is an excellent training area for the neophyte conductor. Learning to properly handle tonal releases at points of phrasing or slight pause $(\frown)$ is of great value to the conductor and to the band. The precision of release, a problem with most band ensembles, can be taught here very effectively.

If you teach a bandstration course, your students can easily learn to write well for the band medium or various ensembles found within this medium by creating original chorale arrangements. An excellent source for this material is *Choral Collection*, selected and edited by Elvera Wonderlich, Eastman School of Music of the University of Rochester, published by Appleton-Century-Crofts, Inc., New York. This collection of four part voice or keyboard chorales includes 156 works of J.S. Bach; chorales of K. H. Graun, G. F. Handel, and Felix Mendelssohn; and various Swedish and Norwegian chorales. Any church hymnal can also be used to create similar warmup material.

Chorales, arranged well, can be used in various ways as band warmups. For instance, *50 Chorales*, arranged by Bill Laas, can be played with woodwinds alone, brass alone, or any other combination of sections you desire to work for tonal balance and intonation. A practical application of a chorale for rehearsal warmup may include the following procedure.

Play the entire chorale through once, alternating full woodwind and brass choirs with each phrase. After adjustments have been made in the two basic tonal choirs of the band, play the chorale again using the entire band on each phrase. Isolate problem areas by having the section having a problem play several phrases alone. For example, if the clarinet choir of the band ensemble is not playing in tune within the section and the balance is not good on all four parts of the chorale, isolate the clarinet choir, having the students listen within this tonal quality alone and making adjustments in intonation and balance as they play. The director must be a part of this exercise, constantly listening and calling out instructions over the group as they play or stopping the group and commenting in detail on adjustments that should be made. If the group can be corrected while playing, valuable rehearsal time may be saved. The use of the chorale warmup technique may consume any amount of time desired, but usually five minutes during each rehearsal will bring about very satisfying results over a period of time.

Any combination of instruments can be worked in the same manner, whether they are playing unison parts or different melodic lines of the chorale. An excellent area to drill is the basic woodwind quintet, which represents five different sections of the band ensemble. When their intonation, tonal quality, and balance are acceptable, you are well on the way to a fine band sound. The brass sextet and the saxophone quartet can be isolated in a similar manner. Problem areas of intonation, such as saxophones and French horns, can be improved by drilling the sections having a problem alone.

Using Folk Songs, Hymns, and Concert Material for Warmup

Similar materials should be rehearsed in the same manner. An excellent source is *The Goldman Band System for Developing Tone, Intonation, and Phrasing, Book II*, Carl Fischer, Inc., New York, New York. It contains simple folk songs and hymns that can be applied as the chorale was. If time is critical, as it might be immediately before a concert, use of some of the slow melodic concert material written for the full ensemble as a warmup medium will produce excellent results. Use this material in the same manner as you would use a chorale, employing a stimulus-response method to gain the musical results desired. It is even possible to effect the same positive results from a contemporary popular song if the situation demands its use for the sake of rehearsal economy or student interest and attention.

When working with a two-band setup where a select group is taken from a larger band, your warmup time may be limited by alternate-day rehearsals. In this case either the three-part warmup or the chorale warmup can be used, instead of combining the two methods. However, the three-part technical warmup should be kept for full band rehearsals if at all possible, and the chorale concept should be used for your select group.

HOW TO IMPROVE BAND INTONATION
DURING YOUR WARMUP PERIOD

Two basic areas of intonation should be considered, intonation within homogeneous sections and heterogeneous intonation, which should be accomplished through your section leaders. Any intonation problem within the band ensemble may be significantly improved by this method, but it must be remembered that daily repetition of this procedure is necessary to effect the maximum positive results. Success is also dependent upon the director's ability, through the stimulus-response method, to use this rehearsal tool with utmost flexibility. What he hears determines the adjustments that will be constantly made in drill procedure. Final performance intonation is not dependent upon the chorale procedure, however. These steps should be followed also in producing the final intonation product: 1) Set a level, such as A = 440, and tune each individual in each class lesson to this level. 2) Tune your section leaders to each other, paying special attention to the oboe and bassoon. If their reeds and embouchures are correct, they will produce a tone very close to A = 440. 3) Tune each section to its section leader. 4) Teach everyone to listen at all times. This is the most important principle of good intonation since all mechanical means will fail if good listening has not been developed.

WHAT TO DO WITH YOUR
PERCUSSION SECTION DURING WARMUPS

The percussion section should be involved actively in the warmups whenever possible to avoid a potential discipline problem and, more importantly, provide a very valuable tool for the director to use in the mass teaching of good musicianship. The percussionist must be involved in all areas of band training, even intonation. A tympanist whose instruments are not properly tuned detracts considerably from the tonal sound the band is attempting to produce. All percussionists should obviously be leaders in the total ensemble in rhythmic and precision study. They must also be involved in the total balance of sound being created within the ensemble. Since many percussion instruments are color instruments and must be used sparingly to preserve their musical value to the group sound, their possible over-use in the warmups must not be construed to be more than an exercise function. When this is musically understood, any or all percussion instruments can be employed at any time. The following explains how to involve the percussion section in the total warmup.

   1) In whole tone and intonation warmup, snare drummers, mallet players, and tympanists can play controlled rolls for each whole note while other instruments not capable of rolls can lightly strike the pulse or the background. The director should use his imagination when employing the percussion section throughout.

2) As the band is playing its tonguing and rhythm warmup, the function of the percussionists is an obvious one, although some instruments may play the entire rhythm while others keep the pulse. Various rudiments can be employed when appropriate. Flams may be added to rhythms to create flam taps, flam paradiddles, flam accents, and so on. Ruff rudiments can be employed in a similar manner, and paradiddles in various forms can be used. Percussionists should be cautioned to keep their rhythms simple and very close in sound to the rhythms being played by band members.

3) As the band plays its fingering warmup, the percussionists can again add their parts to the rhythmic patterns being used. Basically the percussion section will be reinforcing the rhythm of the warmup exercises, becoming a stabilizing influence upon the precision of the exercises being studied. Percussion sound should be kept light throughout these exercises.

CREATING EFFECTIVE LESSON PLANS FOR REHEARSALS

After consideration of all this material, a rehearsal lesson plan may look like this:

1. Warmup—key of A-flat Concert
   Scale in whole notes, up and down
   Tonguing exercise on each scale degree

   Fingering—chromatic scale up and down three times, one octave:

2. Chorale No. 17 (Laas—*50 Chorales*)
   Alternate woodwind and brass choirs and then full band second time
3. *His Honor March*—play through at moderate tempo
4. *Burlesk For Band*—Washburn—work
5. *Selections from Fiddler on the Roof*—read

The above plan is based upon a band rehearsal period of not less than 40 minutes. It is very helpful for both motivation and organization to have your lesson plans for a given rehearsal copied on a chalkboard so the band can follow and anticipate exactly what you are trying to cover in the rehearsal. If your rehearsal area does not have a chalkboard available, you might buy a portable chalkboard with one plain side and the other side having a musical staff painted upon it. I have found this type of chalkboard extremely valuable, and other teachers have borrowed it frequently. It has even been used for Board of Education meetings and other public meetings that were held in areas of the school not equipped with a permanent chalkboard.

The detail into which you desire to go with your written lesson plans is a personal matter. I prefer to keep my written plans brief and base most of my rehearsal work on the stimulus-response approach I have mentioned. Exact plans very seldom work out completely since you are faced daily with unexpected minor problems that call for an adjustment in your plans.

Developing all of the aspects of good musicianship in depth within the band ensemble is a very difficult and almost impossible task. This is one reason we have developed rotating lesson schedules so that these elements can be taught to small groups. The ideal situation would be to have all of your students studying privately since one-to-one teaching in any subject is by far the best method. Each director should work toward the one-to-one relationship with his students as much as possible; but when this is not possible, the teaching tools explained in this chapter can be very helpful. Of course, rehearsals should musically reinforce what the student is learning in class and private lessons. If there is not a close tie between these learning situations, your rehearsal technique will have little success.

TEACHING STYLE AND INTERPRETATION THROUGH STUDY AND PERFORMANCE OF BAND REPERTOIRE

6

Style and interpretation are two different but related entities. Style refers to the characteristics of a composition, which result from the use of various musical materials and the manner in which these materials are treated. Such materials include many types of scales and chords, various types of imitation, forms, rhythmic devices, and so on. Style may relate to a particular period, a particular person, or a particular type of music. It cannot be confined, however, to a specific time or place; many styles originate in one time period but are used in a later time period by subsequent composers. For example, the overall form and style of Prokofiev's *Classical Symphony* originated in the Classical Period and was later emulated by the 20th century composer.

Interpretation is an individual's particular conception of a piece of music. Correct notes and rhythms must be worked out first; then the performer or the conductor must determine the degree of dynamic shading, proper tempos, timbre, phrasing, balance, and stylistic subtleties to be observed. The composer's terms are given; the degree or extent of control over these indications lies in the hands of the conductor. These subtler aspects of the interpretation are rarely indicated in the printed directions given by the composer.

Interpretation is a very personal thing. Every conductor and every teacher has his own preconceived ideas about how a piece of music should sound in performance. There are certain prerequisites that should be followed to properly interpret a given composition. All teachers and conductors should follow the musical guidelines given by the composer since the composition is his creation. When a soloist is involved, he should be given the position of principal interpreter. The conductor, being the secondary interpreter, must complete the interpretation after conferring with the soloist. Of course, modification of this procedure is necessary when you are working with a student soloist.

HOW TO DEVELOP TANGIBLE
OR OBJECTIVE INTERPRETATION

These guidelines should be followed when you are developing a primary interpretation for a given composition:

1) If tempos are given by *metronomic markings*, observe these as closely as is practical. Your students' proficiency on their instruments will determine how precisely you can interpret metronomic markings. You will rarely establish a tempo that is faster than the metronomic marking. If you cannot come within 12 beats per minute of a given rapid tempo, you should not perform the composition. As soon as your band's technical proficiency has improved sufficiently, study and performance of very rapid compositions will be possible. I believe that study of a composition at a tempo far below its metronomic marking does more harm than good to the student musician's esthetic feeling toward the composition.

If no metronomic marking is given, observe carefully all other tempo indications and arrive at an acceptable tempo through your interpretation of these markings. Your interpretation should be developed from consideration of the following influences upon tempo:

a) the period in which the composition was written

b) the composer's style at the time the composition was written

c) the atmosphere or mood the composer is trying to create

d) the rhythmic complexity, the frequency of harmonic change, and the complexity of the counterpoint

2) *Observe all dynamic markings* carefully. The composer's dynamic indications will be relative to your band's level of forte or piano, and so on. Approximate levels of dynamics should be established for your group. They should be determined by the size of your band and by the control of individual tone quality that each student has developed. Establish a satisfactory mezzo forte and then work up or down to produce louder or softer dynamic levels, always being careful to not distort the original mezzo forte tone quality.

3) *Observe any restrictions* the composer has indicated *in instrumentation*; for example, solo passages or indications of two on a part should be followed. These may be doubled in very large groups. Terms such as "divisi" should be observed and carefully balanced.

4) *Observe all markings indicating special effects in tone quality.* These include accents of various types, con sordino markings, stopped horn indications, and so on. Special percussion effects such as striking the

timpani on the side of its body with the wooden end of the timpani stick should be carefully supervised by the conductor. In contemporary compositions, hand clapping, foot stomping, blowing unvibrated air through the instrument, buzzing of brass mouthpieces, and so on are often utilized. *Follow the composer's instructions as exactly as possible.*

5) In summation, seek out all markings and musical terms given by the composer, arranger, or publisher and observe these before adding any refinements of your own to the given interpretation.

DEVELOPING INTANGIBLE OR SUBJECTIVE INTERPRETATION

After you have followed all instructions given by the composer, you can consider intangible or subjective interpretation. This includes all of those elements you may find necessary to add to the performance of the composition in order to refine its style. Additional interpretation must be added for warmth and esthetic feeling. An unmusical performance will result if parts are played exactly as they are written. The following guidelines will help you to develop these secondary steps in interpretation:

1) *Rhythmic considerations*—Terms indicating tempo are relative, not exact. If no metronomic marking is given, you must determine the tempo by stylistic analysis. Terms indicating a change of speed do not designate the rate of change; the conductor determines this. Although fast movements usually employ a steady beat, slow movements normally require some type of rubato to effect feeling. When conducting a slow movement, move your tempo forward toward the climax of each phrase and then relax the tempo gradually as you approach the end of the phrase.

There are certain rhythms or rhythmic patterns that must be interpreted differently from written notation in order to create the proper style for a composition. For example, if a composition is to be performed in a "swing" style, the dotted eighth note followed by the sixteenth must be played as the triplet figure, a quarter note followed by an eighth.

Example 1

2) *Length of notes*—The connection or detachment of notes within a phrase is usually marked with dots, dashes, ties or slurs; these indicate a staccato, marcato, legato, and so on style of articulation. The relative duration of notes or rests is ultimately determined by the conductor after he has studied the score. If a note has no special marking for length, the length should be established by the conductor to create and maintain a given style. For example, not all staccato notes are played one-half the value of the notation ("Bach staccato"). Some pieces call for a *secco*, or dry, staccato, while others may call for slightly detached notes. The best way to determine the length of the notes in a given composition is to study record-

ings of the composition performed by fine groups led by reputable conductors. Then base your interpretation on the composite of the performances you have heard. After a period of time your personal experience will develop within you an almost innate feeling for each composition that you must interpret for your band. This will be derived from either performing the composition yourself or by listening to good performances of the composition.

3) *Tonal considerations*—The tonal quality produced by a group will usually identify the conductor since it is the result of the conductor's individual taste. The *ethnic characteristics* of the composition will affect tonal weight. For example, the heavy texture of German compositions and the light texture of French compositions should be easily discernible through your interpretation. The *emotional or stylistic function* of the composition should also be considered. A composition that is used for an event of considerable pomp will be heavier in tonal quality than a composition that is used for a light-hearted occasion. Consider the tonal weight of the *Coronation March* of Meyerbeer from his opera *Le Prophète* as compared to the light texture of Texidor's *Amparito Roca*. The *tempo* of a composition may also determine its texture. A very fast composition should be played in a light style to assure successful technical performance. Each composition will develop its own texture as you prepare it for performance through your daily interpretation of the number.

4) *Phrasing* can be used by the conductor with great success to achieve his own musical goals. You must *define phrase content* and *determine* the *climax* of each phrase. You should find the most important notes in each phrase and emphasize them. The climax may be the highest or lowest note of the melodic line, or it may occur at the point where an accidental or rhythm change is introduced.

The *use of controlled rubato* in emotional passages when no indication of tempo variation is given is determined by the individual conductor's interpretation. *Unmarked dynamic nuances* within a phrase are also common and are an outgrowth of the conductor's emotional involvement in interpreting the composition. As a musician, you should handle the freedom of these variations carefully, realizing that you should not go beyond a certain point in rhythmic or dynamic nuances or your uncontrolled interpretation may render your performance of a composition trite or unmusical. Handle these extensions of your emotional involvement very carefully; don't allow yourself or your young musicians to overdo this type of interpretive freedom.

5) *Tonal balance*—Four major categories of tonal balance should be considered:

a) *Balance of choirs*—Adjustments in the balance of brass, woodwind, and percussion choirs will change the tonal effect of your band.

b) *Balance of high and low pitches*—Changes in balance between high and low instruments also affect the tonal balance. Don't let the upper part overbalance the lower part, especially in octave or divisi parts.

c) *Adjusting dynamics* to effect tonal balance—Adjust dynamics to the relative strengths of your weaker sections to create tonal balance. For example, lower reeds are often weak, trumpets are often too strong, tubas are often too weak, and flutes cannot play the dynamic level of the forte of the trumpet section without dynamic adjustments. Adjust dynamic markings to bring about proper balance by changing the marking for a strong section from forte to mezzo forte or by changing a weak section from forte to fortissimo.

d) *Relationship of the parts*—The balance between the melody and the bass accompaniment and countermelody and so on must be properly adjusted by the conductor. One successful method of producing this balance is to start with the melody alone and then gradually add the other parts, maintaining a balance with the melody.

Be especially careful to keep a tonal balance in crescendo and diminuendo passages. Control of tonal balance can be easily lost here if you do not carefully control the output of each instrument at all times during the dynamic changes.

6) *Style*—The style of a composition will determine much of your interpretation, including how various rhythms are detached or connected. You may define the length of notes in a specific passage by:
a) playing or singing the passage for your students
b) developing baton techniques that indicate to your students the length of notes in the passage
c) writing in the markings (dashes, dots, and so on) on the printed music

Relate the length of notes to vocal performance whenever possible.

One interpretation that seems consistent is: The slower the tempo, the more connected legato notes can be; the faster the tempo, the more detached the legato notes can be. Staccato notes tend to have greater relative duration in slow passages than in fast passages. However, extreme speed in tongued staccato passages may result in little more than tonguing separation of staccato notes, the time needed to apply the tongue being sufficient separation of the notes.

CHOOSING MATERIALS TO BE USED
IN THE TEACHING OF STYLE

Style is a difficult element of music to teach if it is taken out of context. Unfortunately, this occurs often in music education since so many teachers become slaves to method books. Good method books are valuable tools when they are used in the teaching of specific instrumental skills. But, as in the exclusive use of text books by many academic teachers, a method book can limit a student's creativity and progress if it is slavishly adhered to, page by page. It can also erode a student's interest in the subject. I strongly suggest, therefore, that method books be used in a flexible manner and that materials be selected freely by the teacher from any source deemed valuable in reaching his stylistic goals.

Style has many variations, making it difficult to deal with concisely. The best source for study of a specific style is an original composition or a good transcription written in that style. For example, the Baroque style can be best understood by studying Baroque compositions. After your band has performed several Bach preludes and fugues, it is reasonable to believe that your band members will have developed a good basic understanding of the style. This is dependent, of course, upon proper stylistic pedagogy by the teacher. Other periods may be studied through original or transcribed literature in the same manner.

Specific types of compositions will also need stylistic interpretation. In the study of march literature, a Sousa march will be taught much differently, from the standpoint of musical style, than a circus march by Karl King. A popular composition written in the "swing" style will be performed differently from a popular composition written in the "rock" style. Every composition you prepare for performance will present a different challenge to your interpretive ability.

TEACHING DIFFERENT STYLES OF MARCHES

If your program is a superior one, a large number of styles will be included in your repertoire. Every band plays several types of marches each year. Below is a list of specific types of march compositions with tips on their interpretation:

1) *Concert marches* (orchestral transcriptions and original band compositions). These include marches of all types that were composed to be used in concert rather than marching situations. Proper interpretation of concert marches is determined by many factors, including the composer's ethnic background and his position chronologically in music history, the ethnic background of the composition and the composition's function in original performance, and the original instrumentation of the march and the type of instruments used to perform it.

2) *Quickstep marches*. These include many types of marches composed for marching performances. Among these are Sousa marches, which are invariably performed too fast. A metronomic marking of 116 is very effective in the performance of this type of march since the march retains its dignity and can be utilized for public parades at this speed. Many marches were composed for quasi-military or formal parades and have a tempo limitation involving a military type of marching.

3) *Processional or ceremonial marches.* Marches that fall into the category of processional or ceremonial music should be performed at a slow and dignified tempo; the dignity and seriousness of the occasion demand this. If an actual processional is involved, a metronomic marking of approximately 80 should be observed since this is a comfortable walking tempo.

4) *Circus marches.* A circus march should be performed at a very rapid tempo, and the style should be light since the speed and the technique of the march and the size of circus bands dictate this.

5) *Ethnic and nationalistic marches*, including Spanish or Latin-rhythm marches. A Spanish or Latin-rhythm march is normally played very fast and with lightness of style since it was meant to be used for festive or joyous occasions. The characteristically heavy style of a German march, derived in part from its military overtones, is in complete contrast to the light tonal style of a French or Spanish march. Each country approaches its marches in a style unique to the ethnic backgrounds of its citizens.

6) *Marches for special occasions* (funeral marches, and so on). The occasion will determine the tempo and the tonal color of these marches. For example, a funeral march should be performed at a slow tempo and with a dark tonal quality. A festive march will be performed at a more rapid tempo with a bright or brilliant tone color.

7) *Marches requiring popular or jazz interpretations.* Occasionally a popular or jazz interpretation is needed to perform a march in the proper style. For example, Henry Fillmore's *Lassus Trombone* clearly possesses a rhythmic style found in the popular music of the United States in the early 20th century.

8) *Marches for football games and various sports events.* These march materials usually require little interpretation and are normally played at a rapid tempo and a consistently loud dynamic level in order to reinforce the spirit and excitement of the event.

Interpretation of most marches is a matter of common knowledge and, in most cases, common sense. Yet we hear frequent violations of style in this repertoire, sometimes by conductors of major symphony orchestras. You must determine the style for your band in the performance of marches and then be consistent in your teaching of these compositions in rehearsals. Teaching the style of marches falls mainly into three areas: the tempo, the degree of separation of notes, and the amount of tonal weight desired. If you are cognizant of a march's background, further stylistic interpretation should not be difficult. The meter in which a march was written may determine its approximate tempo. For example, a march in compound meter (the beat being divided equally into threes, as in 6/8) is usually performed at a slower tempo than a march in simple meter (the beat being divided equally into twos, as in 2/4). The purpose for which the march was written has a strong bearing upon its style, and the ethnic background of the composer will also influence its interpretation.

Specific Devices to Use in March Interpretation

After you have observed obvious tempo and dynamic markings, you can employ several devices to improve your band's performance of marches. Each of the following suggestions must be approached somewhat differently in the two meter signatures normally encountered, 6/8 and 2/4 (or 2/2).

1) Don't play ties when the ties extend into short note values on subsequent beats and are immediately followed by rapid articulations or rhythmic patterns.

Example 1 in 6/8

By eliminating the tied-over eighth notes, you will insure clean and rhythmically accurate articulation of the rapid eighth notes that follow. The circled notes will be eliminated in this case.

Example 2 in 6/8

Note the rapid eighth notes that follow the tie. When the tie is eliminated, these eighth notes are played more rhythmically precise. The normal reverberation time of the average auditorium or rehearsal room will fill in the spaces created, thus avoiding a feeling of a broken or disconnected melodic line.

Example 3 in 2/4

Example 3 is very difficult to execute rhythmically. Eliminating the tied sixteenth note will result in improved rhythmic precision.

Example 4 in 2/4

When a rapid melodic passage follows the tied-over sixteenth note (Example 4), execution will be greatly improved by eliminating the tied sixteenth note. You can employ this method when confronted with any situation similar to those in Examples 3 and 4.

2) *Define* clearly the desired *length of individual notes*. This may be done vocally with great success. For example, contrast ♩ ♪ and ♫ within the same march, giving length to the quarter note in the former and using staccato eighth notes in the latter. The quarter note of the pattern ♩ ♪ must be defined in length if it is used exclusively throughout the march. Your interpretation of the march will determine this length.

Quarter notes in 6/8 that follow two sixteenths should be held to full value. This will stabilize the rhythm in passages such as that in Example 5.

Example 5 in 6/8

Eighth notes that follow two sixteenths should also be held to full value to stabilize the rhythm, as in Example 6.

Example 6 in 2/4.

3) *Use of accents* and *spacing* of *accented notes*. Space accented notes, using a "ta" tongue attack. A "da" tongue attack should be used for playing legato passages. Both "da" and "ta" tongue attacks can be produced easily on brass instruments; "ta" attacks are difficult to produce on single-reed instruments and usually result in an unpleasant sound. Single reeds must produce their accents by spacing and by increased air pressure and must not depend upon the tongue for auxiliary help. A feeling of "lifting" the air column between notes will create the spacing desired and also will prepare the next accented attack. The attack is thus produced by release of increased air pressure and not by the tongue. The tongue is only a "stopper" for the air column and has no percussive value in relation to how hard it strikes the front teeth or the reed.

4) Occasional *grandioso slowing of* the *last strain* of a march can be very effective if it is tastefully done.

5) Accentuate rapid woodwind passages in the final strains of marches by having the woodwinds play these passages at a strong forte while the brass play a light mezzo forte. The melodic lines in the brasses will be

clearly heard if they are accented. Accenting in this situation will be produced by considerable spacing of the notes; heavy accents must not be used. The above procedure should be used the first time through a repeated final strain; the second time through the strain, dynamic and tonal balance should be restored.

6) Various balances should be created to bring out specific parts, the accentuation of which are necessary to your interpretation of the number. An excellent example of this technique is its application to Sousa's "The Thunderer." The first half of this march features various sections of the full band as melodic soloists. As each section receives the melody, its dynamic level should be increased, and the dynamic levels of all accompanying instruments should be decreased. "The Thunderer" should be in every band director's repertoire; it presents a unique opportunity to teach balance to your students, regardless of written dynamic levels.

Many excellent marches can be used to teach interpretation in the manner I have described above. I have found Hall's "New Colonial" very helpful in the teaching of note lengths in 6/8 meter. This march is not difficult technically, and it will present you with many opportunities to apply the specific devices I use in march interpretation. The value of eliminating the tied-over eighth note to improve rhythmic precision is evident in the fourth measure of Willson's "76 Trombones." The five ascending eighth notes become even and unrushed as soon as the tied eighth note is replaced by an eighth rest. These devices can be used in any type of composition and should not be construed to be applicable only to march literature.

TEACHING STYLE THROUGH
SELECTIONS FROM BROADWAY MUSICALS

Studying fine arrangements of Broadway musicals is very valuable in teaching style since each arrangement invariably contains several contrasted songs. These contrasts are most obvious in the consecutive use of different meters. One arrangement may contain a march, a waltz in valse tempo, a slow legato love song, an up-tempo number in "swing" style, a song in the "rock" idiom, and a number in an earlier jazz style. It is not unusual for popular composers to use this or a similar conglomeration in the composition of a complete score for a musical. A representative listing of this type of band material is found in the Appendices.

Robert Russell Bennett has done a series of superior arrangements of Gilbert and Sullivan operettas, such as *H.M.S. Pinafore* and *The Mikado*, which contain the same type of stylistic contrast as our contemporary musicals. You may even find a fine example of an English madrigal in this material (*The Mikado Highlights*, measure 68), which affords the conductor the rare opportunity to teach the madrigal through the band medium.

Robert Russell Bennett's arrangements of American musicals are excellent also. His selection for Concert Band of *My Fair Lady* is a classic and offers the following contrasts in style: an introduction followed by "With a Little Bit of Luck" in alla breve; a legato romantic song, "On the Street Where You Live" (measure 63); an excellent setting of "Wouldn't It Be Loverly" in a staccato style and rapid pulse in four (measure 131); an alla breve march, "Get Me to the Church on Time" (measure 169); a legato song with rubato, "I've Grown Accustomed to Her Face" (measure 241); a very rapid use of four, "I Could Have Danced All Night," with excellent accent material in the countermelody (measure 267); a broad two and a final broad four end the arrangement.

The same type of stylistic analysis may be done with Bennett's arrangement of *The Sound of Music*. At measure 139 you will find an excellent study of a modified 3/4 done in one beat to a measure. These valse segments are excellent material for teaching the basic style of compound-single time, the playing of 3/4 or 3/8 in one beat to a measure.

Bennett's arrangement of *Highlights from H.M.S. Pinafore* can give you the opportunity to teach some difficult rhythmic styles. The rhythm found in measure 3, ♩. ♪ ♩ , can be taught by stressing length to the dotted-eighth and pointing out to your students that the sixteenth note in the figure comes exactly on the up-beat, at the exact mathematical center of the beat. The third note of the figure should be legato. Play this figure in the following manner, moving from the sixteenth to the concluding eighth as rapidly as possible.

The section beginning at measure 43 gives you the opportunity to teach the dotted-sixteenth followed by a thirty-second. Here again, if stress is put upon the dotted note to assure its full duration, this difficult rhythm problem for young players can be overcome. The passage at measure 76, a series of rapid repeated patterns of the following rhythm in the reeds

is almost impossible to play stylistically in tempo, especially in the clarinets, unless the dotted notes receive their full duration. Invariably students will try to play this type of passage staccato, resulting in unnecessary technical difficulty and grotesque interpretation. Always insist on full value for rapid dotted notes, and you will not only solve stylistic problems that occur with these rhythms, you will also make the technical problem involved much simpler for your students.

TEACHING STYLE THROUGH POPULAR MUSIC

Teaching style in popular music, whether it is contemporary or several decades old, must be done by study of the original compositions or fine arrangements of these numbers. This area should be entered into with utmost caution since there are so many poor arrangements of popular compositions. If you use inferior arrangements, the validity and success of teaching and performing the style are destroyed, especially if you try to teach a poor arrangement of a contemporary composition to your students. Young students of today spend many hours listening to their popular music; they can immediately recognize a poor arrangement of a contemporary tune. The Appendices list a variety of acceptable "pops" arrangements for concert band.

Some basic comments can be made about interpretation of popular music.

1) *Rhythm.* The major factor that has changed over the past seven decades is the way in which rhythm has been used in development of a style. Attempting to teach a "square," although very capable, young musician to play rhythmic patterns differently from their written notation can be a difficult task. A good example of this is the "swing" style, in which both

♫ and ♫. can be interpreted as ♩♪ . In the "swing" style, as

well as several other jazz styles, two eighth notes preceding a rest can be played ♫ , with the first note legato and the second note clipped off with the tongue. For a student who has been taught never to stop a note with his tongue, playing this interpretation can be difficult. Use of the syllables "Da-Dat" usually will give the proper musical result.

2) *Glissandos and articulation.* Another factor affecting popular music style is the use of glissandos of short or long duration. These glissando figures may ascend or descend. The rapid "drop" can be taught effectively by playing recordings of the Tijuana Brass. Here is a unique style in itself, consisting of very short clipped phrases and light, clean, and tightly controlled articulation. Arrangements of Herb Alpert are excellent stylistic material for serious study by the concert band.

3) *Note duration and dynamic contrasts.* The use of interpretive legato and staccato and very complex combinations of both is another element of the popular style to be mastered. Subtle dynamic contrasts that occur in rapid succession must also be studied in order to gain flexibility over breath control and the freedom of embouchure required to make a legitimate interpretation of such passages.

Using Original Recordings and
Media Presentations as Interpretive Guides

The best sources for the director to study in each popular music style are original recordings done in that style. If these are not available, be very careful in choosing a secondary interpretation. Many of these distort the original style. For example, if you want to emulate the "swing" style of the big bands, find original recordings made by individuals such as Benny Goodman, Harry James, and the Dorsey brothers. Don't use contemporary sources of this style unless they have been checked with the original style and are known to be valid recreations. In the same manner, if you are going to perform the music of Scott Joplin and study objectively the "rag" style, go to original recordings of Joplin to gain understanding of this style. "Rock" should be the easiest style to emulate since it is contemporary and many good recordings and numerous TV and radio presentations are readily available for study. Don't be a "square"; keep in constant contact with the latest happenings in popular music. Your willingness to do this will have a very positive effect on your students' attitude toward you and your program.

Interpreting Early Jazz Styles

Valid interpretations of early jazz styles such as Dixieland and "rag" are not difficult for a good high school band if the band is carefully guided in the development of proper stylistic feeling. Many of the early popular styles can be described as "ricky-tick" (♫. ♪) since their rhythmic squareness and ample use of syncopation produce this feeling. Numerous popular marches of the early 20th century exemplify this rhythmic concept. In teaching "swing," the basic triplet feeling is the most important element to stress, properly seasoned with a smooth legato approach to the tongue. Most "swing" compositions should be played with a legato "Da" attack.

If you as the conductor cannot vocally reproduce the style you want from your band for their immediate guidance and understanding, you had better work on this aspect of your teaching ability. You cannot have your major instrument or a piano at hand at all times when conducting a rehearsal; your most valuable instrument in teaching is your voice, a medium that is always present and extremely effective when properly used. This is one place where "rote" teaching is legitimate and is a very useful interpretive tool. Your group will undoubtedly be "square" if all your teaching is done by words instead of by vocally or instrumentally produced musical sounds and ideas.

The following is an excellent source for interpreting all types of popular music in the concert band idiom: "Jazz in the Concert Band," Rev. George Wiskirchen, Selmer Bandwagon, number 81, Elkhart, Indiana, 1976, p. 14.

Using Your Students to Help Interpret Contemporary Popular Music

"Rock" actually employs all types of interpretation since it is a composite style. There seems to be a type of "rock" for all major styles we find today in popular music. However, since this is a contemporary style, you should have little difficulty in interpreting any individual number if you have done your homework well. Asking your students during rehearsals for interpretive help in regard to numbers they personally know well is an excellent device for many reasons, not the least important of which is their direct involvement in the interpretive creation of the number.

Interpreting Latin Rhythms

In contrast to many popular styles, Latin compositions are played rhythmically precise, rhythms being interpreted as written. The combination of a "swing" number and a Latin composition in the same concert is excellent for developing an interpretive awareness and a rhythmic flexibility within your band. Try programming an arrangement of the theme from the movie "The Third Man" with Benjamin's "Jamaican Rhumba."

Entire books and many short articles have been written about each individual popular style, so the resources for study are readily available to the director if you wish to pursue a style in great detail. The normal time limitation and the extensive literature to be covered in producing the high school program will make such in-depth study by the entire band impractical in most cases. If you do not have an extensive popular music background as a performer, you should also develop your interpretive skills through a continually expanding knowledge of the outstanding artists in each style and their best recordings.

Interpreting Orchestral and Keyboard Transcriptions

Stylistic interpretation of transcriptions can be effected by the director again going to a good recorded source, whether the transcription is orchestral or keyboard. An even better method, which should be a part of teacher training, is extensive orchestral experience for the instrumentalist in both symphonic orchestra and chamber orchestra situations. The universities that offer this training to the teaching candidate certainly do a superior job of preparing the future teacher in interpretive knowledge. All aspects of teaching can best be learned by doing or listening rather than by reading. A teacher who has had the opportunity to perform many different styles certainly has the advantage when he must bring forth an immediate response to a teaching challenge.

Experience as a performer on piano or organ will help you develop an excellent interpretive ability for keyboard transcriptions. If you do not possess this keyboard background, study fine recordings to develop this interpretive skill. Constant refinement of a music literature background in keyboard works will provide you with a knowledge of the best artists on keyboard recordings.

INTERPRETING ORIGINAL BAND COMPOSITIONS

Compositions written specifically for concert band or wind ensemble should be interpreted as closely to the composer's wishes as possible. This requires following the musical indications found in the score very strictly. If definite indications are not given for tempo and so on, the teacher has three choices available in order to create a valid interpretation. First, you can research any information the composer has written about his music or study any commentary a trusted authority has written about the composer's style. Sometimes you may be fortunate enough to find direct references to a particular composition. Second, you can inquire of a proven musician in the field what his interpretation would be, especially if he has performed the composition recently. Third, you can thoroughly study the composition in question and arrive at an interpretation that satisfies you as a musician.

If the third approach is necessary, use your band to help you arrive at your interpretive decision. A good band will sight read the composition well at a moderate speed, giving the director an aural comprehension of the overall sound and style involved. If a band has not been taught exclusively by "rote," it should be able to easily make the adjustments in tempos and other facets of interpretation that you deem necessary to carry out your musical goals. This is admittedly a trial-and-error method, but it can be used very successfully if your group has been intellectually trained. A considerable amount of mutual satisfaction will be felt when you and your band overcome an interpretive problem in this manner.

It is again to your advantage to have had experience playing in a fine band under an exceptional conductor.

INTERPRETING CONTEMPORARY AND
AVANT-GARDE COMPOSITIONS

Most contemporary compositions can be interpreted by employing the same methods used in general interpretation of original band music and transcriptions. Popular music techniques may be used in these serious compositions, so these compositions may require the use of the special interpretations unique to the popular idiom. Avant-garde music, however, presents many new concepts. This experimental music, which may be written in new and unfamiliar notation, is usually not difficult to interpret even though it may be a challenge to prepare and to perform. Various unique sounds may be used by the contemporary composer as part of the musical effect desired. These include blowing "dead" air through an instrument, "buzzing" mouthpieces, and shuffling the feet by the members of the ensemble on the floor at a specific place and for a specific duration. These are not overwhelming interpretive problems since the composer is usually very definite in his instructions to the conductor.

CONCLUSION

As you have observed in this chapter, style and interpretation go far beyond the obvious considerations of tempo, correct reproduction of notation, and dynamics. The subtle aspects of style and interpretation include the relative lengths of notes, articulation in regard to various legato and staccato tonguing approaches, and the weight placed upon the attack and duration of the notes. Your stylistic interpretation of a specific composition is dependent upon two main factors: 1) Your knowledge of the composer's intent and of how others have performed the composition and 2) your right as a musician to a personal interpretation of each composition performed by your group. The latter must be done in good taste and with an academic understanding of the composition being studied. Your interpretation and my interpretation may vary on any given composition, but this variation should not be great and should always be compatible with previous good performances of the number. Good taste, of course, is derived from your knowledge of the style intended originally by the composer and the subsequent interpretations of conductors in performances of the work.

Every piece is a new challenge in interpretation. You will find that interpretation is a continuous process during the preparation of a composition that has not been played previously by your group or experienced by you as a performer or a conductor. The more knowledge you have of the composition, the more successful your interpretation will be.

I have found that my conductor's beat is my most effective tool in creating the style and interpretation I desire in a specific piece of music. I relate all stylistic nuances to my band visually through many esthetic variations in the beat pattern, most of which may be found in any good conducting manual. This visual approach to style and interpretation, once it is understood by my students, creates almost instantaneous interpretation, with very little verbal comment by me. My conductor's beat is a musical instrument, though the actual sound emanates from the instruments of my students. Every movement I create must fit the interpretation I desire, and every sound the band produces must match the movement of my conductor's beat.

Teaching style and interpretation through repertoire is dependent upon the knowledge of the conductor and his ability to communicate this knowledge to his students. The conductor's personal musical experiences and his own initiative to learn and improve his background are very important. You should not be a musical introvert in any way, but should at all times be open to receive, assimilate, and dispense to those who look to you for musical leadership new materials and experiences. It is an exhausting experience, and it takes considerable dedication to develop an outstanding performing group that plays stylistically at all times.

HOW TO DEVELOP
THE SUMMER PROGRAM

7

A well-developed summer program is essential to maintaining a fine and complete band program. The organization of the summer program should be based upon the following:

1) *Starting beginners*—these are normally incoming fifth graders. A student's grade level is based upon the coming school year. Therefore, a student who has just completed the fourth grade is considered to be a fifth grader, and so on.

2) Using a *planned curriculum* for all students, grades six through twelve.

3) *Music education* should be *considered of primary importance*. Entertainment should be considered secondary, and concerts should be given only when they are feasible from a performance standpoint and do not seriously hinder the summer program curriculum.

STARTING YOUR BEGINNERS IN THE SUMMER

If your beginners are tested and selected at the end of the fourth grade, starting them during the summer results in the following advantages:

1) Students and teacher usually have more time to work together during the summer months.

2) Students should have little trouble getting in adequate practice time.

3) Instituting the time-consuming rental program for beginners is easier for the teacher during the summer session when the pressures of the regular program are much lighter.

4) Scheduling of new beginners is also easier during the lighter teaching load of the summer session.

Vacations by the families of beginners may be a problem. It is best to delay the starting of any beginner who may miss more than one or two lessons of summer instruction; start this student in the fall. If the beginner is a strong academic student, he will catch up with the others in a short period of time. This is especially true if your beginner teaching load is light in the fall and classes are small.

Scheduling Beginners

The assembling of instruments, proper placement of reeds, and shaping of embouchures can be very time consuming. Therefore, beginners should be scheduled in classes of an hour in length, especially for the first two lessons. A special time should be established to issue rental instruments so that this task does not take lesson time. A cooperating music dealer may do this for you either by a special meeting with parents and students or by making out rental contracts in advance of your students' first lessons.

Class size should be kept as small as possible. If you must teach the entire summer program for your school district, you may have to schedule beginning classes as large as 10 or 12. Try to meet classes of this size a few extra times and divide them into two or three smaller groups for these meetings. It should be possible after a few lessons to make this division according to student progress, grouping the most advanced students together and so on. It is always advisable to start double reeds privately because of the problems unique to these instruments.

Materials to Be Used

Be sure you have ordered enough beginning method books for your program. If these are not ordered through textbook requisitions (the school district absorbing the cost), they should be ordered through a music dealer, and the students should bring money to pay for their books to their first lessons.

Evaluating Your Beginners

Beginners should be evaluated according to progress, with attendance being a minor factor. I test all of my beginners at their last summer lesson and evaluate them according to the amount of method book material they have mastered. Your syllabus for each instrument should indicate how much progress is expected at the end of a specific period of time. The evaluation given to beginners should include your written recommendation to parents as to whether the student should continue with his present instrument, switch to another instrument (give specific reasons to parents for the possible switch), or discontinue lessons in instrumental music.

SETTING UP YOUR COMPLETE
SUMMER LESSON SCHEDULE

Because of numerous conflicts in your students' summer activities, it is best to have some students choose their own lesson times. This can be done at one of their final lessons during the regular school year by having them choose a day, morning or afternoon, and an exact hour if necessary. Ask each student if he has any conflicts with other daytime activities during the summer months. Also consider that the student may have to arrange for transportation to attend his lessons, which may necessitate having his lessons scheduled on a particular day or at a specific time. If the student has no problem with either of these, you may assume that his summer lessons can be scheduled at any time.

Obviously, if all students choose a specific time, whether they have conflicts or not, intelligent scheduling will become an impossible task. Students who must choose a specific time should have others who have no conflicts scheduled with them. Do this by creating classes of similar proficiency and like instruments.

After you have a complete list of all students who are taking summer lessons (including beginners), divide them into classes. Draw up a chart of lesson times and fill in the specific times requested first. Then fill in those students who must have lessons on a particular day. This should be followed by scheduling students who have requested morning or afternoon times but do not need a specific day assignment. Fill in all others who need no specific times; the majority of your summer students should fall into this category.

Example of Summer Lesson Schedule

Time	Mon.	Tues.	Wed.	Thurs.	Fri.
8:00–8:30	Students' Names	Students' Names	Students' Names	Students' Names	Students' Names
8:30–9:00	Students' Names	Students' Names	Students' Names	Students' Names	Students' Names

etc.

Developing a Curriculum for Each Summer Session

Each summer program should have a definite and comprehensive curriculum. One such planned curriculum, based upon a four-week summer program, follows:

INSTRUMENTAL MUSIC CURRICULUM—Summer, 1976

1st Week: High School (10–12)

1. Warmup (tone)

2. All scales in appropriate rhythmic pattern
3. Discuss rhythm—common time—2/4, 3/4, 4/4, and so on

4. Etude (match rhythm being studied)
5. Sight reading (match rhythm being studied)

   Junior High (8–9)

1. Warmup (tone)
2. All scales to four sharps in appropriate rhythmic pattern
3. Rhythm—common time (see above)
4. Etude (match rhythm being studied)
5. Sight reading (match rhythm being studied)

   Grade School (6–7)

1. Warmup (tone)
2. Key of B♭—scale, arpeggio, and thirds in appropriate rhythm
3. Rhythm—common time (see above)
4. Etude or book assignment (match rhythm being studied)
5. Sight reading (match rhythm being studied)

2nd Week: High School

1. Warmup
2. All arpeggios in appropriate rhythmic pattern
3. Rhythm—alla breve—2/2, ₵, 3/2, and so on

4. Etude in alla breve
5. Sight Reading in alla breve

   Junior High

1. Warmup
2. All arpeggios to four sharps in appropriate rhythmic pattern
3. Rhythm—alla breve (see above)
4. Etude in alla breve
5. Sight Reading in all breve

Grade School

1. Warmup
2. Key of D—scale, arpeggio, and thirds in appropriate rhythm
3. Rhythm—alla breve (see above)
4. Method book assignment in alla breve
5. Sight reading in alla breve

3rd Week: High School

1. Warmup
2. Scales by thirds, all major keys in appropriate rhythmic pattern
3. Rhythm—6/8 in two beats to a measure

4. Etude in 6/8
5. Sight reading in 6/8

Junior High

1. Warmup
2. Scales by thirds to four sharps in appropriate rhythmic pattern
3. Rhythm—6/8 in two beats to a measure (see above)
4. Etude in 6/8
5. Sight reading in 6/8

Grade School

1. Warmup
2. Key of E♭—scale, arpeggio, and thirds in appropriate rhythm
3. Rhythm—6/8 in two beats to a measure (see above)
4. Method book assignment in 6/8
5. Sight reading in 6/8

4th Week: High School

1. Warmup
2. Chromatic scale in appropriate octaves and rhythmic pattern
3. Rhythm—6/8 in six beats to a measure

4. Etude in slow 6/8

5. Sight reading in slow 6/8

   Junior High

1. Warmup

2. Chromatic scale in appropriate octaves and rhythmic pattern

3. Rhythm—6/8 in six beats to a measure (see above)

4. Etude in slow 6/8

5. Sight reading in slow 6/8

   Grade School

1. Warmup

2. Chromatic scale in appropriate octaves and rhythmic pattern

3. Rhythm—6/8 in six beats to a measure

4. Etude in slow 6/8

5. Sight reading in slow 6/8

The above plan contains much flexibility, especially in tempo and rhythmic patterns. The material included may seem to be too much to cover in one lesson period, but if your students come in well prepared, you will be able to use this plan successfully. I have used it and similar summer curriculum plans with considerable success, although I have to be well-organized during every lesson to complete the assignment during a 30- or 45-minute lesson period.

Without a planned curriculum for your summer session, much time can be lost and very little of value can be accomplished musically. I have found that student interest in attending summer lessons is increased if you have a definite plan for the summer lessons and your goals are made clear to your students. My master plan is duplicated, and each student is given a copy as an assignment sheet, specific assignments being written in at lessons. It is also wise to consider that you may have to justify your summer program at some time in the future, and a program that is well-organized and is based upon strong educational and musical goals is most likely to be supported by your Administration and your Board of Education. Your summer program should be directly related to your program for the regular school year and should be organized and carried out to assist and to strengthen that program.

Entertainment Versus Education in Summer Programs

I strongly believe that a summer program should be primarily educational and that summer performances can be added to the curriculum only if it is practical and time permits. It is very difficult to perform concerts during the summer months that will be equal to the standards of your regular school year performances. At the time of your concert date, many students may be on vacations or camping, which has become a very real problem during summer months, especially on weekends. A large number of students may be working to earn money for future college expenses. Some of these jobs may take students out of town on nights when a concert is scheduled or may necessitate the students' working during evenings.

Unfortunately, many school music summer programs have a built-in concert or marching obligation. This can produce many problems for the band director who wants to keep educational integrity in his summer program. Full awareness and understanding of student availability during the summer months can be a difficult thing to put across to school officials and many in your community who feel it is the responsibility of the school band program to supply entertainment during the summer months. I personally believe that performances that may embarrass you or your students should be avoided. When a large number of principal players is missing, a mediocre performance is almost inevitable. Rarely do you have a program with sufficient depth in every section to satisfactorily solve such a problem.

A possible solution to summer performance commitments is a combined band made up of citizens of your community, alumni of your program, and your available band members. If satisfactory rehearsal times can be arranged, performances of acceptable quality may be achieved in this manner.

Using the Summer Program to Effect Band Personnel Changes

The summer session should be a time for reassessment of the entire program. Band lists for the next year should be formulated; deficiencies in instrumentation and player abilities should be corrected. This may necessitate seeking some new beginning students at higher grade levels and accelerating them to fill deficiencies in the band program of the following fall. Such beginning students should be very carefully selected. Your best sources are: 1) strong academic students who have not yet been recruited for the program and 2) switches from other instruments where an excess of players or embouchure problems make such changes possible or advisable. The switching of flute players to bassoon or oboe is usually quite successful. Changing trumpet players to baritone, French horn, or tuba and clarinetists to alto or bass clarinet is usually successful. The most important considerations to be made in these cases are: 1) the musical potential of the students being considered; 2) their academic strengths; and 3) their attitudes toward the switch and toward the overall program. It never pays to make an instrument change against a student's will; this procedure almost always results in the loss of the student from the program.

If carefully selected students are started or switched, it is possible to have an adequate band member within two months and a fine performer within six months to a year. This is obviously dependent upon the quality of your teaching and the overall potential and initiative of the student. In the case of beginners, a strong piano background is also very valuable.

Keeping Summer Attendance Records

Set up an attendance procedure for summer lessons. Give a grade at the beginning of the next school year based upon summer lesson attendance. I prefer to grade my students' summer lessons (with the exception of beginners) entirely on the basis of attendance. Record attendance in three ways: present; excused absence; unexcused absence. Four lessons of present attendance equals an A; four lessons of unexcused absences equals an F; four lessons of excused absences equals a C. Each unexcused absence lowers the grade a full mark; each excused absence lowers the grade one-half mark. With this method, a student with three lessons present and one unexcused absence receives a B, a student with three lessons present and one excused absence receives an A−, and so on. If your students know you are keeping accurate attendance records, they will be more likely to take summer lesson attendance seriously, especially if a grade based upon their attendance is forthcoming.

Comprehensive records of summer attendance can also be very valuable if your Administration or your Board of Education asks you to evaluate your summer program. Its continuance may depend upon your ability to justify its existence and its value to your overall program. If your attendance percentage is high, you have a good chance of saving the summer program. Comprehensive records may be kept in the following manner:

Summer Program—1976

Total Enrollment—253

Total Lessons Given—767 + 82 extra beginners' lessons = 849

Average attendance per week (not including extra beginners' lessons)—192

Percentage of attendance—76%

1st week	2nd week	3rd week	4th week
201	195	179	192
79.4%	77.1%	70.8%	75.9%

This summation is calculated from the following summer lesson attendance records, which are kept for each student. Note the other information included, specifically records of instrument serial numbers and ownership status. Such records are extremely valuable if a student's instrument is lost or stolen, and the information should be kept on permanent file until the student changes instruments or is no longer in the program.

Mondays	Students' Names	Instrument	Inst. No.	Ownership	Attendance	Grade
8:30	Mary Anne Smith	oboe	Loree 2738	School	++++	A
	Julie Jones	oboe	Laubin 487	Own	+++E	A−
9:00	William Pierce	trumpet	Bach 1763	Own	++EE	B
	John Andrews	cornet	Conn 6853	Own	O++E	B−
	Robert Brown	cornet	King 5737	Rental	++OO	C

The suggestions presented here may seem time consuming and somewhat complicated, but they will insure a successful and a continuing summer instrumental program.

DEVELOPING
THE STAGE BAND

8

The stage band is now accepted as a regular part of the music curriculum in many public schools. This development puts the stage band in a different light than the groups that have existed outside regular instrumental programs. Now, in order to have the overall program function smoothly, the stage band should be considered a part of the education system; it should have a close relationship with the concert band program.

A well-developed concert program provides the stage band with the following advantages:

1) A large pool of potential stage band members.

2) Young musicians who are well trained and can read music, not only academically but also stylistically.

3) Various expensive equipment that has been acquired for a comprehensive concert program. I have discovered, however, that some of my students have better and more extensive electronic and percussion equipment than does the school program. I draw upon these individuals when we are using trap sets, amplifiers, and guitar equipment as part of the concert program.

About the only area of stage band performance that is not developed in a comprehensive concert program is improvisation. Here is where you will have to do the most work in developing a functioning stage band.

HOW TO START A STAGE BAND PROGRAM

Use the following steps to set up your stage band program:

1) *Establish* that there is *strong interest among your students* for the formation of a stage band.

2) *Write* an *outline for* the *program*, including possible budget and so on, and present it to your school Administration and Board of Education for approval. Stage Band will undoubtedly be approved

as an activity, but it must have the sanction of school officials to use school facilities and school equipment. If you can convince your school officials that the stage band is to be considered a part of your established instrumental program, a modest budget for equipment and music should not be difficult to obtain.

3) *Meet with* your *cooperating music dealer* and ask his advice in regard to setting up a stage band program. He can give you very valuable information on equipment to use, music to purchase, and what is being done in other school systems in your area.

4) *Consult with other directors* in your area *who have established successful stage band programs.* Ask their advice in regard to specific equipment, instrumentation, and music.

5) *Begin selecting personnel.* This may be done by audition or by selecting those individuals you consider to have the best potential for performance of this type of music. Keep in mind that stage band players must be able to carry a part by themselves and usually must have some developed solo ability.

6) After your stage band has been organized for a few months, *expose your group to a stage band clinic or performances of* other *good high school stage bands* in your area. Your music dealer can tell you what clinicians may be available to you since most of them work through established music companies such as Selmer.

7) *Take your stage band to competition festivals* as soon as it is feasible. This type of experience will have the same positive effect upon a stage band as it has upon your concert bands.

HOW TO JUSTIFY THE CREATION OF A STAGE BAND

Base your justification for the establishment of a stage band on the following:

1) *Educational value* to a well-rounded instrumental music program.

2) *Student interest*, both as performers and as a potential audience.

3) *Functional advantages* of the stage band. The small size of the group and the varied stylistic literature that can be performed should be stressed. Also note the possibility of using the school stage band for such things as dances, thereby saving money for organizations sponsoring such events.

4) *Stress public relations value.*

5) Point out *additional musical challenge and enrichment* education *for* most *talented students*, who many times need supplemental materials to maintain a strong interest in the instrumental pro-

gram. Consider making concert band membership a prerequisite for membership in the stage band. This not only increases the interest and challenge to present band members, but it may also bring to your concert program new talents that have not yet been recruited. This is especially true in the case of percussionists, keyboard specialists, and guitarists.

SEATING ARRANGEMENTS FOR STAGE BAND

Two basic setups are usually recommended for stage bands: the "straight-forward" setup (see Figure 1) and the "V" setup (see Figure 2). I personally prefer the "straight-forward" setup. I believe that it leads to better balance and tighter rhythmic precision. Every performer in the stage band must be able to hear all other performers. This is not always possible in the "V" setup or any other setup that is not straight-forward. In general, brass, woodwind, and rhythm sections should be placed in tight groupings. This is especially true of your rhythm section; it never should be divided, with some members on one side of the winds and some on the other. It is also very important to be sure that any amplifying or speaker equipment that is used is placed in a position that will help balance the ensemble, not complicate its balance.

Avoid spreading your group out over a large area. Always place your group as far forward on the stage as possible and make sure that all brass players are not only playing with bells toward the audience, but that they

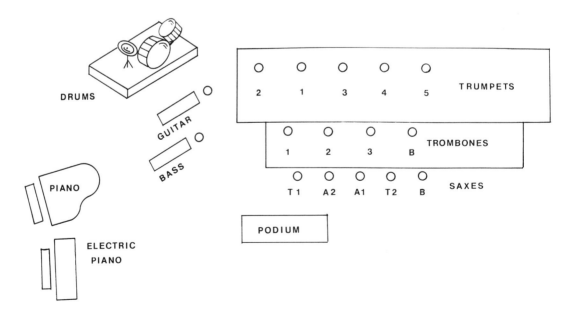

Figure 1. The "straight-forward" setup

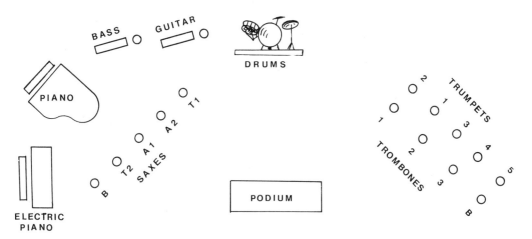

Figure 2. The "V" setup

are not blowing into stands or into bodies in front of them. Any obstruction that blocks the sound from going straight to the audience should be avoided.

See Figures 1 and 2 for possible stage band setups and positioning of specific players and equipment.

DEVELOPING THE MUSICAL ASPECTS OF THE STAGE BAND

Most of the musical aspects of the stage band should have been developed through a strong concert band program. Tone quality and intonation are obviously carry-over elements, as are the basic music reading abilities that have been developed within your concert players. Interpretation, especially of rhythmic notation, will present many new challenges, as will the development of improvisational skills.

Concert band skills that may be utilized include:

1) *Tone quality.* A good basic concert tone quality usually needs additional development of volume and range, plus various controls and uses of vibrato. Vibrato should be matched to the style of each composition, and speed and strength of vibrato matched within the wind sections of the group.

2) *Intonation.* A concert musician who plays in tune will continue to have good intonation if he does not overblow or distort his tone quality in some way during the stage band experience. Encourage your stage band members to add breath support and various vibrato techniques to their tone production without losing their basic concert tonal concept. One of the most difficult problems facing the young musician who wants to perform in both concert groups and stage bands or combos is development of

the ability to adapt to the subtle changes in tone quality that occur. The concert performer often has difficulty handling the tonal requirements of the stage band, and the reverse is true of the stage band performer. It is extremely rare to find an individual who can do both equally well. I believe the secret is in producing a very free and well-supported tone at all times, regardless of the idiom of performance. If this is accomplished, the mind will make the subtle tonal adjustments necessary with relative ease.

3) *Range*. The extreme range of many stage band charts can cause problems of forcing and extreme fatigue; in fact, these extreme ranges can literally destroy a brass player's embouchure. Again, the answer to this problem is blowing freely and using proper support. For example, if this is carefully developed in the concert performer, the trumpet player should have developed a free workable range to g above high c.

4) *Volume*. The loud volume required for stage band playing is relative, as are all dynamic markings, to the level you desire to produce. It is not necessary to play at your loudest volume at all times. This procedure is not only extremely taxing to the performers, but it also can be unpleasant to the ears of many in the audience. Use all dynamic levels with your stage band; don't play loud or very loud all of the time.

5) *Technique*. I believe the most valuable thing a teacher can do in preparing students for stage band performance is to teach them as many scale and chord patterns as possible. This means going beyond major and minor scales and arpeggios to drilling on modal scales and various seventh and ninth chords, plus other scale and chord patterns unique to stage band performance. Any difficult charts will indicate to you very clearly what is needed harmonically and melodically to successfully perform them.

6) *Rhythm*. The rhythmic aspects of stage band charts can be extremely complicated. Work in various types of syncopation and in odd meters can be very helpful. In most cases the eighth note is the clue to rhythmic mastery of a chart, and it is not unusual in advanced charts to run into eighth-note oriented mixed meter, such as 4/4 to 3/8 to 4/4 or 4/4 to 5/8 to 4/4. In advanced charts polymeter may also be encountered. Whether the eighth notes are played evenly or in different lengths is also a rhythmic challenge of stage band charts. A simple example of this is the long-short treatment of eighths in a "swing" style composition.

7) *Interpretation*. This will be the most challenging aspect of stage band performance, not only for the students but also for most high school band directors. If you have not had considerable experience performing in stage bands or combos, you may be moving into foreign territory musically. However, if you are inexperienced in jazz-oriented performance, you need not fear this musical void. You may use the same approach to stage band interpretation as you have used to the various aspects of concert band interpretation. Listening to good charts performed by fine stage bands is the best method for learning the idiom if you have no opportunity to learn as a performer. There are also many excellent books published

today that thoroughly break down each style for you and show you how to teach young people to reproduce the style. Some excellent sources are:

a) Hall, Dr. M.E. *Modern Stage Band Techniques.* Southern Music Company, San Antonio, Texas, 1975.

b) Hall, Dr. M.E. *Teacher's Guide to the High School Stage Band.* H. & A. Selmer, Inc., Elkhart, Indiana, 1961.

c) *Jazz Education in the 70's, A High School Teacher's Guide.* H.& A. Selmer, Inc., Elkhart, Indiana.

d) Polhamus, Al and Art Dedrick. *How the Dance Band Swings.* Kendor Music, Inc., East Aurora, N.Y., 1958.

e) Polhamus, Al and Aubrey Penman. *Basic Theory for Students of School Dance Bands.* Highland Music Company, 1311 North Highland Avenue, Hollywood, California 90028.

f) Wiskirchen, Rev. George. Various articles in *Selmer Bandwagon*, a magazine for which he is jazz editor.

In addition to the many fine commercial recordings available, an excellent recorded source is *The Smithsonian Collection*, P. O. Box 1641, Washington, D. C. 20013. These recordings from the Smithsonian Collection include the following albums: *The Smithsonian Collection of Classic Jazz; King Oliver's Jazz Band/1923; Louis Armstrong and Earl Hines/1928; Fletcher Henderson: Developing an American Orchestra, 1923–1937; Classic Rags and Ragtime Songs.*

8) *Phrasing.* Proper phrasing results from proper interpretation. The type of articulation you use is one of the most important factors in developing your interpretation and phrasing of a particular chart. The most common articulation used in stage band performance is the "du," or legato, tongue attack. The attack "tu" is rarely used; this is an attack the "square" player has great difficulty avoiding. Notes found within slur markings are almost always legato tongued, the slur indication designating the duration of the phrase. A phrase in jazz performance very often ends with an eighth note on the up-beat; this note is usually accented and should be chopped off, often giving it the feeling of a climax to the phrase.

9) *Improvisation.* The heart of jazz performance is the art of improvisation; it is also the most difficult element to teach. Having discussed improvisation with many individuals who do it well, I have drawn the following conclusions about learning and teaching it:

a) *Know* the *scales* and *chord patterns* involved and especially have control of the various aspects of the scale lines. Be sure to include common modal scale lines in your study.

b) *Listen to* and learn to recognize the *harmonic changes,* especially in the piano and in the bass line.

c) *Develop the art of transposition* so that you are able to modulate fluently from one key to another.

d) *Stick closely to* the *melody* line *at first* if one is easily discernible.

As you become more proficient, move to more advanced improvisation.

e) *Listen to* many *recordings by fine jazz artists*; develop a repertory of "riffs," motifs, and so on that will constantly grow with your listening experiences.

Several excellent books on improvisation have been written in recent years:

a) Aebersold, Jamey. *A New Approach to Jazz Improvisation, Volume I.* Schmitt Music Centers, 88 South Tenth Street, Minneapolis, Minnesota 55403.

b) Aebersold, Jamey. *A New Approach to Jazz Improvisation, Volume II, Nothin' But Blues*. Schmitt Music Centers, 88 South Tenth Street, Minneapolis, Minnesota 55403.

Each of the Aebersold books contains an LP record for all instruments. Four more volumes of the series are also available.

c) Baker, David. *Techniques of Improvisation* (4 vols.). Down Beat Workshop Publications, 222 W. Adams Street, Chicago, Illinois 60606.

d) Coker, Jerry. *Improvising Jazz*. Prentice-Hall, Inc., Englewood Cliffs, New Jersey, 1964.

e) *Instant Jazz for the Now Generation, Part III, Improvisation.* Youth Music Foundation, Box 86, Chapin, South Carolina.

This interesting three-part series was written by the Windjammers, a group who taught themselves to improvise. Part I is for beginners, especially junior high students, and gives a solid foundation for developing the art of improvisation. Part II, *Chord Progressions*, logically follows Part I.

10) *Transposition*. Transposition can be taught academically by clef or by interval. First develop a technical proficiency in each of the major and minor keys. When a performer can "think" in any key, transposition should be no problem. Using a "fake" book to study transposition simultaneously accomplishes transposition skills and the learning of basic jazz melodic literature.

CHOOSING THE PROPER LITERATURE

A large number of music publishing companies is producing charts today. These range from beginning stage band charts written especially for young students to the original charts of the best big bands, such as Stan Kenton, Buddy Rich, and Woody Herman. A selected list of stage band charts is found in the Appendices of this book.

DEVELOPING THE COMBO

Most groups that are organized outside the school music curriculum are combos. If the number of students you have available is limited, the combo may be a good starting point for your development of a stage band program. The combo has its limitations in regard to student participation and tonal flexibility. It usually requires more individual orientation to solo-type playing than the stage band. The combo is an excellent medium to use for your advanced students as you are developing the large stage band. It will keep talented players interested and develop immediate interest and initiative in the remainder of your stage band students. If the beginning student talent or experience is extremely limited in your school, you may start your program with a mixed combo of teachers (these need not be music teachers) and students. You should assess your particular situation and use the plan that will work best for you.

Four General Rules for Better Stage Band or Combo Performance

1) Develop a rhythmic "feel" for each style of chart being performed.
2) Use precise articulation at all times, whether it is a legato or a "clipped" style. Many times rapid combinations of these are needed.
3) Always keep good ensemble playing and precision as a top priority.
4) Never sacrifice good tone and intonation for excessive volume.

ADDITIONAL SOURCES FOR STAGE BAND MATERIALS AND INFORMATION

The following are a few of the many sources available for stage band materials:

1) Alfred Publishing Co., Inc., 75 Channel Drive, Port Washington, New York 11050.
2) Big Bells Incorporated, 33 Hovey Avenue, Trenton, New Jersey 08610.
3) Kendor Music Inc., Delevan, New York 14042.
4) Hal Leonard/Pointer Publications, Inc., 64 East Second Street, Winona, Minnesota 55987.
5) J. W. Pepper & Son, Inc., P. O. Box 850, Valley Forge, Pennsylvania 19482.
    Especially the following methods and text books:
    a) *Basic Jazz Improvisation*—Levey
    b) *Developing the School Jazz Ensemble*—LaPorta
    c) *Jazz Phrasing and Interpretation*—Giuffre
    d) *Patterns for Jazz*—Coker, Casale, Campbell, and Greene
    e) *Scales for Jazz Improvisation*—Haerle
    f) *Sound of Rock, The*—Feldstein-Scianni

6) Studio P/R, Inc., 224 S. Lebanon Street, Lebanon, Indiana 46052.
   Includes elementary, junior, and senior high arrangements, plus
   the following methods and texts:

   a) *Evolving Bassist, The*—Reid

   b) *Jazz/Rock Voicings for the Contemporary Keyboard
      Player*—Haerle

   c) *Jazz Trumpet Techniques*—McNeil

   d) *New Approach to Ear Training for Jazz Musicians*—Baker

   e) *No Nonsense Electric Bass*—Cacibauda

   f) *Pentatonic Scales for Jazz Improvisation*—Ricker

   g) *Technique Development in Fourths for Jazz Im-
      provisation*—Ricker

There is no doubt that the stage band has arrived in the public school
music curriculum. You should make every effort to develop some kind of
jazz-oriented organization. Although problems of scheduling and other
problems may discourage you in the beginning, the rewards resulting from
such an endeavor are well worth the effort that must be expended to
produce a successful group.

The Instrumentalist magazine has published many helpful articles in
regard to stage bands. Some of these are:

Baker, David, "Jazz Improvisation—The Weak Link," *The Instrumentalist*,
   vol. 26, November, 1971, p. 21.

Berry, John, "High School Jazz Bands—The State of the Art," *The Instrumentalist*, vol. 26, November, 1971, p. 18.

Blackley, Terry J., "Selecting Music for Jazz Contests," *The Instrumentalist*,
   vol. 27, February, 1972, p. 58.

Brown, Theodore D., "The Evolution of Early Jazz Drumming," *The Instrumentalist*, vol. 27, February, 1973, p. 47.

Burton, Gary, "Improvisation—For Basic Musicianship," *The Instrumentalist*, vol. 27, March, 1973, p. 32.

Colnot, Cliff L., "Understanding Jazz-Rock Articulations," *The Instrumentalist*, vol. 29, March, 1975, p. 103.

Deaton, Gene, "Brass Section in the Jazz Ensemble, The," *The Instrumentalist*, vol. 26, May, 1972, p. 58.

Dedrick, Lyle, "Priorities in Jazz Education," *The Instrumentalist*, vol. 27,
   November, 1972, p. 56.

Delp, Ron, "Adding Extra Percussion to the Stage Band," *The Instrumentalist*, vol. 27, December, 1972, p. 54.

Everett, Thomas G., "Literature for the Jazz Ensemble," *The Instrumentalist*, vol. 29, January, 1975, p. 62.

Everett, Thomas G., "Literature for the Jazz Ensemble, Part II," *The Instrumentalist*, vol. 29, February, 1975, p. 68.

Ferguson, Thomas, "Book Reviews," *The Instrumentalist*, vol. 27, November, 1972, p. 58.

Ferguson, Thomas, "Tips on the Rhythm Section, Part I," *The Instrumentalist*, vol. 26, November, 1971, p. 45.

Ferguson, Thomas, "Tips on the Rhythm Section, Part II," *The Instrumentalist*, vol. 26, December, 1971, p. 50

Hawes, Charles, "Recording the Jazz Band," *The Instrumentalist*, vol. 29, October, 1974, p. 86.

Jones, Morgan, "The Organization of the High School Jazz Band," *The Instrumentalist*, vol. 27, September, 1972, p. 70.

Kaye, Carol, "Teaching Electric Bass," *The Instrumentalist*, vol. 27, October, 1972, p. 60.

Kistner, Kenneth T., "Jazz Interpretation for the Traditionally Oriented Teacher," *The Instrumentalist*, vol. 26, November, 1971, p. 30.

Kuzmich, John Jr., "A Basic Jazz Solo Repertory," *The Instrumentalist*, vol. 29, May, 1975, p. 67.

Kuzmich, John Jr., "A Survey of Charts Available for the Jazz Combo," *The Instrumentalist*, vol. 29, September, 1974, p. 60.

Kuzmich, John Jr., "A Survey of Charts Available for the Jazz Combo, Part II," *The Instrumentalist*, vol. 30, September, 1975, p. 69.

Kuzmich, John Jr., "Jazz/Combo Charts—An Update, Part III," *The Instrumentalist*, vol. 31, January, 1977, p. 61.

Neidig, Kenneth L., and Colnot, Cliff L., "A Woody Herman 'Jazz Seminar,'" *The Instrumentalist*, vol. 29, April, 1975, p. 36.

Rickson, Roger E., "Organizing a Jazz Ensemble Tour," *The Instrumentalist*, vol. 27, January, 1973, p. 57.

Ross, Stewert L., "A Selected Bibliography of Jazz Improvisation Books," *The Instrumentalist*, vol. 29, November, 1974, p. 69.

Shew, Bobby, "Some Thoughts on Jazz Education," *The Instrumentalist*, vol. 29, February, 1975, p. 65.

Snyder, Robert C., "Teaching Melodic Improvisation," *The Instrumentalist*, vol. 30, September, 1975, p. 48.

Suber, Charles, "Jazz Flute," *The Instrumentalist*, vol. 27, November, 1972, p. 36.

Temple, Bruce Gregory, "Jazz Records—Learning by Listening," *The Instrumentalist*, vol. 26, November, 1971, p. 28.

The June issue of *The Instrumentalist* lists all articles published during the previous school year from August to June and is a quick reference for any information you may need.

DEVELOPING
THE MARCHING BAND

9

The well-developed concert band makes the establishment of an effective marching unit a relatively easy task. The musical aspect of the marching band has already been refined within the concert program. Many student musicians who read music well and produce satisfactory tones on their instruments should be available as a personnel pool. If you have carefully balanced the instrumentation of your concert band, instrumentation of a marching band should present little difficulty. Augmentation of your drum section and various aspects of your brass sound may be necessary, but many trained musicians should be available to double on percussion or brass during the marching season without weakening their ability to perform on their primary instruments. Flag lines and color guards can be formed from players of woodwind color instruments such as oboes, bassoons, and alto and bass clarinets. Excess clarinet and flute players may be used for this purpose also. Several members of our band's woodwind section are members of the school's majorette corps, which practices as a separate unit throughout the school year.

With musical and personnel problems solved, all that remains is teaching your band members to march and to perform various physical drills on the field or during the parade route. Your marching band should be established as an independent unit and should not replace the concert band during the football season. Concert rehearsals should continue on a regular basis.

Developing a large marching band may become essential to maintaining your concert program, especially at times of school budget problems. A marching band usually involves the greatest student participation of any of your groups and in turn draws your largest audiences. This can lead to strong community support for your program and can insure continued support from your school officials. Unfortunately, this support often comes from numbers, not necessarily quality. You may have to accept this fact in order to guarantee the continuance of the more musical elements of your band program.

The marching band does not have to be of inferior musical quality;

your well-developed concert program should insure this. A concert carry-over of good tone quality, acceptable intonation, and technical accuracy should occur. My bands, which are based upon concert concepts, have maintained a concert sound when marching. An original Sousa or Fillmore march is performed as musically during a Memorial Day Parade as it is in a concert situation.

The following is a list of basic principles involved in the marching band experience:

1) Playing musically at all times, regardless of the physical situation.
2) Developing precision in marching techniques.
3) Providing spirit for community and school events.
4) Developing good posture and physical conditioning.
5) Developing poise.
6) Stressing neatness in personal appearance.
7) Developing personal discipline, both mental and physical.
8) Creating an equal balance between playing proficiency and marching skills, which fully prepares your students for future participation in college or adult groups.

CONSIDER YOUR RESOURCES AND FACILITIES FIRST

No successful group can be formed without the proper personnel, proper equipment, and satisfactory uniforms. Evaluate these resources first. Next, evaluate the potential for a satisfactory yearly budget for your marching program. A strong marching program cannot succeed without this. Evaluate your facilities for rehearsals and performances. Elaborate shows, which must be seen clearly to be appreciated, should not be done at a football facility where the bleachers or stands are too low for most spectators to view the show properly. Also, consider where and when your marching band is going to rehearse. If the football field is some distance away, you must arrange a satisfactory substitute. This may require having yard lines drawn on some other area nearer to the school building. If you rehearse near a school building during school hours, you should be very careful not to disturb classes. Teachers and non-band students find it very difficult to concentrate in competition with drum cadences and martial music. Ignoring this fact can lead to unnecessary problems for the band director.

ADVANTAGES OF THE
LARGE MARCHING BAND

Charting a show may take longer with a larger band, but drilling time does not increase with the size of your group. The following advantages can be realized when you develop a marching unit of approximately 180 to 200, including 160 playing members plus majorettes and color guard.

1) The volume of sound is greater.

2) Drill and formation possibilities are greater.

3) The total effect upon the students is one of pride and considerable amount of thrill.

4) The total effect upon the school officials and the community usually leads to very strong support of the instrumental program.

5) Your ability to deal with personnel conflicts, such as football, cheerleading, work, and so on is significantly strengthened. Having more personnel enables you to have the flexibility to overcome the loss of some of your regular students from certain performances.

DEVELOPING THE ELEMENTARY SCHOOL MARCHING BAND

A high school marching band will have its best possible foundation with the formation of an elementary school marching band. If this young group is as well trained in marching fundamentals as it is in concert fundamentals, students coming into junior and senior high bands will have learned many of the marching rudiments used by the older groups. These rudiments should be approached in a logical manner according to difficulty, which is much the same approach as is used for developing technical proficiency in rhythm, scale, and chord materials.

A cohort of mine, Mr. Larry Wilson, recently developed a very successful elementary school marching band in our school system. I am deeply indebted to him for many of the ideas found in this chapter, and in particular the following outline for the establishment of an elementary marching band:

1) Membership shall include all instrumental music students in the fifth and sixth grades.

2) Music (two marches for first performance) shall be memorized by all members of the band, thus eliminating the use of lyres.

3) The twirlers and color guard contingent shall be formed during the spring and shall be instructed by volunteers.

4) Uniforms shall be designed and made by a group of volunteers, the core of which shall be elementary band parents.

5) Performances for the first year shall be confined to Memorial Day and community Independence Day programs.

6) Rehearsals shall begin in May and shall be scheduled two days per week immediately after school for a duration of one to two hours.

7) Written parental excuses for any student absences from performances must be handed in to the director at least three weeks prior to a performance of this organization.

With this outline in mind, Mr. Wilson, who is a percussionist, produced an excellent young marching band in approximately six weeks. The most difficult problem to be solved was equipment. A detailed list of drum equipment needed, including the cost of each item, was submitted to school authorities. Money was found in student activities accounts and other places and ultimately approved to finance the project.

As the elementary marching band develops, it will form the core for a much stronger high school marching program. This marching program was established as an addition to a fine elementary concert program, not as a substitute for any portion of the concert training of our young instrumental music students. It will not be overemphasized to the detriment of the overall concert program.

DEVELOPING THE JUNIOR HIGH MARCHING BAND

It is possible to develop a junior high marching band along similar lines. With the feeder system now established for both concert and marching bands, a continuation of the established elementary program is all that is needed. However, if you are teaching in a small school system, you can establish a grade 7 to 12 marching band. This gives you the potential personnel for a 180-piece marching unit even after students with conflicts have been eliminated.

THE TRADITIONAL MARCHING BAND
VERSUS THE "CORPS" APPROACH

Three major concepts should be considered when you are developing your marching band:

1) *The band as used during street parades.* The music and maneuvers are dictated by the character of the event. Use common sense when choosing your music; match it as closely as possible to the nature of the marching event. For example, jazz-type marches should never be played during a Memorial Day parade; traditional military marches should be used.

2) *The traditional marching band at football games.* This concept includes the formation of letters and figures in the style of early football bands.

3) *The modern marching band concept*, based upon drum corps marching techniques. Letters and figures are rarely used; various squad movements and designs are developed from a series of marching rudiments, which are easy to teach and which provide great flexibility when you are designing a show.

The need for the parade band is obvious, and its use is restricted by the nature of the parade. The field unit for football shows is best selected from a combination of traditional marching band techniques and the "corps" concept. The latter has many advantages, and has become the most popular approach in a modified form.

THE PARADE MARCHING BAND

The setup for the block formation of the parade marching band is usually determined by the number of trombone players you have in your group. Six to eight in a row is advisable. If you have less than six trombones, use baritones to complete your front row. Place your sousaphones on the outside positions of your second and third rows. Fill in these rows with horns, baritones, and saxophones. Sousaphones placed anywhere on the inside of the block obstruct the signals given by the drum major. Your next row is your percussion section, which is followed by your trumpets. Clarinets and flutes finish your block formation.

Use more first parts than seconds and thirds to create a satisfactory sound and to allow melody players adequate rest. Strong players should be placed on the outside and equally divided between left and right sides of the block. Keep weaker players inside. Form ranks of like instruments whenever possible; this helps both sound and appearance.

If the marching of your group is limited to an abbreviated program of two or three parades in the spring, preparation may be done in approximately seven days of outside rehearsals at 45 minutes per day. Plan your concert curriculum throughout the school year so that all band members have learned several quickstep marches that can be used for marching performances. Teach your percussion section several good cadences during the school year. They can use these cadences for assembly programs, football and basketball games, and other events.

A Four-Day Practice Schedule

Having previously prepared the musical aspects of your parade obligations, you can use the following plan to prepare your marching:

Day 1—March without instruments; place band members in proper spots for marching; work on attention (one long whistle), forward march (explain long preparation whistle and short execution whistle), halt, and so on. In general, work on keeping in step and keeping lines straight. Teach your band to guide right, left, or center, depending upon your preference.

Day 2—March without instruments; review all elements of Day 1; add a countermarch and a right and left turn. Turns are very difficult if you attempt to use a pinwheel turn with lines that have more than four members. Therefore, I use the following turn in place of the pinwheel:

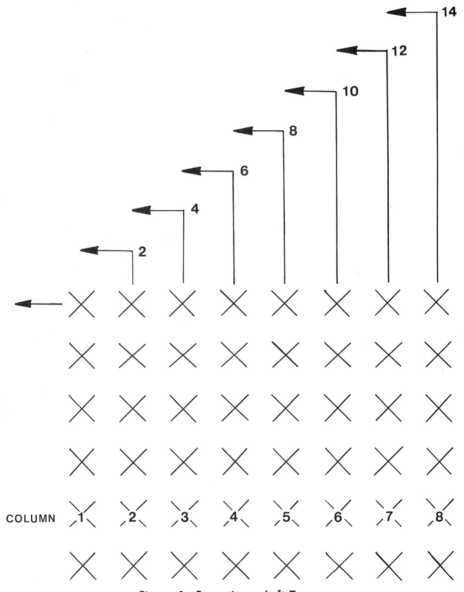

Figure 1. Executing a Left Turn

The pivot man on the inside of the turn executes a right or left flank and marks time. The first man in Column 2 takes two steps forward beyond the original pivot point, executes a flank movement, and marks time. The first man in Column 3 takes four steps forward beyond the original point of pivot, executes a flank movement, and marks time. The first man in Column 4 takes six steps forward, executes a flank movement, and marks time. When the eighth man reaches his pivot point, he executes a flank movement, marches forward immediately, and picks up the seventh man. The seventh and eighth men pick up the sixth man, and so on. Each person in the block must keep a two-step interval between him and all persons adjacent to him at all times. See Figure 1.

Day 3—Review all elements practiced during the first two rehearsals; add instruments and establish attention, carrying, and playing positions for each instrument. Uniformity of positions of like instruments is essential. Add roll-off and play a march or two while standing in formation or marking time.

Day 4—Add playing on the march to all elements already rehearsed.

Remaining Days—Perfect your mini-marching program; establish the order in which marches will be performed; explain and rehearse the specific order of maneuvers needed for this particular parade.

The above mini-marching plan has a prerequisite, which ensures that the older members of your band are reviewing these techniques from previous years. Only students new to your program can be neophytes to simple marching techniques.

THE TRADITIONAL MARCHING BAND ON THE FIELD

The traditional marching band works from the block formation of the parade band. Numbers are given to each performer in the block: first row—A1, A2, A3, A4, A5, A6; second row—B1, B2, B3, B4, B5, B6; and so on. As formations of letters, numbers, and figures are formed, each member learns his position by the placement of his letter-number designation. Band members move from one formation to another either by lines of "follow the leader" (similar to Ohio State's script "Ohio") or by disbursement. The disbursement method is most often used because of the visual effectiveness of the clarity of an organized formation as contrasted with the apparent disorganized confusion between formations. Charting a show is normally the designing of each figure by filling in individual band member designations. See Figure 2.

```
A1   A2   A3   A4   A5   A6   A7   A8

G8

G7

G6

G5

G4   B1   B2   B3   B4

G3

G2

G1

H4

H3

H2

H1
```

Figure 2. Charting by the Traditional Method

The transition from one formation to the next is done with music or with a drum cadence. Once the formation is formed, a number significant to that formation is played; for example, the forming of your school letters combined with the playing of your school fight song.

THE DRUM CORPS STYLE

In addition to the traditional marching band there is the drum corps style of precision marching. It is based upon precision drills and animated kaleidoscopic designs. Because of the added degree of precision required, all formations and maneuvers are charted for complete squads of four, not for individuals as in the traditional marching band. Many fine drum corps of the past were not large, numbering 48 or less. As marching bands began to adapt to this style of show, the number of participants grew to an average of 160 bandsmen plus majorettes and others.

In our school system we had developed only the traditional type of marching band, whose functions included just three parades per year. Recently we found it expedient because of public and school interest to develop a large show band for football games. We chose the drum corps style because it is easy to teach, shows almost immediate results, and has unlimited potential. Within one month we were able to present a show that was not only musically satisfying but drew the largest audience and the most enthusiastic community and school response that we had experienced at any music performance.

Use the following plan to form this corps type of organization:

1) *Personnel needed.* Since you will need a large band to produce the desired sound and visual effects, you need a personnel pool of approximately 160 playing members. We combined our 115-piece high school symphonic band with our 85-piece junior high concert band to create this large number. Out of this total were drawn 160 playing band members, 16 majorettes, 1 drum major, and a color guard of 8. Obvious musical and marching problems occurred at first when we used older and younger players in the same ensemble; but these were quickly worked out, and we had the personnel needed to develop our show.

2) *Squad lists.* Squad lists were developed from those students who had no conflicts. Students with conflicts and excess students in some sections were placed on substitute lists or excused from the activity. Squads were developed from like instruments, as follows:

Squad 1	*Percussion*	*Squad 40*	*Flutes*
	student's name		student's name
	student's name		student's name
	student's name		student's name
	student's name		student's name

3) *Marching Fundamentals.* Marching fundamentals were presented to each instrumental class. Basic maneuvers were explained and drilled within the classroom. Study guides were supplied to each student as follows:

Marching Fundamentals

I. *Marching Rudiments*

    A. Mark Time (MT)—Marching "in place" with the squad facing any direction.

    B. Forward March (FM)—Entire squad moves forward to a new location.

    C. Left Pinwheel (LP)—Entire squad moves in a ¼ circle to the left.

    D. Right Pinwheel (RP)—Entire squad moves in a ¼ circle to the right.

II. *Turn Rudiments*

    All turns are performed by placing the body weight on the ball of the right foot and turning to the left (counterclockwise). The turn is always executed on step 8, 16, 24, etc. of any marching rudiment.

    A. Left Flank (LF)—A 90 degree pivot.

    B. To the Rear (TTR)—A 180 degree pivot.

    C. Right Spin (RS)—A 270 degree pivot.

    D. Full Spin (FS)—A 360 degree pivot.

       Following the pivot turn, each bandsman takes a full 22½-inch step in the new direction with his left foot on the first count of the next rudiment.

III. *Step Size*

    A. Each step should be 22½ inches long.

    B. Bandsmen should move 8 steps per 5 yards.

    C. The arch of the foot should come down on all yard lines, ensuring that each body is exactly perpendicular to the yard lines.

IV. *Squad Formation*

    A. Squads will consist of 4 members of like instruments.

    B. Each member of the squad should be placed 2 steps or 45 inches apart.

    C. Squads are assigned a number for the purpose of identification on show directions.

V. *One-Squad Patterns*

    A. Circle—LP 32 *or* RP 32

    B. Hot Dog—FM 8; LP 16; FM 16; LP 16; FM 8.

    C. Teeny Wienie—FM 8; TTR; FM 8; TTR.

    D. Boomerang—LP 8; TTR; RP 8; TTR.

VI. *Staging Design*

    A. Setup design for any of the squad patterns.

    B. Each member is given a copy of these designs showing his relative position on the field at any point during the show.*

The original for the above outline was developed by Mr. Larry Wilson, who gathered many of his ideas from a series of books by Bill Moffit called *Patterns of Motion*, published by Hal Leonard Publishing Corporation. Each pattern was charted on a field planning chart, also available from Hal Leonard Publishing Corporation. An example of this type of charting is given in Figure 3.

---

*Copyrighted Patterns of Motion material. For further development of these techniques, advanced Patterns of Motion publications are recommended. Patterns of Motion techniques are published by Hal Leonard Publishing Corporation. This material used by permission.

All squads (Hot Dog) LP8; FM16; LP16; FM16; LP8 (64 steps)

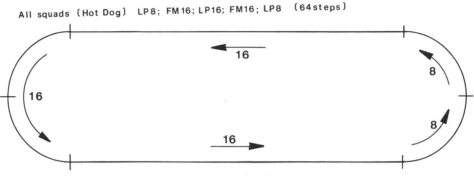

Figure 3. The Hot Dog

Mr. Wilson's charting outline for the first number in our first marching show (a Bicentennial program) is found below:

Field Show

Formation—See Stage Design #1

Music—*Yankee Doodle Boy*

Routing Instructions

4 whistles in tempo

Introduction—All squads MT 16

Letter A to B—All squads FM 32

Letter B to A₁—All even squads FM 32

Odd squads	1,11,21,31	FM 24; MT 8
	3,13,23,33	FM 24; MT 8
	5,15,25,35	FM 16; MT 16
	7,17,27,37	FM 16; MT 16
	9,19,29,39	FM 8; MT 24

See Stage Designs #7 and #8

Letter A₁ to B₁

Squads	10,20,30,40	FM 16; MT 8; RP 8
	8,18,28,38	FM 8; MT 8; RP 8; MT 8
	6,16,26,36	FM 8; MT 16; RP 8
	4,14,24,34	MT 24; RP 8
	2,12,22,32	MT 24; RP 8
	1,11,21,31	MT 16; RP 8; MT 8
	3,13,23,33	MT 24; RP 8
	5,15,25,35	MT 16; RP 8; MT 8
	7,17,27,37	MT 24; RP 8
	9,19,29,39	MT 16; RP 8; MT 8

See Stage Designs #11 and #12

Letter B₁ to C

All squads—Circle—RP 32

All squads—MT 8
  See Stage Design #13
Letter C to C₁
  All squads—Hot Dog—LP 8; FM 16; LP 16; FM 16; LP 8
    (64 steps) See Stage Design #15

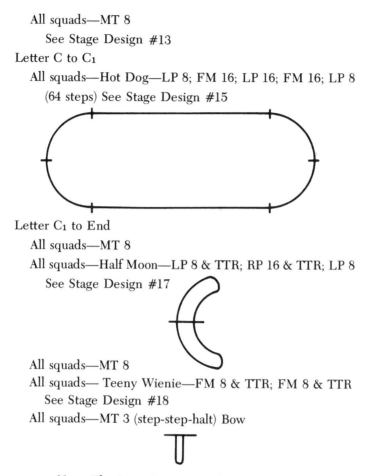

Letter C₁ to End
  All squads—MT 8
  All squads—Half Moon—LP 8 & TTR; RP 16 & TTR; LP 8
    See Stage Design #17

  All squads—MT 8
  All squads— Teeny Wienie—FM 8 & TTR; FM 8 & TTR
    See Stage Design #18
  All squads—MT 3 (step-step-halt) Bow

    Note: The Stage Design numbers are supplied so that each student can easily find every maneuver on his copy of the complete charting of the show.*

Planning a Corps-Type Show

1) General considerations:
    a) Charting can be done with any number divisible by four.
    b) It is not necessary to change the entire show each week.
    c) The total show must display unity and continuity. A feeling of direction is important, just as it is in performing a concert composition.
    d) The show must be based upon its musical content.
    e) Find large blocks of rehearsal time to put your show together.

---

*Copyrighted Patterns of Motion material. For further development of these techniques advanced Patterns of Motion publications are recommended. Patterns of Motion techniques are published by Hal Leonard Publishing Corporation. This material used by permission.

2) Specific order of procedure:

   a) Select a general theme for your show.

   b) Select a fanfare, if needed.

   c) Select entrance music that is dynamic and totally effective.

   d) Chart maneuvers to be used.

   e) Develop the concert portion of your show. This may include such things as special routines for majorettes and use of soloists.

   f) Chart the exit for the conclusion of the show.

3) Musical considerations:

   a) Establish and maintain good intonation.

   b) Emulate good concert tone quality.

   c) Don't neglect proper musical interpretation.

   d) Insist upon exact articulation.

   e) Insist upon accurate technique.

   f) Work for proper balance and blend of the ensemble.

   g) Develop satisfactory volume and projection with the breath; blow through instruments rather than into them; chart so that players with important musical lines are facing the audience.

   h) Continuous playing helps maintain interest, although short percussion bridges are necessary at regular intervals to give embouchures some rest.

   i) Use variety in styles and tempos of the music. Variety in tonal quality should also be utilized; use special percussion equipment such as Latin instruments.

4) Maneuver and drill considerations:

   a) Develop a series of marching maneuvers. Developing a marching band's technique is much like learning rudiments on snare drum; the more specific patterns you master, the more possibilities you have when developing your shows.

   b) Match marching maneuvers to the music in much the same manner as choreography matches dancing to the music in ballet. Use abrupt and quick movements for staccato and marcato styles; use smooth movements for legato music. Circle movements are excellent for legato. Always analyze the music to be used. Chart drills to match the music or find music to match the drill.

   c) Develop proper marching steps—8 steps per 5 yards on a football field. This creates a 22½-inch step, which must be lengthened to 30 inches in parade marching. Knees should be raised approximately half way to horizontal.

d) Placement of instruments—Place instruments in formations for the best possible musical effect. Strong musical ideas must be aimed at your audience.

e) Establish proper positions for all instruments during attention, parade, rest, marching, and playing. Keep trumpets and trombones at a horizontal position when playing. Develop a synchronized movement for instruments when they are moving to and from playing positions.

f) Plan your entrance onto the field.

g) Develop change-of-direction movements, such as flanks, facings, and turns.

h) Develop animated drills—Don't avoid moving from side to side on the field. Bands that have been trained at 8 steps per 5 yards will keep proper step sizes and intervals without yard lines as guides. Your audience is on the sides of the field, not in the end zones.

i) Add simple dance steps to your band's marching technique.

j) Work out specific details of execution for your color guard and majorettes that correspond to the maneuvers being done by the playing part of the band.

SCHEDULING THE MARCHING BAND

Scheduling may be the most difficult aspect of developing the marching band. I strongly believe that the marching band should be considered an auxiliary aspect of the concert program and should not be so overemphasized that it may weaken the existing concert core of the complete instrumental program. Marching band should be limited to specific events during the school year, including home football games and two or three specific parade events in the spring.

Avoid sacrificing a large amount of your concert rehearsal time for marching rehearsals. After school or evening rehearsals may be necessary, even though many conflicts with other activities and work may occur. Study the prevailing attitudes in your community and the specific attitudes of your students toward the time and effort needed for a massive marching program before you require large amounts of rehearsal time outside of school hours. Using alternate regular school rehearsal times for concert and marching rehearsals may be the best compromise. This will guarantee that the concert program will not be tabled during football season.

Supplying Your Marching Band with Proper Equipment

When establishing the large marching band, use conventional instruments that are available in your concert program. Instruments that can only be used for marching must be considered a luxury and should be purchased only if you have an ample budget and if your concert band equipment is first-class. Instruments normally supplied by the school, such as tubas and conventional marching drum equipment, may require a considerable investment. A marching type of tuba (sousaphone) must be available for each of your tuba players at a cost of approximately $800 per instrument. Upright tubas cannot be carried properly, nor is their sound effective on the field. A basic set of quality equipment for a marching percussion section can be purchased for a total of approximately $1,000. Each snare or tenor of an acceptable quality can be purchased for $80 to $100 with a school discount.

Standard Percussion Equipment includes:

1) 1 or 2 pairs of cymbals; 2 pairs allow players to alternate for rest.
2) A minimum of 2 snares for a band of 80, plus 1 for each additional 40 players.
3) A number of tenor drums equal to half of the snares.
4) 1 bass drum (2 with a large band, although two alternating bass drums can be advantageous for any marching unit).

Suggestions for Developing the Percussion Section

1) Use very active percussion parts, but keep them as simple as possible for clarity of sound.
2) Don't allow your percussion to be too loud. When the band is playing, the percussion should be about half as loud as during solo percussion passages.
3) Choose a cadence speed that best fits the event or best fits your band's abilities. Drum cadences should be uncomplicated at very fast tempos. Investigate the several styles of percussion playing that are based upon speed and style; for example, military, fast-step, and Scotch. The percussion section should play like rhythms in fast tempos but can be more diversified in slower tempos.
4) Use visual contact to keep your percussion players together when they are separated by large distances.
5) Alter parts to maintain rhythmic interest. Add notes on the beat to upbeat snare parts; eliminate long rolls by substituting "1 & 2 &" patterns.

6) Add Latin instruments to Latin-rhythm numbers; also use rim and head variations for fancy beats.

7) Keep your percussion section busy all year. Have them learn cadences early in the year and allow them to write their own cadences later. Use some exceptional student cadences for performance. Percussionists need this type of activity to maintain interest and discipline.

Tips on Improving Brass Playing on the March

1) Blow freely; concentrate on proper and plentiful use of the diaphragm muscle and resulting breath support.

2) March on the balls of your feet, not on your heels, to cushion jarring of the lips.

3) Work on erect posture by practicing balancing a book on your head while marching; when the head is held perfectly level and not allowed to move up and down, playing when marching becomes almost as easy on the embouchure as concert playing.

4) Keep the head erect or slightly above horizontal. Blow over the lower lip; keep pressure off the upper lip.

5) Develop depth in your brass section so that endurance and mass of sound are not problems. Instruct your strongest brass players to alternate for occasional rest.

Switching Instruments for Marching Instrumentation

Double reeds, alto and bass clarinets, and an excess of flutes are of little value to a marching band. Many of my students double on other instruments. Double reed to flute and lower clarinet to B-flat soprano clarinet are common doublings. Excess flutes may be used on various saxophones, which are much more effective instruments on the field. Nonessential players can also be used as flag carriers, color guard, majorettes, or additional percussionists (bell lyre, cymbals, and so on).

The Majorette Corps

Majorettes should be handled by another member of your staff, not necessarily a music teacher, who has considerable background in twirling. Our majorettes practice during the entire school year as a separate activity. They have tryouts similar to those of the cheerleaders, and rehearse after school one or two afternoons each week. They rehearse with recordings or tapes made by our band and perform with or without live accompaniment for basketball games and other events. Our majorettes receive letter awards for this activity. When the band marches, the majorette corps is already prepared and only has to be added to the marching band.

Using Other Groups to Assist the Marching Program

It is possible to use many school or community groups to assist your marching program. These can include gymnastic teams, choral ensembles, dance groups, and your school cheerleaders.

Organization and Use of the Color Guard

The color guard is usually formed from members of your concert band who are not essential to your marching sound and who are excellent marchers capable of mastering special drill routines. Color guard uniforms can match those of the band or the majorettes. Abbreviated majorette uniforms for color guard are not considered in good taste. White gloves worn by each member of the color guard add to the sharp appearance of the group.

Follow these suggestions when organizing the color guard:

1) *Position of the flags.* The American flag should always be to the marching right; no other flags are allowed in front of it. It can be placed in front of the center of a complete line of flags. Follow the lead of Veterans' organizations. The United Nations flag should be placed at any position to the left of the American flag. Some states, such as Ohio, require the state flag to be at the immediate left of the American flag.

2) *Position of color guard for parades.* In block formation, the color guard can be the first line of the block or a separate line in front of the block. If the guard is not a part of the block, it can maneuver independently.

3) *Number involved.* The minimum number for color guard is four, two flag bearers and two guards. I prefer a flag line and guard equal to the number in the width of my block.

4) *Arming of the guard.* Guards need not be armed but may use rifles, pistols, or sabres. A sabre in the hands of the commander of your guard can be very effective visually.

5) *Maneuvers of the color guard.* Most maneuvers can be used if the American flag is the only flag used. About face, left face, left flank, to the rear, and so on cannot be used by the color guard if any other flags are carried.

6) *Field entrance.* The color guard can enter as a part of the unit (first line) or lead the unit as a separate line. It can follow the unit only if

the band after entering forms an aisle through which the colors can be presented to the audience.

7) *Field exits*. The colors should precede the band when they are leaving the field.

Selecting and Arranging Your Marching Music

1) Use quality arrangements; there is no reason to use inferior music on the field.
2) Use marches with full chordal treatment or definite melody and counter-melody lines. Most good arrangements will break down into melody, countermelody, and rhythmic background.
3) Find excellent symphonic band compositions and rescore them for field performance. Instrumentation and scoring of some marches may not be satisfactory for marching performances. Woodwind parts may be too technical or in extreme ranges.
4) Avoid upbeats for potentially melodic instruments such as French horns and trombones. Have them play melody or countermelody.
5) Develop pockets of sound by careful placement of instruments.
6) Use occasional silences for musical effect.
7) Avoid consecutive afterbeats and intricate patterns in the percussion.
8) Relate a student's marching assignments to the music he is playing by marking in each marching maneuver.
9) Memorize the music whenever possible.
10) Don't choose music that is too difficult for your group.
11) Develop a marching band library and filing system. Use student librarians. The best system of filing that I have found is explained in "Two Time Savers for the Marching Band Librarian" by Ralph S. Vitt, *The Instrumentalist*, October, 1974, p. 49.

Using a Narrator and the Video Tape Recorder

Using a connecting script and a narrator for your show, especially the concert portion, is very effective. Using a video tape recorder at rehearsals and at the performance can be very helpful for pointing out errors and making improvements in your band's marching technique.

Using Recordings of Marching Music

In choosing published band arrangements and shows, seek out those that are advertised with recordings; recordings in addition to advertising scores make your selection of music much easier and much more effective.

How to Find Detailed Information
on Marching Band Techniques

1) Magazines, such as *The Instrumentalist* and *Music Educators Journal*, publish monthly book reviews that include marching band texts.

2) Almost every music publisher has some useful texts available.

3) A quick source for materials is a large music corporation that handles music of many publishers. Two of these are:

   a) J. W. Pepper & Son, Inc., P. O. Box 850, Valley Forge, Pa. 19482. The *Pepper Marching Band Guide* includes fanfares, march books, marching band music, percussion cadences, marching band texts, manuals for drum majors and majorettes, color guard, and even gun spinning.

   b) Educational Music Bureau, Inc., 434 South Wabash, Chicago, Ill. 60605.

HELPFUL ARTICLES FROM THE INSTRUMENTALIST

Berry, Lemuel S., Jr., "Bibliography of Marching Band Books," *The Instrumentalist*, vol. 29, October, 1974, p. 50.

Bilik, Jerry H., "The Corps Versus the Band," *The Instrumentalist*, vol. 29, June, 1975, p. 41.

Bowles, Richard W., "The Simplicity System of Arranging for Marching Band," *The Instrumentalist*, vol. 27, April, 1973, p. 77.

Brown, Carl R., "The Video Tape Recorder-Teaching Aid," *The Instrumentalist*, vol. 27, October, 1972, p. 54.

Brown, Valerie and Claudette Sisk, "Strutting Techniques for Majorettes," *The Instrumentalist*, vol. 29, October, 1974, p. 44.

Caneva, Donald E., "Individual Attention to Detail," *The Instrumentalist*, vol. 25, May, 1971, p. 59.

Combs, F. Michael, "Organize Your Marching Band Drum Section Early," *The Instrumentalist*, vol. 27, September, 1972, p. 58.

Fink, Ron, "Marching Percussion—An Interview with Larry McCormick," *The Instrumentalist*, vol. 29, March, 1975, p. 91.

Foster, William P., "The Marching Band—Problems and Solutions," *The Instrumentalist*, vol. 27, October, 1972, p. 28.

"Football/Marching Music Guide," *The Instrumentalist*, vol. 27, August, 1972, p. 43.

"Football/Marching Music Guide," *The Instrumentalist*, vol. 28, August, 1973, p. 63.

"Football/Marching Music Guide," *The Instrumentalist*, vol. 29, August, 1974, p. 87.

"Football/Marching Music Guide," *The Instrumentalist*, vol. 29, June, 1975, p. 85.

Gerardi, J. L., "The High School Band at the Professional Football Game," *The Instrumentalist*, vol. 26, May, 1972, p. 28.

Higgins, William, "Drill Teams and Dancing Groups with the Band," *The Instrumentalist*, vol. 26, September, 1971, p. 57.

Kissinger, William D., "Your Halftime Announcer," *The Instrumentalist*, vol. 25, March, 1971, p. 47.

Kreutzer, Bill, "Editing the Marching Band Percussion Part," *The Instrumentalist*, vol. 27, October, 1972, p. 48.

Larrick, Geary, "Which Marching Band Drumming Style Do You Prefer?" *The Instrumentalist*, vol. 26, June, 1972, p. 50.

Sanford, Fred, "Today's Field Percussion," *The Instrumentalist*, vol. 29, June, 1975, p. 50.

Snoeck, Kenneth M., "Corps Style and the Marching Band," *The Instrumentalist*, vol. 29, June, 1975, p. 49.

Snoeck, Kenneth M., "Marching Band Charting for Maximum Musical Effect," *The Instrumentalist*, vol. 27, September, 1972, p. 61.

Sunderman, Norman A., "Planning a Drill Show," *The Instrumentalist*, vol. 26, September, 1971, p. 51.

Tetzlaff, Daniel B., "Brass Playing on the March," *The Instrumentalist*, October, 1972, p. 46.

Vitt, Ralph S., "Two Time Savers for the Marching Band Librarian," *The Instrumentalist*, vol. 29, October, 1974, p. 49.

Wright, Al G., "Marching Band Uniform Trends," *The Instrumentalist*, vol. 26, October, 1971, p. 30.

Wright, Al G., "The Large Marching Band—Bigger Can Be Better," *The Instrumentalist*, vol. 27, October, 1972, p. 26.

SELECTED BIBLIOGRAPHY OF MARCHING BAND TEXTS

Bayless, A., *Fieldshow Flash: A Treatise on Training the High School Marching Band*. New York, New York: Bourne, 1957.

Bilik, Jerry H., *Gridiron Showmanship Marching Band Performance Kit*. Ann Arbor, Michigan: Jerry Bilik Music, Inc., 1974. (An unbound collection of 15 "folios," $25.)

Binion, W. T., Jr., *The High School Marching Band*. West Nyack, New York: Parker Publishing Company, Inc., 1973.

Butts, Carrol M., *How to Arrange and Rehearse Football Band Shows*. West Nyack, New York: Parker Publishing Company, Inc., 1974.

Casavant, A. R., A comprehensive series of books including *Block Progressions* (1965); *Block Specials* (1968); *Fast Break* (1962); *Field Entrances*

(1959); *Precision Drill* (1957); *Precision Drill Line Movements* (1958); *Phalanx Drill Movements* (1959); *Staggered Block Drill* (1961); *Wrapping the Block* (1966). San Antonio, Texas: Southern Music Co. Valley Forge, Pennsylvania: J. W. Pepper & Son.

Cavender, George, *Instrument Placement and Projection for the Modern Marching Band.* Ann Arbor, Michigan: Jerry Bilik Music Co., 1973.

Dale, Carroll R., *Fundamentals of Drill for Marching Bands, Drum Corps, Pep Squads and Other Marching Units.* Chicago, Illinois: Gamble Hinged Music Company, 1941.

Duvalle, W. Clyde, *The High School Band Director's Handbook.* Englewood Cliffs, New Jersey: Prentice-Hall, Inc., 1960.

Dvorak, Raymond F., *The Band on Parade.* New York, New York: Carl Fischer, Inc., 1937.

Fielder, Charles, *Field Tactics for Military Band.* New York, New York: Carl Fischer, Inc., 1937.

Foster, William P., *Band Pageantry—A Guide for the Marching Band.* Winona, Minnesota: Hal Leonard Music, Inc. 1968.

Foster, Robert E., *Multiple-Option Marching Band Techniques.* Port Washington, New York: Alfred Publishing Company, Inc., 1975.

Franklin, Ralph W., *Props Make the Band Show.* Winona, Minnesota: Hal Leonard Music, Inc., 1957.

Hjelmervih, Kenneth, *Marching Bands: How to Organize and Develop Them.* New York, New York: Barnes, 1953.

Hooker, Pat, *Pat Hooker Manual of Basic Dance Steps.* Delevan, New York: Kendor Music, 1960.

Johnson, G., *The Color Guard.* Lake Hiawatha, New Jersey: G. Johnson and Co., 1972.

Johnston, Lawrence, *Parade Technique.* Melville, New York: Belwin Inc., 1944.

Leckrone, Mike, *Koncert Kaleidoscopes on the March*, Vol. I and II. Lebanon, Indiana: Studio P/R, 1973. (Effective programming for "low-bleacher stadiums" and smaller bands.)

Leckrone, Mike, *Quick Steps to Arranging for Marching Band.* Valley Forge, Pennsylvania: J. W. Pepper & Son.

Lee, Jack, *Modern Marching Band Techniques.* Winona, Minnesota: Hal Leonard Music, Inc., 1955.

Marcouiller, Don R., *Marching for Marching Bands.* Dubuque, Iowa: W. C. Brown, 1958.

Moffit, William C., A series including *Master Planning Guide, 80 Piece Band Book*, etc. Winona, Minnesota: Hal Leonard Music, Inc., 1964.

Moffit, William C., a series including *Master Planning Guide, 80 Piece Band Book*, etc. Winona, Minnesota: Hal Leonard Music, Inc., 1964.

Moffit, William C., *Patterns of Motion Staging Designs*. Winona, Minnesota: Hal Leonard Music, Inc., 1966.

Piersol, Frank and Ralph Smith. A series including *12 Easy Precision Drills for Company Fronts for 48-, 64-, 80-, and 96-piece Band*. Winona, Minnesota: Hal Leonard Music, Inc., 1968.

Righter, C. B., *Gridiron Pageantry*. New York, New York: Carl Fischer, Inc.

Roberts, Bob and Charles Scott, *Art of Drum Majoring*. New York, New York: Belwin Inc., 1958.

Spohn, Charles and Richard W. Heine, *The Marching Band*. Boston, Massachusetts: Allyn and Bacon, Inc., 1969.

Weaver, Max and Carol Butts, *Field-Color Entrances for Marching Band*.

Wells, James R., *The Marching Band in Contemporary Music Education*. New York, New York: Interland Publishing, Inc., 1976.

Wettlaufer, J. Maynard, *Building a Show Band*. Rockville Centre, Long Island, New York: Belwin Inc., 1948.

Wright, Al, *Marching Band Fundamentals*. New York, New York: Carl Fischer, Inc., 1967.

Wright, Al, *The Show Band*. Evanston, Illinois: The Instrumentalist Company, 1968.

HOW TO DEVELOP
SYLLABI FOR ALL
BAND INSTRUMENTS

10

Every instrument used in a concert band should be taught with the use of a carefully organized year-by-year syllabus. If you assume that most students start to study a band instrument at the beginning of the fifth grade, each syllabus should cover approximately eight years of the student's study with you.

A good syllabus should include every aspect of the student musician's development. The following general categories should be carefully planned:

1) Development of tone quality

2) Development of a strong sense of good intonation

3) Development of technical abilities:

    a) Proper tonguing technique and speed of tonguing

    b) Proper fingering technique and speed of fingering

    c) Embouchure flexibility and strength

    d) Use of embellishments such as trills, turns, grace notes, and so on

Technical aspects of development, such as tonguing and fingering, must include specific speed to be attained rhythmically and metronomically on each exercise at each level of proficiency.

4) Development of rhythmic skills. These may be the most important skills to be taught since most of our musical problems seem to be based upon rhythmic errors or weaknesses.

5) Development of musical elements of performance:

    a) Various skills in interpretation

    b) Awareness and control of dynamic levels

    c) Knowledge of musical terms of all types

    d) Development of phrasing skills

    e) Development of articulation skills

    f) Accents and various signs indicating such things as length of notes

6) Development of physically related skills:

    a) Proper breathing

    b) Proper posture, both sitting and standing

    c) Development of the ability to play equally well whether the musician is sitting or standing. Proper posture when the musician is sitting should eliminate any great differences between playing in a sitting position and playing in a standing position.

7) Selection of the material to be used to accomplish each of the above.

If a comprehensive syllabus is established and strictly followed, you should have excellent results when your young musicians play together in band ensembles.

ESTABLISHING A YEAR-BY-YEAR PROGRAM
TO DEVELOP PROFICIENT INSTRUMENTALISTS

When you are establishing a syllabus for each of your bands and for each individual instrument, each syllabus should be derived from a detailed plan of behavioral objectives for each level of achievement. These levels can be established by using either the student's academic year in school or the number of years a student has studied a specific instrument. I prefer the latter because it allows me to start a student at any academic grade level if I feel he has the potential to do well on a specific instrument.

Grade levels of playing proficiency can be established in the following manner: Grade I can be based upon materials to be mastered during the student's first year of study, Grade II can be based upon materials to be mastered during the second year of study, and so on. The basic syllabus for each aspect of the program will state the minimum to be achieved after a given number of years of study. Since all human beings are different, the more gifted, the more intelligent, and the more motivated students should be allowed to progress at their own speed. A talented student with considerable initiative could attain a level of proficiency that would be considerably higher than that of his average classmates. I have had many students who progressed through several grade levels in one year. The student should always have this opportunity to progress beyond a stated level of proficiency; but if the stated minimum level is not achieved, the teacher may consider dropping the student from the program.

All syllabi should be divided into two major categories:

1) *General band syllabi* for each of your bands that state the minimum requirements for membership in each organization.

2) *Specific syllabi for each instrument* used in the band program.

DEVELOPING GENERAL BAND SYLLABI

Create a general plan of goals and objectives for each level of band performance. Divide the requirements for membership in each band into tonal, technical, and musical goals and objectives. This can be done in the following manner:

1) *Tonal and intonation goals.* These are general or subjective when compared to technical goals and are based upon the teacher's concepts and standards of good tone and intonation. Specific embouchure exercises on specific instruments may be required; these are found in Chapter 14.

2) *Technical goals:*

   a) Specific *tonguing techniques*, such as single, double, triple, and flutter tonguing and speed of single, double, and triple tonguing.

   b) *Range*—This will vary considerably with specific instruments.

   c) *Fingering technique*—Proficiency in specific keys. Each key should include mastery of scale line, arpeggio, scale by thirds, and the chromatic scale as found within the pitch range of the scale being studied. Each of these should be done with specific rhythms and at specific speeds.

3) *Musical goals.* Musical knowledge to be acquired, including understanding of dynamics, accents, signs for length of notes, musical terms, and so on.

General syllabi for the levels of band performance are given below:

I. *The Elementary Band* (Grade I and II levels for all instruments)

A. *Tone and intonation requirements.* These depend upon the director's judgment, what you consider acceptable achievement in these somewhat intangible areas of student preparation.

B. *Technical goals and objectives for winds*

1) *Tonguing requirements*—Proper tonguing attack is dependent upon your personal standards. Definite goals can be set, however, for speed of consecutive tonguing attacks. For example:

     a) Tongue consecutive eighth notes at m.m. = 120.

     b) Tongue a C, F, or G major scale in eighth notes at m.m. = 72.

2) *Fingering requirements* should include the following:

     a) Mastery of C, F, and G scales in one octave in eighth notes at m.m. = 72.

     b) Mastery of C, F, and G major arpeggios in eighth notes at m.m. = 72. The range will be determined by specific instrumental syllabi.

c) Mastery of C, F, and G scales by thirds in eighth notes in one octave at m.m. = 72.

d) Mastery of chromatic scale in eighth notes at m.m. = 72. The range will be determined by specific instrumental syllabi.

Technique in the keys of B-flat and D major should be mastered by the end of the second year of study in the same manner. Octaves of playing proficiency will be determined by specific instrumental syllabi.

3) *Rhythmic requirements*—Demonstrate the ability to count whole, half, quarter, dotted-quarter followed by eighth, and eighth note rhythms, including equivalent rests. The foot beat should be used properly for all of these rhythms.

C. *Musical knowledge*—Set up specific requirements in regard to terms, symbols, and so on that must be understood before a student can enter the elementary band. A survey of elementary band music will supply a reasonable list, which may include:

1) *Dynamic markings*, such as p, mf, and f, and crescendo and diminuendo markings. Both symbols and complete terms should be learned.

2) Common *tempo markings*, such as allegro, andante, and adagio.

3) Other *musical terms*, such as dolce, ritardando, and accelerando. This aspect of band preparation is important but not nearly as important as proper technical preparation. Therefore, greater emphasis should be placed upon the latter.

D. *Technical goals and objectives for percussion.* At this level all percussion students are normally concentrating on the snare drum. There-fore, requirements should be established in relation to snare drum technique, rhythmic reading, and general knowledge of musical terms.

1) *Rudiments*—All students should be able to perform 12 consecu-tive examples of the following rudiments at m.m. = 108–120:

a) Single-stroke roll, four sixteenth notes to a beat.

b) Long roll, the equivalent of four wrist actions to a beat; double, triple, or multiple bounce can be used.

c) Ruff, 5-stroke, 9-stroke, and 17-stroke rolls done in the same manner as the long roll.

d) Single paradiddle in eighth notes at m.m. = 120.

e) Single ratamacue.

f) Flam, flam-tap, and flam paradiddle (all in eighth notes).

g) Flam accents No. 1 and No. 2.

2) *Rhythmic requirements*—Demonstrate the ability to play the following rhythms with proper reciting syllables: quarter notes, eighth notes, sixteenth notes, eighth and sixteenth combinations (♪♬ , ♬♪), and simple patterns in compound time

(♩. , ♪♪♪ , ♩ ♪).

The above are maximum requirements for percussionists in an elementary band. If you have at least one student who can meet all these requirements, several other students who have not mastered all these techniques could be used on auxiliary percussion parts.

3) *Musical knowledge*—Similar to those requirements of other elementary band members, but sometimes unique to the percussionist's specific part or specific percussion techniques. Dynamic levels and various types of accents are particularly important. The level of music you play with your elementary band will determine the requirements for band members.

The above is a very general syllabus for elementary band. This ensemble should perform at the Grade I and II levels if its membership is fifth and sixth graders. The requirements stated are reasonable average goals for a group of this level. My syllabus for an elementary band would be more specific since I am aware of all of the factors, human and environmental, that may limit or extend the minimum levels of proficiency for such a group in my school system.

II. *The Junior High Band* (Grade III and IV levels for all instruments)

A. *Tone and intonation requirements.* Your standard of tonal quality and intonation for your junior high band will determine whether a student is ready for this level of band participation. See individual syllabi for more specific requirements such as developed vibratos for flute, oboe, and bassoon students.

B. *Technical goals and objectives for winds:*

1) *Tonguing requirements*—Proper tonguing attack is dependent upon your personal standards.

a) Tongue consecutive sixteenth notes at m.m. = 120.

b) Tongue a C, F, G, B-flat, or D major scale in sixteenth notes at m.m. = 80. See specific instrumental syllabi for the number of octaves to be used.

2) *Fingering requirements:*

a) Mastery of the C, F, G, B-flat, and D major scales in sixteenth notes at m.m. = 80. The number of octaves is determined by specific syllabi.

b) Mastery of C, F, G, B-flat, and D major arpeggios in sixteenth notes at m.m. = 80. Range will be determined by specific instrumental syllabi.

c) Mastery of C, F, G, B-flat, and D major scales by thirds in sixteenth notes at m.m. = 80. Range is determined by specific syllabi.

d) Mastery of chromatic scale according to specific instrumental syllabi.

Keys of E-flat, A, A-flat, and E major should be mastered by the end of the second year in junior high band or the fourth year of study. Octaves of playing proficiency will be determined by specific instrumental syllabi.

3) *Rhythmic requirements*—Students should demonstrate the ability to count all rhythmic requirements of the elementary level plus common patterns in sixteenth notes (♫♫ , ♫♩ , ♩♫♫ etc.), common patterns in compound time (♩. , ♩ ♪ , ♫♫♫ etc.), common patterns involved when the eighth note equals the beat, such as 6/8 in six beats to a measure, common patterns involved in alla breve. The simpler patterns found in all four basic types of counting should be understood at this point, including basic syncopation figures.

C. *Musical knowledge*. A survey of your junior high band music will supply a reasonable list of symbols and terms to be added to the musical requirements of the elementary band level.

D. *Technical goals and objectives for percussion*. Add more advanced requirements to the technique, rhythmic reading, and general musical knowledge required of elementary band members. Elementary and intermediate drum cadences and beginning work with a trap set can be added at this level.

1) *Rudiments*—All students should be able to perform 12 consecutive examples of all 26 basic snare drum rudiments at m.m. = 120.

2) *Rhythmic requirements*—All percussionists should be able to demonstrate reading ability in all four major categories of rhythmic reading: common time— 4/4, etc.; alla breve—2/2, etc.; rhythms where the eighth note equals the beat—6/8 in six beats to a measure; compound time—6/8 in two beats to a measure.

The above are maximum requirements for percussionists at the junior high level. If you have two or more students of this ability, weaker percussionists can be used on auxiliary percussion parts. At this point serious attention should be given to specific development of mallet and timpani players. Snare drum players can be switched to these instruments, but the most satisfactory solution may be starting students with considerable keyboard background on these instruments to augment your percussion section. The serious percussionist may be able to do both and should be taught to be proficient on all percussion instruments if possible.

3) *Musical knowledge*—These requirements can be taken from typical junior high band percussion parts of Grade III to Grade IV difficulty and from the study material being used in lessons at that level.

The above is a very general syllabus for junior high band and is not based upon exact behavioral objectives. This ensemble should normally perform Grade III and IV music if its membership is seventh and eighth graders. The requirements stated are reasonable goals for a group at this level. My junior high band syllabus is more specific for the same reasons my elementary band syllabus is more specific.

III. *The Senior High Band* (Grade V and VI levels for all instruments)

A. *Tone and Intonation requirements*. At this point each student should have four years of background on his instrument. Refinement of tone and intonation should have been developed to a standard equal to the level of technical proficiency achieved. Your tonal concept will determine if a student's tone and intonation are acceptable for your senior high band. Fully developed vibrato should be demonstrated on instruments such as flute, oboe, and bassoon. Full saxophone vibrato can be dangerous since it is so often overdone. All winds except those in the clarinet family and French horns may demonstrate tasteful vibrato in solo passages; the degree of vibrato used is dependent upon the type of composition being performed.

B. *Technical goals and objectives for winds:*

1) *Tonguing requirements*—Proper tonguing attack should be refined to a very high degree. All attacks should be well controlled so that they will blend musically with each other, even in accented passages. Too much use of harsh "ta" attacks is quite often a major problem. Use various forms of the "da" attack to improve the overall band sound.

a) All instrumentalists who can employ a double or triple tongue attack should have learned controlled forms of these attacks through specific instrumental syllabi.

b) Each player should demonstrate the use of double tongue in consecutive sixteenths on any chosen pitch at m.m. = 144. Use the following two exercises to evaluate this development, using either of the consonant combinations given:

c) Each player should demonstrate control of the triple tongue on the following exercises at m.m. = circa 96. Use any pitch and either of the consonant combinations given.

During the student's tenure in senior high band he should learn to use these techniques on passages where the pitches change during the exercise. Ultimately he will be able to perform scale passages ascending and descending while employing proper double or triple tonguing syllables. All brasses and flutes should perfect this material. Other instruments should continue to perfect a very rapid single tonguing technique, playing consecutive sixteenths at gradually increasing speeds. Rapid single tonguing coordination should be expected on the major scales of C, F, G, B-flat, D, E-flat, A, A-flat, and E, both ascending and descending in sixteenths at m.m. = circa 84. The number of octaves is determined by specific instrumental syllabi for this level of proficiency.

2) *Fingering requirements*—All techniques should be practiced ascending and descending, with woodwinds slurring and brasses tonguing.

a) Mastery of C, F, G, B-flat, D, E-flat, A, A-flat, and E scales in appropriate octaves in sixteenth notes at m.m. = circa 84.

b) Mastery of arpeggios in the first nine keys, performed in the same manner as the scales; ranges are determined by specific instrumental syllabi.

c) Mastery of scales by thirds in the first nine keys, performed in the same manner as scales.

d) Mastery of the chromatic scale through the normal playing range of the instrument. The student should demonstrate playing proficiency chromatically from the lowest note on his instrument to the extent of his high range in sixteenths at m.m. = 84.

The remaining six major keys should be mastered by all band members during their fifth year of their individual instrument syllabi. Since each is enharmonic with one other key, only three keys need to be learned in regard to fingering technique (D-flat = C-sharp; G-flat = F-sharp; C-flat = B). Various forms of minor scales and arpeggios, dominant seventh and diminished seventh arpeggios, and so on should be studied during the last three years of the syllabus. The only limitations to how much can be taught are the students' innate abilities to learn and their initiative. I have taught my band members pentatonic and whole-tone scales and several of the more common modes, such as Dorian and Mixolydian.

3) *Rhythmic requirements*—All students should now be well-trained in the four basic methods of counting. At this point training should perfect all aspects of rhythmic concepts learned thus far and should advance into odd meter studies and the type of advanced syncopation found in the many forms of popular music your band is to perform. Band music can be used very effectively to teach advanced rhythmic concepts, especially those related to popular music. A survey of the type of band literature you play at the high school level should determine what should be taught rhythmically. The foot should still be used whenever possible to study and demonstrate understanding of advanced rhythmic concepts.

C) *Musical knowledge*—Let this level of musical knowledge be dictated by the band literature you plan to perform. Every term found in each band composition should be reasonably understood by your band members. Although many high school students are reluctant to learn terms, your constant pointing out of these terms as the music is being rehearsed or studied in lessons will be a learning experience for many of your students. The academic understanding of terms by your students is important, but you can control this aspect of performance from the podium. The performance level and success of your group is based primarily upon the technical skills and reading ability of your band members.

D) *Technical goals and objectives for percussion*—At this level of playing experience all rudiments should have been learned and rhythmic facility in the four basic methods of counting should have been established. Rudiments and reading ability should be perfected in speed and accuracy. How advanced your materials at the high school level become is dependent upon your students' abilities and initiative and your knowledge of advanced percussion techniques. Obvious fields of advanced study include:

1) Study of odd meter materials.

2) Study of rhythms used in the many forms of popular and Latin music your band may perform, with special emphasis on advanced syncopation patterns.

3) Study of various playing concepts and techniques used on the trap set.

4) Branching out into the study of other percussion instruments. All of your percussionists should be exposed to tympani and mallet techniques.

5) Emphasis on percussion ensemble material will strengthen any band percussion section.

The senior high band syllabus is so dependent upon the background your students have received in previous band playing that any specific approach to materials and techniques to be used must grow from what your first-year senior band students have learned and mastered technically and musically. If your elementary and junior high programs are well developed and well taught, the high school band can be developed to the level of many college organizations and sound semi-professional in performance. If the foundation in the lower grades is not as strong as I have outlined, your high school program will have to begin where your junior high program ended. Therefore, if you place primary emphasis upon the training and musical experience your elementary and junior high band members receive, an exceptional high school program should evolve as the requirements of your year-by-year syllabi are met.

DEVELOPING SPECIFIC INSTRUMENTAL SYLLABI

After general band syllabi are established, you should develop a syllabus for each band instrument based upon year-by-year minimum achievement objectives. Each syllabus should include all of the elements of the general syllabus plan for band, with the addition of any techniques, exercises, and materials to be used in the development of specific instrumental skills.

Divide each individual instrument syllabus into the following categories:

1) Embouchure: The development of tone and intonation.
2) Tonguing: The development of a proper physical tonguing approach and the development of a rapid tonguing technique.
3) Fingering: The development of fingering technique.
4) Breathing: The development of proper breath support, control, and phrasing as they are related to the breath.
5) The study of ornaments, such as trills, turns, and grace notes.
6) Musical symbols and terms to be learned.
7) Materials to be used: These include warmup routines and technical exercises, method books, solos, and ensembles.
8) A selected bibliography pertaining to each instrument.

DEVELOPING COMPREHENSIVE LISTS OF SOLO, ENSEMBLE, AND METHOD BOOK MATERIALS FOR EACH INSTRUMENT

Comprehensive lists of materials can be developed from various sources.

1) *State manuals* of solo and ensemble competition materials.
2) Various *colleges* with strong music departments print lists of solo, ensemble, and method book materials for their students. You may be able to acquire some of these lists through student teachers of yours, former students who are music majors in college, or through friends you know on college staffs.
3) *Periodicals and magazines*, such as *The Instrumentalist* and *Music Educators Journal*, print lists of materials on occasion and usually have regular reviews of new materials.
4) *Reading clinics* for new band music, set up by state or regional music organizations. *State and regional conferences* usually have materials on display, especially if they invite displays from publishers. Much free material may be obtained in this manner.
5) *All publishing companies* have catalogues and free copies of their published materials available on request.
6) *Visiting other schools* that have strong music programs will supply you with much information on all kinds of materials.
7) Whenever you converse with *another band director, a college music student* or *a professional player*, ask him what new materials he is using.

8) *Live or recorded performances* of various compositions may also expand your repertoire of materials. I became aware of a large amount of the standard literature used in my program in this manner.

If you are an opportunist, your knowledge of solos, ensembles, method books, and étude materials will be constantly growing. There is no substitute, however, for trying the materials yourself and arriving at your own evaluation of their value to your program.

EXPANDING STUDY LITERATURE
THROUGH CLEF READING AND TRANSPOSITION

If you choose your literature carefully, the amount of musical material that you can use in your program can be considerably expanded through teaching your student musicians to read several clefs. A bassoonist, for example, can use trumpet études as extra study material if he is fluent in tenor clef. The B-flat transposition of the trumpet gives you exact trumpet pitches when the bassoonist reads the trumpet part as tenor clef (a major second below if treble clef interval transposition is used; a perfect fifth above if bass clef transposition is used) and adds two flats to the key signature. This, of course, makes it possible for the young bassoonist to play duet or étude materials with a friend who is a trumpet or clarinet player.

Manipulations such as this are possible for all instrumentalists, but especially for those who read more than one clef as a part of their instrumental training. The advanced trombonist who reads fluent tenor or treble clef may also use trumpet literature in the same manner as the bassoonist. Either the bassoonist or the trombonist can be taught to read pitches in treble clef (concert pitches), but these parts cannot then be combined with B-flat instruments for ensemble playing of homogeneous literature.

A trumpet player who can read bass clef baritone fingerings not only can use bass clef materials, he can also play alto saxophone literature by reading it as bass clef and adding three flats to the key signature.

Since I believe in teaching by performance-oriented methods (which includes playing often with my students), I constantly use various clef and interval transpositions to teach my classes. This permits me to play any instrument with a student, regardless of what instrument he plays.

The use of clef and interval transposition by the student not only enables him to enlarge the mass of étude material available to him, it also enables him to play duets or ensembles with various instruments. I have found this to be strong practice motivation for students who are friends but play different instruments. Students as young as junior high have asked me how to play duets with the different instruments their friends play.

Through clef and interval transposition, I have been able to strongly motivate them to practice together.

The following are possible new sources of materials through clef or interval transpositions:

1) Flute—Many selected trumpet, clarinet, oboe, and saxophone compositions can be valuable for flute through 8va transposition. Material that goes below c^1 should be avoided.

2) Bassoon, trombone, and bass-clef baritone—Saxophone literature can be used by changing to bass clef and adding three flats. Carefully selected trumpet and clarinet compositions can be used by changing the clef to tenor clef and adding two flats or by reading the études as concert pitch in treble clef.

3) Trumpet—Carefully selected bass-clef compositions can be played on trumpet by reading bass-clef baritone fingerings. Alto saxophone compositions can be used by reading them as bass clef and adding three flats to the key signature. Be careful of accidentals—they do not always read as written. For example, a c-sharp for alto saxophone must be played as an e-natural when you are using the bass-clef baritone approach.

4) Tuba—Trombone and other bass-clef compositions can be used by the tuba player who can read an octave lower than the printed part. This also makes carefully selected alto saxophone compositions available to the tuba player.

5) Any treble-clef étude composition can be used for a bass-clef instrument by simply changing the clef to bass clef and adding three flats to the key signature. The tuba must read 8^{alt}. All materials must fall within the range of the instrument using the materials after the clef has been changed.

ADAPTING VARIOUS COMPOSITIONS
TO ALL INSTRUMENTS

In expanding instrumental literature resources, and especially étude materials, consider the following:

1) Any instruments whose ranges are comparable can use each other's literature. If the range of any specific instrumental étude is written within the normal playing range of another instrument, it can be used for supplementary material. For example, many saxophone and oboe études are interchangeable; carefully selected cornet or trumpet materials can be used for alto and bass clarinet; selected bassoon, bass-clef baritone, and trombone compositions are interchangeable.

2) Various clef changes make many adaptations possible. Baritonists can use not only bass-clef trombone and selected bassoon compositions but also carefully chosen alto saxophone études. The baritonist can use trumpet literature by reading treble clef trumpet fingerings.

The following are some examples of literature adaptation:

1) Flute, oboe, and saxophone materials are interchangeable if the upper ranges are reasonable.

2) Alto and bass clarinets can use not only clarinet compositions of moderately high range but also trumpet materials. Some excellent examples of the latter are the various études for trumpet by Sigmund Hering, which are very musical études for the lower clarinets. These études especially drill the student on crossing the "break."

3) Alto clarinets can use alto saxophone material that is not consistently above c^3. The Voxman *Selected Duets for Saxophone, Vol. I,* are excellent material for alto clarinet.

4) French horn can use many trumpet materials that have a moderately high range. The Hering études are excellent material for the developing horn student.

5) Many bass and tenor clef compositions for bassoon, bass-clef baritone, and trombone are interchangeable.

6) Trumpet can use any treble-clef material of reasonable range without transposition. Concert pitch études may be read, however, as C-trumpet, transposing upward a major second.

7) Treble-clef baritone not only can play any trumpet composition but also any composition that can be adapted to trumpet.

8) Tuba can use any low-range bass-clef composition without transposition.

9) Percussion keyboard instruments can use any instrumental or vocal material that is within their playing range. Many compositions can be used if they are transposed at sight or rewritten within the range of the keyboard instrument. Music in the relative range of the trumpet is easily adapted to most keyboard instruments, such as marimba or xylophone.

If you use your imagination, and if you train your students to be intelligent readers of music, many more practical literature adaptations can be found for all band instruments.

DEVELOPING
WOODWIND SYLLABI

11

Your syllabus for each instrument can be as brief or as detailed as you desire. The following syllabi are abbreviated, since space is not available here for detailed syllabi. Only the flute syllabus contains a moderate amount of detail. The planned goals for each year of study are given, with special attention given to each aspect of playing to be developed. Some detail is given for the first lesson and the trial beginning period because of their relative importance to the ultimate success of each student.

THE FLUTE SYLLABUS

First Lesson

The student should learn the following during the first week of study:

1) Proper assembling of the flute.

2) Proper placement of the fingers on the flute.

3) The embouchure should be explained and demonstrated by the teacher, using only the head joint of the flute. By the end of the first week of study the student should be able to produce a high note on the open head joint and a note an octave lower with the right hand covering the open end of the head joint, each to a duration of four beats at m.m. = 60.

4) At the end of the first week of study the student should be able to produce a whole note on c^2, b^1, a^1, and g^1 at m.m. = 80, using the foot to count each beat and the tongue to begin each pitch.

5) Practice time should be recorded; one-half hour per day, divided into two or three small segments to avoid excessive fatigue.

Work to Be Completed by the
End of a Six-Week Trial Period

1) Mastery of the first four pages of the *Universal Fundamental Method*, demonstrating acceptable tone quality, acceptable tongue attacks to begin each note, proper fingerings, and a foot beat that controls the rhythm accurately.

Grade I—The First Year of Study

1) Use of natural harmonics to develop proper tone quality and range flexibility.

2) Development of single tonguing of sixteenths at a minimum of m.m. = 60.

3) Study of first three keys on Selmer Scale Sheet for Flutes: C, F, and G major, slurred in eighth notes with the key notes (c in the key of C, for example) receiving a full beat, two octaves ascending and descending at m.m. = 72. This includes study of the scale, arpeggio, scale by thirds, and the chromatic scale within the range of the key being studied.

4) Beginning study of vibrato in pulsations of one and two to a beat at m.m. = 72. Write in breath marks to develop length of breath phrasing (approximately eight beats to each breath at m.m. = 80). Many beginning students will be uncomfortable with this length of breath phrase, but they will develop the breath control of the proper length of phrasing quicker with this realistic approach.

5) Learning of very basic musical terms and symbols as they occur in study material.

6) Materials:

   a) Method books—*Universal Fundamental Method* plus *Rubank Supplementary Studies for Flute*. Both books should be completed by the end of the first year.

   b) Supplement with Grade I solo and ensemble material.

Grade II—The Second Year of Study

1) Continuation of harmonic and vibrato study to improve tone quality.

2) Development of single tonguing of sixteenths at m.m. = 96–120.

3) Mastery of the keys of C, F, G, B-flat, and D major in the same manner as in Grade I at m.m. = 80–96.

4) Vibrato study continued to three or four pulsations to a beat at

m.m. = 60. Continue careful phrasing by marking in all breath marks.

5) Learn additional musical terms and symbols as they occur.

6) Materials:

    a) Method books—*Rubank Intermediate Method for Flute* and *Forty Little Pieces in Progressive Order for Beginner Flutists* by Moyse (excellent for transfer of controlled rhythmic vibrato to melodic material; pulsating background of the beat reinforces rhythmic training.)

    b) Supplement with Grade II solo and ensemble material.

Grade III—The Third Year of Study

1) Harmonic and vibrato exercises to refine tone quality and control.

2) Development of single tonguing of sixteenths at m.m. = 120. Begin study of double tonguing to equal speed of single tonguing by the end of the year.

3) Add keys of E-flat and A; play all material of first seven keys in sixteenths at m.m. = 72.

4) Increase vibrato study to four or five pulsations per beat at m.m. = 60. Continue careful phrasing study.

5) Learn musical terms as encountered.

6) Materials:

    a) Method books—*Advanced Rubank Vol. I* and Koehler's *Thirty-Five Exercises for Flute, Book I.*

    b) Supplement with Grade III solos and ensembles.

Grade IV—The Fourth Year of Study

1) Harmonic and vibrato exercises to refine tone quality and control.

2) Development of double tonguing of sixteenths at m.m. = 144+.

3) Add keys of A-flat and E; play all material of first nine keys in sixteenths at m.m. = 80.

4) Vibrato developed to five or six pulsations per beat at m.m. = 60.

5) Learn musical terms as encountered.

6) Materials:

    a) Method books—*Advanced Rubank Method, Vol. II* and Koehler's *Thirty-Five Exercises for Flute, Book II.*

    b) Supplement with Grade IV solos and ensembles.

Grade V—The Fifth Year of Study

1) Harmonic and vibrato exercises to refine tone quality and control.

2) Development of triple tonguing, using syllables "da-da-ga da-da-ga" or "da-ga-da ga-da-ga" at speed of m.m. = 60 for two sixteenth-note triplets.

3) Add keys of D-flat, B, and G-flat major (C-sharp, C-flat, F-sharp). Develop all techniques in new keys with eighth notes at m.m. = 80.

4) Vibrato should now be well established and free at approximately five and one-half to six vibrations per second.

5) Continue learning new musical terms as encountered.

6) Materials:

   a) Etudes—Soussman's *Complete Method for the Flute, Part II;* Eck's *Flute Trills;* Voxman's *Selected Studies for Flute;* Koehler's *Thirty-Five Exercises for Flute, Book III;* and Cavally's *Melodious and Progressive Studies, Book I.*

   b) Supplement with Grade V solos and ensembles.

Grade VI—The Sixth Year of Study

1) Appropriate warmup material to refine tone and intonation.

2) Use short daily tonguing exercises to maintain good tonguing technique in all types of tonguing.

3) Develop all techniques in all major keys with sixteenths at m.m. = 80.

4) All phrasing carefully designed and effected by breath control.

5) Continue to learn musical terms as encountered.

6) Materials:

   a) *24 Flute Concert Studies From J. S. Bach's Works and Famous Flute Solos* (published by Southern Music Company); Cavally's *Melodious and Progressive Studies, Books II* and *III;* and Andersen's *24 Studies,* Opus 15.

   b) Supplement with Grade VI solos and ensembles.

Grades VII and VIII—The Seventh and Eighth Years of Study

Since these years of study are completely dependent upon what has been accomplished to this point, a syllabus will not be given here. If your students have accomplished all that has been outlined thus far, you can follow this general plan for technical and musical improvement.

1) Study other scales and arpeggios in a manner similar to the major

key study. These may include minor scales in three forms, whole-tone scales, modes, dominant-seventh and diminished-seventh arpeggios, and so on. You may have to make up your own study materials for some of this technical study. I have done this on staff duplicator paper, which allows me to run off over 100 copies of each.

2) Much of the material used at this point should consist of advanced solos and ensembles. Ensemble work, beginning with two homogeneous instruments and expanding to heterogeneous groups such as woodwind quintets, are of greater musical value at this point than more étude study material. All aspects of technique should have been developed to a very high level, freeing the student to spend most of his study time on improving musicianship and learning advanced repertoire.

SELECTED FLUTE BIBLIOGRAPHY

Brown, Carol, "Piccolo Solos," *The Instrumentalist*, vol. 31, November, 1976, p. 50.

Coltman, John W., "Acoustics of the Flute," (Part I), *The Instrumentalist*, vol. 26, January, 1972, p. 36.

Coltman, John W., "Acoustics of the Flute," (Part II), *The Instrumentalist*, vol. 26, February, 1972, p. 37.

Coltman, John W., "The Intonation of Antique and Modern Flutes," (Part I), *The Instrumentalist*, vol. 29, December, 1974, p. 53.

Coltman, John W., "The Intonation of Antique and Modern Flutes," (Part II), *The Instrumentalist*, vol. 29, January, 1975, p. 43.

Coltman, John W., "The Intonation of Antique and Modern Flutes," (Part III), *The Instrumentalist*, vol. 29, February, 1975, p. 47.

Coltman, John W., "The Intonation of Antique and Modern Flutes," (Part IV), *The Instrumentalist*, vol. 29, March, 1975, p. 77.

DeLaney, Charles, *Teacher's Guide for the Flute*, Elkhart, Indiana: Selmer Division of the Magnovox Company, 1969.

Finnigan, Mary M., "Two Approaches to Flutter Tonguing," *The Instrumentalist*, vol. 27, June, 1973, p. 48.

Fletcher, Neville, "Some Acoustical Principles of Flute Technique," *The Instrumentalist*, vol. 28, February, 1974, p. 57.

Goodberg, Robert, "A Long Tone Exercise for Flutists," *The Instrumentalist*, vol. 31, February, 1977, p. 56.

Instructive Talks to Flutists. Elkhart, Indiana: Selmer, Inc., 1955.

Klein, Robert E. "New Books for Flutists," *The Instrumentalist*, vol. 27, May, 1972, p. 42.

Kujala, Walfrid, "Jawboning and the Flute Embouchure," (Part I), *The Instrumentalist*, vol. 26, September, 1971, p. 34.

Kujala, Walfrid, "Jawboning and the Flute Embouchure," (Part II), *The Instrumentalist*, vol. 26, November, 1971, p. 34.

Kujala, Walfrid, "Jawboning and the Flute Embouchure," (Part III), *The Instrumentalist*, vol. 26, December, 1971, p. 38.

Mather, Roger, "Care and Repair of the Flute," (Part I), *The Instrumentalist*, vol. 27, December, 1972, p. 40.

Mather, Roger, "Care and Repair of the Flute," (Part II), *The Instrumentalist*, vol. 27, January, 1973, p. 41.

Mather, Roger, "Care and Repair of the Flute," (Part III), *The Instrumentalist*, vol. 27, March, 1973, p. 66.

Mather, Roger, "Care and Repair of the Flute," (Part IV), *The Instrumentalist*, vol. 27, April, 1973, p. 54.

Oldberg, Elaine, "Notes on Beginning Flute Players," *The Instrumentalist*, vol. 29, October, 1974, p. 54.

Palmer, Harold G., *Teaching Techniques of the Woodwinds*. Melville, N. Y.: Belwin, Inc., 1952.

Pellerite, James, *A Handbook of Literature for the Flute*. Bloomington, Indiana: Zalo Publications, 1963.

Pellerite, James, *A Modern Guide to Fingerings for the Flute*. Bloomington, Indiana: Zalo Publications, 1964.

Simpson, Mary Jean, "A Vibrant Tone for Everyone," *The Instrumentalist*, vol. 29, September, 1975, p. 53.

Simpson, Mary Jean, "Flute Intonation Trouble: Spare Not the Rod," *The Instrumentalist*, vol. 26, March, 1972, p. 63.

Suber, Charles, "Jazz Flute," *The Instrumentalist*, vol. 27, November, 1972, p. 36.

Timm, Everett L., *The Woodwinds*. Boston, Mass.: Allyn and Bacon, Inc., 1964.

Waln, Ronald, "The Flutist's Forte," *The Instrumentalist*, vol. 29, April, 1975, p. 44.

Webb, Robert K., "An Annotated Flute Choir Bibliography," *The Instrumentalist*, vol. 29, June, 1975, p. 63.

Weerts, Richard, *Developing Individual Skills for the High School Band*. West Nyack, N. Y.: Parker Publishing Company, Inc., 1969.

Westphal, Frederick W., *Guide to Teaching Woodwinds*. Dubuque, Iowa: Wm. C. Brown Company, 1962.

Syllabi for the other woodwind instruments can be developed in the same manner as the flute syllabus. This is especially true in developing tonguing and fingering techniques. Only exceptions that are unique to a specific instrument are presented here, followed by a selected bibliography for each instrument. Listings of method books and étude material are found in the Appendices of this book.

THE OBOE SYLLABUS

1) Embouchure: Tone and intonation can be refined in a manner similar to that used on the flute. Proper placement of the reed in the mouth is extremely important. For acceptable tone and intonation, the student should move the reed out of the mouth until only the tip is used. Most students have too much reed free in the mouth, creating a tone quality that is too bright and sharp intonation on many pitches. A correctly made and adjusted reed is essential to creating proper oboe tone and intonation; this usually means that the exceptional young student must study with a professional oboist if one is available. If one is not available, results in this area of student development will be somewhat less than excellent, depending upon your knowledge of oboe reeds and embouchure and your ability to demonstrate proper embouchure and tone quality. You may have to rely on recordings for tonal concept and books or articles for technical knowledge.

2) Single Tonguing: Developed as single tonguing on flute; use "da" approach to rapid tonguing.

3) Fingering: Use edited Selmer Scale Sheet for Clarinet.

4) Breathing: Vibrato and phrasing are developed as on the flute.

5) Musical symbols learned as on the flute.

6) Materials:

     a) Method books and étude material, listed according to grade level:

         Grade I: *Oboe Method, Book One*, Gekeler-Hovey, Belwin, Inc.

         Grade II: *Oboe Method, Book Two*, Gekeler-Hovey, Belwin Inc.

                             Intermediate Method, Skornicka-Koebner, Rubank, Inc.

         Grade III: *Oboe Method, Book Three*, Gekeler-Hovey, Belwin, Inc.

                             Practical Oboe Studies, Book I, Gekeler, Belwin, Inc.

         Grade IV: *Advanced Method*, Voxman-Gower, Rubank, Inc.

Practical Oboe Studies, Book II, Gekeler, Belwin, Inc.

Grade V: *Selected Studies*, Voxman, Rubank, Inc.
            Practical and Progressive Oboe Method, Andraud, Southern Music Co.

Grade VI: *Vade Mecum*, Andraud, Southern Music Co.
            Fifteen Grand Studies for Oboe, Barret, Boosey & Hawkes (sole selling agent)

Grade VII: Advanced solo and ensemble literature.

Grade VIII: Advanced solo and ensemble literature.

b) Supplement each grade level with solos and ensembles appropriate to that level.

SELECTED OBOE BIBLIOGRAPHY

Lehman, Paul R., *Teacher's Guide to the Oboe*. Elkhart, Indiana: H. & A. Selmer, Inc., 1965.

Mayer, R. and T. Rohner, *Oboe Reeds: How to Make and Adjust Them*. Evanston, Illinois: The Instrumentalist Co., 1953.

McGann, Daniel M., "Oboe Reed Binding Materials," *The Instrumentalist*, vol. 29, June, 1975, p. 67.

Moore, E. C., *The Oboe Book*. Kenosha, Wisconsin: G. Leblanc Co., 1957.

Probasco, Robert, "Guidelines for Purchasing an Oboe," *The Instrumentalist*, vol. 28, February, 1974, p. 62.

Probasco, Robert, "Preparing the Oboe Reed for Playing," *The Instrumentalist*, vol. 29, September, 1974, p. 50.

Probasco, Robert C., "Selecting, Soaking, and Adjusting Oboe Reeds," *The Instrumentalist*, vol. 31, February, 1977, p. 60.

Russell, Myron E., *Oboe Reed Making and Problems of the Oboe Player*. Stamford, Connecticut: Jack Spratt Co., 1963.

Spratt, Jack, *How to Make Double Reeds*. Stamford, Connecticut: Jack Spratt Co., 1950.

Sprenkle, Robert and Ledet, David, *The Art of Oboe Playing*. Evanston, Illinois: Summy-Birchard Co., 1961.

Timm, Everett L., *The Woodwinds*. Boston, Mass.: Allyn and Bacon, Inc., 1964.

Waln, Ronald L., "Challenge the Double-Reed Players," *The Instrumentalist*, vol. 26, March, 1972, p. 66.

Westphal, Frederick W., *Guide to Teaching Woodwinds*. Dubuque, Iowa: Wm. C. Brown Company, 1962.

Wheeler, Raymond L., "Obstruction in Oboe Octave Vents," *The Instrumentalist*, vol. 27, December, 1972, p. 44.

THE BASSOON SYLLABUS

1) Embouchure: The condition of the reed will determine tone quality and intonation. Professionally made reeds are the most satisfactory. If professionally made reeds are not available, commercial reeds will have to be used. These must always be adjusted; they are usually much too heavy or thick, especially on the tip. Refer to the selected bibliography that follows for information on making and adjusting double reeds.

2) Tonguing: The reed must be very thin on the tip if acceptable tonguing is to be accomplished. Use a soft "da" approach, especially for rapid tonguing. Develop syllabus goals similar to those stated for flute using only single tongue techniques.

3) Fingering: Printed scale sheets, such as the Selmer Scale Sheet for Clarinet, can be used by editing and changing clef signs and key signatures. I prefer to write my own materials for bass clef instruments and duplicate them by machine.

4) Breathing: Vibrato and phrasing developed in a similar manner to flute.

5) Musical terms: Learn as they are encountered.

6) Materials:

    a) Method books and étude material:

Grade I:	*Bassoon Method, Book One*, Gekeler-Hovey, Belwin, Inc.
Grade II:	*Bassoon Method, Book Two*, Gekeler-Hovey, Belwin, Inc.
	First Book of Practical Studies, McDowell-Hovey, Belwin, Inc.
Grade III:	*Advanced Method, Vol. I*, Voxman-Gower, Rubank, Inc.
	Second Book of Practical Studies, McDowell-Hovey, Belwin, Inc.
Grade IV:	*Practical Method for the Bassoon*, Weissenborn, Carl Fischer.
Grade V:	*25 Studies in All Keys*, Milde, Cundy-Bettoney
	Concert Studies, Books I and II, Milde, Cundy-Bettoney
Grade VI:	Selected advanced trombone and cello materials.
Grade VII:	Advanced solo and ensemble literature.
Grade VIII:	Advanced solo and ensemble literature.

b) Supplement each grade level with solos and ensembles appropriate to that level.

SELECTED BASSOON BIBLIOGRAPHY

Fox, Hugo, *Let's Play Bassoon*. South Whitley, Indiana: Fox Bassoon Company, 1961.

Pence, Homer, *Teacher's Guide to the Bassoon*. Elkhart, Indiana: H. & A. Selmer, Inc., 1963.

Polisi, Joseph W., "Teaching Bassoon Vibrato," *The Instrumentalist*, vol. 31, November, 1976, p. 54.

Spencer, William, *The Art of Bassoon Playing*. Evanston, Illinois: Summy-Birchard Publishing Co., 1958.

Thee, Lawrence E., "The Out-of-Tune Bassoon," *The Instrumentalist*, vol. 27, April, 1973, p. 62.

Weerts, Richard, *Developing Individual Skills for the High School Band*. West Nyack, N.Y.: Parker Publishing Co., Inc., 1969.

Westphal, Frederick W., *Guide to Teaching Woodwinds*. Dubuque, Iowa: Wm. C. Brown Company, 1962.

THE CLARINET SYLLABUS

1) Embouchure: Use the embouchure placement drill as soon as it is technically possible. This should establish one position, in regard to the amount of mouthpiece taken into the mouth, for all registers. Slight modifications are necessary for refinement of tone and intonation. Reed strength should increase from #2 for beginners, to #2½ to #3 for intermediate players, and to #3½ to #4 for advanced players. Lower clarinets usually do not go beyond #3 reeds in strength.

2) Tonguing: Developed as single tonguing is on flute. Use various forms of "da" for all tonguing; the tongue should touch the reed at a point approximately half way between the lip and the tip of the reed. Many methods of tonguing are used; this particular method has been very successful in my teaching, especially in developing speed of tongue attack. Tonguing in the higher register requires a progressively lighter tongue attack, which assures that the reed is not closed by the tongue striking it.

3) Fingering: Use the Selmer Scale Sheet for Clarinet and develop a syllabus similar to that used for flute.

4) Breathing: Teach diaphragmatic breathing, a relaxed throat, and an embouchure that is firm but not pinched.

5) Musical terms: Learn as encountered.

6) Materials:

    a)   Method books and étude materials:

Grade I:	*Universal Fundamental Method*, Pease, Universal
	Supplementary Studies, Endresen, Rubank, Inc.
Grade II:	*Rubank Intermediate Method*, Skornicka, Rubank, Inc.
	First Book of Practical Studies, Hovey, Belwin-Mills
Grade III:	*Rubank Advanced Method, Vol. I*, Voxman-Gower, Rubank, Inc.
	Second Book of Practical Studies, Hovey, Belwin-Mills
Grade IV:	*Rubank Advanced Method, Vol. II*, Gower-Voxman, Rubank, Inc.
	Hendrickson Method, Book II, Hendrickson, Belwin-Mills
Grade V:	*Selected Studies for Clarinet*, Voxman, Rubank, Inc.
	32 Etudes for Clarinet, Rose, Carl Fischer
Grade VI:	*Modern Method for Clarinet, Part II*, Lazarus-Langenus, Cundy-Bettoney
	Classical Studies for Clarinet, Voxman, Rubank, Inc.
	Forty Studies for the Clarinet, Rose, Carl Fischer
Grade VII:	*Modern Method for Clarinet, Part III*, Lazarus-Langenus, Cundy-Bettoney
	Celebrated Method for the Clarinet, Part II, Klose-Bellison, Carl Fischer
Grade VIII:	Same as Grade VII.

    b)   Supplement each grade level with solos and ensembles appropriate to that level.

SELECTED CLARINET BIBLIOGRAPHY

Abramson, Armand R., "Crossing the Clarinet Break," *The Instrumentalist*, vol. 29, November, 1974, p. 57.

Abramson, Armand R., "Guidelines for Selection of Clarinet Fingerings," *The Instrumentalist*, vol. 26, February, 1972, p. 44.

Barzenick, Walter, "Hints on Clarinet Mouthpieces, Reeds, and Maintenance," *The Instrumentalist*, vol. 26, September, 1971, p. 37.

Bonade, Daniel, *The Clarinetist's Compendium*. Kenosha, Wisconsin: Leblanc Publications, Inc., 1962.

Cailliet, Lucien, *The Clarinet and Clarinet Choir*. Kenosha, Wisconsin: Leblanc Publications, Inc., 1955.

Deaton, James W., "Tips for Upper Register Clarinet Playing," *The Instrumentalist*, vol. 27, January, 1973, p. 46.

Drake, Alan H., "A Solution for the Reed Player's Sore Lip," *The Instrumentalist*, vol. 27, June, 1973, p. 49.

Errante, F. Gerard, "New Music for the Clarinet," *The Instrumentalist*, vol. 26, January, 1972, p. 41.

Garofalo, Robert, "Woodwind Instrument Relationships," *The Instrumentalist*, vol. 27, September, 1972, p. 52.

Gillespie, James, "Published Works for Unaccompanied Clarinet—A Graded Checklist," *The Instrumentalist*, vol. 26, May, 1972, p. 47.

Heim, Norman, "The Squeak—The Clarinet Player's Dilemma," *The Instrumentalist*, vol. 29, May, 1975, p. 49.

Heim, Norman M., *A Handbook for Clarinet Performance*. Kenosha, Wisconsin: Leblanc Publications, Inc., 1967.

Hovey, Nilo, *Teacher's Guide to the Clarinet*. Elkhart, Indiana: Selmer, Inc., 1967.

Leeson, Daniel, "The Clarinetist's Repertoire, Part XII," *The Instrumentalist*, vol. 25, May, 1971, p. 84.

Leeson, Daniel, "The Clarinetist's Repertoire, Part XIII," *The Instrumentalist*, vol. 26, December, 1971, p. 40.

Leeson, Daniel, "Mozart Editions and the Clarinet Quintet," *The Instrumentalist*, vol. 29, February, 1975, p. 53.

McCarrell, Lemar K., "The Four Fundamentals of Woodwind Playing," *The Instrumentalist*, vol. 26, November, 1971, p. 38.

McCathren, Donald, *Playing and Teaching the Clarinet Family*. San Antonio, Texas: Southern Music Company, 1959.

Nielsen, Edmund, "Cracks in Woodwind Instruments," *The Instrumentalist*, vol. 29, January, 1975, p. 48.

Norton, Donald B., "A Daily Approach to Clarinet Playing," *The Instrumentalist*, vol. 27, November, 1972, p. 40.

O'Connell, Thomas, "The Short Scrape Concept for Clarinet Reeds," *The Instrumentalist*, vol. 27, October, 1972, p. 44.

Opperman, K., *Repertory of the Clarinet*. New York, New York: G. Ricordi & Company, 1960.

Orcutt, Ronald H. & William A. Roscoe, "Reed Storage—A Simple Solution," *The Instrumentalist*, vol. 26, April, 1972, p. 45.

Pennington, John, "Working with Single Reeds," *The Instrumentalist*, vol. 31, October, 1976, p. 55.

Rasmussen, Mary and Donald Mattran, *A Teacher's Guide to the Literature of Woodwind Instruments*. Durham, New Hampshire: Appleyard Publications, 1966.

Stein, Keith, *The Art of Clarinet Playing*. Evanston, Illinois: Summy-Birchard Co., 1958.

Stella, Martin, "Greater Tonguing Velocity Through Converted Staccatissimo," *The Instrumentalist*, vol. 27, February, 1973, p. 44.

Stubbins, W. H., *The Art of Clarinetistry*. Ann Arbor, Michigan: Ann Arbor Publishers, 1965.

Timm, E., *The Woodwinds*. Boston, Mass.: Allyn Bacon, 1964.

Waln, George, "How to Improve Clarinet Hand Position," *The Instrumentalist*, vol. 26, June, 1972, p. 42.

Waln, George, "A Weak Fundamental in Clarinet Playing," *The Instrumentalist*, vol. 26, October, 1971, p. 49.

West, Charles A., "Controlling Reeds in Dry Climates," *The Instrumentalist*, vol. 31, October, 1976, p. 54.

Westphal, Frederick W., *Guide to Teaching Woodwinds*. Dubuque, Iowa: Wm. C. Brown Company, 1962.

THE ALTO AND BASS CLARINET SYLLABI

Lower clarinet syllabi can be developed from the B-flat clarinet syllabus with one limitation, the high register. The range of the lower clarinets should not rise above c³ except in very advanced solos and difficult band music.

It is standard procedure to start all clarinet students on the B-flat clarinet and to switch some of these students to alto and bass clarinets at a later date. If an emergency need arises for more color instruments, strong academic students not in the band program can be started at the junior or senior high level. However, this procedure should not be necessary if you have developed a successful beginning instrumentation and feeder system.

1) Embouchure: Although the basic embouchure should be the same as on the B-flat clarinet, there are some differences that should be stressed. I use a modified saxophone embouchure on alto clarinet, opening the throat and attempting to round or enlarge the tone of this instrument. Using a #2½ to #3 reed and a rather close-lay mouthpiece will result in a tone that makes your alto clarinets a valuable part of your band tone color. When using the above pro-

cedure, don't go beyond the point where basic tonal focus may be lost. In regard to range, embouchure firmness on the bass clarinet should be inversely proportional to that used on the B-flat clarinet. The B-flat clarinetist feels greater embouchure firmness as the range increases; the bass clarinetist should feel the opposite in embouchure firmness, greater relaxation of the embouchure in the upper register. This should be combined with greater breath support and a lighter tongue attack.

2) Tonguing: Developed as on the B-flat clarinet.

3) Fingering: Use the Selmer Scale Sheet for Clarinet, editing out the higher range when necessary. Be sure all lower clarinetists learn proper chromatic fingerings and alternation of little fingers. Their fingering technique should be as carefully developed as that on the regular B-flat clarinet.

4) Breathing: Developed as on the B-flat clarinet.

5) Musical terms: Learn as encountered.

6) Materials: Standard clarinet literature can be used for beginners. Beginning literature written specifically for alto and bass clarinet is limited. Most beginning and intermediate clarinet materials do not exceed the range limitations of the young alto or bass clarinetist. Advanced materials should be chosen carefully so that they match the practical band range of the lower clarinets. I have found carefully selected trumpet literature to be very successful musical material for these instruments since this literature does not exceed the upper range limitations and crosses the "break" frequently, drilling the students on a smooth transition across this problem area.

    a) Method books and étude materials:

        Grade I: *Universal Fundamental Method for Clarinet*, Pease, Universal

                      Supplementary Studies for Clarinet, Endresen, Rubank, Inc.

        Grade II: *Rubank Intermediate Method for Clarinet*, Skornicka, Rubank, Inc.

                      First Book of Practical Studies for Clarinet, Hovey, Belwin-Mills

        Grade III: *Rubank Advanced Method, Vol. I, for Clarinet*, Voxman-Gower, Rubank, Inc.

                      Forty Progressive Etudes for Trumpet or Cornet, Hering, Carl Fischer

Grade IV: *Rubank Advanced Method, Vol. II, for Clarinet*, Gower-Voxman, Rubank, Inc.

32 Etudes for Trumpet or Cornet, Hering, Carl Fischer

Grade V: *Hendrickson Method, Book II, for Clarinet*, Hendrickson, Belwin-Mills

32 Etudes for Clarinet, Rose, Carl Fischer

Grade VI: Select materials carefully to avoid range problems.

Grade VII: Same as Grade VI.

Grade VIII: Same as Grade VII.

b) Solos written specifically for alto and bass clarinet can be used to supplement Grades I-IV. Transposed clarinet literature is normally used for Grade V-VI solo material.

SELECTED ALTO AND BASS CLARINET BIBLIOGRAPHY

See Selected Clarinet Bibliography for general information books and articles. A selected list of method books written specifically for alto and bass clarinet is found in the Appendices of this book.

THE SAXOPHONE SYLLABUS

1) Embouchure: An open, relaxed throat and proper breath support are essential from the first lesson. Embouchure placement should be carefully established, with special emphasis on an "oo" approach to the quality formation and as little embouchure pressure around the reed-mouthpiece combination as possible. Proper embouchure can be established without pinching and excessive up-and-down pressure on the reed.

2) Tonguing: Use a "doo" approach to tonguing; avoid a "t" attack, which is harsh and may close the tip of the reed. The position of the tongue attack should be similar to that used on the clarinet.

3) Fingering: Use the Selmer Scale Sheets for Saxophone or edited Selmer Scale Sheets for Clarinet. The latter are more successful with very young students playing Grade I and II literature.

4) Breathing: Develop vibrato and phrasing control similar to that on the flute. Saxophone vibrato is usually produced by the jaw and is very difficult for the young student to control. It is better to save vibrato instruction until the student has played for several years.

5) Musical terms: Learn as encountered.
6) Materials:
   a) Method books and étude materials:

      Grade I: *Elementary Method for Saxophone*, Hovey, Rubank, Inc.

      Grade II: *Rubank Intermediate Method*, Skornicka, Rubank, Inc.
                     Method for Saxophone, Book II, Cailliet, Belwin, Inc.
                     First Book of Practical Studies for Saxophone, Hovey, Belwin-Mills

      Grade III: *Advanced Method, Vol. I*, Voxman-Gower, Rubank, Inc.
                     Second Book of Practical Studies for Saxophone, Hovey, Belwin-Mills

      Grade IV: *Advanced Method, Vol. II*, Voxman, Rubank, Inc.
                     Vingt-Quatre Etudes Faciles, Mule, Leduc

      Grade V: *Selected Studies for Saxophone*, Voxman, Rubank, Inc.
                     Thirty-Three Concert Etudes, Vol. I, Iasilli, Carl Fischer

      Grade VI: *Thirty-Three Concert Etudes, Vol. II and III*, Iasilli, Carl Fischer

      Grade VII: Selected solo and ensemble materials.

      Grade VIII: Same as Grade VII.

   b) Supplement with solo and ensemble materials appropriate to each grade level. Baritone saxophone can use alto saxophone materials. Tenor saxophone can use transposed alto saxophone materials.

SELECTED SAXOPHONE BIBLIOGRAPHY

Black, Robert, "The Saxophone in Perspective," *The Instrumentalist*, vol. 25, June, 1971, p. 18.

Hemke, Fred, *Teacher's Guide to the Saxophone*. Elkhart, Indiana: H. & A. Selmer, 1966.

Mule, Marcel, "The Saxophone," *The Instrumentalist*, vol. 12, April, 1958, p. 30.

Pace, Kenneth, "Playing the Saxophone," *The Instrumentalist*, vol. 21, March, 1967, p. 73.

Runyon, Santy, "High Notes for Saxophone," *The Instrumentalist*, vol. 29, December, 1974, p. 56.

Smith, Walter, "Contest Music for Saxophone," *The Instrumentalist*, vol. 29, March, 1975, p. 81.

Smith, Walter, "Contest Music for Saxophone," *The Instrumentalist*, vol. 29, April, 1975, p. 45.

Teal, Larry, *The Art of Saxophone Playing.* Evanston, Illinois: Summy-Birchard Company, 1963.

Waln, George, "Saxophone Playing," *The Instrumentalist*, vol. 19, March, 1965, p. 76.

Weerts, Richard, *Developing Individual Skills for the High School Band.* West Nyack, New York: Parker Publishing Company, Inc., 1969.

DEVELOPING BRASS SYLLABI

12

A similar plan to that used to develop syllabi for woodwinds can be used to develop brass syllabi. The trumpet is treated here in detail, with abbreviated material given for the other brass instruments.

THE TRUMPET SYLLABUS

First Lesson

The student should learn the following during the first week of study:

1) Proper hand position for holding and playing the trumpet: The right hand should be dropped to the side, completely relaxed, and then brought up to the valves, the thumb remaining straight and placed against the first-valve casing. The three slightly curved fingers of the right hand are placed over the valves, the first joints being used to depress the valves. The little finger remains free and relaxed and should not be placed in the loop of the little finger rest since placing the little finger in the loop restricts the third-valve finger. Use the loop only for "one-hand" emergencies.

2) The embouchure should be explained and demonstrated by the teacher, using only the mouthpiece at first. By the end of the first week of study the student should be able to "buzz" different pitches on the mouthpiece to a duration of four beats at m.m. = 60 for each pitch. Having the student try to "buzz" simple melodies, such as "America," is a good procedure at this point.

3) At the end of the first week of study the student should be able to produce a whole note on c^1, d^1, e^1, $f^{\sharp 1}$, and g^1 at m.m. = 80, using the foot to count each beat and the tongue to start each pitch.

4) Practice time should be recorded—one-half hour per day, divided into two small segments to avoid excessive fatigue.

Work to Be Completed by the End of a Six-Week Trial Period

1) Mastery of the first six pages of the *Universal Fundamental Method*, demonstrating acceptable tone quality, proper tongue attacks to begin each note, proper fingerings, and a foot beat that controls the rhythm accurately. *Do not force* the *range upward* at any time.

Grade I—The First Year of Study

1) Use natural slur exercises to develop proper tone quality and range flexibility. Range should be developed to f^2.

2) Development of single tonguing of sixteenths at a minimum of m.m. = 60.

3) Study of first three keys on an edited Selmer Scale Sheet for Clarinet: C, F, and G major, tongued in eighth notes with key notes receiving a full beat, one octave ascending and descending at m.m. = 72. This includes study of the scale, arpeggio, scale by thirds, and chromatic scale within the range of the key being studied.

4) Study of diaphragmatic breathing; write in all breath marks to develop length of breath phrasing (approximately eight beats to each breath at m.m. = 80).

5) Learn musical terms as encountered.

6) Materials:

   a) Method books—*Universal Fundamental Method* with *Edwards-Hovey Method, Book One* as supplementary review material. Both books should be completed by the end of the first year.

   b) Supplement with Grade I solo and ensemble material.

Grade II—The Second Year of Study

1) Continuation of embouchure-building natural slurs, extending the range to g^2. Freely executed embouchure slurs develop embouchure strength and flexibility and assure establishment of good tone quality.

2) Development of single tonguing of sixteenths at m.m. = 96–120.

3) Mastery of the keys of C, F, G, B-flat, and D major in the same manner as in Grade I at m.m. = 80–96.

4) Continue careful phrasing by marking in all breath marks.

5) Learn musical terms as encountered.
6) Materials:
   a) Method books—*Rubank Intermediate Method* and the Getchell-Hovey *First Book of Practical Studies for Cornet and Trumpet.*
   b) Supplement with Grade II solo and ensemble material.

Grade III—The Third Year of Study.

1) Continued use of natural slur exercises to develop range and flexibility.
2) Development of single tonguing of sixteenths at m.m. = 120. Begin study of double tonguing, equaling speed of single tonguing by the end of the year.
3) Add keys of E-flat and A; play all material of first seven keys in sixteenths at m.m. = 72. Intonation problems encountered on c-sharp^1, d^1, and e^1 can be corrected by use of first and third valve sleeves or triggers.
4) Continue careful phrasing study, working toward greater breath support and control.
5) Learn musical terms as encountered.
6) Materials:
   a) Method books—*Rubank Advanced Method, Vol. I* and *Forty Progressive Etudes for Trumpet and Cornet* by Hering.
   b) Supplement with Grade III solo and ensemble material.

Grade IV—The Fourth Year of Study

1) Continued use of natural slur exercises to develop range and flexibility.
2) Development of double tonguing of sixteenths at m.m. = 144+.
3) Add keys of A-flat and E; play all material of first nine keys in sixteenths at m.m. = 80.
4) Continue careful study of breath phrasing.
5) Learn musical terms as encountered.
6) Materials:
   a) Method books—*Edwards-Hovey Method, Book Two* and Getchell-Hovey *Second Book of Practical Studies for Cornet and Trumpet.*
   b) Supplement with Grade IV solo and ensemble materials.

Grade V—The Fifth Year of Study

1) Advanced natural slur exercises, extending the range to c^3 and above. Simple natural slurs are used for warmup before any other material is played.

2) Develop triple tonguing, using syllables "da-da-ga da-da-ga" or "da-ga-da ga-da-ga" at a speed of m.m. = 60 for two sixteenth-note triplets. A legato approach to development of double and triple tonguing will result in faster execution and less throat and tongue tension.

3) Add keys of D-flat, B, and G-flat major and their enharmonic keys. Develop all techniques in new keys with eighth notes at m.m. = 80.

4) Continued emphasis on breath phrasing and support. By this point in the student's development the tone should "float" on the air column.

5) Learn new musical terms as encountered.

6) Materials:

   a) Etudes and method book—*Rubank Advanced Method, Vol. II* and *24 Advanced Etudes* by Hering.

   b) Supplement with Grade V solos and ensembles.

Grade VI—The Sixth Year of Study

1) Appropriate warmup material to refine tone and intonation.

2) Use short daily tonguing exercises to maintain good tonguing technique in all types of tonguing.

3) Develop all techniques in all major keys with sixteenths at m.m. = 80.

4) All phrasing carefully designed and effected by breath control.

5) Learn musical terms as encountered.

6) Materials:

   a) Etude materials—*Selected Studies for Cornet or Trumpet* by Voxman and *Twenty-Eight Melodious and Technical Etudes* by Hering.

   b) Supplement with Grade VI solos and ensembles.

Grades VII and VIII—The Seventh and Eighth Years of Study

Embouchure, tonguing techniques, and fingering techniques in all major keys should be well developed. The student should now concentrate upon interpretation and learning new literature. Technique may be strengthened by the study of various other scales and arpeggios. Dominant and diminished seventh chord study is of particular importance.

Selected materials:

a) Method books and études—Arban's *Célèbre Method;* Saint-Jacome's Grand Method, Part II; and Clarke's *Technical Studies for the Cornet.*

b) Various advanced solo and ensemble materials.

SELECTED TRUMPET BIBLIOGRAPHY

Bach, Vincent, "The Art of Trumpet Playing," *Selmer Bandwagon*, vol. 15, April, 1967, p. 16.

Brown, Merrill, "Repertoire for Brass Soloists, Part I," *The Instrumentalist*, vol. 31, December, 1976, p. 66.

Brown, Merrill, "Repertoire for Brass Soloists, Part II," *The Instrumentalist*, vol. 31, January, 1977, p. 51.

Carse, A. A., *Musical Wind Instruments*. London: MacMillan and Co., Ltd., 1939.

Day, Donald K., "A Comprehensive Bibliography of Music for Brass Quintet—Addendum," *The Instrumentalist*, vol. 29, October, 1974, p. 59.

Decker, Charles F., "Trumpet Research: A Selective Bibliography," *The Instrumentalist*, vol. 27, May, 1973, p. 56.

Farkas, Philip, *The Art of Brass Playing*. Bloomington, Indiana: Brass Publications, 1962.

Faulkner, Maurice, "Tips on Teaching Beginning Brass," *The Instrumentalist*, vol. 30, September, 1975, p. 60.

Geiringer, Carl, *Musical Instruments*. Trans. by Bernard Miall. New York: Oxford University Press, 1945.

Getchell, Robert, *Teacher's Guide to the Brass Instruments*. Elkhart, Indiana: H. & A. Selmer Inc., 1959.

Hardin, Burton, "Brass Embouchure," *The Instrumentalist*, vol. 29, February, 1975, p. 56.

Instrumentalist, The, vol. 31, April, 1977, pp. 38-60.

Lieberman, William B. and Robert C. Jones, "Dental Appliances as an Aid to Brass Playing," *The Instrumentalist*, vol. 26, October, 1971, p. 52.

Moore, E. C. (Revised by Dr. James Neilson), *The Brass Book*. Kenosha, Wisconsin: Leblanc Publications, Inc., 1964.

Neilson, James, *Warm-Up Procedures for the Brass Player*. Kenosha, Wisconsin: G. Leblanc Corporation, 1962.

Pietzsch, Hermann, *The Trumpet*. Germany: C. F. Schmidt, cop. 1901.

Rasmussen, Mary, *A Teacher's Guide to the Literature of Brass Instruments*. Durham, New Hampshire: Appleyard Publications, 1968.

Roberts, Chester, "Elements of Brass Intonation," *The Instrumentalist*, vol. 29, March, 1975, p. 86.

Sachs, Curt, *The History of Musical Instruments*. New York: W. W. Norton & Co., Inc., 1940.

Sandor, Edward P., "The Closed-Throat Syndrome," *The Instrumentalist*, vol. 31, November, 1976, p. 58.

Smith, Douglas, "Trumpet Embouchure Change," *The Instrumentalist*, vol. 26, June, 1972, p. 46.

Stoutamire, Albert, "Deviled Tongue," *The Instrumentalist*, vol. 26, April, 1972, p. 48.

Weerts, Richard, *Developing Individual Skills for the High School Band*. West Nyack, New York: Parker Publishing Company, Inc., 1969.

Winik, Steven, "Music for Brass Trio," *The Instrumentalist*, vol. 27, January, 1973, p. 48.

Winslow, Robert W. and John E. Green, *Playing and Teaching Brass Instruments*. Englewood Cliffs, New Jersey: Prentice-Hall, Inc., 1961.

Winter, James H., *The Brass Instruments*. Boston, Massachusetts: Allyn and Bacon, Inc., 1964.

Zorn, Jay D., "Exploring the Trumpet's Upper Register," *The Instrumentalist*, vol. 29, June, 1975, p. 70.

THE FRENCH HORN SYLLABUS

1) Embouchure: Use natural lip slurs for development of embouchure flexibility and good tone quality. The range of these slur exercises should increase grade by grade; basic slurs should be used for preliminary warmup throughout all grade levels. An "oo" approach to a completely open throat and a relaxed embouchure, plus strong breath support, will lead to a round, "floating" tone quality. This is difficult to do with such a small mouthpiece and narrow-bore lead pipe; I tell my students to think of the size of the bell, not the mouthpiece and lead pipe, when they are developing a concept of French horn tone quality.

2) Tonguing: Developed as on the trumpet. A "doo" approach to tonguing is helpful since "too" is not only harsh but tends to produce "cracked" attacks. A legato approach to French horn tonguing is especially important in rapid tonguing passages and for tonguing in the lower register.

3) Fingering: Use an edited Selmer Scale Sheet for Clarinet and develop a syllabus similar to that used on trumpet.

4) Breathing: Teach diaphragmatic breathing, a relaxed throat, and as free an embouchure as possible. The center of the embouchure should feel very relaxed, and only enough firmness to keep the lips in place should occur at the corners of the embouchure. Strong breath support should overcome any feeling of insecurity resulting from the use of such a free embouchure. Without this breath support, this approach to embouchure will not be successful.

5) Musical terms: Learn as encountered.

6) Materials:

a) Method books and étude materials: More than one method book can be suggested at some levels; trumpet literature can be used for the French horn successfully.

Grade I: *Pottag-Hovey, Book One,* Pottag-Hovey, Belwin-Mills

Primary Studies for the French Horn, Horner, Elkan-Vogel

Universal Fundamental Method for the Cornet or Trumpet, Pease, Universal

Supplementary Studies, French Horn, Endresen, Rubank, Inc.

Grade II: *Intermediate Method, French Horn,* Skornicka-Erdman, Rubank, Inc.

First Book of Practical Studies for the French Horn, Getchell, Belwin, Inc.

Grade III: *Advanced Method, French Horn, Vol. I,* Gower-Voxman, Rubank, Inc.

Second Book of Practical Studies for the French Horn, Getchell, Belwin, Inc.

Forty Progressive Etudes for Trumpet or Cornet, Hering, Carl Fischer, Inc.

Grade IV: *Pottag-Hovey Method, Book Two,* Pottag-Hovey, Belwin-Mills

32 Etudes for Trumpet or Cornet, Hering, Carl Fischer, Inc.

Grade V: *Advanced Method, French Horn, Vol. II,* Gower-Voxman, Rubank, Inc.

Preparatory Melodies to Solo Work for French Horn, Pottag, Belwin, Inc.

22 Etudes for French Horn, Mueller-Pottag, Belwin, Inc.

Grade VI: *Selected Studies for French Horn,* Voxman, Rubank, Inc.

> 48 *Etudes for French Horn*, Reynolds, G. Schirmer, Inc.

Grade VII: Other selected advanced étude materials.

Grade VIII: Same as Grade VII.

b) Supplement each grade level with solos and ensembles appropriate to that level.

SELECTED FRENCH HORN BIBLIOGRAPHY

Bergstone, Frederick, "A Recommended Selected List of French Horn Literature," *The Instrumentalist*, vol. 27, June, 1973, p. 51.

Brown, Merrill, "Repertoire for Brass Soloists, Part II," *The Instrumentalist*, vol. 31, January, 1977, p. 51.

Chambers, James, "Horn Tone and Technique," *Woodwind World*, vol. 4, June, 1962, p. 11.

Day, Donald K., "A Comprehensive Bibliography for the Brass Quintet—Addendum," *The Instrumentalist*, vol. 29, October, 1974, p. 59.

Erlenbach, Julius, "Daily Warm-Ups for the Young Horn Student," *The Instrumentalist*, vol. 25, May, 1971, p. 48.

Erlenbach, Julius, "French Horn Maintenance," *The Instrumentalist*, vol. 29, May, 1975, p. 51.

Farkas, Philip, *The Art of Brass Playing*. Bloomington, Indiana: Brass Publications, 1962.

Farkas, Philip, *The Art of French Horn Playing*. Evanston, Illinois: Summy-Birchard Publishing Company, 1956.

Getchell, Robert, *Teacher's Guide to the Brass Instruments*. Elkhart, Indiana: H. & A. Selmer, Inc., 1959.

Hunt, Norman J., *Guide to Teaching Brass*. Dubuque, Iowa: Wm. C. Brown Company, 1968.

Moore, E. C. (Revised by Dr. James Neilson), *The Brass Book*. Kenosha, Wisconsin: G. Leblanc Corporation, 1964.

Murray, Thomas W., "Pursuing the Ideal Horn Tone," *The Instrumentalist*, vol. 31, October, 1976, p. 58.

Neilson, James, *The Overtone Principle*. Kenosha, Wisconsin: G. Leblanc Corporation, 1962.

Neilson, James, *Warm-Up Procedures for the Brass Player*. Kenosha, Wisconsin: G. Leblanc Corporation, 1962.

Rasmussen, Mary, *A Teacher's Guide to the Literature of Brass Instruments*. Durham, New Hampshire: Appleyard Publications, 1968.

Rumery, Kenneth R., "Improved Use of the Double Horn," *The Instrumentalist*, vol. 29, November, 1974, p. 61.

Rumery, Kenneth R., "Improving the French Horn Section," *The Instrumentalist*, vol. 27, April, 1973, p. 65.

Seiffert, Stephen, "Tuning the Double Horn," *The Instrumentalist*, vol. 29, April, 1975, p. 54.

Weerts, Richard, *Developing Individual Skills for the High School Band.* West Nyack, New York: Parker Publishing Company, Inc., 1969.

Winik, Steven, "Music for Brass Trio," *The Instrumentalist*, vol. 27, January, 1973, p. 48.

Winslow, Robert W. and John E. Green, *Playing and Teaching Brass Instruments.* Englewood Cliffs, New Jersey: Prentice-Hall, Inc., 1961.

Winter, James H., *The Brass Instruments*. Boston, Mass.: Allyn and Bacon, Inc., 1964.

THE TROMBONE SYLLABUS

1) Embouchure: Use natural lip slurs for development of flexibility, range, and tone quality. Slur exercises should increase in range at each grade level. The trombonist's warmup should include basic slur exercises at every grade level. Diaphragmatic breath support, freedom of the center of the embouchure, and flexibility of the corners of the embouchure will lead to excellent tone quality and flexibility.

2) Tonguing: Developed as on the trumpet.

3) Slide technique: This should be developed in much the same manner as fingering techniques on other brass instruments. It is especially important to move the slide very quickly. Keep the right arm, and particularly the right wrist, relaxed and flexible. The first basic warmup routine for trombone (small f, small e, small f, small e-flat, and so on) is an excellent method for teaching proper slide positions. Teach alternate positions whenever possible and urge your trombonists to buy f-attachment trombones. Emphasize the double trombone's advantages in simplifying slide position changes.

4) Breathing: Diaphragmatic breathing is extremely important on trombone because of the heroic nature of many trombone parts. Long natural slur exercises will help to develop the breath support needed.

5) Musical terms: Learn as encountered.

6) Materials:

    a) Method books and étude materials:

        Grade I: *Universal Fundamental Method for Trombone,* Pease, Universal

> *Supplementary Studies for Trombone*, Endresen, Rubank

Grade II: *Intermediate Method for Trombone*, Skornicka-Boltz, Rubank

First Book of Practical Studies for Trombone, Bordner, Belwin

Grade III: *Advanced Method for Trombone, Vol. I*, Gower-Voxman, Rubank

Second Book of Practical Studies for Trombone, Bordner, Belwin-Mills

Grade IV: *Advanced Method for Trombone, Vol. II*, Gower-Voxman, Rubank

55 Phrasing Studies for Trombone, Cimera, Belwin

221 Progressive Studies for Trombone, Cimera, Belwin

Selected Kopprasch Studies (with F attachment), ed. Fote, Kendor Music, Inc.

Grade V: *Melodious Etudes for Trombone, Book I*, Bordogni-Rochut, Carl Fischer

Sixty Studies, Books I and *II*, Kopprasch, Carl Fischer

36 Studies for Trombone with F Attachment, Blume-Fink, Carl Fischer

Grade VI: *Selected Studies for Trombone*, Voxman, Rubank

Melodious Etudes for Trombone, Books II and *III*, Bordogni-Rochut, Carl Fischer

Grade VII: Other selected advanced étude materials.

Grade VIII: Same as Grade VII.

b) Supplement each grade level with solos and ensembles appropriate to that level.

SELECTED TROMBONE BIBLIOGRAPHY

Bate, Philip, *The Trumpet and Trombone*. New York, New York: W. W. Norton & Company, Inc., 1966.

Brown, Merrill, "Repertoire for Brass Soloists, Part II," *The Instrumentalist*, vol. 31, January, 1977, p. 51.

Dalkert, Charles, "Improved Holding Position—Better Sound," *The Instrumentalist*, vol. 28, February, 1974, p. 48.

Day, Donald K., "A Comprehensive Bibliography for the Brass Quintet—Addendum," *The Instrumentalist*, vol. 29, October, 1974, p. 59.

Everett, Thomas G., "Solo Literature for the Bass Trombone—a Selected Bibliography," *The Instrumentalist*, vol. 26, December, 1971, p. 43.

Farkas, Philip, *The Art of Brass Playing*. Bloomington, Indiana: Brass Publications, 1962.

Fink, Reginald H., *The Trombonist's Handbook*. Athens, Ohio: Accura Music, 1977.

Fote, Richard, "Principles of Trombone Legato," *The Instrumentalist*, vol. 28, February, 1974, p. 47.

Getchell, Robert, *Teacher's Guide to the Brass Instruments*. Elkhart, Indiana: H. & A. Selmer, Inc., 1959.

Giardinelli, Robert, "Trombone Care and Maintenance," *The Instrumentalist*, vol. 28, February, 1974, p. 51.

Kleinhammer, Edward, *The Art of Trombone Playing*. Evanston, Illinois: Summy-Birchard, 1963.

Moore, E. C. (Revised by Dr. James Neilson), *The Brass Book*. Kenosha, Wisconsin: G. Leblanc Corporation, 1964.

Poolos, J.G., "Trombone Articulation—Legato Style," *The Instrumentalist*, vol. 27, March, 1973, p. 74.

Rasmussen, Mary, *A Teacher's Guide to the Literature of Brass Instruments*, Durham, New Hampshire: Appleyard Publications, 1968.

Rosenberg, Marvin, "Alternate Trombone Positions—First Year of Study," *The Instrumentalist*, vol. 26, May, 1972, p. 52.

Smith, Glenn P., "Original Unaccompanied Trombone Ensemble Music," *The Instrumentalist*, vol. 28, February, 1974, p. 52.

Stevens, Milton, "Vocalization—An Introduction to Avant-Garde Techniques on the Trombone," *The Instrumentalist*, vol. 28, February, 1974, p. 44.

Swett, Jim, "A Selected, Annotated List of Published Trombone Literature," *The Instrumentalist*, vol. 28, February, 1974, p. 76.

Weerts, Richard, *Developing Individual Skills for the High School Band*. West Nyack, New York: Parker Publishing Company, Inc., 1969.

Winik, Steven, "Music for Brass Trio," *The Instrumentalist*, vol. 27, January, 1973, p. 48.

Winslow, Robert W. and John E. Green, *Playing and Teaching Brass Instruments*. Englewood Cliffs, New Jersey: Prentice-Hall, Inc., 1961.

Winter, James H., *The Brass Instruments*. Boston, Mass.: Allyn and Bacon, Inc., 1964.

THE BARITONE (EUPHONIUM) SYLLABUS

1) Embouchure: The baritone embouchure is similar to the trombone embouchure, but the lips are drawn inward a bit more toward the

center of the mouthpiece and are generally more relaxed in the middle. The mouthpiece of the baritone should have a deeper cup than that normally used on the trombone. These adjustments lead to the characteristically more mellow tone produced by the fine baritonist. The common switch from trumpet to baritone usually requires a considerable change in embouchure, although the rare student who plays very freely on trumpet will have little difficulty making the adjustment. Natural lip slurs, similar to those used on the trumpet and trombone, should be used throughout all grade levels. The euphonium has a larger bore and bell, uses a mouthpiece with a deeper cup, and should produce a correspondingly larger tone than the baritone horn.

2) Tonguing: Developed as on the trumpet or trombone.

3) Fingering: Develop fingering techniques as planned in the trumpet syllabus. An edited Selmer Scale Sheet for Clarinet can be used for treble-clef; I have written out my own sheets for bass-clef baritone and trombone. The treble-clef baritone reads and fingers exactly the same as the trumpet. The bass-clef baritone reads and fingers the same as the tuba fingerings an octave lower. Alternate fingerings can be used extensively on the baritone to improve intonation; these fingerings do not distort the tone quality as many alternate fingerings do on the trumpet. The four-valve euphonium is uncommon in most public schools; its added lower range is not practical in most high school band music. The fourth valve with a compensating device does, however, correct intonation on notes using 1-3 or 1-2-3 valve combinations. Teach all of your baritonists both clefs if possible. The amount of good trumpet and trombone literature that can be used by the baritonist is extensive.

4) Breathing: Teach diaphragmatic breathing as taught on the trombone.

5) Musical terms: Learn as encountered.

6) Materials: Use the trumpet syllabus for treble-clef players and the trombone syllabus for bass-clef players. There are good methods and études written specifically for baritone (see the Appendices of this book), but I have found trumpet and trombone literature to be excellent practical and musical material for this instrument.

SELECTED BARITONE (EUPHONIUM) BIBLIOGRAPHY

Information relative to baritone teaching and playing can be found in the selected bibliographies for trumpet and trombone. The following are especially useful:

Brown, Merrill, "Repertoire for Brass Soloists," *The Instrumentalist*, vol. 31, January, 1977, p. 51.

Duvall, W. Clyde, *The High School Band Director's Handbook*. Englewood Cliffs, New Jersey: Prentice-Hall, Inc., 1960.

Farkas, Philip, *The Art of Brass Playing*. Bloomington, Indiana: Brass Publications, 1962.

Getchell, Robert, *Teacher's Guide to the Brass Instruments*. Elkhart, Indiana: H. & A. Selmer Inc., 1959.

Moore, E.C. (Revised by Dr. James Neilson), *The Brass Book*. Kenosha, Wisconsin: Leblanc Publications Inc., 1964.

Rasmussen, Mary, *A Teacher's Guide to the Literature of Brass Instruments*. Durham, New Hampshire: Appleyard Publications, 1968.

Weerts, Richard, *Developing Individual Skills for the High School Band*. West Nyack, New York: Parker Publishing Company, Inc., 1969.

Winslow, Robert W. and John E. Green, *Playing and Teaching Brass Instruments*. Englewood Cliffs, New Jersey: Prentice-Hall, Inc., 1961.

Winter, James H., *The Brass Instruments*. Boston, Mass.: Allyn and Bacon, Inc., 1964.

THE TUBA SYLLABUS

Use light-weight fiberglass Sousaphones for marching and bell-front upright BB-flat tubas for concert bands. Standard Bach mouthpieces are excellent for all basses. If the size of your students is a problem in the lower grades, use the E-flat tuba. This smaller instrument fingers like the trumpet if the student thinks treble clef when reading a tuba part and changes key signatures by subtracting three flats or adding three sharps. An extra trumpet player can be switched to tuba for instrumentation purposes in this manner. Another way to overcome the size problem is to start the young student on baritone with a tuba method book and switch him when he is physically big enough to handle the BB-flat tuba.

1) Embouchure: Lip slurs are somewhat impractical for tuba; use long tones as a substitute in warmups and tonal development exercises. Tuba tone quality should be as clear and musical as that of any other brass instrument. The obvious volume of breath support needed to play the tuba should produce a clear, centered tone quality, with the embouchure relaxed and the center of the lips moving slightly forward toward the cup of the mouthpiece. Enough overall embouchure firmness must be maintained, however, to keep the cheeks from puffing and to provide the air column with a reasonable focus. This is especially true in the middle and upper register of the tuba, where the center of the lips must

be kept close together to produce the proper pitch with good tone quality. I have had my tuba players practice occasionally on a euphonium to develop better focus of the tone quality. Tune each valve slide on the tuba to effect good intonation; be sure your open pitches are in tune when you purchase a new tuba.

2) Tonguing: Develop as on other brass instruments. Slower metronomic markings may be necessary in specific exercises. A "doo" approach to tonguing will result in a more musical tonguing attack and more rapid tonguing ability.

3) Fingering: I write out my own scale materials for my tuba players and duplicate them by machine. My tuba players are required to learn the same fingering technique as other brass players. They need this technical background to play difficult band music. The four-valve tuba is advantageous in correcting faulty intonation, lowering the practical playing range, and in some cases simplifying fingerings. Substitute the fourth valve for 1-3 to improve intonation. A tuba with short-action valves can be an advantage in fast fingering techniques.

4) Breathing: Emphasis should be on deep diaphragmatic breathing since the tuba obviously takes more air to support the tone properly than is necessary on any other brass or wind instrument.

5) Musical terms: Learn as encountered.

6) Materials:

    a) Method books and étude materials:

Grade I:	*Elementary Method, E♭ or BB♭ Bass,* Hovey, Rubank, Inc.
	Supplementary Studies, E♭ or BB♭ Bass, Endresen, Rubank, Inc.
Grade II:	*Intermediate Method, E♭ or BB♭ Bass,* Skornicka-Boltz, Rubank, Inc.
	First Book of Practical Studies for Tuba, Getchell-Hovey, Belwin, Inc.
Grade III:	*Advanced Method, Vol. I,* Gower-Voxman, Rubank, Inc.
	Second Book of Practical Studies for Tuba, Getchell-Hovey, Belwin, Inc.
Grade IV:	*Advanced Method, Vol. II,* Gower-Voxman, Rubank, Inc.
	VanderCook Etudes for E♭ or BB♭ Bass, VanderCook, Rubank, Inc.
Grade V:	*26 Melodic Studies in Varied Rhythms and Keys,* Blazhevich, Carl Fischer

                70 Studies for BB-flat Tuba, Vol. I, Blazhevich, Robert King

Grade VI: *70 Studies for BB-flat Tuba, Vol. II,* Blazhevich, Robert King

                66 Etudes in All Major and Minor Keys, Slama, Carl Fischer

Grade VII: Various selected advanced étude and solo materials.

Grade VIII: Same as Grade VII.

  b) Supplement each grade level with appropriate solo and ensemble material.

SELECTED TUBA BIBLIOGRAPHY

Bell, William J., *A Handbook of Information on Intonation.* Elkhorn, Wisconsin: The Getzen Company, Inc., 1965.

Brown, Merrill, "Repertoire for Brass Soloists, Part II," *The Instrumentalist,* vol. 31, January, 1977, p. 51.

Conner, Rex, "How to Care for a Rotary-Valved Tuba," *The Instrumentalist,* vol. 26, November, 1971, p. 40.

Farkas, Philip, *The Art of Brass Playing.* Bloomington, Indiana: Brass Publications, 1962.

Getchell, Robert, *Teacher's Guide to the Brass Instruments.* Elkhart, Indiana: H. & A. Selmer Inc., 1959.

Moore, E. C. (Revised by Dr. James Neilson), *The Brass Book.* Kenosha, Wisconsin: Leblanc Publications Inc., 1964.

Morris, R. Winston, "A Basic Repertoire and Studies for the Serious Tubist," *The Instrumentalist,* vol. 27, February, 1973, p. 33.

Morris, R. Winston, "A Tuba Clinic with Harvey Phillips," *The Instrumentalist,* vol. 29, January, 1975, p. 51.

Morris, R. Winston, "The Tuba Family," *The Instrumentalist,* vol. 27, February, 1973, p. 33.

Pitts, Larry P., "Using the First Valve Slide to Adjust Tuba Intonation," *The Instrumentalist,* vol. 29, April, 1975, p. 52.

Rasmussen, Mary, *A Teacher's Guide to the Literature of Brass Instruments.* Durham, New Hampshire: Appleyard Publications, 1968.

Weerts, Richard, *Developing Individual Skills for the High School Band.* West Nyack, New York: Parker Publishing Company, Inc., 1969.

Weldon, Constance, "The Tuba Ensemble," *The Instrumentalist,* vol. 27, February, 1973, p. 35.

Winslow, Robert W. and John E. Green, *Playing and Teaching Brass Instruments*. Englewood Cliffs, New Jersey: Prentice-Hall, Inc., 1961.

Winter, James H., *The Brass Instruments*. Boston, Mass.: Allyn and Bacon, Inc., 1964.

DEVELOPING PERCUSSION SYLLABI

13

One of the most difficult tasks facing the band director who is a wind player is the teaching of percussion instruments. Fortunately, there is a large amount of published material pertaining to each of the percussion instruments. A syllabus similar to the woodwind and brass syllabi can be developed for the snare drum. Developing practical syllabi for other percussion instruments may be difficult since most percussionists study snare drum during the elementary stages of their development. Other percussion instruments are studied later.

THE SNARE DRUM SYLLABUS

After formal academic study of the snare drum I came to two conclusions: 1) I would have to develop at least an intermediate proficiency on snare to be successful in teaching the instrument, and 2) a syllabus would have to be developed that would be successful for the teacher with a wind instrument background. The following is the method that evolved for the lower grades; it has not only worked successfully for me but has also been of great value to my college student teachers who were wind players.

1) Teaching the Rudiments

Grade I—The First Year of Study

Each of the following is presented during the *first half of the year*; all exercises are developed to m.m. = 120. Each student receives a copy of the material as shown. Musical notation is not used in this preliminary rudiment study; the student is studying notation of quarter, eighth, and sixteenth notes in various rhythmic patterns from a selected method book. Rapid introduction of this material during the first few months of study increases student interest and motivation.

Snare Drum Rudiments

(1) The long roll   L L R R L L R R   etc.
1 & 2 & 3 & 4 &

(2) The single-stroke roll   L R L R L R L R   etc.
1 & 2 & 3 & 4 &

(3) The ruff   L L R – R R L   etc.
1 & 2   1 & 2

(4) The 5-stroke roll   L L R R L ⸘   R R L L R ⸘   etc.
1 & 2 & 3 4   1 & 2 & 3 4

(5) The 9-stroke roll   L L R R L L R R L ⸘   R R L L R R L L R ⸘   etc.
1 & 2 & 3 & 4 & 5 6   1 & 2 & 3 & 4 & 5 6

(6) The 7-stroke roll   L L R R L L R ⸘   R R L L R R L ⸘   etc.
1 & 2 & 3 & 4 5   1 & 2 & 3 & 4 5

(7) Single paradiddle   L R L L – R L R R   etc.
   >   >
1 & 2 &   1 & 2 &

(8) Double paradiddle   L R L R L L – R L R L R R   etc.
   >   >   >   >
1 & 2 & 3 &   1 & 2 & 3 &

(9) Triple paradiddle   L R L R L R L L – R L R L R L R R   etc.
   >   >   >   >   >   >
1 & 2 & 3 & 4 &   1 & 2 & 3 & 4 &

(10) Paradiddle exercise   S–D–T–D–S   S–D–T–D–S
L–R–L–R–L   R–L–R–L–R

(The paradiddle exercise combines all three forms of paradiddles into one drill—single, double, triple, double, single—using all possible stickings for each form.)

Each of the following exercises is added during the *second half of the year*. The double bounce is used for roll and ruff rudiments from this point onward. Notation is used when the flam is introduced. Notation to various rolls can be introduced at any time; the transfer from these exercises to actual notation should be accomplished as soon as possible.

(11) Ruff with bounce   LL R – RR L   etc.
1 & 2 &

(12) 5-stroke roll with bounce   LL RR L – RR LL R   etc.
1 & 2   1 & 2

(13) 9-stroke roll with bounce   LL RR LL RR L – RR LL RR LL R   etc.
1 & 2 & 3   1 & 2 & 3

(14) 7-stroke roll with bounce   LL RR LL R – RR LL RR L   etc.
1 & 2 & 1 & 2 &

(15) 13-stroke roll   LL RR LL RR LL RR L – RR LL RR LL RR LL
    with bounce   1   &   2   &   3   &   4   1   &   2   &   3   &

    R etc.
    4

(16) 17-stroke roll   LL RR LL RR LL RR LL RR L – RR LL   etc.
    with bounce   1   &   2   &   3   &   4   &   5

(17) 15-stroke roll   LL RR LL RR LL RR LL R – RR LL   etc.
    with bounce   1   &   2   &   3   &   4   &

(18) Flam
    LR   RL etc.
    1   2

(19) Flam-tap
    LR R RL L etc.
    1   &   2   &

(20) Flam Accent
    No. 2
    LR R RL L etc.
    1 lee 2 lee

(21) Flam Accent
    No. 1
    LR L R RL R L etc.
    1 la lee 2 la lee

After the above material has been mastered, the remainder of the 26 rudiments should be introduced.

Grade II—The Second Year of Study

This is spent perfecting these rudiments at a very moderate tempo. Academic understanding and proper sticking are most important during this year, not development of speed. Appropriate Grade II method books and étude materials are used to develop reading skills.

Grades III and IV—The Third and Fourth Years of Study

The following study sheets are given to each student. A group of rudiments is studied each week. These are: roll rudiments, first week; flam rudiments, second week; ruff rudiments, third week; and so on. These are rotated, the main object being to develop speed of execution and speed of recognizing and reading the notation of the rudiments in étude materials. All rolls are assigned rhythmic syllables, as are all rhythms being studied.

These syllables are spoken as the student plays. They become as essential to the percussionist as the foot beat is to the young wind player.

Rudiments Involving the Roll

(Do each exercise for at least 12 beats at m.m. = 120. Sticking may be started with either the right or the left hand.)

(1) Long roll

    le&a2e&a le&a2e&a etc.
    LRLRLRLR LRLRLRLR

(2) 5-stroke roll (off beat)

    1 &a 2 &a 1 &a 2 &a etc.
    R LR L RL R LR L RL

5-stroke roll (on beat)

    1 e & 2 e & 3 e & 4 e & etc.
    L R L R L R L R L R L R

(3) 7-stroke roll

    le&a 2e&a
    LRLR LRLR

(4) 9-stroke roll

    le&a2 le&a2 etc.
    LRLRL RLRLR

(5) 11-stroke roll

    le&a2e le&a2e etc.
    LRLRLR LRLRLR

(6) 13-stroke roll

    le&a2e& le&a2e& etc.
    LRLRLRL RLRLRLR

(7) 15-stroke roll

    le&a2e&a le&a2e&a etc.
    LRLRLRLR LRLRLRLR

(8) 17-stroke roll

    le&a2e&a3 4 le&a2e&a3 4 etc.
    LRLRLRLRL   RLRLRLRLR

Rudiments Involving the Flam

(Do each exercise for at least 12 beats at m.m. = 120. Stress the use of a high and a low stick when playing flams.)

(1) Flam
etc.
1   2
LR RL

(2) Flam tap
etc.
1 & 2 &
LR R RL L

(3) Flam accent no. 2
etc.
1   lee 2   lee
LR R   RL L

(4) Flam accent no. 1
etc.
1 la lee 2 la lee
LR L R RL R L

(5) Flam paradiddle
etc.
1 & 2 & 1 & 2 &
1 e & a 2 e & a
LR L R R RL R L L

(6) Flamacue
etc.
1 & 2 & 3
1 e & a 2
LR L R L LR

The Single Stroke Roll and the Paradiddles

(1) Single-stroke roll
etc.
1 e & a 2 e & a
L R L R L R L R

(2) Single paradiddle
etc.
1 e & a 2 e & a
L R L L R L R R

(3) Double paradiddle
etc.
1 talataleeta 2 talataleeta
L R L R L L R L R L R R

(4) Triple paradiddle
etc.
1 e & a 2 e & a 1 e & a 2 e & a
L R L R L R L L R L R L R L R R

(5) Paradiddle combination exercise   SDTDS SDTDS
                                        LRLRL RLRLR

Rudiments Involving the Ruff

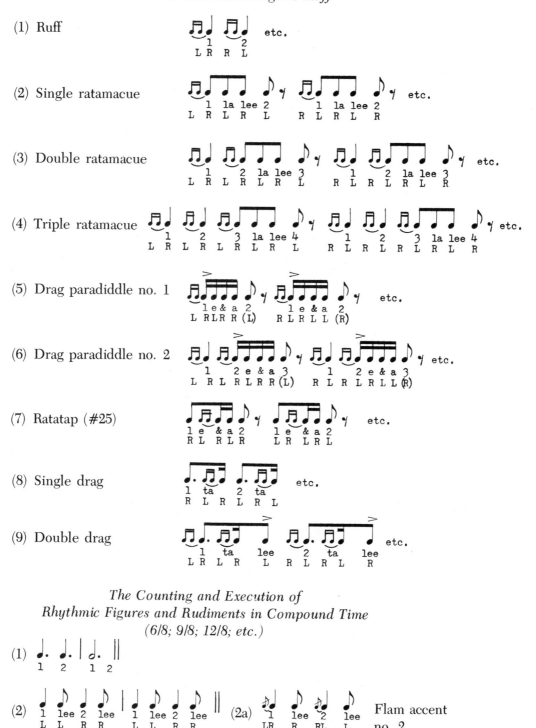

(1) Ruff

(2) Single ratamacue

(3) Double ratamacue

(4) Triple ratamacue

(5) Drag paradiddle no. 1

(6) Drag paradiddle no. 2

(7) Ratatap (#25)

(8) Single drag

(9) Double drag

The Counting and Execution of
Rhythmic Figures and Rudiments in Compound Time
(6/8; 9/8; 12/8; etc.)

(1)

(2)   (2a)   Flam accent no. 2

(3) 1 la lee 2 la lee   1 la lee 2 la lee   (3a) 1 la lee 2 la lee   Flam accent
     L R L   R L R   L R L   R L R   RL R L   LR L R   no. 1

(4) 1 talataleeta 2 talataleeta   (4a) 1talataleeta   2   13-stroke roll
     L R L R L R L R L R L R   LR L R L R   L   (slow tempo)

(5) 1ta la lee 2 lata lee   (9) 1   leeta 2   leeta 1   5-stroke roll

(6) 1 la leeta 2talata lee   (10) 1talataleeta 1   2   25-stroke roll
                                                     2talataleeta   (slow tempo)

(7) 1 lataleeta 2 lataleeta   (11) 1 la lee 2   7-stroke roll
                                                                            (fast tempo)

(8) 1 ta lee 2 ta lee   (12) 1 la lee 1   2   13-stroke roll
                                                     2 la lee   (fast tempo)

(8a) 1 ta lee 2 ta lee   Double drag
      LR LR L RL RL R

The above materials should cover basic counting and rudiment study through Grades III and IV. At advanced levels of instruction, rudiments should have been mastered, but reading study should continue through Grade V to VIII materials. If you have a percussionist on your staff, advanced rudimental variations can be taught to advanced students; this study can include advanced techniques in marching band cadences and on the trap set.

Various methods of multiple bounce can also be taught, using three, four, five, and so on bounces to a stroke to create a connected roll technique. Although I teach my younger students to strictly alternate hands in rhythms and repeated rudimental patterns, many professionals do not practice the strict alternation method. My advanced players are informed of this difference and told to use freedom in regard to alternation. I feel very strongly that students should be proficient snare drummers in the rudiments before they adopt multiple bounce and free alternation techniques.

2) First Lesson Considerations

I teach the traditional grip to all of my beginning snare drum students. Every student, if possible, should be taught the matched grip technique as soon as his traditional grip is well established. Matched grip is very important to the percussion doubler, the marching percussionist, and the traps player. The traditional grip is the most often used concert technique.

A student may begin to feel groupings of two (2/4), groupings of three (3/4), and groupings of four (4/4) at his first lesson. Three exercises of quarter notes divided in such a manner are excellent material for the first week of study. Use any good stick with a 2B designation for your beginners. Have all students develop the technique of "drawing the stick out" of the pad or head from the first lesson. This will lead to precise and clear tone quality.

3) Musical Terms

All percussionists should learn musical terms as they occur in their playing materials. This is especially true in regard to tempo markings, dynamic markings, and stylistic indications found in their band music.

4) Materials

a) Method books and étude materials.

Grade I:	*Drum Method, Book I*, Harr, M. M. Cole
	Three R's for Snare Drum, Book One, Ostling, Belwin, Inc.
Grade II:	*Breeze Easy Method for Snare Drum, Book II*, Kinyon, Belwin, Inc.
	Three R's for Snare Drum, Book Two, Ostling, Belwin, Inc.
Grade III:	*Intermediate Method, Drums*, Buggert, Rubank, Inc.
	Modern School for Snare Drum, Goldenberg, Chappell & Co.
Grade IV:	*Drum Method, Book II*, Harr, M. M. Cole
	Rubank Advanced Method, Whistler, Rubank, Inc.
Grade V:	*Ludwig Collection of Drum Solos*, Ludwig, Ludwig Drum Co.
	Drum Rhythms, Krupa, Mills
Grade VI:	*Adventures in Solo Drumming*, Schinstine, Southern Music Co.
	Practical Percussion Studies, Tilles, Henry Adler, Inc.

Grade VII: Selected advanced étude and solo materials.

Grade VIII: Same as Grade VII.

b) Supplement with solo and ensemble material appropriate to each
grade level.

THE TIMPANI SYLLABUS

A detailed yearly syllabus for timpani may be impractical. Many
elementary schools do not have timpani available, so timpani players are
often started in junior high. Most high school timpanists are specialists and
may be switches from snare drum or recruited at the high school level from
strong academic students with good senses of pitch. Tuning can be taught
by solfeggio with emphasis on singing common intervals or by using scale-
degree numbers, with 5 up to 1 (perfect fourth) or 5 down to 1 (perfect
fifth) being of primary importance. Each timpanist should be supplied with
his own pitch pipe, although emergency tuning can use orchestral bells or
lower brass instruments. Use pedal timpani, and be sure that they are
properly tuned to their fundamental pitches and that each head is tuned to
the same pitch at each point directly in front of the tuning knobs. Each
timpanist should have several pairs of sticks of varying hardness; any good
timpani manual should have detailed information on the different types of
sticks that should be used.

The following are several recommended timpani method books:

Grades I-II	*Timpani Method*, Harr, M. M. Cole
	Ludwig Timpani Instructor, Ludwig, Ludwig
Grades III-IV	*Modern Method for Timpani*, Goodman, Mills
	Timpani Instruction Manual, Harr, Slingerland
Grades V-VI	*Timp Tunes* (19 Pieces), Schinstine, Southern Music Co.
	The Solo Timpanist: 26 Etudes, Firth, Carl Fischer

THE MALLET INSTRUMENT SYLLABUS

Mallet players are usually recruited at higher levels of your band
program because of the lack of instruments to play in elementary or junior
high schools or because of the lack of parts to be covered in easier band
music. One possible exception is an occasional bell part, which usually
requires very little technical skill. Strong academic students with piano
backgrounds are excellent recruits for mallet instruments since they are
familiar with the keyboard and only need to learn mallet technique. A
mallet player should be able to double on auxiliary percussion parts because extensive mallet parts are encountered in a small percentage of your
band music.

An exceptional amount of good original material is available for the mallet player, in addition to various instrumental method books, études, and solos that lie within the proper range of the mallet instrument being studied. A year-by-year syllabus can be developed if instruments are available. If a detailed syllabus is used, pattern technical study after brass and woodwind scale sheet work, including study of scales, arpeggios, scales by thirds, and the chromatic scale. Edited Selmer Scale Sheets can be very useful.

The following are some recommended method books for mallet study:

Grade I-II	*Music for Marimba, Book I,* Jolliff, Rubank
	Music for Marimba, Book II, Jolliff, Rubank
	A Simple and Practical Method for Xylophone, Marimba and Bells, Dorn, G. Schirmer, Inc.
	Modern Method for Bells, Xylophone, Marimba and Chimes, Gardner, Carl Fischer
Grades III-IV	*Music for Marimba, Book III,* Jolliff, Rubank
	Mallet Student Level III, Feldstein, Belwin-Mills
	Modern School of Xylophone, Marimba, Vibraphone, Goldenberg, Chappell
	Percussion Keyboard Technique, McMillan, Pro Art
	Foundation Studies for Vibes, Xylophone, Marimba, Gornston, Gornston
	305 Selected Melodious Studies for French Horn, Pottag-Andraud, Southern Music Co.
Grades V-VI	*Masterpieces for Marimba,* McMillan, Pro Art
	Mallet Technique for Xylophone, Marimba and Vibraphone, Firth, Carl Fischer
	Studies & Melodious Etudes for Mallets, Level III, Feldstein, Belwin-Mills

Other percussion instruments, such as bass drum, cymbals, triangle, and various Latin instruments, can be included in the regular snare drum syllabus. These parts are usually covered by students whose basic background has been snare drum. Many books and articles have been written to help the student and the teacher understand the special techniques of these auxiliary instruments. A selected bibliography of these follows:

Denov, Sam, *The Art of Playing the Cymbals.* New York, New York: Henry Adler, Inc., 1963.

Jerger, Jacob M., *Bongo Playing Made Easy.* Niles, Illinois: Slingerland Drum Co., 1962.

Morales, Humberto, and Henry Adler, *Latin Rhythm Instruments and How to Play Them*. New York, New York: Henry Adler, Inc., 1958.

Noonan, John, *Notes on Striking Cymbals*. North Quincy, Massachusetts: Avedis Zildjian Co., 1962.

Walters, Harold, *Simplified Rudiments for Latin American Instruments*. Chicago, Illinois: Rubank, Inc., 1951.

Weill, LeRoy S., *Latin-American Drum Rhythms, Modern Style*. New York, New York: Remick Music Corp., 1959.

SELECTED GENERAL PERCUSSION BIBLIOGRAPHY

Applebaum, Terry, "Flams, Ruffs and Rolls," *The Instrumentalist*, vol. 29, January, 1975, p. 56.

Barnett, Wallace, *The Mallet Percussions and How to Use Them*. Chicago, Illinois: J. C. Deagan, Inc., 1968.

Bartlett, Harry R., *Guide to Teaching Percussion*. Dubuque, Iowa: Wm. C. Brown Company, 1964.

Bircher, John, Jr., "Chamber Percussion: Approach to Musicality," *The Instrumentalist*, vol. 26, March, 1972, p. 74.

Britton, Mervin W., "Developing a Good Snare Drum Roll," *The Instrumentalist*, vol. 26, November, 1971, p. 43.

Brown, Merrill, "Repertoire for Percussionists," *The Instrumentalist*, vol. 31, February, 1977, p. 67.

Burns, Roy, "The Super Soft Roll and How to Develop It," *The Instrumentalist*, vol. 26, May, 1972, p. 54.

Collins, Myron D. and John E. Green, *Playing and Teaching Percussion Instruments*. Englewood Cliffs, New Jersey: Prentice-Hall, Inc., 1962.

Combs, F. Michael, "Keyboard Percussion in the School Music Program," *The Instrumentalist*, vol. 26, April, 1972, p. 52.

Combs, F. Michael, "Percussionists and the Contest/Festival," *The Instrumentalist*, vol. 27, March, 1973, p. 76.

Combs, F. Michael, "Review of Percussion Materials," *The Instrumentalist*, vol. 26, December, 1971, p. 48.

Combs, F. Michael, "Selecting a Snare Drum Method Book," *The Instrumentalist*, vol. 27, December, 1972, p. 50.

Combs, F. Michael, "The Set Drummer—Advice From the Pros," *The Instrumentalist*, vol. 27, April, 1973, p. 58.

Combs, F. Michael "Snare Drum Method Books," *The Instrumentalist*, vol. 29, September, 1974, p. 53.

Delp, Ron, "The Conga Drum," *The Instrumentalist*, vol. 29, February, 1975, p. 58.

Ervin, Karen, "Developing Keyboard Mallet Technique," *The Instrumentalist*, vol. 29, April, 1975, p. 56.

Fink, Ron, "Careers in Percussion," *The Instrumentalist*, vol. 28, February, 1974, p. 65.

Gilbert, Donald K., "How and When to Teach Rolls," *The Instrumentalist*, vol. 31, March, 1977, p. 100.

Glassock, Lynn, "Selecting Suspended Cymbals," *The Instrumentalist*, vol. 29, November, 1974, p. 67.

Harr, Haskell, "How to Apply Drum Rudiments to 6/8 Meter," *The Instrumentalist*, vol. 27, June, 1973, p. 54.

Knaack, Donald, "How to Organize a High School Percussion Ensemble," *The Instrumentalist*, vol. 25, May, 1971, p. 57.

Lawrence, Paul, "Understanding Ruffs and Drags," *The Instrumentalist*, vol. 31, November, 1976, p. 62.

McKenzie, Jack and H. Payson, *Music Educator's Guide to Percussion*. Rockville Centre, Long Island, New York: Belwin, Inc., 1964.

McKinney, Jim, "A Band Director's Guide to Percussion Texts," *The Instrumentalist*, vol. 29, June, 1975, p. 75.

McKinney, James R., "Play a Multiple Percussion Solo," *The Instrumentalist*, vol. 31, January, 1977, p. 54.

Noonan, John, *Notes on Striking Cymbals*. North Quincy, Massachusetts: Avedis Zildjian Co., 1962.

Peters, Gordon, "Care and Maintenance of Percussion Instruments," *The Instrumentalist*, vol. 29, May, 1975, p. 56.

Peters, Gordon B., *Treatise on Percussion*. Unpublished Master's Thesis, Eastman School of Music of the University of Rochester, 1962.

Publications, Catelogue P1, Publication Department, Ludwig Industries, Chicago, Illinois.

Pullis, Joe M., "Developing the Rudimental Snare Drum Grip," *The Instrumentalist*, vol. 26, October, 1971, p. 47.

Schinstine, William, "Three Way Flams," *The Instrumentalist*, vol. 27, November, 1972, p. 47.

Snider, Larry, "Concepts for the Inexperienced Mallet Player," *The Instrumentalist*, vol. 29, December, 1974, p. 62.

Special Issue on Percussion, Selmer Bandwagon, Number 83, Elkhart, Indiana, 1977.

Spohn, Charles L., *The Percussion*. Boston, Massachusetts: Allyn and Bacon, Inc., 1967.

Weerts, Richard, *Developing Individual Skills for the High School Band*. West Nyack, New York: Parker Publishing Company, Inc., 1969.

HOW TO TEACH
GENERAL BAND SKILLS
IN LESSON AND SMALL ENSEMBLE
SITUATIONS

14

Most comprehensive teaching of our future or present band members is done in small groups or private lessons. It is difficult during band rehearsals to teach the more subtle aspects of individual musicianship and the skills needed to play specific instruments. Therefore, the rotating instrumental music schedule, or a similar method of small class instruction, should be established.

Band skills are not any different from the musical skills needed to perform in small ensembles or as a soloist. All of these musical situations require development of tone quality, intonation, interpretation, posture, breath control, and the technical skills of tonguing, fingering, and performing the proper articulations and dynamic nuances. The best working conditions for teaching these skills would seem to be the private lesson, but the most readily available and the most practical teaching climate is the class lesson of six or fewer students. Ensemble skills can be developed best in class situations, not in private lessons. The teacher must take part as a performer to create an ensemble situation in a private lesson. Although there are advantages to this procedure, it is somewhat misleading and unrealistic to have part of the ensemble be a professional. The student will learn to follow the teacher instead of developing solid leadership skills himself. When students alone make up the ensemble, problems occur that do not surface in a private lesson.

USING WARMUP, PRACTICE, AND LESSON ROUTINES

All lessons should be tightly structured by various routines that will develop the many aspects of the complete musician. These should include routines for developing the following skills.

1) *Tone quality*—Each student should be carefully controlled in his use of proper warmup materials on his specific instrument. He should be trained to *never* play other materials until at least a few minutes of proper warmup are completed. Many embouchure and tone quality problems can be avoided by strict enforcement of proper warmup procedures.

2) *Intonation*—Good tonal development will usually lead to good intonation. Once the tone production of a student is established and progressing in a proper manner, his instrument should be thoroughly checked for out-of-tune notes. This may be done by use of a Strobotuner or a Stroboconn or the teacher can check the instrument by playing it himself if he is satisfactorily proficient on the specific instrument. Any notes that may be out of tune on the instrument should be corrected by a competent repairman. If this cannot be done, the student who has a well-developed tone quality and firmly established embouchure control should be made aware of the notes that are out of tune on his instrument. By working with an instrument similar to a Strobotuner, he can learn to adjust pitches up or down to correct faulty intonation on his instrument. Careful purchase of a good instrument and strictly developed embouchure and tone production control will lead to a performer with few intonation problems.

3) *Tonguing*—Tonguing exercises should be presented very early in the development of the instrumentalist. I begin young students on some tonguing exercises a few weeks after they start study of an instrument. Proper placement of the tongue in tonguing is very important, as is the development of tonguing speed. Relaxation of the tongue as a muscle should be stressed continually when tonguing technique is being developed.

4) *Flexibility exercises*—All wind instruments require a considerable degree of embouchure flexibility. This is particularly important to the brass player since rapid pitch changes are rarely helped by fingering changes, as they may be on woodwind instruments. Exercises must be developed and presented to the student within weeks of his beginning study of a brass or woodwind instrument. The use of flexibility exercises very early in the development of a young player will also lead to proper tone production. Flexibility on a woodwind instrument is greatly enhanced by fingering technique, which may be specifically developed through rapid work in scales, scales by thirds, arpeggios, and chromatic scales played throughout the range of the instrument.

5) *Fingering technique*—Fingering technique can be developed on all wind instruments by early use of scale and arpeggio exercises. These may be introduced within a few weeks of the student's starting study of his instrument. At first the exercises are done very slowly, within the technical capabilities of the student. As the student progresses through quarter notes, eighth notes, and sixteenth notes, his technical study in various keys

should be increased in speed by use of shorter note values and faster metronomic speeds.

6) *Articulation studies*—Articulations should be introduced within a few weeks of the student's beginning study of his instrument. Use of various articulation patterns in playing scale and arpeggio studies develops articulation skills and fingering skills at the same time. Simple articulations should be introduced at first; for example, tonguing all notes, slurring all notes, slurring in four-note groups, and using a repeated pattern of two slurred notes followed by two tongued notes. Strict attention to exact articulation should be stressed at all times.

7) *Dynamic awareness* should be developed at an early age. This may be combined with breath-control exercises, which stress and reproduce contrasting dynamic levels. For example, a mezzo-forte can be explained to the student as the average dynamic level or loudness he creates when practicing with proper tone quality. Louder dynamics may be thought of as being above or greater than this sound in intensity, and softer dynamics as being below or less than this sound. It should also be stressed that the louder the sound, the greater the volume of breath required to produce it with proper tone quality and the softer the sound, the less the volume of breath needed. When dynamics are being properly produced, all aspects of playing should remain constant except for the volume and speed of the breath flowing through the instrument.

8) *Breath support* can also be taught through routines, but care should be taken to constantly reinforce the student's understanding that the breath support felt in the area of the diaphragm is not necessarily relative to the loudness with which one plays. I have experienced a feeling of more support or effort on the breathing apparatus when I am supporting very soft dynamic playing, especially in the upper register of a brass instrument.

Proper use of the breathing apparatus should be explained in detail to every class. Draw a rough diagram of the body on the chalkboard. (See Figure 1.) Explain the position and use of the diaphragm muscle in this manner: When the lungs expand with air, they expand not only outward against the rib cage but also downward, forcing the diaphragm muscle downward and, in turn, forcing the organs of the abdomen downward and away from the breathing apparatus expansion. What appears to be air expanding the abdomen is actually the diaphragm muscle forcing the organs of the abdomen downward and outward, allowing the lungs greater expansion downward.

When you are exhaling, or supporting the tone with breath, the diaphragm moves upward, putting the air in the lungs under pressure. The abdominal wall will move inward and upward at the same time. Caution the student against the opposite type of breathing, where the chest expands and the abdominal wall moves in and up when you are inhaling and

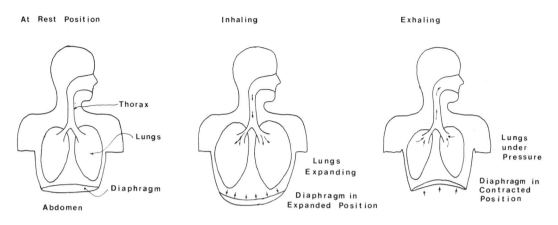

Figure 1. Body During Breathing Exercise

the chest and abdomen fall when you are exhaling. "Lift" is necessary for proper breath support, not "pushing downward."

This entire process can be explained to your students as: Fill and expand like a balloon when you are inhaling; place the air in your "balloon" under pressure when you are exhaling by lifting with the diaphragm muscle and literally squeezing the air out of your "balloon" by pressure. Emphasize that the embouchure is in no way involved and should remain relaxed at all times so the air being controlled by the breathing apparatus can flow freely through a relaxed throat and lips. Use only enough lip firmness to assure the air proper passage through the mouthpiece and through the body of the instrument. The combination of a well-developed breathing apparatus, a relaxed throat, and a "free-blowing" embouchure will develop startling results in tone production and control, especially at dynamic extremes.

9) *Proper posture* should be required at all times. Stress to your students that correct posture leads to the best possible musical results with the least physical effort. There is no doubt that when the body is held erect the breathing apparatus is able to work at utmost efficiency. The physical production of good tone quality should be the primary objective of correct posture; the appearance of your students should be a secondary objective.

Using an Outline for Practice and Lesson Routines

Practice and lesson routines can be considered on three different levels of complexity:

1) Simple routines for all winds or for percussion.

2) More detailed routines for woodwinds, brass, or percussion.

3) Complex routines for specific instruments.

The following is a simple outline that can be used by instrumental students at any level as a guide for proper practicing and lesson routines.

Practice Routine for Winds

1) Warmup (total of 10 minutes).

    a) Tone and intonation development (2 minutes).

    b) Tonguing exercise for development of tonguing control and speed (2 minutes).

    c) Fingering technique development—scale, arpeggio, scale by thirds, and chromatic scale in a specific key each week (6 minutes).

2) Etude work, especially stressing rhythm (10 to 15 minutes).

3) Ensemble or band music work (10 to 15 minutes).

This simple routine can be followed for a practice or a lesson session of 30 to 40 minutes. Stress the importance of following the warmup portion of the routine very closely so that tone quality, tonguing, and fingering are equally warmed up and developed. Neglect of any part of the warmup routine at any level may lead to weaknesses in the technical development of the student.

Simple Practice Routine for Percussionists

1) Rudiments for the week (10 minutes).

2) Etude (10 to 15 minutes).

3) Ensemble or band music (10 to 15 minutes).

Keyboard percussionists can use a routine similar to (1c) of the Practice Routine for Winds.

Expanding the Simple Practice Outline for Woodwinds and Brasses

After presenting the simple outline to your students, expand it for each class. Variations will occur between woodwinds and brasses and also between specific instruments. The following suggestions should aid you in the preliminary expansion of the outline.

1) *Warmup:*

    a) *Tone and intonation*—Use long tones or natural slurs, depending upon the specific instrument involved in the tonal portion of the warmup. Brasses can use various lip slurs; woodwinds can use a scale in one octave in whole or half notes, applying vibrato to the exercise when appropriate.

Vibrato should be done in pulsations of two, three, four, and so on to a beat.

b) *The tonguing exercise*—Use various repeated rhythms played on each degree of a one-octave scale, ascending and descending. These may include the following rhythmic patterns:

Double and triple tonguing can be used when appropriate. Faster tonguing can be developed with the rapid single, double, or triple tongue by using a legato approach, stressing a "da" tongue and a continuous air column. The tempo of the exercise is dependent upon the proficiency of the class, although tonguing speed should be constantly pushed to the maximum with each class.

c) *Fingering technique*—Use a scale, an arpeggio, and a scale by thirds in a key chosen for one week of study. Also use a chromatic scale, played from the tonic note of the key being studied to an octave or two above this tonic note. Various rhythmic patterns can be used, and various speeds employed, depending upon the proficiency of the students involved. The chromatic scale can be played in eighth notes, triplets, or sixteenth notes. An interesting variation to this exercise can be introduced by dividing the class in half and having one half of the class ascending as the other half is descending. Students become proficient at playing chromatically when this exercise is practiced at rapid speeds.

Scales can be played in harmony in classes by combining two or more scales built a third apart. Arpeggios can be played in harmony by starting one student on the root, another on the third, another on the fifth, and so on. Scales by thirds can be played as a round, thus producing harmony. Simply start student "A" at the beginning of a scale by thirds, start student "B" at the beginning after "A" has played four notes, start student "C" at the beginning after "B" has played four notes, and so on. All exercises such as these must be varied to maintain student interest; playing them in harmony is an excellent way to increase student interest in practicing and perfecting sometimes uninteresting scale-like materials.

Use of various articulation patterns also creates interest and improves the student's ability to recognize and play articulations correctly. Dynamic variations can also be used for variety and will lead to better understanding of dynamic levels and nuances. Constant variation will keep the student alert and interested when he is playing any part of his warmup routine.

2) *Etude work* should include a thorough study of an étude chosen for

each week, stressing rhythms, articulations, key and accidentals, and any special techniques required to play the étude, such as trills and turns.

3) Detailed *study of* an *ensemble or* a *selected* piece of *band music* to be performed should end the lesson and practice routine. Study of your band music in small groups need not be a "rote" drill for concert performances. Every piece of band music you play has specific interpretative, pedagogical, and technical problems that are unique to that composition and can also be unique to certain instruments in the band ensemble. Working out specific interpretative or technical problems directly related to specific instruments is very difficult in the full band. Once such problems are worked out in small classes, your band will immediately sound better and band rehearsal time will not be wasted for other instrumentalists not involved in specific problems. The latter may often become spectators during your rehearsals and lose interest in playing with the group if large amounts of rehearsal time are spent on the problems of a few band members. For example, imagine the brass player who must sit through 20 minutes of remedial work that the conductor must do with some difficult woodwind passages. The happy band player is usually the one who is constantly directly involved in actual playing during the full band rehearsal. A small amount of specific study of band music problems during each homogeneous lesson can be very valuable to the ultimate success of your band's performances.

Developing Specific Routines for Each Instrument

Since each instrument of your band has technical problems unique to it, routines for technical development can be based upon a simple lesson outline but will vary considerably with each instrument. Therefore, the following are practice and lesson routines for specific instruments.

1) The Flute

a) *Warmup with vibrato*—Warmup with the major scale of the week played in whole notes at approximately m.m. = 72, pulsating a vibrato in eighth-note rhythm, eight pulsations for each whole note. Descending, use three pulsations per beat. This may be increased with advanced players to four, five or six pulsations per beat, with the tempo at the higher pulsation rate being m.m. = 60. This exercise will result in a well-supported tone quality, and a controlled vibrato will be developed by all flute players at approximately the speed at which a free vibrato is produced by the advanced player—between five and six pulsations per second. This exercise should not exceed two minutes in duration after the student understands exactly how to produce the pulsations. Explain that this exercise is used to develop proper tone quality, which includes a workable vibrato and ultimately leads to proper intonation. Intonation changes in the instrument (tuning) should be effected during this part of the warmup, and any notes that are intonation problems should be brought to the attention of the student and adjusted by embouchure changes or other effective methods such as alternate fingerings. For example, keeping the entire right hand down during the playing of an open c-sharp helps the tone quality and intonation of this pitch on the flute. This exercise can be varied by use of major or minor scales, arpeggios of different types, scales by thirds, chromatic scales, and so on. This primary warmup exercise can also be played in harmony.

b) *Tonguing exercise*—A tonguing exercise as part of the flute warmup can be played in various rhythmic patterns but usually should consist of four beats of consecutive eighths, triplet eighths, or sixteenths played on each degree of a major or minor scale. Double tonguing and triple tonguing can be used in this flute warmup procedure. The tonguing exercise should use one octave of the scale and can be varied by using sixteenths ascending and triplet eighths descending. This element of warmup should not exceed two minutes in duration once the student has the exercise well in hand. Variation for interest may include the use of arpeggios, scales by thirds, or chromatic scales. All of these can be played in harmony.

c) *Warming up the fingers*—Develop finger flexibility and speed in a technical warmup consisting of the scale, arpeggio, and scale by thirds in a chosen key. Follow this by playing a chromatic scale that covers the range of the scale being studied. Each of these exercises is played ascending and descending through two octaves. Younger students can play the fingering exercises in one octave and in slower note values. As the student progresses, the range and speed with which the exercise is played increases, the ultimate speed being determined by the technical limitations of each student. Push the student to his "breaking point" in these technical warmup exercises. Technical facility will increase through these exercises to the point where the student will seldom be required in band playing to approach his technical limit.

Having warmed up the embouchure (tone and intonation), the tongue (rapid tonguing exercise), and the fingers (scales, arpeggios, and thirds) for approximately ten minutes, the student should be prepared to play the remainder of his lesson. This type of warmup is developing skills in tone production, tonguing, and fingering on a day-by-day basis. Other specific flute exercises can be added to the warmup; for example, an embouchure slurring exercise using only harmonics. The following is an example of a flute warmup and lesson routine:

Flute Warmup and Lesson Routine

I) Optional harmonic exercise:

II) Warmup—key of F major (total of ten minutes)

A) Scale in whole or half notes, with vibrato pulsations, in one or two octaves. This exercise is used specifically to develop tone and intonation. (Maximum of two minutes.)

B) Tonguing exercise—one octave in the following rhythmic pattern on each scale degree. (Two minutes.)

   ascending

descending

C) Finger warmup—All fingering studies should be played in as many octaves as possible, both ascending and descending. (Total of six minutes.)

1) Scale in two octaves. Use the following rhythmic pattern for each octave:

2) Arpeggios in sixteenths, slurred in groups of four:

3) Scale by thirds in two octaves in sixteenths, slurred or using a slurring and tonguing articulation pattern, such as the following (descending).

4) Chromatic scale from tonic to tonic within the range of the key. Practice in eighths, triplet eighths, or sixteenths.

(Use Selmer Scale Sheets for flute for this warmup study.)

III) Etude (ten minutes)

IV) Band music or ensemble (ten minutes)

2) The Oboe and the Bassoon

a) Tonal warmup should be done as on the flute, including vibrato.

b) Tonguing is done in a similar manner to the flute but is limited to rapid single tonguing.

c) Finger flexibility is developed in a similar manner to the flute.

d) Etude and band or ensemble music should be played as on the flute.

Special half-hole drills can be utilized in this warmup if they are a problem for a specific student. Other exercises, such as "flick" key drills for bassoonists to effect octave or register changes, can be included in the warmup routine when appropriate.

To provide oboe materials, edit Selmer Scale Sheets for either clarinet or flute. Simply place parentheses around the area of scale, arpeggio, thirds, or chromatic scale you wish the student to practice. Bassoon materials may have to be made up by the teacher since Selmer does not publish bass clef scale sheets at the present time. I have drawn up my own bass clef scale sheets, similar to the examples that follow.

3) The Clarinet

a) Optional embouchure placement drill—Use the embouchure placement drill shown below before progressing to the remainder of this warmup. The purpose of this exercise is to find the place on the mouthpiece that will produce a clean, free tone quality throughout the range of the instrument without changing the amount of mouthpiece taken into the mouth at any place in the clarinet range. If too much mouthpiece is taken, the extreme lower register will squeak or overblow to a higher harmonic; if too little mouthpiece is taken, the extreme upper register will not respond.

If this exercise is done properly, little or no change in the amount of mouthpiece taken into the mouth will be necessary to play the entire range. Tone quality in the lower register will brighten and "fuzziness" caused by taking too little mouthpiece will disappear. Better intonation between octaves should also be developed through this exercise. Play each octave of the following drill in slow, lightly tongued quarter notes, starting with the highest note in each series.

   b) Tonal warmup should be done within one or two octaves of the chosen scale in whole or half notes without vibrato.

   c) Tonguing is done in a similar manner to tonguing on the flute but is limited to rapid single tonguing. Stress a legato approach to rapid tonguing by using a whole note before the rapid tonguing exercise and using a "da" tongue attack. Ask your student not to change his approach to the use of the air column when he is changing from the whole note to the rapid tonguing exercise; he should simply add the tongue attack to a legato air stream.

ascending:

descending:

   d) Finger flexibility and speed are developed in a similar manner to flute, with special emphasis on rapid arpeggios, especially those that move across the "break." Extensive arpeggio study and drill are especially important to the development of the clarinet fingering technique. Play scale materials in as many octaves as possible. Drill on the chromatic scale as played within the range of your scale study for the week. For example, in the key of F major in three octaves: Play the chromatic scale from small f to f^3 using quarter notes, eighth notes, triplet eighths, and sixteenth notes as your student progresses in technical facility. The chromatic scale played in any number of octaves breaks down beautifully into two, three, four, or six notes to a beat. Be sure to use special chromatic fingerings for f^1 to f-sharp^1 (f-sharp is played with two side keys added to thumb f), b-flat to b-natural, and f^2 to f-sharp^2 (trill key, right hand, is added to b-flat or f^2 fingerings). Use Selmer Scale Sheets for clarinet for this routine.

   e) Etude and band or ensemble work done as in flute outline.

4) The Alto and Bass Clarinets

All techniques used in the clarinet routine can be used for the larger clarinets, but the upper range and speed are limited to somewhat less than you would expect from the B-flat clarinetist. However, don't neglect the extreme upper registers of the alto and bass clarinets; they can be played successfully by the student who practices the proper materials faithfully.

Have your students take as much mouthpiece as possible into their mouths so that the tonal quality of your lower clarinets is bright and clear rather than "fuzzy" and without edge. The clarinet embouchure placement drill is not successfully applied to these larger instruments.

Use half-hole fingerings for pitches above c^3. The first finger of the left hand should be down for half-hole fingerings, whereas this finger is not used for these pitches on the regular B-flat clarinet. Alto and bass clarinetists should be expected to play all the alternate fingerings used on the B-flat clarinet. These should include proper alternation of the little fingers from e through g-sharp and from b^1 through d-sharp^2, and proper chromatic fingerings.

5) The Saxophones

Use Selmer Scale Sheets for the saxophone for the following routine.

a) Saxophones should employ a very light jaw vibrato in their opening warmup exercise similar to the flute vibrato and tone exercise (flute vibrato employs diaphragmatic vibrato). Have your saxophonists use an "oo" approach to tonal focus, especially in the high register when the intonation tends to be sharp in left hand fingerings and especially on a^2. An open throat approach is absolutely necessary to play a saxophone in tune in the upper register. Special octave exercises will help produce acceptable intonation in sharp upper register notes.

b) Tonguing on the saxophone will follow the procedure used on the clarinet, employing a rapid single tongue with a legato "da" approach.

c) Scale exercises should be developed in a similar manner to clarinet.

d) Etude and band or ensemble material should follow the warmup.

6) The Cornet or Trumpet

a) *Warm up with natural slurs*—All brass players should begin their warmups each day with a simple natural slur exercise. This can be followed by more difficult slur exercises that gradually increase in range. These exercises should be played mezzo-piano, and the student should constantly be reminded to blow as freely as possible. The tone should "float" on the air column, and the throat and embouchure should remain as relaxed as possible. The following are some of the many slur exercises that can be used. All are done on each of the seven possible valve combinations, descending in half steps (0; 2; 1; 1&2; 2&3; 1&3; 1, 2&3). The third valve is not used by itself. Use vowel syllables as marked, especially with younger players. This part of the warmup routine should not exceed two minutes in duration.

TA OO A   TA OO A   E   A   OO   TA OO A   A   E   A   OO   TA OO A A   E   E   E   A   OO

b) *Tonguing exercises*—Single tonguing speed should be developed first. After this is well established, use double and triple tonguing exercises in your warmup routine. A legato approach is best when the student is developing speed; use "da" for single tonguing, "da-ga" for double tonguing, and "da-da-ga" for triple tonguing. A whole note preceding the tonguing exercise will insure a legato approach to the air column when tonguing rapidly. Tell the student to simply add the tongue to the legato air stream. Start with the following exercise for this portion of your warmup:

ascending:

descending:

c) *Warming up the fingers*—Edit Selmer Scale Sheets for clarinet by placing parentheses around that portion of the scale, arpeggio, or scale by thirds that the player is to study. Play the scale in one octave three times in succession, ascending and descending. Increase the speed of the exercise as the player's proficiency improves. Use the following rhythmic pattern for the scale exercise:

younger student:

advanced student:

The range of the arpeggios should increase as the player's range increases:

Scales by thirds should be placed in one octave, ascending and descending:

The chromatic scale should be practiced from tonic to tonic within the key being studied:

All exercises should be played ascending and descending, and brasses will usually tongue all notes. Various articulations can be used, however, on any of these technical exercises.

d) Etude and band or ensemble material should be chosen to fill out the remainder of the lesson, using 10 to 15 minutes for the étude and 10 to 15 minutes for the band or ensemble music. The following is an example of a trumpet warmup and lesson routine.

Trumpet Warmup and Lesson Routine

I) Warmup slurs (two minutes)
II) Tonguing exercise (two minutes)
III) Finger technique—key of F major (total of six minutes)

   A) Scale in one octave, three times ascending and descending; all tongued.

   B) Arpeggio to limit of student's range; all tongued.

   C) Scale by thirds in one octave, ascending and descending; all tongued.

   D) Chromatic scale, ascending and descending, within range of key; all tongued.

IV) Etude (ten minutes)
V) Band music or ensemble (ten minutes)

7) The French Horn

a) *Warm up with natural slurs*—These exercises should be done as on the trumpet, but the exercises must be specially written for the harmonic series of the French horn. Work for an open throat, embouchure freedom, and as much breath support as possible to round the tone. Thinking the vowel sound "oo" is helpful in producing the roundness of tone and freedom of embouchure required to produce a proper French horn sound. A modified "oo" (low register), "a" (middle register), and "ee" (upper register) are helpful in effecting pitch changes during natural slurs. I use the trumpet descending chromatic valve sequence when doing these exercises (0; 2; 1; 1&2; 2&3; 1&3; 1, 2&3).

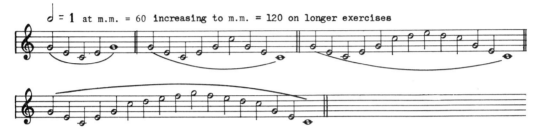

b) *Tonguing exercises* are done as on trumpet except that the tongue attack must be light or the student's tone will crack. This is especially true in the low register. The use of a legato attack, "du," for rapid tonguing brings excellent results.

c) *Finger warmup*—All techniques in a chosen key should be done as on the trumpet. Special exercises using double horn fingering can be added.

d) Etude and band or ensemble material should follow.

The basic warmup routine for the French horn can be patterned after the trumpet routine.

8) The Trombone

a) *Warm up with natural slurs*—The seven slide positions are substituted for the descending chromatic valve sequence. All slur exercises are started in first position and continue chromatically downward through seventh position. Warmup exercises are done on the B-flat trombone; the F attachment is not used, although exercises employing the thumb mechanism can be added to the basic warmup routine.

b) *Tonguing exercises*—Tonguing is done as on the trumpet.

c) *Warming up slide positions*—The technique to be studied is basically the same as on trumpet, but the exercises are written in bass clef. The following are examples of the various techniques to be studied in the key of B-flat.

Have your younger players use the following slide study for warmup of tone and for learning correct slide positions. This exercise should be done in whole or half notes.

Middle register—
(Ta)

Low register—
(too)

High register—
(tee)

d) Appropriate étude and band or ensemble materials should follow the basic warmup.

The basic trombone warmup and lesson routine will be very similar to that of the trumpet; substitute slide positions for valves when necessary.

9) The Baritone

Use *trumpet* warmups, technical *materials*, and études *to teach treble-clef baritone*. For *bass-clef baritone*, use trumpet warmups and technical materials that have been transposed to bass-clef or *use trombone materials* that have been modified for valves. The bass-clef baritone should use trombone études if bass-clef baritone materials are not available.

10) The Tuba

a) *Warmup slurs*, similar to those on trumpet or trombone, are usually not successfully done by younger players on the tuba. The tuba warmup is more practical when it uses a one-octave scale played in whole or half notes, ascending and descending.

b) *Tonguing exercises* can be patterned after the trumpet tonguing routine.

c) *Fingering warmup*—Each of the technical exercises used in the trumpet warmup should be transposed to the tuba range. Basic development of tuba technique is done the same as on trumpet. Examples in the key of E-flat major follow:

d) Etudes and band or ensemble materials should follow the basic warmup routine.

11) The Snare Drum

a) Rhythmic patterns using single strokes can be very effective preliminary warmup exercises. Basic rhythmic problems may be worked out in this manner. (Five minutes.)

b) Rudiment or *rudiments for the week*—This portion of the warmup routine can be done very slowly for basic warmup. For example, a 5-stroke roll can be done with single strokes (Left; Left; Right; Right; Left), then bounced as an open roll, and finally closed as the speed increases. I have used groups of rudiments for this portion of the warmup. One week all flam rudiments are studied, another week all rudiments involving the ruff are used, and so on. (Five minutes.)

c) *Etudes*—Etudes chosen to include rudiments being studied make the overall lesson plan more cohesive. (Ten minutes.)

d) *Band music or ensembles.* (Ten minutes.)

12) The Timpani and Percussion
Keyboard Instruments

a) Appropriate warmup exercises can be patterned after the snare drum routine. All percussionists will benefit from a five-minute rhythmic study at the beginning of the lesson.

b) Keyboard instruments can have the technical aspect of their routine patterned after woodwind and brass routines, employing scales, arpeggios, scales by thirds, and chromatic scales.

Various aspects of timpani techniques, such as tuning and cross-sticking exercises, can be employed in this technical part of the timpani warmup routine. (Five minutes.)

c) *Etude material*—Choose appropriate études for timpani or keyboard. Keyboard can use étude material of any treble-clef instrument that matches the range of the keyboard instrument being studied. Various brass and woodwind études can be transcribed for keyboard instruments. Trumpet and oboe literature is especially useful. (Ten minutes.)

d) *Band or ensemble materials* should end the lesson (Ten minutes.)

The amount of time spent on any part of these routines can be changed to fit your lesson needs. Your syllabus for each band instrument will assist you in making up lesson routines.

TEACHING RHYTHM THROUGH
SMALL ENSEMBLES AND LESSONS

It is very difficult to teach rhythm in detail during band rehearsals. If a band is going to be a successful ensemble and perform music of at least moderate difficulty, each of its members must be well trained in basic rhythmic skills before being placed in a band rehearsal. The major part of this training should be done in small ensembles and homogeneous classes of six or fewer students.

Rhythm can be approached in small classes in various ways, each of which should be founded on intellectual concepts. Teaching rhythm is not unlike teaching mathematics because of the exactness required in interpreting rhythmic notation. A very structured formal approach can be used by following these steps:

1) *Divide common rhythmic situations into four main categories:*

a) Those where the quarter note equals one beat. These include 2/4, 3/4, 4/4, 5/4, and so on meter signatures.

b) Those where the eighth note equals one beat. These include 3/8, 6/8, 9/8, and so on meter signatures.

c) Those where the half note equals one beat. These include 2/2 (alla breve or "cut time"), 3/2, 4/2, and so on meter signatures.

d) Those where a dotted note equals one beat. These include 3/8 in one beat to a measure, 3/4 in one beat to a measure, 6/8 in two beats to a measure, and so on.

2) Teach (1a) thoroughly and use it as the basis for understanding all the other rhythms.

3) All meter signatures such as 3/8 and 6/8 that are to be played with the *eighth note equaling one beat* should be *taught using the principle of doubling* the value of the notation learned in the basic 2/4, 3/4, and so on notation. For example, when the eighth note equals one beat, the quarter note receives two beats, the dotted-quarter receives three beats, and so on. Each of these notes receives exactly twice the value it did in the original rhythms. When faced with the problem of playing 6/8 in six beats to a measure, simply tell the student to "double everything."

4) All meter signatures such as 2/2 (*alla breve*) should be *taught as* "*cutting in half*" all the *values of* the basic 2/4, 3/4, or 4/4 *meters*. A whole

note will receive two beats instead of four, a half note one beat instead of two and so on. The young student in particular can learn to play alla breve properly in this manner. Although it is pointed out that the half note equals the beat or the pulse, the "cutting-in-half" principle is stressed throughout the study of this type of rhythm.

5) In playing meters where a *dotted note equals* the *beat* or pulse and the background is divisible by three, a new method of notation interpretation is needed. It is usually confusing to the student to attempt to relate the dotted note values to the basic 2/4, 3/4, and so on concepts he has already mastered. I find it easier to teach these meters by listing the basic values involved: A dotted-quarter equals one beat, a dotted-half equals two beats, a "triplet" of eighth notes equals one beat, a quarter note followed by an eighth note equals one beat, and so on. Since the student must now think in divisions of three, this type of rhythm is not related to the basic rhythm (quarter note equals one beat) he has learned. No simple solution to the rhythmic problems we encounter can be applied, such as cutting values in half or doubling values.

6) Unusual situations are then taught individually as they are encountered. Odd and mixed or changing meters are taught by "keeping the eighth note constant" and similar instructions.

7) Rhythmic flash cards, rhythmic syllables, or clapping exercises can be employed to reinforce your rhythmic teaching.

All of the above rhythmic suggestions should be taught in small groups, where individual student problems involving basic rhythmic concepts can be corrected. It is also very important to keep a constant and controlled beat or pulse during the study of rhythm in lessons or in practice. I have found no better control mechanism for rhythmic development than tapping the foot. I insist on the proper controlled "foot-beat" in lessons. I avoid problems later with excessive foot tapping in rehearsals and performances by telling the student that the conductor's beat takes the place of the foot under these circumstances.

The small homogeneous class is the medium through which most of my detailed teaching is done. If you carefully plan every minute of this valuable teaching time, your students in full band rehearsals will be well prepared to play most of their music at sight. Only interpretation, balance, and other large ensemble problems remain to be solved during full band rehearsals. The most valuable concept involved in this type of teaching is the carefully structured organization of lesson and practice time. If the time you meet with your students and the time they practice on their own is efficiently used, your combined efforts will result in first-class musical performances.

HOW TO DEVELOP
AN OUTSTANDING BAND
THROUGH SOLO AND
ENSEMBLE COMPETITIONS

15

The motivation produced by pressure placed on a student to prepare for solo competitions can greatly improve individual proficiency. Students who have become active in competition invariably become the leaders in your band. They not only develop technical proficiency but also the poise and confidence needed to be section leaders. Solos in a band are handled easily since the pressure is so much less than in a solo competition. The confidence and performing ability of your soloists instills confidence in the other members of your band because their performance is reinforced by the presence of soloists in their section.

By involving members of your band in ensemble performance and competition, you strengthen your band in a similar manner. Although the benefits derived from small ensemble performances are usually not as great as those derived from the solo experience, ensemble performers do feel some of the pressures of the soloist. They work harder to prepare their part of the ensemble and ultimately improve their own proficiency and confidence to perform under pressure.

USING ENSEMBLES IN THE LOWER GRADES
TO DEVELOP INTEREST IN THE HIGH SCHOOL PROGRAM

Getting an early start in preparing a solo or ensemble performer is extremely important. I believe students with strong talent should be encouraged to play solos and ensembles at the fifth grade level. If they overcome nervousness and develop performing confidence at this age, they usually have little difficulty becoming successful performers in junior and senior high school. The level of their technical proficiency, their ability to read music accurately, and their confidence in their performing ability is greatly enhanced. They progress much faster than students who do not participate in solo and ensemble work and soon become the leaders of the grade school band.

Some of the many ways solos and ensembles can be used in the lower grades are:

1) *Preparing strong grade school musicians for solo and ensemble competitions* involves them at the highest level of individual achievement available and prepares them for participation in grade school All-County or All-State groups. This preparation also provides the leadership necessary for a successful grade school band program.

2) *Using elementary soloists or ensembles for local concerts* and musical events increases the motivation of the students. Although the benefits may not be as great, the motivation resulting from the pressure on the performers of an upcoming local performance is almost as strong as the motivation experienced in solo and ensemble competitions.

3) Use of your *advanced* high school *soloists and ensembles for elementary performances or* special elementary *assembly programs* not only benefits the performers but also motivates elementary students to improve on their instruments so they can someday perform concerts at similar levels of proficiency.

4) *High school soloists*, woodwind *and* brass quintets, percussion ensembles, and saxophone *ensembles can be utilized for demonstrations at the elementary level* when you begin your yearly recruiting program. This will create interest in joining the band program and will help the beginner choose the instrument he wishes to play. It also benefits the high school musicians, who are motivated to improve their performance abilities for this performance.

HOW TO USE SOLO AND ENSEMBLE RECITALS
AND CLASS DEMONSTRATIONS
AS MOTIVATING TOOLS

Any opportunities you can provide for your soloists and ensembles to perform in public or in a classroom situation will motivate these students to excel. Performing opportunities can be created in the following ways:

1) *Recitals for the public.* These can be performed *with* the *assistance of* your entire *band*. A "concerto" program featuring soloists with band accompaniment can be very successful if a reasonably large audience will attend. Preparing a recital of this type, which can involve many hours of rehearsal, can be a disappointing and negative experience if a very small audience attends your program. Presenting a few numbers performed by your stage band and your concert band in a "concerto" program will draw a larger audience. The following is an example of such a program:

Organ prelude from the pit

King Cotton	Sousa	Concert Band
Concertino	von Weber-Reed	Clarinet Soloist Band accompaniment
Three Bluejackets	Williams	Trumpet Trio Band accompaniment
Menuet and Rondo	Balay	Woodwind Quintet (from the pit)
Suite for Brass Quintet	Scheidt	Brass Quintet (from the pit)
Queen Bee	Nestico	Stage Band (from the pit)
Another Shade of Blue	D. Fenno	Stage Band
That Old Black Magic	B. May	Stage Band
Concerto in C Major	Vivaldi-Reed	Piccolo Soloist Band Accompaniment
Slaughter on 10th Avenue	Rodgers-Lang	Piano Soloist Band Accompaniment
Flute Cocktail	Simeone	Flute Trio Band Accompaniment
Selections from "Raisin"	Arr. Holcombe	Concert Band

2) *Christmas concerts* are excellent times *to feature soloists and small ensembles*. Vocal or instrumental soloists can be featured with band accompaniment. Organ or piano soloists can be used as a prelude to your main program or as unaccompanied soloists during the program. A brass or woodwind quintet can be featured as a prelude to a Christmas concert with considerable success.

3) *A band concert can feature ensembles*, such as woodwind quintets and brass quintets, programmed between the numbers presented by the entire band. However, in a large auditorium your ensemble can suffer from the contrast in volume with your band.

4) A *recital* for the public featuring soloists *accompanied by keyboard and* various *small ensembles* can develop into a beautiful program if you are not concerned about the size of your audience. Interest in such a program would have to be developed in most communities.

5) *Use* your *soloists and ensembles at* various *clinics or meetings of music teachers* as demonstration groups. You can be sure that under these circumstances your students will prepare themselves well.

6) Your *soloists or ensembles* can be *utilized to help* in *teaching* any other part of the *complete school program*. Although classroom demonstrations are difficult to plan outside the music department, they are not impossible. An English or Social Studies teacher may be interested in

presenting live music related to the unit being taught. The impact of a live performance is much greater than that produced by records or films.

7) Various *events* may occur *during* the *school year* in which small ensembles or soloists can be more successful than a full band. It is much easier to use an ensemble for assembly entrance and exit music than it is to use a large band.

8) Programs for various *community events, club meetings,* and so on that call for some of your musicians to be featured as a part of the formal program can utilize a small ensemble or soloists much more effectively than they can a larger band.

9) *Soloists and ensembles* can be *utilized within the music program* to present special lessons to general music classes, music theory classes, and so on. Live performance always creates additional interest in the subject matter being presented by a classroom teacher.

HOW TO PREPARE THE STUDENT
FOR SOLO AND ENSEMBLE COMPETITION

Use the following steps in recruiting soloists and members for your performing ensembles:

1) *Encourage all students to take part* in some aspect of solo or ensemble performance. Your most talented students will probably have the greatest success, but the experience will be valuable for any of your band members. Many students who claim that they become too nervous to play solos might be willing to form homogeneous ensembles such as flute trios, clarinet quartets, trumpet trios, and trombone trios and quartets. Other ensembles, such as woodwind quintets, require stronger soloists because of the heterogeneous nature of such ensembles.

2) *Point out* the *value of solo ratings* and small ensemble experience *when* a *student is recommended for All-County or All-State groups.* Many of these organizations are "paper" groups, chosen without audition from detailed recommendations submitted by directors. If an audition is required, the student with solo experience will probably do better than the student without solo experience. Some solo experience in district or state competition festivals is almost mandatory for selection to one of these groups.

3) *Post* a *sign-up sheet for* all students who desire to play *solos or ensembles.* Before your students have signed this sheet, it should be explained that they are expected to complete the preparation and performance of their solos or ensembles. You can use an alternate method by personally selecting soloists and ensemble members and requesting their pledges to perform for the particular solo and ensemble competition assigned. However, students not originally chosen should not be prevented

from gaining this experience if they desire to be involved, regardless of their individual ability. If a student is very weak musically, he should be briefed on his weaknesses and warned that he might receive a poor grade on his solo performance. This will help you avoid any psychological problems with the student after the performance or any adverse reaction from parents.

4) *Set up* definite *times to meet each solo and ensemble* at least six weeks before the competition. Plan to meet each person or group at least two or three times per week. This extra work can rarely be done during regular rotating class lessons. Posting a tentative schedule of the times you have available is an effective way of establishing extra meetings with your students. Have each soloist or ensemble choose two or three times per week to meet with you by signing up for available posted times.

5) *If accompaniment is needed, contact* available *pianists* as soon as your soloists have their compositions assigned. Give the accompanists their music immediately so that they may be as well prepared as the soloists. Accompaniment tapes can be used, but they greatly inhibit a musical performance since the student must follow the tape and consequently loses interpretive flexibility in his performance.

6) *Have* your *soloists and accompanists meet* at least two to *three weeks before* the solo *competition*. Try to work out a schedule so that soloists will have at least two one-hour meetings per week with their accompanists. The number of meetings varies according to the difficulty of the solo and the experience of the soloist in working with accompaniment.

7) If a *registration fee* is to be paid by the soloists and the ensemble members, collect the money as soon as possible. Tell each performer what the individual fee is for his event and set a deadline for payment. If you or your school prepay the solo and ensemble fees for the festival to the host school, be sure you receive reimbursement from the performing students before the event is completed. It can be difficult to collect festival fees from your students after they have performed.

8) *Set up awards* such as solo medals *for* your *soloists* and plan to present them at an awards assembly before the student body. School and community recognition for solo and ensemble achievements is necessary for the continuation and growth of your solo and ensemble program. Be sure to give your soloists and ensemble members recognition for their achievements in your local newspaper.

Musical Preparation of Soloists

Three aspects of preparation are involved in a solo performance:

1) Memorization and preparation of all *major scales* required at a specific grade level. The more difficult the solo, the more scale preparation is expected.

2) Preparation of *the solo* itself. This includes all musical and technical aspects of the solo. Special attention must be given to technique, interpretation, and tonal quality needed for the specific solo.

3) *Sight reading.* If your student has been well taught and is playing a solo at the proper level of difficulty, sight reading at that grade level should be no problem. However, specific preparation on unusual musical symbols such as double sharps or double flats and extra drill on odd or mixed meter are valuable to the soloist. A favorite trap placed in sight reading at the more difficult levels is a 3/8 bar in a 2/4 or 4/4 melody where the eighth note remains constant. If rests also complicate this mixed-meter melody, a student not specifically prepared for this type of sight reading could have considerable difficulty and lose an "A" rating because of this rhythmic problem.

Sight reading that can be interpreted rhythmically in two different ways should be pointed out to the student. A melody in 6/8, for example, could be played in six beats to a measure or two beats to a measure. If the sight reading example does not have written indications as to which note receives the beat and a metronomic marking in relation to that note, the student should be advised to ask the adjudicator which rhythmic interpretation he desires the student to use.

A good sight reader can be developed by very careful teaching and by the student's continued reading of various new materials each time he practices by himself. The teacher must provide the student with a strong background in technique and rhythm. Sight reading in lessons and in band rehearsals also develops better readers. The more music a student plays, the better reader he becomes.

Musical Preparation of Ensembles

Ensemble performers do not usually need to prepare scales or perform sight reading, although good sight reading certainly separates the "rote" groups from the real musicians. In preparation of an ensemble, all the basic elements of music considered in band performance should be stressed:

1) *Tone quality*—Each member of the ensemble must not only produce a good tone on his individual instrument but must match his tone quality to that of other members of the ensemble. In performing a French composition, for example, all members of the ensemble should produce the light and bright tone quality needed to properly interpret the composition. A German composition may require all members of the ensemble to produce a dark and somewhat heavy tone quality. Good musicians are always cognizant of the need to match their tone qualities to those of other members of their ensemble.

2) *Intonation*—Start with a basic A = 440 intonation level. Once all members of the ensemble are tuned to the same pitch, seek notes that need individual adjustment. Some will be quite obvious such as the "throat" register B-flat produced on most clarinets and the sharp c^2 and g^2 produced on most oboes if the oboist takes too much reed into his mouth. Most intonation difficulties of this type can be corrected by proper embouchure development and ear training of each member of your ensemble. If they are fine soloists, their intonation will be much better than that of less-developed players.

3) *Technique*—Each member of your ensemble must have developed the technical proficiency to play on the grade level of difficulty that the ensemble is attempting. If any member is technically weak, it can easily cost the group an "A" rating. Choose your ensemble players very carefully for such groups as woodwind quintets and brass sextets. The players must be equal in their proficiency on their individual instruments. Equal proficiency is not as critical with homogeneous groups, where the players on third or fourth parts may not need to be as strong as the first or second players.

4) *Interpretation*—You must be sure that each member of any given ensemble plays the same interpretation. This is especially true in imitative passages where length of notes, style of melodic line, and weight given individual notes must match. Usually, the first player to play a particular motif will set the interpretation for the group. All others should match this interpretation as exactly as possible. Matching interpretations in ensemble or conductus-style passages is equally necessary or the ensemble will not hold together well.

5) *Balance*—Each member should carefully balance his part with all others in the ensemble, being especially aware of simultaneous differences in dynamic levels that are written into the music. There are many times in ensemble playing when a particular part that may or may not be marked with dynamic indications of balance should be emphasized. You should work carefully during your meetings with each ensemble to assure that proper balance is understood and maintained at all times.

Choosing Effective Music
for Your Soloists and Ensembles

Choose the music for each soloist and each ensemble carefully. Match the composition to the strengths of the soloist or the ensemble. For example, a trumpet soloist with a fine tone but limited technique should be given a solo such as the first movement of the Hindemith Sonata for Trumpet and Piano. On the other hand, the Hummel Concerto for Trumpet requires considerable technique. Avoid compositions with extended double or triple tonguing passages unless your soloist is very strong in tonguing technique. The Mozart Concerto K. 191 is excellent material for the trombonist or bassoonist with limited technique. The Mozart Concerto for Clarinet K. 622 can be chosen for a student with tonal and expressive strengths and technical limitations. Spohr's Concerto No. 1 and Concerto No. 2, on the other hand, require considerable technique. It is difficult to cover tonal and intonational deficiencies with any choice of solo, so these elements of musicianship should be stressed with younger players who are not ready to attempt solos of considerable technical difficulty.

Measure the potential of each member of an ensemble and choose music that best displays the ensemble's strengths and avoids its weaknesses. Ensemble music can be chosen to display the strengths of a particular member of the ensemble who is an exceptional musician. Specific music can also be chosen to hide the weaknesses of any member of the group. The basic preparation of each student will determine strengths and weaknesses in most cases. This fact emphasizes the importance of careful and comprehensive teaching at each lesson. Well-prepared individual students will lead to strong soloists and fine musical ensembles and will ultimately create and maintain first-class bands in your school system.

A representative list of solos and ensembles is found in the Appendices of this book.

PLANNING CONCERT PROGRAMS AND PREPARING BUDGETS

16

The work of the band director can be divided into the following general categories:

1) *Musical*—All aspects of teaching and performing music.

2) *External business*—Those aspects of your program that reach outside the music department.

3) *Internal business*—Those aspects of your program that are executed within the confines of your teaching areas or within the music department.

4) *Personal and professional growth*—Development of your personal resources by reading, traveling, attending concerts, attending workshops, and so on.

Each of these categories is equally important and should be organized carefully and efficiently. All available resources should be employed to help you reach the goals of your complete program. The most important of these resources is people, and your ability to utilize their various talents will have a strong influence on the ultimate success of your program.

HOW TO SUCCESSFULLY RUN
THE EXTERNAL BUSINESS ASPECTS
OF YOUR BAND PROGRAM

Use of your prime resource, people, is especially helpful in carrying out the external business of your band program. Organize each category of external business in the following manner:

1) Divide your external business into specific categories.

2) Determine those tasks that must be accomplished.

3) Utilize people who may be of help to each category.

Preparing Concert Programs and Publicity

Concert programs present these tasks that need to be completed:

1) *Organization of program content*—Choose the compositions to be performed and place them in an interesting sequence on your concert program. The content of your program should be varied, not only for the music education of your students, but also to maintain the interest of your audience. Program organization should take change of pace into consideration:

   a) A slow melodic composition should be followed by a march, a Latin composition, or another number with a rapid tempo.

   b) A long composition requiring considerable concentration by the audience should be followed by a short composition that requires little listening effort.

   c) Stylistic variation throughout the program is very important. If you perform a Bach, Mozart, or Wagner number, you should follow it with a popular composition, a number that is light stylistically, or a number in complete contrast to the first composition. You will lose the attention of your audience with back-to-back programming of heavy numbers or numbers of a similar style.

   d) You can vary the simple and compound divisions of meter and beat by following a 2/4 or 4/4 composition with a number in 6/8 or 9/8.

   e) You can utilize soloists and guest conductors for variety.

   f) Lighting variations, slide projection, and various other audio-visual techniques can be employed.

Opening and closing your program with a march-like composition is also very effective. Musical comedy selections or popular compositions with exciting conclusions are very successful for concluding a concert. Your audience should leave such a program with the feeling that they would like to hear more.

The following is an example of varied programming.

On the Alert March	Edwin Franko Goldman
Prelude and Fugue in G Minor	Bach-Moehlmann
Night Soliloquy	Kent Kennan
———— ———— , flute soloist	
H. M. S. Pinafore	Sullivan-R. R. Bennett
El Conquistador (Spanish March)	Robert Tarver

Intermission (15 minutes)

George Washington Bicentennial March	John Philip Sousa
Symphonic Suite	Clifton Williams

Jamaican Rhumba	Benjamin-Lang
Funny Girl (Overture)	Styne-R.R. Bennett
Selections from Shaft	Hayes-Lowden
(Guest traps and guitars)	

2) *Use of Program Notes*—Use an announcer to introduce each number on your program. Supply your announcer with a microphone and brief program notes consisting of two or three sentences about each composition. I have alternated using an announcer and doing the program notes myself, using a microphone placed at my conducting left. (Be careful to have the microphone off when the band is playing.) Verbal program notes not only add interest and variety to your program, they also give you an opportunity to communicate personally with your audience. A cold atmosphere is created by the high school conductor who never verbally communicates with his audience during an entire program. Take advantage of any opportunities to develop personal rapport with your audience.

3) *Organization of the printed program*—Your printed program for a concert can be as simple as one page that lists the titles of the compositions you are performing and the composers and/or arrangers. My programs are printed (duplicated) by a school A.B. Dick machine, which is used to duplicate materials when more than 20 copies are needed. This machine reproduces a simple typed page in black print and is much easier to use than a standard mimeograph machine. Since the cost of printing is no problem, my programs consist of several pages:

a) A title page set up as follows:

THE

_____ CENTRAL SCHOOL

MUSIC DEPARTMENT

presents its

ANNUAL FALL BAND CONCERT

under the direction

of

Director's Name

Guest Conductor (optional)

Guest Soloist (optional)

Announcer (optional)

_____ Evening, month/day, year

b) A page listing the program to be performed:

PROGRAM
Symphonic Band

Washington Post March   John Philip Sousa

etc.

c) A page for each organization's personnel, listed in concert order and according to seating:

Senior Symphonic Band

Flutes	*Alto Clarinets*	*Cornets*
Jayne Smith (picc.)	etc.	etc.
Kathy Brown		
Anne Keller		
etc.		

d) A concluding page of acknowledgments:

ACKNOWLEDGMENTS

Lighting Design	*Stage Crew*
Names (including faculty help)	Names
Posters and Publicity	*Ushers*
Names	Names
Programs	*Band Officers*
Names (including faculty help)	Names
Recording	*Band Librarians*
Names	Names

You may add announcements of coming events on the bottom of your acknowledgments page.

e) Optional program notes can be included in the printed program. I prefer verbal program notes used in the manner explained earlier in this chapter. The lighting for the audience is usually not adequate for reading, and the constant rustling of paper can be distracting.

How to Publicize Your Programs

Your environmental teaching situation will usually dictate what methods are available for publicizing a program. The following are some of the possibilities:

1) *Posters* made by artistic volunteers from your program. You should be able to requisition poster paper, magic markers, and other materials needed from your school's central supply.

2) *Press releases.* I personally write all band press releases to be printed in our local newspaper, whether they are concert publicity or acknowledgments of students' musical accomplishments. I deliver them to the editor personally, and he prints them as submitted. This usually guarantees front-page coverage. Our school student newspaper also covers band activities. The students write these articles, and I proofread them before they are submitted. We also print a school district bulletin, which is delivered to all homes in the district several times each year. I write regular articles covering band events for this publication.

3) Announcements on *local radio and television stations.*

4) Add announcements of coming events to the *acknowledgments page* of a current program and include verbal announcements of coming events in your *concert program notes.*

5) Communicate with the homes of your students. This can be done by writing a concise duplicated *letter* written *to parents,* and having students deliver them to their own homes. Probably not all students will carry out their responsibilities in this case, but the cost of postage would be prohibitive.

6) *Flyers* consisting of the basic information found on the title page of your program can be very effective. They can be distributed throughout the business area of your community, placed under windshield wipers of cars, handed to shoppers on the street, and so on.

7) Use any *audio-visual means* available *within* your *school* to communicate concert information to your student body and to your staff. A short assembly program before a concert is an effective way of advertising if you use music that is appealing to the student body. For example, use a "rock" composition featuring guitars and an exciting "trap" percussionist, but give the student body only enough to arouse a strong interest in hearing the entire program at your evening concert.

Making Effective Use
of Individual Talents and Abilities

Three categories of people are important to the success of your programs:

1) *The performers,* including any available soloists, ensembles, or student conductors. Soloists and guest conductors may include professionals and college practice-teachers.

2) *The audience.* Not only must you get your audience to the concert, you must offer them program content that will insure their return to your next concert.

3) Those *individuals who help with* the *business aspects* of your program. These include:

   a) The students who will be your *ushers.* Set up a reciprocal plan with your choral director to use chorus members who are not in band as ushers.

b) All *individuals who* help to *type and print* the *programs*. The chairman of our business department supervises the typing of the programs, and the typing is usually done by band members who are taking business courses. The printing or duplicating is done by a member of our school business office staff. Stapling of the completed programs is done by a committee of my students who have study halls at the time the printing is completed. Some volunteers stay after school, if necessary, to complete the job. Programs are then boxed and placed at the rear of the auditorium for distribution by the ushers.

c) *Lighting design* is worked out for each program by our drama instructor and members of his theater classes. Members of these classes are in charge of lighting and special effects at the programs.

d) The *stage crew* is composed of members of the band. A chairman is appointed and given copies of the seating arrangements. Approximately 10 to 12 individuals are then appointed to set up certain parts of the band; it is advantageous to have them set up the areas in which they sit as performers. An entire setup change from one organization to another takes approximately five minutes in this system. The complete band setup is divided into seven setup areas as follows: row one; row two; row three and four, left; row three and four, right; riser one; riser two; riser three. One or two stage crew members are assigned to each area. Each member of the crew is given a copy of the complete setup, with his area of responsibility outlined in red. The chairman of the stage crew checks the entire setup from the podium as it is being changed, giving verbal directions for any corrections. (See Figure 1.)

e) *Recording* your *programs* properly is a very important job. Be sure you employ an individual who not only understands the equipment involved but also knows exactly how you want your program recorded. Good recordings of your programs can be used in your teaching and can also serve as a permanent record of your group's accomplishments.

f) *Posters* can be made by artistic members of your group. Appoint a poster chairman, give that person the responsibility of forming and supervising a poster committee, and supply the materials needed to complete this task. Brief the poster chairman carefully on exactly how he is to carry out his responsibilities.

g) Your *band officers* can be *utilized as chairmen of* your concert committees. They have been selected by their peers as leaders of the group and should be delegated responsibilities whenever possible. Four or five officers can carry out most of the business aspects of a concert's preparation, thereby freeing the conductor to concentrate on the musical aspects of the program. If you are to be successful in delegating a large portion of your concert preparation, you must personally brief every committee chairman carefully and thoroughly on his portion of the work to be done, stressing that the success of the program is dependent upon his completing the tasks correctly and on time.

h) Your *school maintenance staff* can be a valuable source of assistance, especially when last-minute equipment problems arise. Develop close personal relationships with these individuals so that when you call on them for assistance they will respond immediately.

i) Your *concert announcer* can be any student not in your performing organization. A person with public speaking ability or training who is a member of the chorus or the drama department will make a fine announcer. A student who presents an attractive personal appearance is an especially strong asset to the overall effectiveness of the concert program.

PREPARING REQUISITIONS AND BUDGETS

A *budget* can be defined as an estimate of expenses for a given period. It can be an itemized allotment of funds or a total sum of money set aside for a specific purpose. A *requisition* is a written request for supplies, equipment, and so on. It demands exact detail, with specifications and costs given for each item.

For purposes of clarity, the budget as referred to here will be considered the total amount of money needed or approved, and a requisition will be considered a specific and itemized order or request for materials to be ordered within that budget.

Methods of preparing requisitions and budgets vary greatly from school to school. Some schools demand an itemized list of everything to be requisitioned in the coming year. Others establish an amount of money that will be alloted to the music department for a given year, and the department keeps a running account of how much has been spent. The budget in this case is a lump sum, and approval of detailed items to be purchased is not required before the budget for the coming year is approved. The only detailed accounting required is on the ordering requisitions.

1. 100-piece Symphonic Band (Set before program begins)

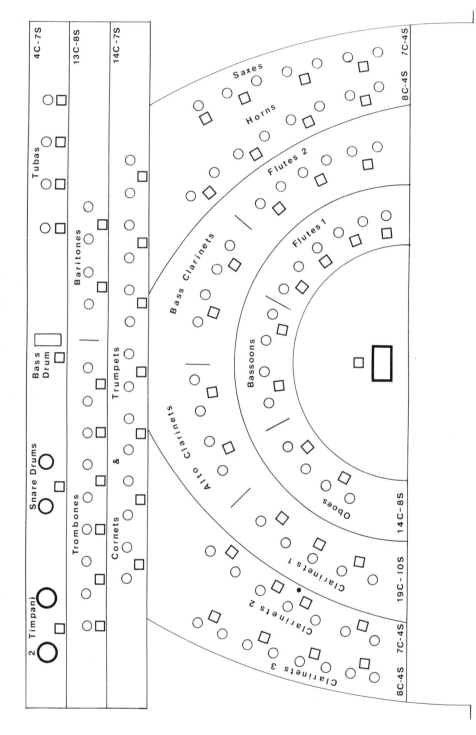

2. 70-piece Concert Band (Change above to this plan)

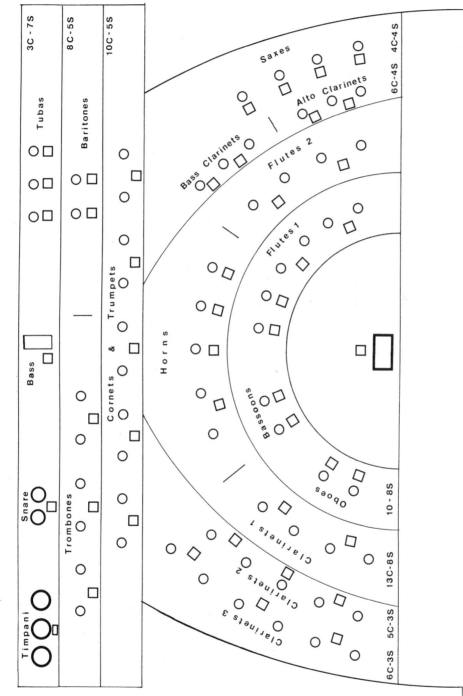

Figure 1. Stage Crew Plan

255

A total budget is usually divided into several smaller budgets, each requiring a specific type of requisition. These include:

1) *Textbook Requisitions*—You should order all of your method books through the textbook requisition, defining them as paperbacks, which will last a maximum of three years. A specific requisition form may be required in your school. If not, you can follow this example:

Textbook Requisition (19XX–XX)

Instrumental Music (9–12)

Director's Name

Instrument	Title	Author	Publisher	No. to Order	Unit Cost	Total
Flute	Selected Studies	Voxman	Rubank	6	$2.50	$15.00
Oboe	48 Famous Studies	Ferling	Southern Music Co.	3	4.00	12.00

2) *Library Requisitions*—Normally, any reference texts pertaining to your program will be ordered through the library budget. See your librarian about this. I have ordered soft-cover reference texts through textbook requisitions and hard-cover texts through the library budget.

3) *Instructional Supplies*—These are ordered from your regular music department budget when needed. An example of a supply requisition follows:

INSTRUCTIONAL SUPPLIES

ORDER FROM: _____ Company

_____ Street address

_____ City, State, zip code

Quantity and Unit	Catalog Number	Item (Complete Description)	Unit Cost	Total Cost
100 sheets	C-10	Music manuscript paper, concert size, 10 line.	$_____	$_____
100 boxes	——	Music filing boxes, concert size, ½ inch thick.	_____	_____
1 set	#5336	Bass clarinet pads, tan.	_____	_____

All items under $25 are considered supplies; any item over $25 is considered equipment. Supplies can include instrument mouthpieces, pads for woodwind instruments, sheet cork, screw driver kits, band folios, marching folios, small percussion equipment such as bass drum or tympani sticks and cymbal thongs, valve oil, cork grease, manuscript paper, filing boxes, band music, solos, ensembles, stage band arrangements, music lyres, double-reed cane, and pad and cork cement.

4) *Other Supplies* such as paper clips, rubber bands, scotch tape, and poster paper are requisitioned when needed from the school central supply on a central supply form. No previous itemized requisition is needed for these materials.

5) *Equipment Requisitions*—This category usually involves the largest amount of money in your total budget. It includes musical instruments, phonographs, recording equipment, tuning devices, uniforms, music stands, risers, storage equipment, filing cabinets, acoustical shells, and any item of furniture or storage cabinet that must be purchased. Any item costing over $25 may need a written statement of justification. Because of the budget difficulties of recent years, all equipment may have to be listed according to priority of need. If your first priority is a French horn, it is the first item approved. In times of financial stress it may be the only item approved. The following is an example of an equipment requisition form:

EQUIPMENT

Quantity   Cat. No.   Make   Item   Vendor   Cost

Written justification and a priority list should be done as follows:

Your Name—Instrumental Music
Justification of requisitioned equipment:
Priority 1. _____French horn—$600
   If you check the inventory of our French horns, you
will find several listed in poor condition because of age and
normal usage. Any instrument that is more than 15 years
old will probably be worn out if it has been used daily.
Several of our French horns are practically unplayable.
Their age and condition do not merit another overhaul.
They should be replaced, one or two at a time, until our
equipment is again in first-class playing condition.
Priority 2. One _____ upright tuba—$1,250
   We have two upright tubas for concert use. We carry
four tuba players in our performing concert band and des-
perately need proper instruments for each to play.
Sousaphones are available, but they do not meet the musi-
cal needs of our concert band because of intonation prob-
lems and harshness of tone quality.
Priority 3. One tympani—23 inch—$300

6) *Maintenance and Repair Requisitions*—These include instrument repairs, overhauls, and uniform cleaning. Set up a repair fund based upon a deterioration figure of approximately 3 percent of the total estimated value of your equipment. The general repair fund, which does not include overhauls, will be used for repairs as needed during the regular school year.

7) *Audio-Visual Materials*—These may be included in another portion of your budget or might be a separate requisition if you have an organized audio-visual department. Items covered here will include records, tapes, films, and transparencies.

8) *Building Improvements*—These will include any equipment built by school district employees and any remodeling of rooms, rehearsal areas, and so on that is done by school employees. This usually requires a complete description of the work to be done, including at least rough plans and specifications. My music storage and instrument storage areas were developed by our maintenance staff from plans and diagrams I drew.

9) *Transportation Requests*—An itemized list of school transportation that will be needed by your organizations in the coming year may be required for total budget purposes even though the moneys needed here may not be included as part of the music department budget. This information may include description of transportation needed, number of trips, number of buses per trip, time involved in each trip, and total mileage.

10) *Conference Expenses*—Somewhere in your budget your expenses as a director for conferences, All-County and All-State music festivals, and so on, should be itemized for the following year.

11) *Student Registrations, School Professional Fees,* and so on—I believe that any student who is selected for an All-County or All-State group should have his registration fees paid by the school or by music department funds. These registration fees are included in my regular requisitions, which also list state competition fees for our concert bands and school membership fees for student participation in state and county music activities. You can list these items in this manner:

FEES, REGISTRATIONS, AND SO ON

Description	Cost
School membership—New York State School Music Association	$ _____
All-County Student Registrations 10 students @ $_____ = $ _____	$ _____
State Competition—Student registrations for band 120 students @ $ _____ = $ _____	$ _____

12) *Awards*—Somewhere in your total budget you should have an itemized requisition for awards such as letters, pins, solo medals, ensemble medals, and so on as follows:

Description	Source	Cost
10 All-County pins @ $ _____	Supplier	$ _____
25 Solo Awards @ $_____	Supplier	$ _____

    1 John Philip Sousa Award   Supplier $ _____

    25 Senior Pin Awards @ $ _____   Supplier $ _____

13) *Periodical Requisitions*—These include student or teacher magazine subscriptions and are usually done through the librarian as follows:

> *No. of copies   Length of sub.   Title   Publisher   New or Renewal*

The *requisition process* usually *consists of three elements:*

1) The *original requisition*, which is normally an itemized budget for the next school year. An item may or may not be ordered from this requisition, depending upon its approval and whether you have marked it to be ordered immediately. These requisitions can be completed as early as the beginning of the second semester or as late as March or April. All requisitions must be in before the total school budget is voted upon in the spring.

2) *Regular requisitions*, which are used during the school year to order materials marked "when needed" on the original budget requisition. These may include the date, school building, department or individual ordering, suggested supplier, delivery instructions, and detailed information on requisitioned items. The latter may be broken down in the following manner:

Quantity and Unit   Cat. No.   Complete Description   Unit Price   Total Price

3) *Local purchase orders*, which are used when an emergency arises and materials are needed immediately. In such a case, your business office gives you a local purchase order, which allows you to purchase the materials directly from the vendor without going through the usual channels of requisition approval.

THE BAND BOOSTERS CLUB
AND ITS RELATIONSHIP TO THE BAND PROGRAM

A Band Boosters' or Music Boosters' Club can be a valuable asset, or it can have a negative effect on your program. The ultimate results of its creation will depend upon how it is organized and whether it is effectively controlled. I prefer a Boosters' Club to be a Music Boosters' Club rather than just a Band Boosters' club since the potential base for membership is much greater when all music organizations within the school system are included. The possibility for your Boosters' Club functioning effectively is greatly enhanced by the inclusion of bands and choruses at all levels of the music program.

Steps to Follow When Establishing a Boosters' Club

Follow this procedure when you are establishing your Boosters' Club:

1) *Spend* some *time investigating* the *potential interest* for establishing such an organization *in your community*. Obtain at least verbal commitments from influential individuals who are willing to help found a Boosters' Club. Be sure that their motives are in agreement with your definition of the function of a Music Boosters' Club, and that they are not motivated by any factors that might have a negative effect on your program in the future.

2) *Investigate other Music Booster organizations* that have been successful in school systems and communities similar to yours. Obtain copies of their plans of organization, by-laws, constitutions, and so on and discuss the pros and cons of their function with the directors involved.

3) *Draw up* a tentative *plan of organization* for your Club based on educationally and musically sound goals and objectives. Present your plan in written form to your Administration and your Board of Education for approval.

4) After approval by school officials, *set up* a well-publicized *meeting* with members of your community interested in forming a Music Boosters' Club. Although you hope to have parents of your students form the core of the organization, stress in your publicity that being an adult resident of your school district is the only prerequisite for membership. Also, consider a student membership status. You may find students within your school system who are interested in supporting the music program even though they are not active performers. Members of your music organization may also want to be actively involved in the planning aspects of the Boosters' contributions to your program.

5) Once a personnel base is established for your Boosters' Club, *draw up a constitution* that includes the following:

   a) General goals and objectives of the Club.

   b) A process for election of officers and establishment of committees.

   c) Definitions of the responsibilities of each officer of the Club.

   d) A member of the music department to act as liaison between the Boosters' Club and your Administration and Board of Education.

   e) Membership eligibility and a small membership fee. Each of our members pays a token sum of $1 per year in dues.

   f) Meeting times and frequency of meetings.

   g) A formal plan of organization for each meeting. This is usually based upon Robert's Rules of Order.

   h) A treasury and a set procedure for the handling of moneys.

Clearly explain at your organizational meeting your idea of the basic functions of the Music Boosters' Club. This should be supported by your

Administration and your Board of Education. Spelling out the ground rules before the organization becomes fully functional is extremely important and can assure your ability to handle tactfully any difficult situation that may arise in regard to the Club's functions in the future.

Defining the General Functions of a Music Boosters Club

Stating your school and music department position in relation to the functions of a Music Boosters' Club at the time of the Club's organization may prevent failure of the Club to be a positive influence on your program. Some points you can consider when developing a professional position regarding these functions are:

1) The *student is* the *most important* element of any public school organization. All Club decisions should be aimed at student welfare, both educationally and musically. The individual must be stressed since every student is different in his needs as well as his talents.

2) Our general *band philosophy* is simply: a) to give all of our students an enriching experience that is both pleasurable and educational and b) to develop each individual to the highest degree of proficiency that his talents will allow.

3) Club *support* of band, solo, and ensemble *competitions and* participation in *music education events outside* of the *school district* is important. The value of these experiences should be explained in detail to your Club.

4) Stress that the proper way to reach the goals of your program is to develop and maintain a large and proficient concert band program as the core of the instrumental music program.

5) The Club can give assistance in obtaining proper equipment for your groups.

6) The Club can actively take part in making the program more attractive for students by planning field trips and band tours, providing opportunities for musical and educational experiences, and planning social events for your groups during the school year.

7) Stress the school and music department opposition to attempts to use students' musical talents for self-serving interests of Club members instead of for educationally sound projects. Examples of self-serving interests are a merchant who promotes a special concert for sales purposes and a local organization that promotes a parade that primarily benefits that organization and is not community oriented.

Developing a Set of Goals and Objectives for Your Boosters' Club

Goals and objectives are usually general in nature but are influenced by specific local needs, which are constantly changing.

1) General goals and objectives:

    a) Enthusiastic interest in and support of your program, including the endorsement of the educational and musical programs of your school system and a commitment for auxiliary financial assistance.

    b) Sponsoring of projects stressing educational and musical values, including trips and educational programs.

    c) Maintaining musical standards established by your program through cooperation with the Music Department, Administration, and the Board of Education.

    d) Alleviating the work load for music teachers through establishment of a uniform committee, a sales committee, and so on.

    e) Providing financial help for music students through scholarships.

2) Specific goals and objectives:

    a) Helping obtain needed equipment.

    b) Helping effect improvement in facilities (for example, support of a bond issue for school remodeling).

    c) Assisting in establishment of new performing groups for your program. This may consist of financial help or official Club support of the need to establish a new group.

    d) Supply new uniforms or add accessories to present uniforms.

Establishing Specific Functions for Your Boosters' Club

Some of the successful functions of our Music Boosters' Club are:

1) *Supervising* and assisting with *sales and money-making projects.* Receipts from sales can be kept in an independent Music Boosters' fund outside the school. We have found it advantageous, however, to channel all moneys received into a student music activities account within the school. A system of checks and balances is created when the money is controlled jointly by school officials and the Music Boosters' Club.

2) *Assistance in planning field trips* of educational and social value. *Chaperoning* of this is particularly important.

3) Assistance with *distribution and collection of band uniforms.* A well-organized uniform committee can lighten the load of the director considerably.

4) Helping to *publicize concerts and* other *music department events.*

5) *Serving refreshments* to the audience *after each performance.* Our Music Boosters serve punch and cookies after each concert, a function that adds class to the overall program and has been well received by the public.

6) *Setting up* Club-funded *scholarships.*

a) Our Club has established a scholarship award of several hundred dollars to the outstanding music major graduating each year. A committee of music teachers, Music Boosters, and guidance counselors determines the recipient of this award, which is presented by a representative of the Booster's Club at our school's annual graduation awards program. Not only is the student music major benefited in this manner, but the function of the Music Boosters' Club takes on added meaning in the eyes of school officials and the public.

b) A scholarship fund has been established by the Booster's Club to send one instrumental and one vocal student to a summer music camp each year. Candidates must formally apply for this scholarship, stating in an essay of not less than 250 words their reasons for wanting to attend a summer music camp. A committee of music teachers, Music Boosters, and guidance counselors selects the recipients through review of musical and academic records and the students' essays, which are judged solely on content.

After your Club has functioned for a period of time, the following suggestions can help you to maintain a successful Music Boosters' Club:

1) *Work* diligently *to expand* the *membership* of your Club. If your Club suffers from small membership, although community support of the music program is very strong, you should formulate an active and well-developed recruitment plan that includes publicized activities that will attract new members.

2) *Establish a* Music Boosters' Club *credo of music education*, based upon the welfare and educational enrichment of your students. Point out that methods of instruction, supervision, and program content should be determined by the professional musicians and administrators who are employed for that purpose. The basic function of the Music Boosters' Club should be limited to being supportive of an educationally sound music program and helping with the work involved in maintaining fine musical and educational experiences for your young musicians. If its power becomes greater, the Music Boosters' Club may become a negative influence upon the smooth administration of your band program.

3) *Work for improved communications* between the Boosters' Club and students, teachers, and school officials involved in daily music education. Even though you may think your lines of communication are well established, misunderstandings can occur because of breakdowns in communications.

Avoid the Possible Negative Aspects
of a Music Boosters' Club

1) Don't allow your Boosters' Club to become a *pressure group*, creating tensions in the relationships among your Music Department, Administration, and Board of Education.

2) Don't permit your Boosters' Club to become *politically oriented* so that power and control are sought by individuals for personal reasons.

3) Don't allow your Boosters' Club to dictate *its own music education philosophies* to the Music Department or to school officials.

An active Music Boosters' Club can be a great asset to a successful program if it is properly organized and carefully supervised. However, it can become a negative influence on your music program if its members attempt to dictate the policy or philosophy of music education to your school system.

ORGANIZING THE BAND'S
INTERNAL BUSINESS MACHINE

17

The internal business of a band program includes the following:

1) The music library
2) Field trips and assembly programs
3) The rotating lesson schedule
4) An evaluation and grading system

It is your responsibility to organize and develop these aspects of the band program, although you can enlist responsible students to assist you.

DEVELOPING AND MAINTAINING
A FINE MUSIC LIBRARY

Your music library is one of the most important elements of a successful program. It should be well organized, constantly expanded, and kept up to date with the addition of recent compositions, especially in the field of popular music. If your library is an extensive one, organizing it and keeping it in order will be a time-consuming job. Your library will not only include band arrangements but will also contain solos, ensembles, and method books. Each of these categories must be organized separately, and adequate storage space must be provided to keep each category in order.

The Band Music Library

Follow these steps in creating and maintaining your band music library:

1) *Organize* all of your band music into categories *according to size*. Band arrangements are published in three sizes: march, octavo, and concert. Have cabinets built to hold each size of music. All march-size compositions should be filed together on shelves which are built approximately ten inches apart in height and octavo-size music should be filed on shelves

which are approximately twelve inches apart. Concert-size arrangements are then filed on the remaining shelves, which are approximately fourteen inches apart in height. Each arrangement should be filed in a box that is made for one of these three sizes. Filing boxes of this type can be obtained from Instrumental Music, Inc., 1416 Lake Street, Evanston, Illinois. The size of the arrangement becomes the first symbol of the filing system: "M" = March-size, "O" = Octavo-size, and "C" = Concert-size.

2) *Organize* each size of arrangement into categories *according to type of composition*. With march-size marches, I use three difficulty levels: Easy, Medium, and Difficult. Each is designated with one of the letters, "E," "M," or "D." The system I developed for octavo- and concert-size arrangements is much more complicated. Since there were so many arrangements of these sizes in my library, I decided to file them according to type of composition, finally arriving at the following code system:

C	= Christmas Music
CB	= Original Concert Band Compositions
CM	= Concert Marches (octavo- or concert-size marches)
EB	= Ensemble with Band Accompaniment
KT	= Keyboard Transcriptions
LR	= Latin-Rhythm Compositions
MC	= Musical Comedy or Broadway Show Arrangements
N	= Novelty Arrangements
OT	= Orchestral Transcriptions
P	= Popular Music Arrangements
PCM	= Parade, or Ceremonial Music
POB	= Piano or Organ Soloist with Band Accompaniment
SB	= Soloist with Band Accompaniment

3) *Organize* each "type" category *into levels of difficulty*. I use six levels of difficulty, designated by Roman numerals from I to VI where I represents the easiest compositions and VI represents the most difficult.

4) The final designation, which gives my library code system the possibility of infinite expansion, is simply an Arabic numeral that is added at the end of the filing code as a composition is added to my library.

Now the code system is developed so that any composition can be filed at any time and you will never need to reorganize your system or develop a new system to replace it. The following are examples of compositions filed in this manner. Each states the title of the composition, its composer and/or arranger, the publisher, and its library code number.

Yankee Doodle Boy	Cohan-Van Auken	Leonard	M-(E)-31
On the Alert	Goldman	CF	M-(M)-39

Liberty Bell	Sousa	CF	M-(D)-4
Sleigh Ride	Anderson	Mills	O-(C)-III-1
Toccata Marziale	Vaughan Williams	B & H	C-(CB)-VI-1
Moorside March	Holst-Jacob	B & H	C-(CM)-IV-5
Flute Cocktail (Fl. trio)	Simeone	Shawnee	C-(EB)-IV-5
Chorale and Fugue in G Minor	Bach-Aubert	Schirmer	C-(KT)-VI-2
Bolero Espanole	Lecuone	Marks	C-(LR)-V-10
Westside Story	Bernstein-Duthoit	Chappell	C-(MC)-V-2
Badinage for Brasses	Walters	Rubank	C-(N)-III-2
Cosi Fan Tutti	Mozart-Moehlmann	Fitzsimons	C-(OT)-VI-11
Lawrence of Arabia	Jarre-Reed	Gower	C-(P)-IV-1
March and Chorus from *Judas Maccabaeus*	Handel- R. F. Goldman	CF	C-(PCM)-IV-1
Warsaw Concerto	Addinsell-Leidzen	Chappell	C-(POB)-V-2
Concerto in C Major for Piccolo and Band	Vivaldi-Reed	Colombo	C-(SB)-VI-2

5) After each of your band arrangements has been placed in an appropriate filing box, *mark* the *box with* the following *information*:

    a) Name of composition

    b) Name of composer and/or arranger

    c) Name of publisher

    d) Filing code number

    e) Any other pertinent information you desire to include such as the exact number of parts in the arrangement, performance information, and the type of score provided. The filing boxes manufactured by Instrumental Music, Inc. provide spaces for all of the above information.

6) *Find* two or three capable *students and use them as* your *librarians*. Teach them the following music library information:

    a) How to file arrangements by concert order

    b) How to file by your band library code system

    c) How to mark boxes for new band arrangements

7) If you do not have adequate cabinets to receive your band arrangements, have them built to your specifications by your school maintenance

staff. In this manner, you may specify exactly what you desire and the cost to your budget is considerably less than commercially manufactured cabinets. My band music filing cabinets were built to specifications which best utilized the wall space available in my band room. Therefore, the following pictures are to be construed as suggestions to help you in building such a filing area. (See Figures 1 and 2.) Large doors with locks were added to the shelf areas so that these areas may be closed and locked.

The following two filing racks (See Figures 3 and 4) may be used for storage of band folders or for sorting and filing band arrangements.

8) *Continue building* your *band music library* by yearly addition of several numbers in each category.

The Solo Library

As part of my yearly supplies requisition I order several solos for each instrument at each grade level of difficulty. Two copies of each solo are

Figure 1. Cabinet for Filing All Three Sizes of Band Music

Figure 2. Cabinet for Filing Only Concert-Size Band Music

Figure 3. Permanent Filing Rack Built Into Wall Space

Figure 4. Portable Filing Rack

ordered so that when a solo is chosen for competition a copy is available for both the soloist and the adjudicator. All solos are simply filed according to instrument and difficulty. For example, the *Golden Concerto* by Nelhybel is marked: Trumpet Solo—Grade VI. Representative lists of solos for each instrument are found in the Appendices of this book.

Solos for each instrument at each grade level of difficulty are filed in manila folders that are marked with the name of the instrument and the difficulty level. For example, a folder may be marked: Flute Solo—Grade VI. As your solo library grows, you may find it expedient to file the solos for each instrument and level of difficulty alphabetically according to composer. As each category becomes larger, more manila folders should be added to hold your expanding solo library.

I use a special metal filing cabinet for solos and ensembles of the type used by the business office of our school for filing records which are kept in manila folders (see Figure 5). This cabinet can be ordered from Beco

Figure 5. Metal Filing Cabinet for Solo and Ensemble Storage

Interiors, 1285 East Second Street, Jamestown, New York, 14701.

Organize your solo library according to concert order and difficulty. Reading from left to right, the top shelf will begin with Piccolo Solos—Grade I, Piccolo Solos—Grade II, and so on, and then progress to Flute Solos—Grade I, Flute Solos—Grade II, and so on. After each instrument is filed in concert order, the solos within each instrumental category should be filed from Grade I (easy) to Grade VI (difficult). When the filing of all woodwind, brass, and percussion solos has been completed, the remainder of the cabinet space can be used for ensembles.

The Ensemble Library

Ensembles should be filed in a similar manner to solos, according to concert order and order of difficulty. Thus, piccolo and flute ensembles would be filed first. An additional category for filing will now be necessary.

You should file each instrumental group according to duets, trios, quartets, quintets, and so on. Mixed ensembles such as woodwind quintet literature should be filed at the end of the homogeneous ensembles. Your ensemble library may be filed in three ways:

1) Flute ensembles can follow flute solo literature, and so on;

2) All woodwind ensembles can follow at the end of the woodwind solo library, and so on;

3) Ensemble literature can be filed in concert order at the end of the entire solo library.

Use whichever of these methods is most convenient for you.

After you have set up your solo and ensemble libraries, train your librarians to file the music properly for you. Flexibility, according to your choice of filing system, can be employed in any of these library setups. A possible outline for your solo and ensemble library follows:

Piccolo Solos—Grades I–VI

Flute Solos—Grades I–VI

Flute Duets—Grades I-VI

Flute Trios—Grades I-VI

Flute Quartets—Grades I-VI

Flute Quintets—Grades I-VI

Oboe Solos—Grades I-VI

E-flat Clarinet Solos—Grades I-VI

Clarinet Solos—Grades I-VI

Clarinet Duets, Trios, and Quartets—Grades I-VI (as flute ensembles)

Alto Clarinet Solos—Grades I-VI

Bass Clarinet Solos—Grades I-VI

Mixed Clarinet Ensembles—Grades I-VI (as flute ensembles)

Bassoon Solos—Grades I-VI

Alto Saxophone Solos—Grades I-VI

Alto Saxophone Duets, Trios, etc,—Grades I-VI (as flute ensembles)

Tenor Saxophone Solos—Grades I-VI

Baritone Saxophone Solos—Grades I-VI

Mixed Saxophone Ensembles—Grades I-VI (as flute ensembles)

French Horn Solos—Grades I-VI

French Horn Duets, Trios, and Quartets—Grades I-VI (as flute ensembles)

Cornet or Trumpet Solos—Grades I-VI

Cornet Ensembles—Grades I-VI (as horn ensembles)

Trombone Solos—Grades I-VI

Trombone Ensembles—Grades I-VI (as horn ensembles)

Baritone Solos—Grades I-VI

(Differences between bass and treble clef may be recognized.)

Tuba Solos—Grades I-VI

Mixed Brass Duets, Trios, Quartets, Quintets, Sextets, and Septets—Grades I-VI (as horn ensembles)

Snare Drum Solos—Grades I-VI

Timpani Solos—Grades I-VI

Mallet Solos—Grades I-VI

Mixed Percussion Ensembles—Grades I-VI (as horn ensembles)

You should expand your solo and ensemble libraries by yearly requisition of a few new additions to each instrumental category and level of difficulty found in your present structure.

The Method Book Library

My method books are ordered as textbook requisitions. Each year I order a number of selected method books for each instrument at each difficulty level. When making out each new textbook requisition I also order single copies of method books which are unfamiliar to me, thereby building a reference library for myself. If an exceptional book is found, additional copies are then ordered for my students. All method books are used until they are completely worn out. By having the school buy the method books for each student and by building a large and flexible method book library, I am able to change method books with a class or a student at any time such a change seems educationally desirable. A representative list of method books for each instrument at each difficulty level is found in the Appendices of this book.

Method books are filed in concert order in a cabinet that I had built specifically for this part of my library. I rejected filing cabinets because of the expense and because I found my type of cabinet more efficient. A

Flute	Oboe-Bassoon
Clarinet	Saxophone
French Horn	Cornet
Trombone	Baritone-Tuba
Snare	Timpani-Bell Lyre
Conductor	Conductor

Figure 6. Diagram of Method Book Storage Cabinet

Figure 7. The Permanent Method Book Cabinet

diagram and picture of my method book cabinet are found in Figures 6 and 7. Fingering charts for each instrument are filed with the method books. All method books for a specific instrument are filed according to difficulty with all like copies filed together. As a student finishes a method book it is collected and filed for future use by another student much like paperback textbooks are used by academic classroom teachers.

ORGANIZING FIELD TRIPS AND ASSEMBLY PROGRAMS

Field trips and assembly programs are an essential part of your program for two major reasons: 1) the educational value derived by your students and 2) the boost to the morale of your group and the motivation to work in preparation for the trip or the assembly.

Organizing Field Trips

Field trips can include performances by your group, or they can be organized entirely for educational enrichment, but a combination of these two elements is most beneficial. The length of your trip in regard to distance and time must be carefully considered. The following check list will help you organize a successful field trip:

1) *Choose* the *content and location of* the *field trip experience* carefully. Be sure your plan contains strong educational value so that you will have the full support of your Administration and Board of Education in the planning and execution of your venture.

2) *Draw up* a carefully planned and timed *itinerary* for your trip. Considerable research may be necessary to gain knowledge of exact distances involved and various expenses for transportation, meals, housing and possible admission fees to various planned events.

3) *Arrange* any *contacts* you will have on your trip *with other schools*. If you are to present programs for other schools in assemblies or as an evening concert, these must be properly set up with the school officials and the music directors of the schools you are to visit.

4) *Arrange* tentative *transportation* for your group. If you can use school buses for your trip, your expenses will be much less than if you must hire buses. In most cases your school will absorb the cost of use of local buses and drivers.

5) If your trip will involve considerable expenses, *plan* very carefully *how* these *expenses will be met*. Money-raising activities might be necessary, and should be planned several months in advance of your trip.

6) *Reserve dates* for your trip *on* the *school calendar*, preferably a school year in advance. School calendars are very full today and you do not want any conflicts with scheduling which might cause you to lose some of your students to another activity.

7) *Chaperones* may be needed for your trip. They *must be contacted* and a chaperone list must be drawn up. Each chaperone should be assigned approximately ten students if your trip is lengthy, entails housing, and will consist of at least one night's stay. Chaperones may be easily obtained by asking your students which of their parents are interested in helping with this task. If you have a Music Boosters' Club, they can take care of the chaperone recruitment and assignment.

8) *Housing lists* may be necessary if an overnight trip is involved. These should be done in detail and will be most successful if you allow your students to choose their own roommates. A confidential list of problem students may be drawn up which would include any suspected problems of drinking, drugs, and smoking. Such a list alerts your chaperones to special observation of possible problem students.

9) You may also desire to draw up *bus lists* that include seating. Again, it is advantageous in most cases to let the students choose their bus partners. Students forced into pairings without regard for friendships will probably enjoy your trip much less and may become discipline problems. Conversely, some student pairings may have to be avoided because of possible discipline problems when certain students are together for a period of time. Use a reasonable degree of common sense and compassion for the students involved whenever making up housing or busing lists.

10) *Complete arrangements for* any admission fees to *special concerts, museums,* and so on. Contact box offices far in advance to arrange for handling of a large group and to secure a group fee if possible.

11) *Complete arrangements for* any *meals* which you plan to eat *at restaurants*. Plan far in advance for the serving of a large group and for possible special rates for your meals.

12) *Present* your *completed itinerary to* your *Administration and Board of Education for approval*. Be sure to include a list of chaperones secured, transportation and meal expenses, and any other pertinent information.

13) As soon as your trip is formally approved, begin sending home a series of *bulletins to* your band *parents* keeping them informed in detail. *Have* each *communication approved by* your *Administration* before releasing it to parents and supply each administrator with a copy of each communication.

14) *Formulate* a very *specific* list of *rules of conduct for* the *trip*, that must be strictly adhered to by your students. Have them approved by your Administration and then dispense them to all of your students and their parents. Spell out specific penalties if rules are not followed. Flagrant violations should result in sending the student home immediately or dismissing the student from your group upon return home and review of the case by your Administration.

The following sample itinerary is included to help you with the planning of a successful field trip.

SENIOR BAND FIELD TRIP TO (DESTINATION)

(Date)

Final Itinerary

7:30 A.M.—Load equipment on buses.

8:00 A.M.—Leave from front circle of high school by bus (each student should bring his/her own box lunch plus beverage).

9:00 A.M.—Arrive at (location of first event); warm up and prepare for assembly program concert.

9:30–10:30 A.M.—Play assembly program concert.

10:30–11:00 A.M.—Concert cleanup and loading of buses.

11:00 A.M.—Leave for (location of second event).

12:00 P.M.—Arrive at (industrial plant or second event); have lunch on buses.

1:15 P.M.—Group tour of industrial plant.

3:00 P.M.—Depart for (location of third event).

3:45 P.M.—Tour and program at planetarium (or third event).

5:00 P.M.—Dinner at (restaurant).

6:30 P.M.—Depart for (theater or fourth event).

7:15 P.M.—Enter (theater or ——) for performance of Mozart's opera *The Marriage of Figaro* (or a similar experience).

8:00–11:00 P.M.—Performance of opera (or fourth event).

11:00 P.M.—Depart from theater for home school.

1:30 A.M.—Arrive at front circle of home school. Parents meet students and transport them to respective homes.

The above is a one-day field trip itinerary that was both specific and detailed in its original form. Some of the events have been mentioned by name so that you can see the educational diversity of such a trip. The original itinerary included specific locations with addresses, detailed information about each event, admission fees when needed, restaurant menus when possible, and special instructions for students and chaperones.

Field trips of more than one day's duration may be set up in a similar manner by developing detailed day-by-day itinerary plans. If your trip will necessitate your students' missing some days of school classes, an alphabetized list of the students in your band should be supplied to classroom teachers so that they can plan accordingly. *Teachers* appreciate this courtesy, and their passive *approval* of your trip and its value to the overall education of the students is necessary if such trips are to become a regular part of your school program.

Parental support will be ensured by keeping parents fully informed of your plans and their educational value. Your bulletins to the parents may include a blank to be signed and returned by those parents who desire to volunteer as chaperones for your trip. A signed parental consent for each student to make the trip with your band is also helpful since you are assured when using this procedure that all parents are fully aware of their child's participation in the event.

Assembly Programs

Assembly programs are not difficult to set up in your own school, although school officials usually want at least several weeks of notice as to date and time. This type of performance is strong motivation for your students since they are playing for their peers. At least one or two of these programs should be done each school year. If programming which is interesting to your general student body is used, many of these students will also attend your evening concerts. This usually means programming of contemporary popular music and marches. Using numbers which feature traps and guitars is excellent, especially if the numbers used are popular at the time of your performance.

An assembly program should be approximately 40 to 50 minutes in length, and should move rapidly. Your band can play the students into the auditorium at the beginning of the assembly with march material currently being studied and use a similar procedure at the end for dismissal. In this manner, more of your prepared music can be presented to the student body.

Using your band members to play students in and out of regular school assemblies is an excellent way to gain more performance experience and to cultivate the support of your student body and its teachers. A small band can be used for such assemblies. I have the members of my woodwind and brass quintets and my saxophone and percussion ensembles on standby to cover these performances. They are the strongest musicians in the band and can be assembled on very short notice to play almost any musical requests coming from the organizers of the assembly program being presented.

If an assembly program is to be presented at another school, use the following procedures:

1) *Set up* the exact *time of performance* with the school officials and the director involved. Ask for at least one-half hour setup and warmup time on stage before the assembly begins.

2) *Send* a *band seating chart to* the *school* if they are willing to set the stage for you. If this is not possible, supply your own stage crew but notify the other school as to how many chairs and stands you

will need so that this equipment is on stage and available when you arrive.

3) *Send a list of* additional *equipment* you would be able to use if it is readily available at the other school. This includes large percussion equipment, risers, and microphones.

4) *Send any request for special lighting* which may be needed for your program.

5) Be sure to *arrange for* any *meals* in their school cafeteria if necessitated by your time schedule.

6) *Set up* your *transportation request* for school buses several weeks in advance of your exchange concert so that no conflicts can occur in securing transportation for the trip. You may have to request a certain concert time at the other school in order to avoid any conflicts in the busing schedules of your school. If your school does not have buses, you must solve the transportation problem in some other manner. Such a situation is rare today and would make performing an assembly program at another school very difficult.

7) Usually, trips of this nature are not long distances from the school and chaperones are not needed.

8) *Equipment loading* for such trips should be *done by band members*. Your percussionists, for example, should be responsible for loading and unloading all percussion equipment. You should, however, check with each section taking equipment and write up a personal checklist of all equipment to be loaded. This includes making sure that all music for the assembly program has been loaded properly. You may also want to take a small repair kit or tuners. Assign students to be responsible for loading of music, repair kits or tuners, and so on, but be sure to check with them in regard to their responsibilities before departing from your school.

HOW TO USE THE ROTATING
LESSON SCHEDULE TO BEST ADVANTAGE

The rotating instrumental music lesson schedule is an absolute necessity to the success of your program. The only alternative to some form of rotating schedule is to have all of your students study privately. Under some difficult circumstances rotating schedules are not permitted, and you must then draw your students from study halls for their lessons. This procedure is very poor since homogeneous grouping according to instrument and talent is almost impossible. It should be used only if you have no choice.

Setting up a workable rotating schedule is not difficult, if you carefully consider the following:

1) *Determine* the *number of weeks* your *schedule is to cover.* This should not exceed five or six since you must have the flexibility to change students' class assignments at regular intervals. These changes are determined by the progress of individual students or by the type of material you are teaching. For example, I have a certain time each year when I try to assign as many students as possible to performing ensembles. In some cases, this requires considerable schedule juggling, especially in the case of woodwind quintets or brass sextets. This assumes that your schedule starts the school year with homogeneous grouping according to instrument. The shorter rotating schedule also makes it possible to add or drop students without too much confusion.

2) *Determine* the *number of periods you will rotate* in your teaching schedule. In my schedule I have two non-rotating periods; band rehearsals and music theory classes. All of the other periods in the school day are available for rotation. Since I rotate five or six instrumental classes, my individual schedules run for five or six weeks. Because the rotating schedule is set up in this manner, my new schedules always start with the same class having their lesson first period, which avoids considerable confusion for the teachers and the students who must interpret the schedules.

3) *Set up* your *classes homogeneously* according to instrument and level of playing ability at the beginning of the school year. For example, first cornets in one class, second cornets in another, and so on. Keep the class size as small as possible. After you have determined the total number of rotating classes you can teach in a week, divide your total number of students accordingly. Hopefully, your classes will number from two students to not more than five. I feel that classes of three are ideal, although I can seldom keep the number in a class that low. It is also advantageous to schedule specific instruments on the same day throughout the year. When a student always has his lesson on a particular day he is not likely to forget his lesson time. If you constantly juggle the day on which a student is to take his lesson, he will become confused and lesson attendance will suffer.

I usually schedule my French horns, trombones, and baritones on Mondays since these heavy horns are not normally taken home for practicing until the weekend. Consequently, these Monday lessons are freshly prepared. Tuesdays are reserved for flute and clarinet classes; Wednesdays for oboe, bassoon, alto, and bass clarinet classes; and Thursdays for cornets, saxophones, and tubas (tubas usually practice their lessons at school and are better prepared later in the school week). Fridays are reserved for percussion, beginners, and any left over classes. Meeting your percussion students on Fridays allows you to prepare them for special routines immediately prior to football or basketball games or weekend marching assignments. Fridays are the weakest teaching days considering the number of Fridays you may not have school and the fatigue of both the students and teacher at the end of the school week. Therefore, the bulk of the performing students have their lessons on the first four days of the week, and beginners are picked up on Fridays since their immediate importance to your band program is less.

4) *Supply* each *student with his own copy of* the *rotating schedule.* Also *post* a full *set of* your *rotating schedules* in the band room areas. *Make* enough additional *copies* of these schedules *for* all *classroom teachers and* for each member of the *Administration.* You may want to leave a full set of your schedules at the switchboard in your main office and in your office class-list file. This makes it possible for office personnel to locate a student quickly in case of an emergency. It is also good procedure to place an explanatory letter in each teacher's mailbox at the beginning of the school year. New teachers, especially, will appreciate this since rotating lesson schedules are usually unfamiliar to them.

An example of my rotating schedules is found below:

INSTRUMENTAL MUSIC ROTATING SCHEDULE

(Day of week)   (Teacher's name)

Period	(month and day)	(date)	(date)	(date)	(date)	(date)
1	A	F	E	D	C	B
2	B	A	F	E	D	C
3	C	B	A	F	E	D
4	Senior Band Rehearsal					
5AB	Work Period					
5C	Lunch					
6DE	D	C	B	A	F	E
7	E	D	C	B	A	F
8	F	E	D	C	B	A

A
(students' names)

D
(students' names)

B
(students' names)

E
(students' names)

C
(students' names)

F
(students' names)

If you are also teaching music theory courses, one or more of the rotating periods can be scheduled for this. The period designated as a "work period" is also flexible and can be used as a teaching period.

DEVELOPING AN EFFECTIVE
EVALUATION AND GRADING SYSTEM

Evaluation and grading are two methods of measuring a student's progress. Grading is an everyday or short-term evaluation, whereas true evaluation seems to be related to long-term or periodic measurement of a student's improvement. An evaluation of a student's developed ability may be done at any time. You may desire to evaluate your students at the end of each semester of study or at the end of each year. Evaluations can also be done at the beginning or end of educational levels. For example, you may desire to evaluate each instrumental music student before he is placed in an elementary band, a junior high band, or a senior high band.

Grading, on the other hand, can be thought of as the evaluation of a student at his weekly lesson or at the end of each school grading period.

You should develop a definite plan of evaluation and evaluate your entire band program at predetermined intervals. An evaluation test can be administered before a beginning student is placed in an elementary band. Another evaluation test can be given by the end of the sixth grade before each instrumental student is assigned to a junior high band. The most important evaluation test I administer is at the end of the eighth grade, before an instrumental student is assigned to a senior high band.

The *evaluation* test *for each level is determined by* the *syllabus* you have developed for each instrument. And, in turn, the syllabus for each instrument is determined by what you expect the student to be able to perform at a given level of his instrumental music education. Both the evaluation and the syllabus should be based upon educational and musical behavioral objectives.

A suggested evaluation test for each level follows:

Level 1—The End of the Fifth Grade
or One Full Year of Study

1) All woodwind players will perform the major scales of C, F, and G in two octaves at m.m. = 80 in quarter and eighth notes, the tonic notes being sustained for one beat and all other notes for one-half beat. Arpeggios and thirds of these keys will be performed through two octaves at the same tempo in eighth notes.

2) All brass players will perform the scales, arpeggios, and thirds in the keys of C, F, and G major at m.m. = 80 in quarter notes for the tonic notes and eighth notes for all other notes. Arpeggios and thirds of these keys will be performed through one octave in eighth notes.

3) All percussionists (snare drummers at this point) will play 12 consecutive patterns of the following rudiments in a tempo of m.m. =

80: long roll (12 beats), 5-stroke roll, 9-stroke roll, 17-stroke roll, flam, flam-tap, single-stroke roll, ruff, single paradiddle, double paradiddle, and triple paradiddle.

4) Brass and woodwind players will prepare an étude (selected by the teacher) that will clearly indicate knowledge and playing ability of the following note values and equivalent rests: whole notes, dotted-half notes, half notes, quarter notes, eighth notes, and dotted-quarter notes.

5) Percussionists will prepare an étude of not less than five lines that will clearly indicate knowledge and playing control of several of the rudiments named in (3) and the following rhythmic patterns: combinations of quarter notes (rests) and eighth notes (rests), and sixteenth note patterns (♪♪♪♪ ; ♩♪♪ ; ♪♪♩ ; and so on).

6) All performers will sight read a simple étude appropriate to this level of evaluation and realistic as to the level of band music performance that will be expected from elementary school band members.

7) Percussionists will perform all of their evaluation on a snare drum or a drum pad and demonstrate knowledge of rhythmic syllables by counting aloud with proper syllables during the evaluation.

8) All woodwind and brass players will demonstrate their counting understanding by proper use of the foot during the evaluation.

Level 2—The End of the Sixth Grade or Two Full Years of Study

1) The scales, arpeggios, and thirds of the major keys of B-flat and D will be added to the evaluation, and all five keys will now be performed by all woodwind and brass players in the same manner as Level 1.

2) All percussionists will now be responsible for all rudiments covered in Level 1 plus the following: 7-stroke roll, 15-stroke roll, 11-stroke roll, 13-stroke roll, flam accents 1 and 2, and single, double, and triple ratamacues. All of these are to be performed as in Level 1.

3) Brass and woodwind études will be chosen by the teacher to include common sixteenth note patterns and simple compound time patterns (♩. ; ♩. ; ♪♪♪ ; ♩ ♪ ; and so on).

4) Percussionists' étude material should include several of the added rudiments and compound time rhythmic patterns as in (3) above.

5) Sight reading material should be realistic as to the level of band

music performance which will be expected from junior high band members.

6) Percussionists will perform on pads or a snare drum and will demonstrate knowledge of rhythmic syllables in both simple and compound meters.

7) All wind players will continue to demonstrate their counting knowledge by proper use of the foot throughout the evaluation.

8) Knowledge of the chromatic scale will be evaluated at this point by performance in one octave for brasses and woodwinds (c^1 to c^2, and so on) and from low e to the "break" on clarinets.

Level 3—The End of the Seventh Grade or Three Full Years of Study

This level of evaluation is optional since no band level change is usually encountered here. Major keys of E-flat and A are now added for winds. Percussion add the following rudiments: 6-stroke roll, 10-stroke roll, flam paradiddles and flamacue, and single and double drags. At this point all winds will prepare scale-related work in sixteenth notes at m.m. = 60. Etudes will be chosen by the teacher to demonstrate the level attained in étude study. Sight reading will also be based upon the present level attained. Chromatic scales will be extended through the playing range of woodwind and brass players, and be performed in sixteenth notes at m.m. = 60.

Level 4—The End of the Eighth Grade or Four Full Years of Study

This evaluation will determine membership in a high school band, and it is, therefore, the most important evaluation in relation to the success of your high school program. If proper teaching and learning has occurred to this point, this evaluation is only a formality. Your students will know the required material so well that all should score well.

The Senior Band Test

The following requirements are to be performed as noted in Level 3, the pulse being m.m. = 60:

All major scales prepared through keys of four flats and four sharps

All major arpeggios prepared through keys of four flats and four sharps

All major scales by thirds prepared through keys of four flats and four sharps

Chromatic scale prepared through the range of the particular instrument

One prepared étude (chosen by teacher)

Sight reading (chosen by teacher)

Percussionists:

Prepare all 26 rudiments in repeated patterns of 12 examples

Prepared étude (chosen by teacher)

Sight reading (chosen by teacher)

The above Senior Band Entrance Test will be given to each candidate in the spring of the student's eighth grade school year. A composite score of 75 percent must be attained for membership in Senior Band. Exceptions are made, however, when a student has studied an instrument for only a short period of time but shows above-average potential.

Evaluations in high school can be done each year. I prefer to do them during the first four lessons of the school year in the following manner:

First week—All scales through seven flats and seven sharps (proba-bly, new freshmen cannot play the advanced keys since they will normally be taught during ninth grade classes). Scales should be performed at m.m. = 60, with eighth note values used for tonic notes and sixteenth notes used for all other notes.

Second week—All arpeggios in a similar manner.

Third week—All scales by thirds in a similar manner.

Fourth week—Chromatic scale in sixteenth notes, étude and sight reading.

Grading Procedures

Grading is usually done with letters or numbers, although pass-fail is used in some school systems. I personally prefer letters for elementary students and numbers for junior and senior high students. Several grades should be taken at each lesson: one for practice time, one for warmups, one for technique, one for étude assignment (method book material included), and one for band performance. Therefore, an elementary student can be graded in the following manner: an A for three hours of preparation (prac-tice time), an A for warmups (evaluation of tone quality can be included here), a B for scale-type work, an A for his étude (usually indicating five or fewer errors in performing the étude), and a B for band performance (a subjective grade based upon comparison with other band members' per-formance of band music on like instruments).

Junior high students can be graded on a letter or number basis deter-mined by school grading policy. Since Junior High Band is usually consid-ered an exploratory subject, a letter grade is more practical. Several grades should be given for each lesson and should include a grade for practice time (homework preparation), warmup and tone quality evaluation, technique, étude material, and a subjective band grade.

I prefer to grade the high school student on a numerical basis. I find it much more exact, and it gives you the opportunity to clearly indicate the smallest differences between student performances. Several grades should be taken at each lesson, based upon the same criteria as the junior high grading.

This type of academic grading may seem tedious to many band directors, but it is absolutely necessary if you are to attain an academic credit status for your high school band program. My band members receive one full credit per year for Senior Band, which is the same amount of academic credit toward graduation that is given for each year of math, science, and so on. Figuring report card grades is not a difficult task, even though you may have to average as many as 20 to 30 grades for each marking period. Since almost all band students will receive grades in the 90's or the 80's, the mathematical reciprocal of the number grade can be used when figuring the averages. If you use a hand calculator, your grades can be averaged in a very short time. Use the following method for reciprocal calculation of averages:

Student's grades:	90	85	92	96	88
Reciprocal:	10	15	8	4	12

Add second group of numbers: Total = 49

Divide by number of grades: $49/5 = 10$ (approx.)

Subtract 10 from 100: Student's average grade = 90

Whichever method of grading you choose, you must first consider the grading system used by your school. Ultimately, your grades must be converted to that system. Therefore, the 90 indicated above may be converted to an A− if your school uses letter grades. I prefer using numbers and converting when necessary to another system because numbers give you a much more accurate evaluation of your students' abilities.

Use the class book provided by your school to record all grades and enter these grades into this book in the same manner as the regular academic teachers record their grades. If you follow the same procedures with your class book (grade book) and your plan book as your regular academic teachers do, you will have a strong chance of having Band considered an academic subject, thereby receiving full academic credit for your students' participation in the course.

HOW TO OPERATE INSTRUMENT MAINTENANCE AND REPAIR PROGRAMS

18

Although the field of instrument repair is the domain of the professionally trained instrument repairman, instrument maintenance and minor repairs must often be done by the band director. All maintenance and repairs fall into the following categories:

1) Overhauls—to be done by the professional repairman at his shop.

2) Major repairs—to be done by the professional repairman in most cases.

3) Minor repairs—can be done in most cases by the band director. Such repairs include:

   a) Woodwinds—replacing pads, replacing springs, recorking tenons, replacing various corks which are used for adjustment on woodwinds, adjusting screws on some woodwind mechanisms, especially on flutes and oboes, and minor repairs of bent bridge keys or other keys which are not seating properly. Severely bent key mechanisms should be professionally repaired.

   b) Brass—replacing water-key corks, replacing water-key and valve springs, replacing felt or cork washers in brass valve mechanisms, freeing frozen tuning slides, and removing stuck mouthpieces. Dents in trombone slides or in valve casings of other brasses should be repaired by the professional repairman.

   c) Percussion—replacing drum heads, adjusting snare tensions, replacing worn cymbal thongs, and minor repair of any other percussion equipment.

4) General instrument maintenance:

   a) Woodwinds (maintenance manuals are available from most instrument manufacturers)—*complete overhauls* should be done every two to three years, periodic *oiling of* all moving *rods*, regular check for possible *replacement of pads* with broken skin or pads which have turned brown and are no longer soft enough to seal openings properly, periodic *check* of *tenon corks* and replacement when necessary to prevent leakage between joints, *check* of *mouthpiece cork* for leakage, and occasional *strengthening of springs* where key movement seems weak or slow. *Head-joint corks in flutes* should be regularly adjusted to assure proper intonation between registers. All *woodwinds should be swabbed* out after each playing because excess saliva accumulating on the pads and drying can cause pads to harden and crack. A periodic *check* should be made of *double octave mechanisms* on saxophones and lower clarinets for proper adjustments. *Bocal cork and tenon cork* should be *checked* frequently *on the bassoon.* The pianissimo key pad should also be checked for possible replacement at frequent intervals. *Check* the *corks* between the joints *of* an *oboe* for leakage.

b) Brass—*valves* should be *oiled* at least every two days by wiping the valve dry with a clean cloth and applying a couple of drops of valve oil to each valve. At periods of several weeks or one month, valves should be removed and *valve casings cleaned* by a swab dipped in rubbing alcohol. Each piston should also be cleaned with alcohol. *Threads of valve caps* at top and bottom should be *lubricated* with vaseline at regular intervals so that they will not freeze. All *valve slides* should be *lubricated* with slide cream or vaseline at least once each month so that they remain easily operable. *Trombone slides* should be *lubricated* properly at all times. A small atomizer bottle with water in it can be used to lubricate a cold cream solution which has been placed on the slide. Slide oil is not as successful since it tends to dry up sooner. *Check* and adjust *strings for rotary valves and* for the *trombone f-attachment* at regular intervals. Replace any worn strings so that they do not break in performing situations. *Check water-key corks* for excessive wear or leakage. Check *mouthpieces* for dirt, food particles, and so on, which might distort tone. Also check for dents in the circular end of the mouthpiece which is inserted into the brass instrument. A graduated metal tool which can be used to straighten all sizes of mouthpieces can be made by your Industrial Arts Department. All *brass instruments* should be *cleaned out* at least *once a month* with lukewarm water; do not use hot water—it may damage the lacquer. A "snake" (sometimes called a microcleaner) should be run through smaller horns. "Snakes" are made of flexible metal with small brushes on each end, and are specially made for trumpet, trombone, and so on.

c) Percussion instruments—*Drum heads* should be washed with a damp cloth at regular intervals. Do not saturate the head; only attempt to clean off the excess dirt, which may cause the head to vibrate at less than 100 percent efficiency. *Proper tuning of drum heads* and *adjustments of snare and pedal tensions* will insure good mechanical performance of the snare and the timpani. Be sure *timpani* are *left with* their *pedals partially depressed* to allow the heads to adjust to changes in temperature and humidity.

The *cracking of wooden instruments* is one of the most serious ways damage can occur to your band equipment. Always swab a wooden instrument thoroughly after playing and avoid taking it out in temperatures below 55 degrees since the expansion and contraction of the wooden instrument when it is played in cold temperatures frequently leads to serious cracking. Oil wooden instruments with pure olive oil, which may be purchased at any drug store. Oil both the outside and the bore of the instrument, but avoid getting oil on the pads. Pinning or banding of serious cracks should be done by the professional repairman.

PROVIDING PROPER INSTRUMENT STORAGE

Cabinets should be built or purchased to store all band instruments when they are in the school building. Such storage should include locker areas for personal instruments as well as school-owned instruments. Buying cabinets to house all your band instruments can be an expensive proposition. I elected to build storage according to specifications that were drawn up with regard to space available in my band area and the inventory of band instruments to be stored during an average year. Such cabinets can be built with doors which can be locked, but I found it more convenient to keep the storage area locked or supervised when open and to build storage cabinets without doors. Each segment of the cabinetry was designed for a certain size instrument case, and all lockers were marked with a number.

Figure 1. Instrument Storage Lockers

Students were assigned specific numbers and were required to keep their instruments in these assigned lockers. See Figure 1.

We purchased a percussion center for storage of our smaller drum equipment. The center is kept locked when not in use, can be moved easily on its casters, and is used during performances as a table for small equipment. See Figure 2.

Figure 2. Percussion Center

SETTING UP A REPAIR DEPARTMENT

A repair area can be built into a music area. It can be quite extensive, including several storage cabinets, a large work bench area, drawers for storage of small repair items and tools, and so on. If you do not have a built-in repair area, a smaller work bench area, as shown in Figure 3, can be built by your school maintenance staff. The top of the cabinet can be used as a work bench, and the drawers and cabinet area below can be used to store repair equipment. I have found such a repair cabinet to be quite adequate when built to my specifications to fit into an area of my band room. A repair area of this type is very inexpensive.

Your repair department should have pads available for each woodwind instrument, water-key corks, various thicknesses of sheet cork for woodwind repair, cork grease, key oil, valve oil, slide oil, penetrating oil, bore oil, pure olive oil, various screws for woodwinds, screws for French horn

Figure 3. Work Bench and Repair Cabinet

valves, flat springs, needle springs, assorted micro-cork washers, cymbal thongs, extra snare and batter heads for snare drum, rubber bands, scotch tape, masking tape, pad and cork cement, French horn string, reed string for oboe and bassoon, and reed wire for bassoon.

Your *tools* should include various sizes of screw drivers, a small pair of pliers, a wooden mallet, a rubber mallet, a leak light, a Bunsen burner, cleaning "snakes" for brass instruments, mouthpiece cleaning brushes, a mouthpiece puller, a graduated tool for taking dents out of mouthpieces, a carborundum sharpening stone, double-reed making tools including proper reed knives, a simple vise, and a crochet needle for work with needle springs.

A complete list of tools and supplies may be found on pages 9 and 10 of Erick D. Brand's *Band Instrument Repairing Manual*. Mr. Brand's manual is used by many professional repairmen and is considered one of the best repair manuals available.

LEARNING THE ELEMENTAL BUSINESS OF PROPER EMERGENCY INSTRUMENT REPAIR

The following is a list of possible emergency instrument repairs that you may face:

1) *Pad replacement*—Keys should be removed to properly replace

pads. However, if an emergency exists you may carefully "pop" out a defective pad with a small screwdriver blade and replace the pad without taking keys off. Be careful not to injure the metal or the wood of the instrument. Hold the key down firmly after replacing the pad so that the pad may seat properly before the glue dries.

2) *Cork replacement on tenons* of the clarinet—Clean the tenon thoroughly, cut a piece of cork of the proper thickness needed, glue the cork in place and hold until dry by tightly winding rubber bands around the tenon cork.

3) *Repair of bent bridge and side keys of the clarinet*—Use a dime to gently force the metal back into place. Severe damage should be repaired by the professional.

4) *French horn and trombone string repair on rotary valve*—Memorize the proper winding of the string around screws and posts so that you may change a string quickly when an emergency arises.

5) *Adjustment of flute or oboe adjustment screws*—Check adjustment screws first when a leakage occurs in these instruments. Always carry a small screwdriver to make these emergency adjustments.

6) *Recorking of bassoon bocals*—Choose the proper thickness of cork needed. A cork which is a bit too thick can always be sanded down with fine sand paper to the exact thickness needed for a firm connection after installation on the bocal.

7) *Repair of oboe joint cork*—Oboe joints may be repaired by winding strong thread tightly around the worn cork, building it up so that the joint is tight again. This thread-binding technique will keep the joint tight for a long period of time and prevents the need to replace the cork immediately.

8) *Adjustment of flute head-joint cork*—The position of the flute head-joint cork should be checked at regular intervals. Use the flute cleaning rod to assist you. Place the blunt end of the rod in the open end of the head joint, and adjust the cork to the position where the mark on the rod cuts the tone hole exactly in half transversely.

RECOMMENDING PURCHASE OF
PRIVATE INSTRUMENTS AND MOUTHPIECES

The parents of young music students should always contact the band director before purchasing an instrument. I carefully check any instrument that one of my students is considering purchasing. Such a check-out includes not only a physical check of all parts of the instrument for defects but the playing of the instrument as well, checking all chromatic fingerings throughout its entire playing range. Such a check-out is especially important if the student is buying a used instrument from a private individual.

Any defects should be corrected by the seller or an appropriate adjustment should be made in the selling price of the instrument.

I have selected two or three medium-priced to expensive models of each instrument to recommend to my students. Very rarely can a low-priced instrument be purchased which is not inferior in tone quality, intonation, or workmanship. I played a model of each instrument I selected, checking it for basic tonal quality, intonation, and ease of response. I also selected woodwind and brass mouthpieces in a similar manner, by actually playing each and experiencing the various responses when combined with specific models of instruments. No single woodwind or brass mouthpiece will be satisfactory for all students on a specific instrument. The mouthpiece should be matched to the student's needs both physically and musically. Usually, a mouthpiece which will enlarge and darken the tone quality is advantageous. For example, the trumpet player may use several mouthpieces to create the different tonal requirements of orchestral, band, or jazz performance.

It is advantageous to have all of your players of one particular instrument playing on the same model of instrument or models which match closely in intonation and tonal quality. Similar mouthpieces will also help to develop a section that blends well within itself. Matched sections can overcome most personal differences in tone quality. Sections which are very heterogeneous in regard to the model of instrument usually find it very difficult to blend and to play with acceptable intonation.

Teaching Woodwinds, an excellent 1976 publication of the New York State Education Department Bureau of General Education Curriculum Development, contains fine material and resources relating to the purchasing, maintenance, and repair of instruments and mouthpieces. One of these manuals would be of great value to any band director since it covers very thoroughly every aspect of teaching the woodwind instruments and contains many valuable resources, including books, method books, records, and filmstrips.

LEARNING THE PROS AND CONS OF REEDS

The best method of evaluating reeds is playing them. Many reeds may be satisfactory if they are adjusted by careful shaving with a reed knife. Such adjustments should be made through a combination of your knowledge of reed adjustment and the physical feeling when you play the reed. A reed clipper can be used to prolong the life of a clarinet or saxophone reed which has become too soft on the tip. Oboe and bassoon reeds can be adjusted in a similar manner by cutting off a small portion of the tip of the reed with a sharp reed knife.

Clarinet Reeds

The following characteristics may be helpful in identifying good reeds:

The cane should be a deep yellow in color, with flecks of brown in the bark of the stem (the uncut bottom of the reed). Light or greenish yellow indicates that the cane is either poor in quality or improperly aged.

Small, darker grains should run parallel to the sides of the reed (not diagonally) all the way to the tip. Reeds with brown spots should be avoided.

Reeds made from French cane in a "straight cut" are the best. They have a thickness in the heel of the cut section, an even taper to the tip, a ridge or peak running down the center of the cut portion and tapering off each side, and a decided resistance point beginning approximately ¼"–⅜" back from the tip.

The reed should be perfectly symmetrical in shape and cut so that the entire reed will vibrate in controlled wavelengths, thus producing optimum tone quality and response.[1]

Similar statements can be made about choosing saxophone reeds. Some clarinet or saxophone reeds may not be flat on the back, which results in the reed responding very poorly. This can be corrected by placing the back of the reed on a piece of fine sandpaper that is placed on a piece of glass or an absolutely flat surface. Applying equal pressure on all sides of the reed while lightly sanding it down should result in the back of the reed becoming an evenly flat surface.

Oboe Reeds

Although commercial oboe reeds are available, I have found none to be as successful as reeds made by a professional oboist or reeds made by a student who was taught reed making by a professional player.

The oboist must be a mechanic and should have the following tools and materials to make reeds and adjust them: a scraping knife, a chopping knife (a single-edged razor blade may be used), a sharpening stone, a cutting block or billot, a plaque, a piece of fishskin, oboe reed string, clear nail polish, and a mandrel. The advanced oboist should buy a shaper to shape his own reeds. Eventually this saves money and guarantees that properly shaped cane will be available at all times.

Some of the problems encountered in adjusting oboe reeds and their possible solutions are:

A reed which is too open, too stiff, and therefore hard to play can be improved by scraping the back of it on either side of the spine. This

---

[1] *Teaching Woodwinds* (Albany: The University of the State of New York/ The State Education Department Bureau of General Education Curriculum Development, 1976), p. 55.

will close the reed a bit, and general scraping of the tip and of the thicker area behind the tip will ease resistance as required.

A reed which is too closed can usually be played easily enough, but often suffers from volume limitations or difficulty in low register playing. Trimming about 1 mm. from the tip may help, or—if this is not sufficient—the reed can be opened a little more by *gently* pinching the flat sides of the tube at the winding with a pair of pliers. Inserting a mandrel into the tube before pinching it with pliers will prevent accidental crushing and also help to reshape the tube properly.

A reed which fails to produce a sound although appearing to be intact and in proper adjustment may give evidence of air leaking out between the blades. In this case, a 1½ x ¾-inch piece of fishskin should be wrapped around the bottom of the cane portion of the reed, overlapping the winding. The whole area may be coated with clear nail polish to insure permanent adherence to the reed. . . . debris will accumulate inside and the reed will fail to respond. This material can usually be removed with a thin pipe cleaner, stripped clean of lint and drawn through the reed *from the bottom to the top.*[2]

Use 47 mm. tubes for your reeds. They will produce a 440-A level of intonation if the reed is properly made. Detailed information can be found in *The Art of Oboe Playing* by Sprenkle and Ledet and other resources listed in the selected bibliography at the end of this chapter.

Bassoon Reeds

Although various commercial bassoon reeds are available, I have found none that compare with the reeds made by a professional bassoonist. While adjudicating, I have observed several young bassoonists having satisfactory success with plastic reeds. These should not be used, however, by serious intermediate and advanced students.

Excellent information on selecting and adjusting bassoon reeds can be found in *The Art of Bassoon Playing* by William Spencer. *Teaching Woodwinds* has comprehensive information on reed selection and adjustment on pages 116–123 and includes an explanation of *the crow test* and *the pop test*.

The tools and materials needed to make and adjust bassoon reeds are similar to those used for oboe reeds, with the addition of a reamer and soft brass reed wire.

TEACHING YOUR DOUBLE-REED PLAYERS TO MAKE THEIR OWN REEDS

The most satisfactory solution to the problem of reed making is to have your serious oboists and bassoonists study with a professional player. Un-

---

[2]*Ibid.*, pp. 30–31.

less you are a double-reed player, it is very difficult to teach the art of reed making successfully. If you must assume this burden, refer to such resources as *The Art of Oboe Playing* (Sprenkle and Ledet) and *The Art of Bassoon Playing* (Spencer) or similar resources found in the bibliography at the end of this chapter. A wiser alternative might be to find several commercially made reeds which are reasonably satisfactory and teach your student to adjust them to their own requirements.

DEVELOPING WORKING RELATIONSHIPS WITH INSTRUMENTAL DEALERS, REPAIRMEN AND INDUSTRIAL ARTS PERSONNEL

Three types of individuals are invaluable to the band director in solving the problems of instrument purchase, maintenance, and repair:

1) *The Instrumental Dealer*—A close professional relationship with one or more dealers should assure good instruments, equipment, and supplies being sold to your students at reasonable prices. Small equipment and supplies can be sold to your students during school hours if you have a school store.

2) *The Professional Repairman*—Every music department should have a repairman available for instrument repairs which cannot be handled by the director or other individuals within your school system. Usually a good music dealer will have his own repairman or a source for repairs which may give service in a reasonable length of time (one to two weeks in most cases).

3) *Industrial Arts Personnel*—These individuals are usually talented in some aspect of basic repair, which may make it possible to avoid sending a damaged instrument out for repair. This procedure saves time and money for your music department and your students. Cultivate a close professional relationship with Industrial Arts personnel because their help with emergency repairs can be invaluable.

SELECTED BIBLIOGRAPHY

Artley, Joe, *How to Make Double Reeds for Oboe, English Horn, and Bassoon*. Stamford, Connecticut, Jack Spratt Music Company, 1961.

Bach, Vincent, "How to Choose the Best Mouthpiece Cup," *Selmer Bandwagon*, vol. 14, May, 1966, p. 16.

Brand, Eric D., *Band Instrument Repairing Manual*. Elkhart, Indiana: Eric D. Brand, 1946.

Brilhart, Arnold, "A Mouthpiece Maker Speaks to Teachers," *Selmer Bandwagon*, vol. 14, May, 1966.

Christlieb, Don, *Notes on the Bassoon Reed: Machinery, Measurement Analysis;* rev. ed. Published by the author, 1966.

Eby, W.M., *The Clarinet and Its Care*. New York, Walter Jacobs Company, 1927. (Available from Big Three Music Corporation.)

Farkas, Philip, *The Art of Brass Playing*. Bloomington, Indiana, Brass Publications, 1962.

Farkas, Philip, *The Art of French Horn Playing*. Evanston, Illinois, Summy-Birchard Publishing Company, 1956.

Holdsworth, Frank, "Clarinet Mouthpieces," *Woodwind World*, vol. 13, no. 5, Holiday 1974, pp. 16, 17, 26, 27, 28.

Hovey, Nilo, *Teacher's Guide to the Clarinet*. Elkhart, Indiana, H. & A. Selmer, Inc., 1967.

How to Care for Your Instrument. Elkhart, Indiana, Conn Corporation, n.d.

Kleinhammer, Edward, *The Art of Trombone Playing*. Evanston, Illinois, Summy-Birchard Co., 1962.

Mayer, R. & T. Rohner, *Oboe Reeds: How to Make and Adjust Them*. Evanston, Illinois, The Instrumentalist Co., 1953.

Opperman, Kalmen, *Handbook for Making and Adjusting Single Reeds*. New York, Chappell and Company, 1956.

Proper Selection of Clarinet and Saxophone Mouthpieces, The. Elkhart, Indiana, Conn Corporation, 1965.

Putnik, Edwin, *The Art of Flute Playing*. Evanston, Illinois, Summy-Birchard Company, 1970.

Russell, Myron E., *Oboe Reed Making and Problems of the Oboe Player*. Stamford, Connecticut, Jack Spratt Co., 1963.

Selection and Care of Clarinet and Saxophone Mouthpieces, The. Kenosha, Wisconsin, Leblanc Publications, Inc., n.d.

Spencer, William, *The Art of Bassoon Playing*. Rev. by Frederick A. Mueller. Evanston, Illinois, Summy-Birchard Publishing Company, 1969.

Spratt, Jack, *How to Make Double Reeds*. Stamford, Connecticut, Jack Spratt Co., 1950.

Spratt, Jack, *How to Make Your Own Clarinet Reeds*. Stamford, Connecticut, Spratt Music Publishers, 1956.

Sprenkle, Robert & David Ledet, *The Art of Oboe Playing*. Evanston, Illinois, Summy-Birchard Company, 1961.

Stanley, Burton, "Instrument Repair for the Band Man," (A series), *The New York State School Music News*, April, 1972, p. 36+.

Stanton, Robert, *Oboe Player's Encyclopedia*. Oneonta, New York, Swift-Dorr Publications, n.d.

Stein, Keith, *The Art of Clarinet Playing*. Evanston, Illinois, Summy-Birchard Company, 1958.

Teaching Woodwinds. The University of the State of New York/ The State Education Department Bureau of General Education Curriculum Development/ Albany, 1976.

Teal, Larry, *The Art of Saxophone Playing*. Evanston, Illinois, Summy-Birchard Company, 1963.

Tiede, Clayton H., *The Practical Band Instrument Repair Manual.* Dubuque, Iowa: William C. Brown Company, 1962.

Weerts, Richard, *Developing Individual Skills for the High School Band.* West Nyack, N.Y., Parker Publishing Company, Inc., 1969.

Winter, James H., "The French Horn Mouthpiece," *Woodwind World*, vol. 6, September, 1964, p. 3.

GIVING VOCATIONAL GUIDANCE
TO BAND MEMBERS AND
TRAINING PRACTICE TEACHERS

19

One of the most important and most difficult tasks in music education is the proper preparation of students who are interested in pursuing a career in music. Their long range goals should be discussed and their abilities to succeed realistically evaluated. It is difficult to be objective when recommending a music career to a talented student. Some school systems measure your program's success by how many students you send into music careers, even though employment opportunities in many areas of music are not good at the present time. Current conditions in the public schools not only offer few job openings, but job security for even the best teachers is being constantly threatened by cutbacks in staff and in music programs. Finding job security in any field of performance has always been very difficult. Nevertheless, the challenge of career preparation does exist, and adequate steps should be taken to meet this challenge.

A January 1975 MENC newsletter, *Music Power*, distributed two music career questionnaires, one to music educators and the other to students. Over 90 percent of the educators replied that students were not adequately informed about music careers. Both music educators and students replied that music teachers should be primarily responsible for music career information. The second choice of music educators was a combination of music teachers, guidance counselors, and professional performers. Students listed performers as their second choice.

INFORMING YOUR STUDENTS
ABOUT CAREER OPPORTUNITIES IN MUSIC

These are some of the ways that you can prepare yourself for accomplishing this task:

1) Attend workshops concerning music career information and preparation.

2) Invite people actively involved in music careers to speak to your students.

3) Locate articles written by people in various music careers and make copies of them for your interested students.

4) Use audio-visual aids concerning music careers.

5) Prepare a packet of career information for your students to study.

6) Expose your students to as many relevant outside experiences as possible. These can include all types of performances, a visit to a large music store or a music publishing house, a visit to an institution which actively uses music therapy, a visit to a radio or TV studio.

7) If your students are interested in music education, involve them in as many aspects of your program as possible. This can include teaching younger students, conducting your groups, working with your music library, arranging for the band, repairing instruments, and helping with the business aspects of your program.

8) If students desire to be performers, especially symphony orchestra members, have them study with a professional on their instrument. Encourage them to attend symphony orchestra rehearsals and auditions. If your students are studying with a member of the orchestra, such experiences are not difficult to arrange.

9) Obtain current information from the colleges or universities that your students desire to enter. Students should be informed early in high school as to the prerequisites required and the curriculum they will have to study at the college level in order to reach their tentative goals.

Careers in Music

Some of the many careers possible in the field of music or related fields are listed below:

MUSIC CAREERS

Performance	*Teaching*	*Business*
soloist (popular or concert)	private instruction	music publisher
	elementary schools	agent
clinician	secondary schools	personal manager
small ensemble (concert)	college level	administration
combo	administration or	sales and marketing
symphony orchestra performer	supervision	retail sales (clerk or
	choral director	manager)
symphony orchestra manager or librarian	band director	advertising
	orchestra director	promotion

band (esp. military)
studio orchestra (radio, TV, films)
big band (popular)
conductor
dancer
actor/actress
comedian
impersonator
accompanist

Creative

producer
arranger
composer
songwriter
radio/TV director

stage band director
marching band director
academic music subjects
drama director

Church-related

clergyman
religious education director
organist
choir director

publicity
instrument manufacturing
instrument repair
piano tuning and repair
recording (technical)
music librarian

Medical

occupational therapist
recreational therapist

Commentary

editor
reporter
critic
disc jockey

General information which is dispensed to your students should include:

1) Employment opportunities
2) Security
3) Academic and musical requirements
4) Training needed
5) Salaries
6) Matching career with vocational goals
7) The life style desired and personal goals (Will they be achieved through this career?)

DEVELOPING A MUSIC SEQUENCE AND A SYLLABUS FOR EACH COURSE INVOLVED

All students pursuing a career in music should have the opportunity to study a music-major sequence in high school. This usually includes being a member of one major performing group and taking from one to three years of theory or music history-related courses. Each potential music major should have as much piano background as possible. I encourage my music majors to study piano privately with a professional teacher for up to eight years, even though their major may be a wind instrument. This type of piano background supplies strong preparation for any theory or keyboard courses required at the college level. Many of my best students have passed their college keyboard requirements upon entrance into a music school.

As much vocal experience as possible should also be strongly encouraged. A music major who cannot sight-sing is going to be greatly handicapped in a good music school. We schedule our choruses and bands so that students may be members of both organizations.

The Music Sequence

I have developed and am presently teaching a comprehensive sequence in our school system. It goes beyond the average high school music curriculum in content, but has been well received by both average and superior academic students. Depth of content beyond the teaching outlines is determined by the quality of students in class during a given year.

Each course is set up so that the text and outline are used in lecture and study on Mondays, Tuesdays, and Wednesdays. Thursdays a test is given over material covered during the week. Fridays are used in each subject as enrichment days for music literature listening and student exposure to broadening musical experiences and concepts.

Each of these courses covers all that is outlined in the New York State Syllabus, plus much more in-depth study. Theory I and Theory II are alternated yearly with Comprehensive Foundations of Music, a course combining theory, music literature and a detailed study of forms. All courses are taught from detailed outlines I have developed. A brief outline of the three-course sequence is given below.

I. Theory I

    A. Text—McHose, Allen Irvine, *Basic Principles of the Technique of 18th and 19th Century Composition.* New York, N.Y., Appleton-Century Crofts, Inc., 1951. (out of print)

        1. Two weeks of Elementary Acoustics

        2. Part I—The Elements of Time and Rhythm

            a. Includes study of beat, meter, conducting beat, simple and compound divisions of beat, the tie, syncopation, superimposed backgrounds and superimposed meters, the divided beat, mixed meter, polymeter, and unusual meters.

        3. Part II—The Tonal Elements

            a. Includes study of intervals, the chord, major and minor triads, tonality, nonharmonic tones, diminished triad, classification of root movement, study of triads in tonic , 1st and 2nd classifications, the augmented triad, 3rd and 4th classifications, modulation, and modes.

    B. Study is divided into three parts:

        1. text

        2. rhythmic, melodic, and beginning harmonic dictation

        3. beginning harmony and analytical technique

    C. Also taught are elements of music not included above; e.g., clefs, key signatures, other basic rudiments of music, and a detailed unit in orchestration and bandstration.

II. Theory II

    A. Text—Piston, Walter, *Harmony*. New York, N.Y., W.W. Norton & Company, Inc., 1962.

        1. Includes study of scales and intervals, triads, harmonic progression, tonality, modality, chords of the 6th—the figured bass, the harmonic structure of a phrase, harmonization of a given part, nonharmonic tones, the six-four chord, cadences, harmonic rhythm, modulation, the dominant seventh chord, secondary dominants, irregular resolutions, the diminished seventh chord, the incomplete major ninth, the complete dominant ninth, the sequence, nondominant harmony—seventh, ninth, eleventh and thirteenth chords, the raised supertonic and submediant, the neopolitan sixth, augmented chords, other chromatic chords, extention of tonality.

    B. Study is divided into four parts

        1. text

        2. more advanced rhythmic, melodic, and harmonic dictation

        3. harmonization and beginning composition

        4. orchestration and bandstration

    C. Any elements which might be in New York State Syllabus and not covered above.

III. Comprehensive Foundations of Music

    A. Various texts which are appropriate, including:

        1. Miller, Hugh M., *History of Music*. New York, N.Y., Barnes and Noble Books, 1973.

        2. Copland, Aaron, *What to Listen for in Music*. New York, N.Y., Mentor Books, 1953.

B. A year-long program is divided into two phases:
1. Elements of Music
    a. Tracing the development of rhythm, melody, harmony, and tone quality.
        1) done by periods of music history found below.
2. Introduction to the Structure, Materials, and Music Literature of music
    a. study of form, music literature, and composers by style periods:
        1) Medieval Period (500–1450)
        2) Renaissance Period (1450–1600)
        3) Baroque Period (1600–1750)
        4) Classical Period (1750–1825)
        5) Romantic Period (1825–1900)
        6) Contemporary Period (1900–   )

My music sequence has also included an Instrumental Music Regents Exam, given at the end of each school year to instrumentalists who qualify through participation in New York State School Music Association solo or ensemble competitions. A student successfully passing this exam receives New York State Regents credit for instrumental music for that year. The exam is made up locally and approved by the New York State Board of Regents. It is divided into four parts, each counting 25 percent: 1) performance; 2) elementary music theory learned in instrumental lessons; 3) musical terms; 4) music literature we have studied in band. Study guides covering the material to be tested are supplied to the students several weeks before the exam is given. Regents Applied Music credit is also available to the student studying privately who fulfills practice requirements.

HOW TO WRITE EFFECTIVE RECOMMENDATIONS FOR YOUR STUDENTS

Whether a recommendation is written for college entrance or for a high school experience, such as All-State groups, selection committees are interested not only in musical ability but also in well-rounded, well-disciplined students. Therefore, your recommendation should include the following aspects of the complete student:

1) musical ability and musical accomplishments
2) academic ability and academic accomplishments

3) extra-curricular activities

4) a statement concerning the character of the student

5) special honors received during high school

Most recommendations are best written in short concise statements rather than complete sentences. Many colleges, however, may prefer a formal statement of recommendation written in paragraph form. The following is the general content of a recommendation I wrote recently for a student of mine applying for an All-State group. Names and specific instruments have been deleted. I would use the information given in sentence form for all college recommendations.

> Musical ability and accomplishments: Finest _____ I have had in twenty years of teaching; _____ has studied four years privately with _____ _____ , Principal _____ of the _____ Philharmonic; has studied _____ for a total of seven years; first chair in my concert band since ninth grade; selected through audition for five Area All-State and five All-County instrumental groups; has attained eight 6A ratings in state solo competitions; member of school 6A woodwind quintet for three years; has studied piano privately for seven years, the last three of which have been with State Piano Chairman, _____ _____ ; _____ has received two 6A ratings in State piano solo competition; _____ has completed two years of music theory courses, maintaining an A+ average.
>
> Academic ability and accomplishments: high honor roll academic student; exceptional talents in math, science and creative subjects.
>
> Extra-curricular activities: member of girl's varsity tennis and track teams; active in drama productions and French Club.
>
> Special honors: National Honor Society; International Thespian Society.
>
> Character: Fine young lady in every respect; recommended without reservation.

Your students should be informed at an early age that recommendations must be based upon specific accomplishments. Statements given in a recommendation must be objective since subjective statements, i.e. "Mary is a fine clarinetist" or "John is an excellent academic student," are of little value to the person reading a recommendation. Character statements, however, are usually subjective.

HOW TO TRAIN AND USE PRACTICE-TEACHERS

Working with the college senior who is a Music Education major can be very rewarding. You can give this young teacher the practical experience and knowledge he needs to be well prepared for a teaching career, and at the same time he can bring to your program his experiences and his specific knowledge of his major instrument. Conversely, a candidate who is weak musically or academically or has some serious character flaw can become a very negative experience for your program. If you develop a reputation for giving the student-teacher a strong background and valuable experience, you have an excellent chance of having the cooperating college send their best students to you.

Your basic responsibilities to the practice-teacher are to supply information and opportunities for experience and to evaluate objectively all aspects of his work with you.

Dispensing Information to the Practice-Teacher

Brief your practice-teacher thoroughly on the following:

1) Attitudes and responsibilities of a teacher in your school system and proper staff relations.

2) Routine school procedures: general discipline procedure, student passes of all types, attendance taking, announcements, study hall, detention and other monitoring assignments, chaperoning school events, checking out AV equipment, decorating bulletin boards, and typing and posting instrumental music rotating schedules.

3) Class management and discipline.

4) Proper use of students' personal files; backgrounds of your students which influence teaching success.

5) Use of school machines (duplicating and so on) and audio-visual equipment (movie projectors, overhead projectors, and tape equipment).

6) School library resources.

7) Your music library: repertoire used at various levels, method books used at various levels, solo and ensemble material, and your filing system.

8) Your rehearsal and lesson techniques.

9) Lesson plans and grade book procedures.

10) Basic elements of instrument repair.

11) All-County and All-State participation.

12) Solo and ensemble competitions.

13) Band competitions, including materials to use and proper preparation.

14) Membership in professional groups, such as MENC.

15) Awareness of and familiarity with valuable periodicals such as *The Instrumentalist, Selmer Bandwagon,* and *Music Educators Journal.*

16) Recommend books and any other materials which may be helpful to the student-teacher in his future teaching career. One of the reasons for writing this book was to put materials and ideas in concise form not only for the experienced band director but also for the practice-teacher. Most of the material in this book has been presented to my practice-teachers during their work with me.

17) Let your student-teacher know exactly what you expect of him during his apprenticeship with you. Establish a rapport with him that will insure that your work together progresses smoothly without unnecessary apprehensions or inhibitions in his daily work or adverse reactions to your suggestions and constructive criticism. Your practice-teacher must develop a confidence and a trust in you so that he will freely discuss his problems with you.

Supplying Adequate Experience
for the Practice-Teacher

The practice-teacher should not be "used" to lighten the load of the supervising teacher. All assignments given to him should lead to his becoming a better teacher. Therefore, assignments in his weaker areas of preparation, such as minor instruments, should not be neglected by having him teach his major instrument for the majority of his teaching experience with you. The practice-teacher gains the most by strengthening his weaknesses, not by having his strengths exploited.

Expose the young teacher to every aspect of your teaching assignment. If he has not had adequate college preparation in any phase of the work he hopes to do, it is your responsibility to make him and his college aware of the deficiencies. You may improve the teacher training program of your cooperating college by your objective comments.

You should evaluate your practice-teacher as soon as possible through a comprehensive review of his background in high school and college and in all courses and instruments he has studied, through knowledge of his professional experiences, and through a constant stimulus-response condition between the young teacher and yourself. This can best be accomplished by a long and candid conversation with the practice-teacher immediately after his arrival at your school. Your assignments to the young teacher will at first be determined by his background and later by what you have taught him and expect him to be able to do. If he is a strong student-teacher, he should be able to take over every aspect of your job with some success after his practice-teaching period is concluded.

Schedule your practice-teacher so that he may have experience in the following areas:

1) Opportunities to develop a teaching personality through *personal contact with students* in rehearsals and in the classroom. Development of a good rapport between the practice-teacher and the students is very important.

2) *Teaching in a lesson situation.* Start by having the student teacher teach a part of the complete lesson, and gradually increase his responsibility until he is able to teach the entire lesson.

3) Have the practice-teacher *conduct* a portion of the *band rehearsal* at first. A good place to begin is with the warmup chorale or warmup routine, followed by a march or a similar composition that is easy to conduct with a relatively simple score. All scores should be assigned for study at first so that the student-teacher is not sight-reading on the podium. His inexperience and insecurity could lead to disaster if he is not properly prepared. Gradually expand his responsibility so that he is capable of conducting the entire rehearsal by the end of his practice-teaching experience.

4) Reinforce the practice-teacher's learning experiences by *constant evaluation* of his work, *constructive criticism* in private after each experience, and suggestions on how he may improve.

5) *Assign* some *long term projects* to the practice-teacher. He may have the complete responsibility for introducing, rehearsing, and ultimately performing a chosen number in a formal concert. Giving him a few classes which he will meet each week for several weeks gives him the opportunity to measure the progress these students make under his guidance. This is one area where the young teacher's major instrument could be utilized, since you are usually assured that his teaching will be successful in his major.

6) During the last week of the practice-teacher's work with you, have him take over the entire work load that you normally carry (if this is feasible). Under these circumstances, you can not only evaluate whether your practice-teacher is ready to assume a teaching position of his own but the practice-teacher can realistically measure his own preparation and his adaptability to the job situation.

7) In concert situations do not substitute a practice-teacher's ability to perform on his major instrument for conducting experience. If

the young musician is going to be a teacher, using his established abilities on his major instrument in place of allowing him to gain experience in minor areas can lead to short-term false security concerning his future. He will not be judged in a teaching situation on how he performs on his major instrument, but on how his students perform.

Meeting the Evaluation Responsibilities of Practice-Teacher Supervision

My practice-teachers were in residence at our school for 40 complete school days. During that time they were exposed to all aspects and all levels of the instrumental program. They were required by their college to have a detailed set of lesson plans or assignments for each week of work. I met with the practice-teachers at regular intervals to set up their schedules one week in advance of the work to be done.

The supervising teacher's responsibilities to the practice-teacher go beyond the classroom. In addition to meeting with the college supervisor several times during the practice-teaching period, the following three reports are required.

1) A weekly written report to the student's college supervisor. The following is an example of this report.*

STATE UNIVERSITY COLLEGE

FREDONIA, NEW YORK 14063

NAME OF STUDENT ....   REPORT DATE ....

SCHOOL ....   DATES ABSENT ....

EVALUATED BY ....

Evaluate by selecting the appropriate letter for each item. Indicate "not observed" or "does not apply" by leaving the evaluation space blank.

E—Excellent   S—Satisfactory   I—Improving   N—Needs Improvement

MUSICIANSHIP   COMMENTS

1. General musicianship
2. Use of singing voice
3. Use of piano

---

*Weekly Practice—Teacher Report (State University College, Fredonia, New York). Reproduced by permission.

	4. Conducting ability
	5. Skill in sight reading
	6. Use of applied major
	7. Use of minor instruments

TEACHING ACTIVITIES

	1. Preparation of lessons
	2. Class control and management
	3. Instructional skills
	4. Provides for needs of students
	5. Use of English (include spelling)
	6. General informational background
	7. Ability to adapt materials and methods to appropriate levels
	8. Use of audio-visual aids
	9. Participation in special programs

PERSONAL QUALITIES

	1. General appearance
	2. Emotional stability
	3. Poise and self control
	4. Sense of humor
	5. Judgment and tact
	6. Health and physical stamina
	7. Initiative and resourcefulness
	8. Spontaneity
	9. Dependability
	10. Speech
	11. Promptness
	12. Reaction to criticism

This copy to be mailed each Friday to the Student's College Supervisor

2) A final practice-teaching report on the student's progress while working with you, including his teaching assignments, his attendance, your evaluation of his teaching ability, a recommendation of the type of position in which he would be most successful, and a summary of his strengths and weaknesses as a future professional, as a musician, as a teacher, and as a person.

3) A letter of recommendation to the college placement office, including your professional relationship with the student, his musical ability, his academic ability, his ability to plan, organize and pre-

sent lessons, his personal qualities, and your general evaluation of him and his potential.

A well-organized college music department will send you a detailed set of instructions and suggestions when working with their student-teachers. I have had a long and successful relationship with the State University College, Fredonia, New York, and am indebted to their staff for the experiences in student-teacher supervision, which are the basis for much of the material found in this chapter.

SELECTED BIBLIOGRAPHY

Csida, Joseph. *The Music/Record Career Handbook*. First Place Music Publishers, Studio City, California, 1973.

Music: A Teaching Career. (incl. filmstrip) Music Educators National Conference, Washington, D.C., 1969.

Teacher Education in Music. Music Educators National Conference, Washington, D.C., 1970.

Pamphlets

"A Career in Music Education." Music Educators National Conference, Washington, D.C., 1965.

"Careers in Music." Music Educators National Conference, Washington, D.C., 1970.

USEFUL AIDS
AND GUIDELINES FOR
THE INSTRUMENTAL TEACHER

20

UTILIZING CONDUCTING TIPS,
SCORE STUDY AND READING TIPS

Conducting is an art in itself. The conductor should develop a "feel" for each composition he may conduct, but he should always stay close to a basic conducting beat pattern. Conducting is much like improvisation; the performer often sticks close to the melody and follows the harmonic background, but he has the freedom to be creative. As the interpretation of each conductor will vary on any given composition, your appearance when you conduct will be different from any other conductor when conducting the same composition.

Conducting Tips

Choose conducting patterns which esthetically satisfy you as the conducting performer and then train your students to produce their musical interpretation from their visual understanding of your conducting techniques.

1) The differences between *staccato and legato* conducting *patterns* should be just as contrasted as the sounds produced when such marks are encountered. The smoothness of the conductor's beat should match the smoothness of the sound he wants produced.

2) *Dynamic nuances* should be produced in a similar manner, the beat becoming larger as the intensity increases.

3) Rapid *tempos* call for smaller beat patterns, just as slow tempos will require larger beat patterns. Any good conducting text will stress matching the size of the beat pattern with the type of sound you desire from your group.

4) *Using rubato*, whether or not it is indicated by the composer, leads

312

to more expressive playing by your students when individual notes must be stressed or when phrases must vary in tempo to create expressive playing.

5) *Spacing or lifting between notes*, which may be necessary in slower marcato playing, can also be indicated by your hand motion when conducting.

6) *Accents* can be effectively drawn from your group when you use accents in your conducting beat.

Conducting techniques can be developed by observation and by reading good conducting texts and articles. But I have discovered that developing an esthetic feeling for each musical phrase performed and then re-creating this feeling through my conducting in any manner which brings effective results from my group is the best method of producing very musical performances.

Score Study

Use the following steps in preparing a score for performance or for detailed study:

1) If you have a well-developed band program, your band should sight read well. I *sight read a new score with* my *band* before I do any outside study of the score. This not only is good experience for the conductor but also tests your band's ability to sight read when the conductor is sight reading. Such sight reading experiences occur in certain types of band competitions when neither you nor your band may have the opportunity to see a piece of music before you play it.

2) *Mark* all *key changes in red.*

3) *Circle all dynamic markings in red* as they occur. Mark the dynamics in your full score in two or three places, one at the top, one in the middle, and one at the bottom of the page.

4) *Mark all tempos and tempo changes in red*, as above. Include indications of possible divided beat and so on. Be sure your band members mark their parts in the same manner so that they are completely prepared for an abrupt change in your beat pattern.

5) *Mark* all *important entrances* (especially those that must be cued) *in red*, using one of the following signs: $<$; $($; $\downarrow$; $[$. Like signs are used for similar entrances occurring at the same time. These four signs are alternated in whatever manner is necessary to maintain clarity in your score marking.

Reading Tips

The following tips will improve the reading of both the conductor and his band members:

1) *Approach* the *reading of music as a language*; treat notes as letters, small patterns of a few notes as words, and patterns extending over several

beats as phrases. Work toward the reading of all music by phrases, grasping several beats at each glance. Many students are slow in reading music because they read every note individually or read very few notes with each glance. I believe that the technique which makes a person a rapid reader of literature with a high degree of comprehension is very similar to the technique which should be used to teach people to read music more rapidly and more accurately.

2) *Know your technique.* The earlier a student learns the many types of scales, arpeggios, scales by thirds, and rhythmic patterns he will encounter, the sooner he will become a fine reader of music. His training should also include visual comprehension of melodic and harmonic patterns, making it possible for him to read patterns rather than individual notes. Such reading skill is developed through a combination of mental comprehension and physical practice. If the fingers and the embouchure will not cover the required technique rapidly enough, no degree of mental comprehension will result in a strong reader. Conversely, no degree of physical dexterity will result in a good reader without a high degree of mental comprehension. Techniques to be mastered should include: major scales; three forms of minor scales; modes; major, minor, diminished, and augmented triads; dominant and diminished seventh chords; the chromatic scale; and whole tone scales.

3) *Transposition* to several different keys *by clef or interval* will improve reading ability. This procedure tends to free the individual from many inhibitions which may block the mind from reading exact notes as printed, and it creates a mental flexibility not developed without using transposition techniques.

4) *Improvisation* can also be used as a tool in developing better reading skills. This technique develops mental flexibility and actively utilizes scale and chord knowledge and skills.

5) Use hymns and Bach chorales to *develop vertical reading* as a conducting skill. Playing this type of material on piano or organ will develop fundamental skills in vertical score reading.

6) *Sight read* at every opportunity. Nothing seems to develop reading skills faster than active daily sight reading.

7) *Exactness should be a primary goal* in training the young player to read. Articulation and length of note values should be strictly taught. Beginning with his first lesson, the student should be taught to play rhythmic patterns exactly, using the foot to count during lessons and practice. Inexact teaching or learning of rhythmic values invariably leads to poor sight reading ability in the student's future.

USING AUDIO-VISUAL EQUIPMENT
TO DEVELOP YOUR BAND

The following audio-visual equipment can be used in your work with students:

1) *Tuners*—An audio and a visual tuner should be available. I tune my audio tuner to 440-A and then tune the visual tuner to the audio tuner. The student can choose to use the audio or the visual tuner to check his intonation. The visual tuner can be used to check every chromatic pitch on any instrument, but the audio tuner is usually limited to Concert B-flat and Concert A.

2) *Television video tapes*—Video tapes are especially helpful if you want your band to see themselves in rehearsal or performance. Many posture problems can be pointed out and corrected in this manner. In these days of television domination it may be more successful to teach with video tape and sound than to try to correct problems by sound alone. When the students can see as well as hear themselves they concentrate more on the replay of their performance. If sound on the video tape is not satisfactory, you can use a good tape recorder which is synchronized to the video tape picture. Video tapes are exceptionally valuable when you are working with a marching band.

3) Use an *electric metronome* whenever possible for your students' study of tempo. Caution the students that the electric metronome is fragile, and that it must be treated with care. Metronomes are excellent for setting tempos, but they can be restrictive to esthetic playing if complete tempo inflexibility is created. However, a student with a weak sense of rhythm may benefit greatly by considerable practice with a metronome.

4) Every band area should have a good *tape recorder* and/or *cassette recorder* available to record concerts, rehearsals, lessons, solos, and ensembles. The recording of rehearsals tends to improve the attentiveness of your students during subsequent rehearsals if you do not record too frequently. If you do, it will destroy the uniqueness of a recorded rehearsal or lesson and greatly reduce the psychological advantage of recording. Be sure you requisition an adequate supply of tapes each year. Tapes used by the general education areas of a school are usually made for voice recording and create very poor music reproduction.

USING PROFESSIONAL PUBLICATIONS
AND RECORDS IN YOUR TEACHING

Some of the publications which have been very helpful are:

High Fidelity and Musical America. ABC Leisure Magazines, Inc., The Publish-House, Great Barrington, Massachusetts.

The Instrumentalist. The Instrumentalist Co., 1418 Lake St., Evanston, Illinois.

Ludwig Drummer. Ludwig Drum Company, 1728 North Damen Avenue., Chicago, Illinois.

Music Educators Journal. Music Educators National Conference, Reston, Virginia.

New York Times (Sunday Edition). New York, New York.

Opera News. Metropolitan Opera Guild, 1865 Broadway, New York, New York.

Selmer Bandwagon. Selmer, Elkhart, Indiana.

Woodwind World. Swift-Dorr Publications, Inc., 17 Suncrest Terrace, Oneonta, New York.

Some school systems will furnish subscriptions to you through annual requisitions if the magazines are kept in the band area and are available for student use. I receive several of those listed through annual school period-ical requisitions, including *The Instrumentalist* and *Opera News.* Informa-tional periodicals, such as *Conn Chord* or *Selmer Bandwagon,* may be obtained through local music dealers or directly from the music company involved.

I post several pages from the Sunday Edition of the *New York Times* on my band bulletin board each week. This gives my students the oppor-tunity to learn what is being currently performed in New York City. Many times they see compositions listed which we are studying or have recently performed, especially compositions from Broadway musicals. Such expo-sure makes my teaching of such compositions more meaningful.

Periodicals such as those listed give my students current information on compositions, composers, performers, and recordings.

Using Recordings in Your Teaching

Although live performance is always the best teacher, records may be successfully used if live performers are not available. In addition to the obvious sources for recordings, most music companies advertise recordings which can be valuable in the teaching of specific instruments. A record library of this type of teaching aid should be developed as part of the band library. Some sources for recordings are:

1) Accompaniments Unlimited, Inc., Grosse Pointe Woods, Michi-gan, 48236—A source for tape recordings of piano accompani-ments to instrumental and vocal solos. These are valuable if you do not have strong accompanists available, and your soloists are required to be accompanied.

2) Crest LPs from the Conn Corporation, 1101 East Beardsley Street, Elkhart, Indiana 46514.

3) Coronet label, Coronet Recording Co., 4971 North High Street, Columbus, Ohio—various recordings.

4) Golden Crest Recital Series.

5) Lanier Records and Selmer Educational Recordings, Selmer Di-

vision of the Magnavox Company, Box 310, Elkhart, Indiana 46514.

6) Mark Educational Recordings, Inc., 4249 Cameron Road, Buffalo, New York 14221. A series of valuable recordings for teaching, including solo recitals on most band instruments.

7) Musical Heritage Society, Inc., 1991 Broadway, New York, New York 10023.

8) Music Minus One Recordings, 43 West 61st Street, New York, New York 10023. These recorded accompaniments for instrumentalists and vocalists include: band or orchestra accompaniments minus a soloist, woodwind quintets minus one of their members, and solos with piano accompaniment minus the soloist.

9) Schwann Artist Issue Catalogue, W. Schwann, Inc., 137 Newbury Street, Boston, Massachusetts 02116.

10) Zalo Publications, P.O. Box 913, Bloomington, Indiana 47401.

The following is a brief list of the many instrumental recordings which may be of value in your teaching of band students, and especially in your preparation of soloists and small ensembles:

Flute

"A Baroque Recital," James Pellerite, flutist, Wallace Hornibrook, harpsichord. Coronet S 1505.

"Flute Contest Music," Charles DeLaney, flutist. Selmer No. 2900 and No. 2942.

"The Flute Family," Harry Moskovitz, flutist. Mark Educational Recording MRS23 396.

"Flute Solos with Band," James Pellerite, flutist, Indiana University Wind Ensemble. Coronet S 1724.

"Flutists' Showcase." Golden Crest Record CR 4020.

"James Pellerite Flute Recital," James Pellerite, flutist, Ashley Miller, pianist. Golden Crest RE-7010.

"James Pellerite Plays Flute." Coronet LP 1291 (Zalo Publications).

"A Musical Soiree at the Court of Sans-Souci," Jean-Pierre Rampal, flutist, Jacques Roussel, Orchestre Musica Antiqua. Mercury SR 90408.

"Music for the Flute," William Kincaid, flutist. Columbia LP-ML 4339.

"Sonatas and Fantasies for Flute," Jean-Pierre Rampal, flutist. Epic BC 1299.

"Twentieth Century Music for Flute," Jean-Pierre Rampal, flutist. Musical Heritage Society MHS 906.

"William Kincaid Plays the Flute," Award Artist Series AAS-705 and AAS-706.

Oboe

"Art of the Oboe," Marcel Tabuteau, oboist. Coronet ST 1717.

"The Baroque Oboe," Harold Gomberg, oboist, Seiji Ozawa, Columbia Chamber Orchestra. Columbia MS 6832.

"Favorite Baroque Oboe Concertos," Pierre Pierlot, oboist. Victrola VICS-1691.

"Mozart Oboe Concerto," John DeLancie, oboist. Columbia K 314.

"Oboe Recital," Arno Mariotti, oboist. Golden Crest Recital Series RE 7027.

"Recital Music for the Oboe," Donald Jaeger, oboist. Mark Educational Recordings.

"Wayne Rapier Plays Oboe." Coronet S 1409.

Bassoon

"The Baroque Bassoon," Robert Thompson, bassoon, Thomas Trobaugh, harpsichord. The Musical Heritage Society MHS 1853.

"Concerto in B♭, K. 191" (W.A. Mozart), Leonard Sharrow, bassoon. RCA-Victor LM-1030.

"Leonard Sharrow Plays Bassoon." Coronet LP #1294.

"Recital Music for Bassoon," Robert Quayle, bassoon, James Staples, piano. Mark Educational Recording MRS 32286.

Clarinet

"The Capitol University Clarinet Choir," David Hite, conductor. Selmer No. 4490.

"Clarinet Contest Music," Donald E. McGinnis, clarinet. Selmer No. 2944.

"Contest Solos for the Clarinet Family," Donald E. McCathren, clarinet, Alfred Reed, contrabass clarinet. Selmer Educational Recording.

"Mozart Concerto for Clarinet and Orchestra, in A, K. 622; Clarinet Quintet in A, K. 581," Benny Goodman, clarinet, Boston Symphony Orchestra, Charles Munch, conductor. RCA Victor LM 2073.

"Music for Clarinet Choir," State University College at Fredonia, New York Clarinet Choir. Mark Educational Recording MES 22085.

"New Directions for Woodwind Choir," Bundy Woodwind Ensemble, Nilo Hovey, conducting. Selmer No. 4404.

"Recital Music for Clarinet," William Willett, clarinet. Mark Educational Recording MRS 32638.

"Robert McGinnis Plays the Clarinet." Award Artist Series AAS33-702.

Saxophone

"American Music," Donald Sinta, alto saxophone. Mark Educational Recording MRS 22868.

"A Classical Recital on the Saxophone," Sigurd Rascher, saxophone. Concert Hall Society #1156.

"Contest Music for Saxophone," Fred Hemke, saxophone. Selmer No. 4150.

"Eugene Rousseau Plays Saxophone." Coronet LP 1292.

"Eugene Rousseau—The Virtuoso Saxophone." Coronet LP 1601.

"Marcel Mule Saxophone Recital." Selmer Division of Magnavox Company.

"Paul Brodie, Saxophone." Golden Crest Recital Series RE 7028.

"Sigurd Rascher Plays the Saxophone." Award Artist Series AAS-703.

Woodwind Quintet

"Boston Woodwind Quintet." Boston #B-407.

"The Philadelphia Woodwind Quintet." Columbia ML 5093.

Cornet and Trumpet

"The Art of the Baroque Trumpet," Edward Tarr and Robert Bodenroder, trumpets. Nonesuch H-71217.

"Baroque Masterpieces for Trumpet and Organ," Edward Tarr, trumpet, George Kent, organ. Nonesuch H-71279.

"Baroque Trumpet Concerti," Maurice Andre, trumpet, Chamber Orchestra of the North German Radio, Gabor Otvos, conductor. Turnabout Vox TV-S 34529.

"Concerto for Trumpet in E-flat" (Haydn), Helmut Wobitsch, trumpet, Orchestra of the Vienna State Opera, Anton Heiller, conductor. Haydn Society HSLP-1038.

"The Contemporary Trumpet," Thomas Stevens, trumpet. Avant AV 1003.

"Leonard Smith Plays the Cornet." Award Artist Series AAS-701.

"Music for Trumpet and Orchestra," Roger Voisin, trumpet. Kapp #KS 3383 and #KS 3384.

"Trumpet Concertos," Edward Tarr, trumpet. Nonesuch H-71270.

"Trumpet Solos," Jack Hyatt, trumpet. Coronet LP #1246.

French Horn

"The Art of Dennis Brain." Seraphim Record #60040.

"The Art of Dennis Brain, Vol. 2." Seraphim Record #60073.

"Concerto for Horn and Orchestra" (Hindemith), Dennis Brain, horn, The Philharmonia Orchestra, Paul Hindemith, conductor. Time-Life records "The Music of Today" STL3-145.

"French Horn Solos," Philip Farkas, French horn. Coronet LP #1293.

"Horn Concerto No. 1 in E-flat, Op. 11" (R. Strauss), Mason Jones, soloist, The Philadelphia Orchestra, Eugene Ormandy, conductor. Columbia M 32233.

"James Chambers Plays the French Horn." Award Artist Series AAS 704.

"John Barrows, French Horn." Golden Crest #7002.

"Mozart: The Four Horn Concertos," Mason Jones, soloist, Philadelphia Orchestra, Eugene Ormandy, conductor. Columbia MS 6785.

"Music for Horns," Horn Club of Los Angeles. Seraphim S-60095.

Trombone

"Davis Shuman, Trombone," with WQXR Strings. Golden Crest Record # RE 7011.

"John Swallow, Trombone, and Harriet Wingreen, Piano." Golden Crest Record # RE 7015.

Baritone

"Leonard Falcone and His Baritone." Golden Crest Record # RE 7001.

"Leonard Falcone and His Baritone," Volume II. Golden Crest Record # RE 7016.

Tuba

"Bill Bell and His Tuba." Golden Crest Record CR 4027.

"Harvey Phillips, Tuba." Golden Crest Record # 7006.

"Peter Popiel, Tuba, and Henry Fuchs, Piano." Mark Educational Recording MRS 28437.

"Tuba Solos," Rex Conner, tuba. Coronet LP #1259.

Percussion

"Ithaca Percussion Ensemble." Golden Crest #4016.

"Percussion Music," Saul Feldstein, percussionist. Golden Crest #CR-1005.

"Ruffles and Flourishes," Eastman Symphonic Wind Ensemble, Frederick Fennell, conductor. Mercury #50112.

"The 26 Standard American Drum Rudiments and Selected Solos," Frank Arsenault, percussionist. Ludwig Drum Company, Chicago, Illinois.

Brass Ensemble

"Gabrieli," The Philadelphia Brass Ensemble, The Cleveland Brass Ensemble, and the Chicago Brass Ensemble. Columbia MS 7209.

"The Glorious Sound of Brass," The Philadelphia Brass Ensemble. MS 6941.

"The Los Angeles Brass Society." Avant AV 1001.

"The Magnificent Sound of Baroque Brass," London Festival Brass Ensemble. London SPC 21087.

"Music for Organ, Brass and Percussion," E. Power Biggs, organ, The Columbia Brass and Percussion Ensemble, Maurice Peress, conductor. Columbia M 31193.

"The Pacific Brass Quintet." Avant AV 1004.

"The Venetian Brass Album," Members of the Los Angeles Philharmonic Orchestra and the San Francisco Symphony Orchestra. Avant AV 1007.

Miscellaneous Ensemble Recordings

"The Chamber Music Society of Lincoln Center," Charles Wadsworth, Artistic Director. Elliott Carter: "Eight Études for Woodwind Quartet," Paula Robison, flute; Leonard Arner, oboe; Gervase de Peyer, clarinet; Loren Glickman, bassoon. Robert Schumann: "Fantasy Pieces for Clarinet and Piano, Op. 73," Gervase de Peyer, clarinet. The Classics Record Library SQL 5707-02.

"First-Chair Encores Volume 2," Eugene Ormandy and the Philadelphia Orchestra. Columbia MS 6977.

Saint-Saens "Septet in E-flat major, opus 65, for trumpet, string quartet, bass and piano," and Poulenc "Sonata for trumpet, trombone and horn," Harry Glantz, trumpet; Gordon Pulis, trombone; Arthur Berv, horn. Stradivari Records STR 605.

Telemann—"4 Concertos for Diverse Solo Instruments," "First-Chair Soloists," The Philadelphia Orchestra, Eugene Ormandy, conductor. RCA LSC-3057.

"20th Century Music for Winds." Paul Hindemith: "Konzertmusik for Piano, Brass and Two Harps, Op. 49"; Igor Stravinsky: "Octet for Winds"; Darius Milhaud: "Symphony No. 5 for 10 Wind Instruments." Chamber Harmony Ensemble, Prague, Libor Pesek, conductor. Parliament PLPS 608.

Band Recordings

"American Concert Band Masterpieces," Frederick Fennell, Eastman Symphonic Wind Ensemble. Mercury MG 50079.

"British Band Classics," Frederick Fennell, Eastman Symphonic Wind Ensemble. Mercury MG 50088.

"Concert Music for Strings and Brass" and "Symphony in B-Flat for Concert Band" (Hindemith), The Philharmonia Orchestra, Paul Hindemith, conductor. Seraphim 60005.

"La Fiesta Mexicana," Frederick Fennell, Eastman Symphonic Wind Ensemble. Mercury MG 50084.

"Wagner for Band," Frederick Fennell, Eastman Wind Ensemble. Mercury MG 50276.

"Winds in Hi-Fi," Frederick Fennell, Eastman Wind Ensemble. Mercury MG 50173.

In addition to the many sources for discovering new recordings, periodicals such as *The Instrumentalist* have monthly reviews of recordings which may be of interest to the band director.

APPENDIX A

SELECTED METHOD BOOKS, ETUDES, AND SUPPLEMENTARY MATERIALS

Flute

Elementary

Eck	*Eck Method for Flute*	Belwin-Mills
Endresen	*Supplementary Studies*	Rubank
Gekeler-Hovey	*Belwin Flute Method, Book One*	Belwin
Gekeler-Hovey	*Belwin Flute Method, Book Two*	Belwin
Melnik-James	*Universal Fundamental Method*	Universal
Moyse	*Forty Little Pieces in Progressive Order for Beginner Flutists (piano accompaniment)*	G. Schirmer
Pares-Whistler	*Pares Scales for Flute or Piccolo*	Rubank

Intermediate

Andersen	*Eighteen Studies for the Flute, Op. 41*	G. Schirmer
Berbiguier-Barrere	*Eighteen Exercises and Etudes for the Flute*	G. Schirmer
Cavally (revised by)	*Melodious & Progressive Studies, Book I*	Southern
Eck	*Flute Trills*	Belwin
Gekeler-Hovey	*Belwin Flute Method, Books Two and Three*	Belwin
Koehler	*35 Exercises for Flute, Opus 33, Book 1*	Carl Fischer
Moyse	*24 Short Melodious Studies with Variations*	Belwin
Moyse	*24 Small Melodious Studies*	Leduc
Skornicka-Petersen	*Rubank Intermediate Method*	Rubank
Soussmann-Popp	*Complete Method for the Flute, Part II*	Carl Fischer
Voxman-Gower	*Rubank Advanced Method, Vol. I*	Rubank
Voxman	*Selected Duets for Flute, Volume I*	Rubank

Advanced

Altes	*26 Selected Studies for Flute*	G. Schirmer
Andersen	*24 Progressive Studies for Flute, Op. 33*	Southern
Andersen-Barrere	*18 Studies for the Flute, Opus 41*	G. Schirmer
Andersen-Cavally	*24 Instructive Studies for Flute, Op. 30*	Southern
Andersen-Wummer	*24 Studies, Opus 15, for Solo Flute*	International
Andraud	*24 Flute Concert Studies*	Southern
Cavally (revised by)	*Melodious and Progressive Studies for Flute, Books II and III*	Southern
Cavally (revised by)	*24 Short Concert Pieces for Flute and Piano*	Southern
Demersseman-Moyse	*Cinquante Etudes Melodiques, Op. 4*	Leduc
Koehler	*35 Exercises for Flute, Opus 33, Books 2 & 3*	Carl Fischer
Leeuwen-Andraud	*The Modern Flutist*	Southern
Moyse	*Vingt-Quatre Petites Etudes Melodiques*	Leduc
Soussmann-Popp	*Complete Method for the Flute, Part III*	Carl Fischer
Voxman	*Rubank Advanced Method, Vol. II*	Rubank
Voxman (editor)	*Selected Duets for Flute, Vol. II*	Rubank
Voxman	*Selected Studies for Flute*	Rubank
Wummer	*Twelve Daily Exercises for Flute*	Boston Music Co.

Oboe

Elementary

Gekeler	*First Book of Practical Studies for Oboe*	Belwin
Gekeler	*Gekeler Method for Oboe, Book I*	Belwin-Mills
Gekeler-Hovey	*Belwin Oboe Method, Book One*	Belwin
Hovey	*Rubank Elementary Method, Oboe*	Rubank

Intermediate

Barrett	*The Barrett Oboe Method*	Pepper (source)
Gekeler	*Gekeler Method for Oboe, Books II and III*	Belwin
Gekeler	*Second Book of Practical Studies for Oboe*	Belwin
Gekeler-Hovey	*Belwin Oboe Method, Books Two and Three*	Belwin
Pares-Whistler	*Pares Scales for Oboe*	Rubank

Skornicka-Koebner	*Rubank Intermediate Method for Oboe*	Rubank

Advanced

Andraud	*Practical and Progressive Oboe Method*	Southern
Andraud	*Vade-Mecum*	Southern
Barret	*Fifteen Grand Studies for Oboe* (Optional bassoon accompaniment)	Boosey & Hawkes
Bassi	*27 Virtuoso Studies for Oboe*	Carl Fischer
Ferling-Andraud	*48 Famous Studies for Oboe or Saxophone*	Southern
Gillet	*Studies for the Advanced Teaching of the Oboe*	Leduc
Labate	*Etudes and Scales for Advanced Oboists*	Carl Fischer
Lamotte	*Eighteen Etudes for Oboe*	Presser
Luft	*Twenty-Four Etudes in Duet Form for Two Saxophones or Oboes*	Carl Fischer
Tabate	*16 Daily Exercises for Oboe*	Carl Fischer
Voxman	*Selected Studies for Oboe*	Rubank
Voxman-Gower	*Rubank Advanced Method, Vol. I & II*	Rubank

Transfer Method for Beginners

Fitch	*The Study of the Oboe*	George Wahr

Bassoon

Elementary

Gekeler-Hovey	*Belwin Bassoon Method, Book One*	Belwin
Lentz	*Lentz Method for Bassoon, Book One*	Belwin
McDowell-Hovey	*First Book of Practical Studies for Bassoon*	Belwin
Skornicka	*Rubank Elementary Method, Bassoon*	Rubank

Intermediate

Gekeler-Hovey	*Belwin Bassoon Method, Book Two*	Belwin
McDowell-Hovey	*Second Book of Practical Studies for Bassoon*	Belwin
Voxman	*Rubank Intermediate Method, Bassoon*	Rubank
Voxman-Gower	*Rubank Advanced Method, Vol. I*	Rubank

Advanced

Collins	*Jancourt Bassoon Studies*	Belwin
Gambaro-Kovar	*18 Studies for Bassoon*	International
Gekeler-Hovey	*Belwin Bassoon Method, Book Three*	Belwin
Kopprasch-Kovar	*60 Studies for Bassoon* (2 volumes)	International
Kovar	*24 Daily Exercises for Bassoon*	Kovar
Lee	*Forty Progressive Etudes, Book I*	Carl Fischer
Milde	*Concert Studies, Books I & II*	Cundy-Bettoney
Milde	*25 Studies in All Keys*	Cundy-Bettoney
Orefici	*Studi Melodici per Fagotto* (2 volumes)	Leduc
Slama	*66 Etudes*	Carl Fischer
Vaulet	*20 Studies for Bassoon*	Rubank
Weissenborn	*Bassoon Studies, Opus 8, Volume Two*	Carl Fischer
Weissenborn	*Practical Method for the Bassoon*	Carl Fischer

Clarinet

Elementary

DeCaprio	*Beginning Method for Clarinet*	Remick
Hendrickson	*Hendrickson Method for Clarinet, Book One*	Belwin
Pease	*Universal Fundamental Method for the Clarinet*	Universal
Waln	*Beginning Method for Clarinet*	Belwin-Mills

Intermediate

Cailliet	*Cailliet Clarinet Studies*	Belwin
Endresen	*Supplementary Studies for Clarinet*	Rubank
Hendrickson	*Hendrickson Method for Clarinet, Book Two*	Belwin-Mills
Hovey	*First Book of Practical Studies for Clarinet*	Belwin-Mills
Hovey	*Second Book of Practical Studies for Clarinet*	Belwin-Mills
Hovey	*Section Studies for B♭ Clarinets*	Belwin
Klose-Bellison	*Celebrated Method for the Clarinet, Part I*	Carl Fischer
Langenus	*Complete Method for the Boehm Clarinet, Book I*	Carl Fischer
Lazarus-Langenus	*Modern Method for Clarinet, Part I*	Cundy-Bettoney
LoPresti	*20 Melodic Studies for Clarinet*	Luverne
Pares-Whistler	*Pares Scales for Clarinet*	Rubank

Pease	*Universal's Follow-Up Method for the Clarinet*	Universal
Skornicka-Miller	*Rubank Intermediate Method, Clarinet*	Rubank
Voxman	*Selected Duets for Clarinet, Volume I*	Rubank
Voxman-Gower	*Rubank Advanced Method, Clarinet, Vol. I*	Rubank
Waln	*Melodious Etudes and Chord Studies*	Kjos

Advanced

Bitsch	*Twelve Rhythmical Studies for Clarinet*	Leduc
Cavallini	*Thirty Caprices for the Clarinet*	Carl Fischer
Giampieri	*Klose' Methodo Completo*	Ricordi
Jean-Jean	*18 Etudes for the Clarinet*	Alfred
Jean-Jean	*Etudes Progressives et Melodiques*	Leduc
Klose-Bellison	*Celebrated Method for the Clarinet Part II*	Carl Fischer
Kroepsch-Bellison	*416 Progressive Daily Studies*	Carl Fischer
Langenus	*Complete Method for the Boehm Clarinet, Parts II* and *III*	Carl Fischer
Lazarus-Bellison	*Method for Clarinet, Part III*	Carl Fischer
Lazarus-Langenus	*Modern Method for Clarinet, Parts II & III*	Cundy-Bettoney
Rode-Rose	*20 Grand Etudes*	M. Baron
Rose	*Forty Studies for the Clarinet* (two books)	Carl Fischer
Rose	*Thirty-Two Etudes for Clarinet*	Carl Fischer
Voxman (ed.)	*Classical Studies for Clarinet*	Rubank
Voxman-Gower	*Rubank Advanced Method, Clarinet, Vol. II*	Rubank
Voxman (ed.)	*Selected Duets for Clarinet, Vol. II*	Rubank
Voxman (ed.)	*Selected Studies for Clarinet*	Rubank
Zitek-Voxman	*Sixteen Modern Etudes for Clarinet, Op. 14*	Rubank

Alto and Bass Clarinet

Elementary

(Use Clarinet Materials)

Intermediate

Mimart	*Method for Alto and Bass Clarinet and Sarrusophones*	Cundy-Bettoney

Rhoads (adapted by)	*Baermann for the Alto and Bass Clarinet*	Southern
Rhoads	*Etudes for Technical Facility for Alto and Bass Clarinet*	Southern
Voxman	*Introducing the Alto or Bass Clarinet* (A transfer method)	Rubank

Advanced

Rhoads (ed.)	*18 Selected Etudes for Alto and Bass Clarinet*	Southern
Rhoads	*25 Technical Studies for Alto and Bass Clarinet*	Southern
Saunders-Siennicki	*Understanding the Low Clarinets*	Shawnee Press

Saxophone

Elementary

Cailliet	*Cailliet Method for Saxophone, Book One*	Belwin
Hovey	*First Book of Practical Studies for Saxophone*	Belwin
Hovey	*Rubank Elementary Method, Saxophone*	Rubank
Melnik	*Universal Fundamental Method for Saxophone*	Universal
Rousseau	*Saxophone Method for Beginning Students*	Leblanc

Intermediate

Cailliet	*Cailliet Method for Saxophone, Book Two*	Belwin
Hovey	*Second Book of Practical Studies for Saxophone*	Belwin-Mills
Klose	*Twenty-five Daily Studies*	Carl Fischer
Lee	*Melodic and Progressive Exercises for Saxophone*	Cundy-Bettoney
Mule	*Vingt-Quatre Etudes Faciles*	Leduc
Skornicka	*Rubank Intermediate Method, Saxophone*	Rubank
Voxman (ed.)	*Selected Duets for Saxophone, Volume I*	Rubank
Voxman-Gower	*Rubank Advanced Method, Saxophone, Vol. I*	Rubank

Advanced

Berbiguier-Mule	*18 Exercises or Etudes*	Leduc
Cavallini-Iasilli	*30 Caprices*	Carl Fischer
Karg-Elert	*25 Capricen und Sonate fur Saxophon Solo*	C. F. Peters
Labanchi-Iasilli	*Thirty-three Concert Etudes (in three books)*	Carl Fischer
Luft	*Twenty-Four Etudes in Duet Form for Two Saxophones or Oboes*	Carl Fischer
Mule	*Cinquante-Trois Etudes* (3 vols.)	Leduc
Mule	*Enseignement du Saxophone*	Leduc
Pares-Hovey	*Daily Exercises for Saxophone*	Belwin-Mills
Parisi-Iasilli	*Forty Technical and Melodious Studies for Saxophone (Bks. I & II)*	Southern
Rascher	*158 Exercises*	Hansen
Rascher	*Top Tones for the Saxophone*	Carl Fischer
Rossari-Iasilli	*Fifty-three Melodious Etudes (in two books)*	Southern
Teal	*The Saxophonist's Workbook*	U. of Mich. Music Press
Traxler	*Grand Virtuoso Sax Studies*	Belwin
Voxman	*Rubank Advanced Method, Saxophone, Vol. II*	Rubank
Voxman (ed.)	*Selected Duets for Saxophone, Volume II*	Rubank
Voxman	*Selected Studies for Saxophone*	Rubank

French Horn

Elementary

Eidson-Hovey	*French Horn Method, Book One*	Belwin
Endresen	*Supplementary Studies, French Horn*	Rubank
Getchell	*First Book of Practical Studies for the French Horn*	Belwin
Horner	*Primary Studies for the French Horn*	Elkan-Vogel
Pease	*Universal Fundamental Method for French Horn*	Universal
Pottag-Hovey	*Pottag-Hovey Method, Book One*	Belwin-Mills
Skornicka	*Rubank Elementary Method, French Horn*	Rubank

Intermediate

Boyd (arr.)	*Golden Melodies for French Horn*	Witmark

Eidson-Hovey	*French Horn Method, Book Two*	Belwin
Getchell	*Second Book of Practical Studies for the French Horn*	Belwin
Getchell-Hovey	*Section Studies for French Horns*	Belwin
Gower-Voxman	*Rubank Advanced Method, French Horn, Vol. I*	Rubank
Jones	*First Solos for the Horn Player*	G. Schirmer
Maxime-Alphonse	*200 Modern French Horn Etudes (Books 1, 2 & 3)*	Leduc
Pottag	*Daily Exercises for French Horn*	Belwin
Pottag	*Sixty French Horn Duets, Books One & Two*	Belwin
Skornicka-Erdman	*Rubank Intermediate Method, French Horn*	Rubank
Voxman	*Selected Duets for French Horn, Vol. I*	Rubank

Advanced

Bitsch	*Twelve Etudes for French Horn*	Leduc
Eidson-Hovey	*French Horn Method, Book Three*	Belwin
Franz-Gebhardt	*Complete Method for the French Horn*	Cundy-Bettoney
Gower-Voxman	*Rubank Advanced Method, French Horn, Vol. II*	Rubank
Kopprasch	*60 Selected Studies, Books I and II*	Carl Fischer
Kopprasch-Franz	*50 Etudes, Opus 6, for French Horn*	Southern
Maxime-Alphonse	*200 Modern French Horn Etudes (Books 4, 5 & 6)*	Leduc
Mueller-Pottag	*22 Etudes for French Horn, Op. 64*	Belwin
Muller	*Twelve Etudes for French Horn*	Sansone
Pottag	*French Horn Passages, Volume Two*	Belwin
Pottag (ed.)	*Preparatory Melodies to Solo Work for French Horn*	Belwin
Pottag-Hovey	*Pottag-Hovey Method, Book Two, for French Horn*	Belwin
Reynolds	*48 Etudes for French Horn*	G. Schirmer
Voxman (ed.)	*Selected Duets for French Horn Vol. II*	Rubank
Voxman	*Selected Studies for French Horn*	Rubank

Trumpet or Cornet

Elementary

| Edwards-Hovey | *Edwards-Hovey Method for Cornet or Trumpet, Book I* | Belwin |
| Getchell-Hovey | *First Book of Practical Studies for Cornet and Trumpet* | Belwin |

Hering	*The Beginning Trumpeter,* *Book One*	Carl Fischer
Hering	*Miniature Classics for Two Trumpets* *(or Cornets)*	Carl Fischer
Hering	*More Miniature Classics for Two* *Trumpets (or Cornets)*	Carl Fischer
Pease	*Universal Fundamental Method for* *the Cornet and Trumpet*	Universal
Robinson	*Rubank Elementary Method,* *Cornet or Trumpet*	Rubank
Whistler	*Modern Arban-St. Jacome Course* *for Cornet and Trumpet*	Rubank

Intermediate

Beeler	*Method for the Cornet (Trumpet)*	Remick
Edwards-Hovey	*Edwards-Hovey Method, Book Two,* *for Cornet or Trumpet*	Belwin-Mills
Getchell-Hovey	*Second Book of Practical Studies for* *Cornet and Trumpet*	Belwin-Mills
Gower-Voxman	*Rubank Advanced Method, Cornet* *or Trumpet, Vol. I*	Rubank
Hering	*The Advancing Trumpeter,* *Book Two*	Carl Fischer
Hering (ed.)	*Bach for Two Trumpets*	Carl Fischer
Hering	*Forty Progressive Etudes for* *Trumpet or Cornet*	Carl Fischer
Hering	*The Progressing Trumpeter*	Carl Fischer
Hering	*Thirty-Two Etudes for Trumpet* *or Cornet*	Carl Fischer
Little	*Embouchure Builder for Trumpet* *(Cornet)*	Pro Art
Pares-Whistler	*Pares Scales for Cornet or Trumpet*	Rubank
Pease	*Universal's Follow-Up Method* *for the Cornet or Trumpet*	Universal
Skornicka	*Rubank Intermediate Method,* *Cornet or Trumpet*	Rubank

Sylvius	*20 Original Duets for Trumpet*
	    or Cornet in B♭
	    (published in two books)
		Sam Fox

Teal	*Studies in Time Division*	University Music
		    Press,
		    Ann Arbor,
		    Michigan

VanderCook	*VanderCook Etudes for Cornet* *or Trumpet*	Rubank
VanderCook	*VanderCook Progressive Duets* *for Cornet or Trumpet*	Rubank

Voxman (ed.)	*Selected Duets for Cornet or Trumpet, Volume I*	Rubank

Advanced

Amsden	*Amsden's Celebrated Practice Duets*	Barnhouse
Arban	*Arban's Complete Conservatory Method*	Carl Fischer
Cassel-Gearhart	*Trumpet Sessions* (Fun for 2, 3, and 4 trumpets)	Shawnee
Clarke	*Technical Studies for the Cornet*	Carl Fischer
Colin	*Advanced Lip Flexibilities, Vol. I*	New Sounds in Modern Music
Dalby	*Advanced Trumpet Studies*	Belwin
Duhem	*Twenty-Four Etudes*	Cundy-Bettoney
Gates	*Odd Meter Etudes for all Instruments in Treble Clef*	Fox
Glantz	*48 Studies for the Advanced Trumpeter*	Witmark
Gower-Voxman	*Rubank Advanced Method, Cornet or Trumpet, Vol. II*	Rubank
Hering	*Twenty-Eight Melodious and Technical Etudes for Trumpet or Cornet*	Carl Fischer
Hering	*24 Advanced Etudes for the Trumpet or Cornet*	Carl Fischer
Reinhardt (ed.)	*Donald S. Reinhardt's Selection of Concone Studies*	Elkan-Vogel
Saint-Jacome	*Saint Jacome's Grand Method, Part II*	Carl Fischer
Schlossberg	*Daily Drills and Technical Studies for Trumpet*	M. Baron
Smith	*Top Tones for the Trumpet*	Carl Fischer
Voxman (ed.)	*Selected Duets for Cornet or Trumpet, Vol. II*	Rubank
Voxman (ed.)	*Selected Studies for Cornet or Trumpet*	Rubank
Williams	*Supplementary Studies for Advanced Students of the Trumpet or Cornet*	Colin

Trombone

Elementary

Beeler	*Method for the Trombone, Vol. I*	Remick
Cimera-Hovey	*Cimera-Hovey Method for Trombone, Book One*	Belwin

Endresen	*Supplementary Studies for Trombone*	Rubank
Long	*Rubank Elementary Method for Trombone*	Rubank
Pease	*Universal Fundamental Method for Trombone and Baritone*	Universal

Intermediate

Beeler	*Method for the Trombone, Vol. II*	Remick
Bordner	*First Book of Practical Studies for Trombone or Baritone*	Belwin
Bordner	*Second Book of Practical Studies for Trombone*	Belwin-Mills
Gower-Voxman	*Rubank Advanced Method, Trombone or Baritone, Vol. I*	Rubank
Henning	*Twenty-Four Easy Duets*	Cundy-Bettoney (Carl Fischer)
Hering	*40 Progressive Etudes for Trombone*	Carl Fischer
Skornicka-Boltz	*Rubank Intermediate Method for Trombone*	Rubank
Voxman (ed.)	*Selected Duets for Trombone, Vol. I*	Rubank
Welke (ed.)	*VanderCook Etudes for Trombone or Baritone*	Rubank

Advanced

Amsden	*Amsden's Celebrated Practice Duets* (bass-clef)	Barnhouse
Bellstedt-Simon	*Twelve Famous Technical Studies*	Colin
Bitsch	*15 Rhythmic Etudes*	Leduc
Blazhevich	*Clef Studies for Trombone*	Leeds
Blazhevich	*Sequences for Trombone, Part I and Part II*	Carl Fischer
Blazhevich	*26 Melodic Studies in Varied Rhythms and Keys*	Carl Fischer
Blecer	*Thirty-One Brilliant Studies*	Cundy-Bettoney
Blecer	*Twelve Concert Duets*	Cundy-Bettoney
Blume-Fink	*36 Studies for Trombone with F Attachment*	Carl Fischer
Bordogni-Rochut	*Melodious Etudes for Trombone* (three books)	Carl Fischer
Cimera	*55 Phrasing Studies for Trombone*	Belwin
Cimera	*221 Progressive Studies for Trombone*	Belwin
Cornette	*Six Concert Duets for Trombone (or Baritone)*	Cundy-Bettoney
Cornette	*6 Grand Studies*	Cundy-Bettoney

Dieppo	*Nine Progressive Studies*	Cundy-Bettoney
Endresen	*Solo Studies and Advanced Etudes*	Cole
Gearhart-Cassel-Hornibrook	*Bass Clef Sessions*	Shawnee
Gower-Voxman	*Rubank Advanced Method, Trombone or Baritone, Vol. II*	Rubank
Harvey	*Advanced Studies*	Belwin
Kopprasch	*Sixty Studies, Books I & II*	Carl Fischer
Mueller	*Technical Studies for Trombone*	Carl Fischer
Ostrander	*Allen Ostrander Method for Bass Trombone and F Attachment for Tenor Trombone*	Carl Fischer
Ostrander	*Melodious Etudes for Bass Trombone*	Carl Fischer
Randall-Mantia	*Arban's Famous Method for Trombone, Part II*	Carl Fischer
Remington	*Warmup Exercises*	Pyraminx
Seidel	*Twenty-Four Studies*	Cundy-Bettoney
Slama	*66 Etudes*	Carl Fischer
Tyrrell	*40 Progressive Studies*	Boosey & Hawkes
Vobaron	*Thirty-Four Etudes*	Cundy-Bettoney
Voxman (ed.)	*Selected Duets for Trombone or Baritone, Vol. II*	Rubank
Voxman (ed.)	*Selected Studies for Trombone*	Rubank
Wagner	*Twenty-Seven Progressive Studies*	Cundy-Bettoney

Baritone (Bass Cleff)
(Any Trombone Materials Can Be Used)

Elementary

Beeler	*Method for the Baritone, Book I*	Remick
Hindsley	*Basic Method for the Baritone*	Carl Fischer
Long	*Rubank Elementary Method for Trombone or Baritone*	Rubank
Pease	*Universal Fundamental Method for Trombone*	Universal

Intermediate

Beeler	*Method for the Baritone, Book II*	Remick
Kopprasch-Gumbert-Herbst	*60 Selected Studies for B♭ Baritone, Book I*	Carl Fischer
Ronka	*Daily Lip Drills and Studies for the Euphonium*	Carl Fischer

Advanced

Kopprasch-
  Gumbert-Herbst
	60 Selected Studies for B♭ Baritone,
	  Book II
		Carl Fischer

Vobaron	*32 Melodies for Baritone*	Carl Fischer
Voxman	*Selected Studies for Baritone*	Rubank

Tuba

Elementary

Beeler	*Method for Tuba, Volume I*	Remick
Bell	*Foundation to Tuba and* *Sousaphone Playing*	Carl Fischer
Endresen	*Supplementary Studies, E♭ or* *BB♭ Bass*	Rubank
Getchell-Hovey	*First Book of Practical Studies for* *Tuba*	Belwin
Hovey	*Rubank Elementary Method, E♭* *or BB♭ Bass*	Rubank
Hovey	*Universal Fundamental Method*	Universal

Intermediate

Beeler	*Method for the Tuba, Volume II*	Remick
Getchell-Hovey	*Second Book of Practical Studies* *for Tuba*	Belwin
Nelhybel	*11 Duets for Tuba*	Boston Music Co.
Ronka	*Studies and Lip Drills for Tuba*	Carl Fischer
Skornicka-Boltz	*Rubank Intermediate Method,* *E♭ or BB♭ Bass*	Rubank
VanderCook	*VanderCook Etudes for E♭ or* *BB♭ Bass*	Rubank

Advanced

Arban-Prescott	*Arban-Prescott Method*	Carl Fischer
Blazhevich	*70 Studies for BB flat Tuba*	Robert King
Cimera	*73 Advanced Tuba Studies*	Belwin
Gower-Voxman	*Rubank Advanced Method, E♭ or* *BB♭ Bass, Vol. I*	Rubank
Gower-Voxman	*Rubank Advanced Method, E♭ or* *BB♭ Bass, Vol. II*	Rubank

Adaptable Trombone Materials

Bitsch	*15 Rhythmic Etudes*	Leduc

Blazhevich	*26 Melodic Studies in Varied Rhythms and Keys*	Carl Fischer
Bordogni-Rochut	*Melodious Etudes for Trombone, Vol. II & III*	Carl Fischer
Slama	*66 Etudes in All Major and Minor Keys*	Carl Fischer

Snare Drum

Elementary

Buggert	*Buggert Method, Book 1*	Belwin
Gardner	*Modern Method, Part I*	Carl Fischer
Gardner	*Progressive Studies for the Snare Drum, Book I*	Carl Fischer
Harr	*Haskell W. Harr Drum Method, Book 1*	Cole
Ostling	*Three R's for Snare Drum, Book One*	Belwin
Whistler	*Reviewing the Rudiments*	Rubank
Yoder	*Rubank Elementary Method, Drums*	Rubank

Intermediate

Brown-Musser	*Percussion Studies (Percussion Ensembles)*	Kendor
Buggert	*Buggert Method, Books 2 & 3*	Belwin
Buggert	*110 Progressive Studies for Snare Drum, Books I & II*	Belwin
Buggert	*Rubank Intermediate Method, Drums*	Rubank
Burns-Malin	*Practical Method of Developing Finger Control*	Henry Adler
Fennell	*The Drummer's Heritage*	Carl Fischer
Gardner	*Progressive Studies for the Snare Drum, Book II*	Carl Fischer
Goldenberg	*Modern School for Snare Drum*	Chappell
Harr	*Haskell W. Harr Drum Method, Book Two*	Cole
Kinyon	*Breeze Easy Method for Drums, Book 2*	Witmark
Ludwig	*Collection Drum Solos*	Ludwig Drum Co.
Moore	*The Art of Drumming*	Ludwig
Ostling	*Three R's for Snare Drum, Book II*	Belwin
Prentice	*The School Band Drummer*	Belwin
Whistler	*Rubank Advanced Method*	Rubank
Wilcoxon	*Drummer on Parade*	Wilcoxon

Advanced

Gardner	*Progressive Studies for the Snare Drum, Books 3 & 4*	Carl Fischer
Harris	*The Solo Drummer*	G. Ricordi
Krupa	*Drum Rhythms*	Mills
Schinstine	*Adventures in Solo Drumming*	Southern
Schinstine	*Cadences for All Occasions*	Southern
Tilles	*Practical Percussion Studies*	Henry Adler
Wilcoxon	*Modern Rudimental Swing Solos for the Advanced Drummer*	Wilcoxon

Timpani

Firth	*Solo Timpanist*	Carl Fischer
Gardner	*Modern Method for Timpani*	Carl Fischer
Goodman	*Modern Method for Timpani*	Mills
Harr	*Slingerland Timpani Instruction Manual*	Slingerland Drum Co.
Harr	*Timpani Method*	Cole
Ludwig	*Timpani Instructor*	Ludwig
Schinstine	*Timp Tunes*	Southern
Whistler	*Rubank Elementary Method, Timpani*	Rubank

Mallet Instruments

Elementary

Goldenberg	*Modern School for Xylophone, Marimba and Vibraphone*	Chappell
Gornston	*Foundation Studies for Vibes, Xylophone or Marimba*	Gornston
Pease	*Bell Lyre & Orchestral Bell Method, Book 1*	Rubank
Peterson	*Elementary Method, Marimba or Xylophone*	Rubank
Schaefer	*Xylophone and Marimba Method, Volume I*	Henry Adler
Whaley	*Fundamental Studies for Mallets*	J R Publications

Intermediate

Firth	*Mallet Technique for Xylophone, Marimba, and Vibraphone*	Carl Fischer
Gardner	*Gardner Modern Method, Part II, Bells, Xylophone, Vibraphone, Chimes*	Carl Fischer

| Jolliff | *Intermediate Method for Marimba, Xylophone, Vibes* | Rubank |

Advanced

Bailey	*Mental and Manual Calisthenics for the Modern Mallet Player*	Henry Adler
McMillan	*Masterpieces for Marimba*	Pepper (source)
McMillan	*Percussion Keyboard Technique*	Pepper (source)
Strelsin	*New Method of Velocity for Xylophone, Marimba and Vibraphone*	Carl Fischer

Special Techniques

Denov	*The Art of Playing the Cymbals*	Belwin-Mills
Feldstein	*Begin to Play Rock & Jazz on the Drum Set*	Alfred
Gornston	*Foot Cymbal and Bass Drum Control*	Sam Fox
Jerger	*Bongo Playing Made Easy*	Slingerland Drum Co.
Morales-Adler	*Latin-American Rhythm Instruments and How to Play Them*	Henry Adler
Morey-Collins Dedrick (ed.)	*Student's Guide to Dance & Stage Band Drumming*	Kendor
Rale	*Latin-American Rhythms for the Drummer*	Remick
Weill	*Latin-American Drum Rhythms, Modern Style*	Remick

APPENDIX B

SELECTED SOLOS FOR BAND INSTRUMENTS

Flute

Grade I

Lully-Felix	*Dances for the King*	Edition Musicus
Schubert-Isaac	*Three Themes from Schubert*	Carl Fischer
Tschaikowsky-Maganini	*Three Pieces from Album for Children*	Edition Musicus

Grade II

Bartok-Harris	*Evening in the Country*	Ludwig Music Pub.
Beethoven-Katz	*Six Allemandes*	Omega Music Edition (Sam Fox Publishing Co.)
Gossec	*Gavotte*	Rubank, Inc.

Grade III

Handel	*Sonata II*	Cundy-Bettony Co.
Kuhlau	*Menuett*	Cundy-Bettony Co.
Moyse (arr.)	*Album of Sonatinas*	G. Schirmer, Inc.
Mozart	*Minuet in D Major*	Cundy-Bettony Co.

Grade IV

Bizet	*Minuet (L'Arlesienne Suite No. 2)*	Rubank, Inc.
Frackenpohl	*Ballad and Tango*	Southern Music Co.
Handel	*Sonata IV*	Cundy-Bettony Co.
Marcello-Slater	*Sonata in F*	Oxford University Press
Quantz	*Sonata in B Flat*	Forberg (Derby Music Service)
Tuthill	*Flute Song*	Southern Music Co.
Vaughan Williams	*Suite de Ballet*	Oxford University Press

339

Grade V

Haydn-Moyse	*Concerto in D Major*	Southern Music Co.
Kronke-Eck	*Suite in Ancient Style*	Belwin-Mills
Quantz	*Sonata No. 1 in A Minor*	Cundy-Bettony Co.
Telemann-Wummer	*Suite in A Minor*	Southern Music Co.
Vivaldi	*Sonata No. 6 in G Minor*	McGinnis & Marx (Pietro Deiro Publications)

Grade VI

Bach, J. S.	*Sonata I*	Cundy-Bettony Co.
Boccherini	*Concerto in D, Op. 27*	Southern Music Co.
Chaminade	*Concertino, Op. 107*	Carl Fischer
Faure	*Fantasie, Op. 79*	Southern Music Co.
Frederick the Great	*Sonata in A, No. 117*	Sikorsky, Hamburg (Belwin-Mills)
Handel	*Sonata I*	Cundy-Bettony Co.
Hindemith	*Sonata*	Schott & Co. (Belwin-Mills)
Kennan	*Night Soliloquy*	Carl Fischer
Mozart	*Concerto in D*	Cundy-Bettony Co.
Mozart	*Concerto in G*	Cundy-Bettony Co.

Oboe

Grade I

Labate	*Canzona*	Carl Fischer
Telemann-Stouffer	*Minuet*	Kendor Music Inc.
Vivaldi	*Rain*	Edition Musicus

Grade II

Bach, J. S.	*Minuets 1 & 2*	Ludwig Music Pub.
Benson	*Evening Piece*	Boosey-Hawkes, Inc.
Lully	*Dances for the King*	Edition Musicus
Mozart-Scarmolin	*Allegretto*	Ludwig Music Pub.

Grade III

Beethoven-Hanson	*Bagatelle*	Ludwig Music Pub.
Corelli	*Air and Dance*	Edition Musicus
Handel-Hanson	*Minuet and Allegretto*	Ludwig Music Pub.
Haydn-Pearson	*A Haydn Suite*	Chappell & Co.
Mozart	*Andante from Piano Sonata No. 1*	Carl Fischer

Grade IV

Krenek	*Two Themes by Handel*	Belwin-Mills
Labate	Pastorale	Carl Fischer
Telemann-Schovogt	*Sonata*	Oxford University Press
Tschaikowsky	*Andantino*	Carl Fischer

Grade V

Bartok	*Bagpiper*	Belwin-Mills
Handel	*Concerto Grosso in B Flat (No. 8)*	Albert J. Andraud (Southern Music Co.)
Handel	*Sonata No. I*	Cundy-Bettony Co.
Telemann	*Concerto in F Minor*	Albert J. Andraud (Southern Music Co.)
Vivaldi-Marx	*Sonata No. 6 in G Minor*	McGinnis & Marx (Pietro Deiro Publications)

Grade VI

Bach-Tottcher	*Concerto in F Major*	Franco Colombo, Inc.
Cimarosa	*Concerto*	Boosey-Hawkes, Inc.
Fischer-Carse	*Concerto in C Major*	Galaxy Music Co.
Gilhaud	*First Concertino*	Rubank, Inc.
Handel	*Sonata No. 3*	Albert J. Andraud
Haydn-Rothwell	*Concerto in C*	Franco Colombo, Inc.
Marcello	*Concerto in C Minor*	Albert J. Andraud
St. Verroust	*4th Solo de Concert*	Albert J. Andraud

Bassoon

Grade I

| Bach-Stouffer | *Minuet from 6th French Suite* | Kendor Music Inc. |
| Weber | *The Elephant Dance* | Belwin-Mills |

Grade II

Benson	*Song and Dance*	Boosey-Hawkes, Inc.
Gossec-Buchtel	*Gavotte*	Neil A. Kjos Music Co.
Kuhlau-Buchtel	*Minuet*	Neil A. Kjos Music Co.
Weinberger	*Sonatina*	Carl Fischer

Grade III

| Bakaleinikoff | *Three Pieces* | Belwin-Mills |
| Beethoven | *Minuet* | Fillmore Music House Ed. (Carl Fischer) |

| Kesnar | *The Clown Festival* | Cundy-Bettony Co. |
| Weissenborn | *Song Without Words* | Carl Fischer |

Grade IV

Galliard	*Sonata No. 2*	McGinnis & Marx
Jancourt	*Reverie Op. 61*	Cundy-Bettony Co.
Telemann	*Sonata*	International Music Co.

Grade V

Bach, J. C.	*Concerto in E♭*	Presto Music Service
Hindemith	*Sonata*	Schott & Co.
Stamitz	*Concerto in F*	Frederick Charles, Inc.

Grade VI

Mozart	*Concerto K. 191*	Cundy-Bettony Co.
Mozart-Spratt	*Concerto No. 2 in B♭*	Spratt Music Publishers
Vivaldi	*Concerto in La Minor F VIII, No. 7*	G. Ricardi & Co. (Belwin-Mills)
Weber	*Hungarian Fantasie, Op. 35*	Cundy-Bettony Co.

Clarinet

Grade I

Langenus	*Lullaby*	Carl Fischer
Rienicke-Kaplan	*Lullaby and Moderato*	Spratt Music Publishers
Stuart	*Famous Clarinet Favorites*	Boston Music Co.

Grade II

Bartok-Suchoff	*Eleven Easy Pieces*	Belwin-Mills
Corelli-Maganini	*Suite in B♭ Major*	Edition Musicus
Handel-Hovey-Leonard	*Sarabande and Gavotte*	Belwin-Mills
Rameau-Scarmolin	*La Villageoise*	Ludwig Music Pub.

Grade III

Collis	*Little Concerto No. 1*	Charles Hansen Music Corp.
Handel-Hovey-Leonard	*Sarabande and Bouree*	Belwin-Mills
Mozart-Langenus	*Minuet K. 334*	Carl Fischer
White	*Petite Suite*	Sam Fox Publishing Co.

Grade IV

| Handel-Worley | *Sonata in F Major* | Edition Musicus |

Telemann-Voxman	*Sonata in C Minor*	Rubank, Inc.
Wagner-Bellison	*Adagio*	G. Ricardi & Co.
Whitney	*Roaming River*	Bourne, Inc.

Grade V

Brahms	*Sonata No. 2 in E♮ Op. 120*	Carl Fischer
Hahn	*Sarabande and Theme Varie*	Albert J. Andraud
Hindemith	*Sonata for Clarinet and Piano*	Associated Music Pub., Inc.
Jean-Jean	*Arabesques*	Alfred Music Co., Inc.
Mozart-Giampieri	*Divertimento, K. 581*	G. Ricardi & Co.
Poulenc	*Sonata for Clarinet and Piano*	M. Baron Co.
Weber	*Concerto No. 1, Op. 73*	Carl Fischer

Grade VI

Cavallini	*Adagio and Tarantella*	Cundy-Bettony Co.
Debussy	*Premier Rhapsody*	Durand (Elkan-Vogel Co.)
Messager	*Solo De Concours*	Albert J. Andraud
Mozart	*Concerto for Clarinet K. 622*	Carl Fischer
Spohr	*Concerto No. 2, Op. 57 in E♭*	Carl Fischer
Stravinsky	*Three Pieces for Clarinet (unacc.)*	Carl Fischer
Weber	*Concertino*	Carl Fischer
Weber	*Concerto No. 2, Op. 74*	Carl Fischer

Alto Clarinet

Grade I

Handel-Barr	*Sarabande from Concerto in F Minor*	Ludwig Music Pub.
Purcell-Kaplan	*Saraband*	Spratt Music Publishers
Weber	*The Elephant Dance*	Belwin-Mills

Grade II

Dvorak-Leonard	*Slavonic Dance*	Belwin-Mills
Mozart-Voxman	*Menuetto from Divertimento No. 1*	Rubank, Inc.
Reed	*Intermezzo*	Carl Fischer

Grade III

Corelli-Voxman	*Sarabande and Gigue*	Rubank, Inc.
Ravel-Bettoney	*Pavane pour une infante defunte*	Cundy-Bettony Co.

White   *Petite Suite*   Sam Fox Publishing Co.

Grade IV

Frangkiser   *Evening*   Belwin-Mills
Galliard-Gee   *Hornpipe and Allegro*   Southern Music Co.
Petit-Findlay   *Premiere Etude De Concours*   Cundy-Bettony Co.
Schmutz   *Praeludium*   Carl Fischer

Grades V and VI

Escudie-Prendiville   *Third Fantasia*   Cundy-Bettony Co.
Lacome-Andraud   *Rigaudon*   Southern Music Co.
Lecail-Voxman   *Fantaisie Concertante*   Rubank, Inc.
Von Weber   *Concertino*   Carl Fischer

Bass Clarinet

Grade I

Cui-Leonard   *Orientale*   Belwin-Mills
Haydn-Kaplan   *Arietta & Minuet*   Spratt Music Publishers
Knight-Buchtel   *Rocked in the Cradle of the*   Neil A. Kjos Music Co.
                         Deep

Grade II

Handel-Ayres   *Andante and Bouree*   C.L. Barnhouse, Inc.
Mozart-Barnes   *Per Questa Bella Mano, K. 612*   Spratt Music Publishers
Petrie-Walters   *Asleep in the Deep*   Rubank, Inc.
Prokofieff-Hummel   *Romance and Troika*   Rubank, Inc.

Grade III

German-Voxman   *Pastorale and Bourree*   Rubank, Inc.
Kesnar   *A Clown Festival*   Cundy-Bettony Co.
Rathaus   *In Ancient Style*   Belwin-Mills
White   *Petite Suite*   Sam Fox Publishing Co.

Grade IV

Bennett   *Deepwood*   Carl Fischer
Desportes   *Andante and Allegro*   Southern Music Co.
Galliard-Kreiselman   *Sonata No. 1 and Sonata No. 2*   McGinnis & Marx
Mozart-Andraud   *Adagio Religioso*   Southern Music Co.
Vivaldi-Ayres   *Sonata No. 6*   C.L. Barnhouse, Inc.

Grade V

Bozza   *Ballade*   Southern Music Co.

Frangkiser	*Concert Theme*	Belwin-Mills
Galliard-Kreiselman	*Sonata No. 5*	McGinnis & Marx
Long	*Undercurrent*	Rubank, Inc.

Grade VI

Eccles-Goldberg	*Sonata in G Minor*	Belwin-Mills
Galliard-Kreiselman	*Sonata No. 3*	McGinnis & Marx
Marty	*Premiere Fantasie*	Cundy-Bettony Co.

Alto Saxophone

Grade I

Barnes	*The Young Artist*	Boosey-Hawkes, Inc.
Mozart-Rascher	*Ave Verum Corpus*	Belwin-Mills
Purcell-Buchtel	*Nymphs and Shepherds*	Neil A. Kjos Music Co.

Grade II

Bach-Rascher	*Minuet*	Belwin-Mills
Bartok-Harris	*Evening in the Country*	Ludwig Music Pub.
Rameau-Scarmolin	*La Villageoise*	Ludwig Music Pub.

Grade III

Bizet-Buchtel	*Minuet from L'Arlesienne*	Neil A. Kjos Music Co.
Corelli-Maganini	*Air and Dance*	Edition Musicus
Haydn-Rascher	*The Oxen Minuet*	Belwin-Mills
Purcell-Rascher	*Two Bourrees*	Bourne, Inc.
Rameau-Rascher	*Rigaudon*	Chappell & Co.

Grade IV

Corelli-Maganini	*Suite in B♭*	Edition Musicus
Gershwin-Rascher	*Second Prelude*	New World Music Corp.
Handel-Mule	*The Harmonious Blacksmith*	LeDuc
Whitney	*Rumba*	Bourne, Inc.

Grade V

Gossec-Mule	*La Fete Du Village*	LeDuc
Handel-Rascher	*Sonata No. 3*	Chappell & Co.
Tcherepnine	*Sonatine Sportive*	LeDuc

Grade VI

| Glazounov-Petiot | *Concerto* | LeDuc |
| Glaser-Rascher | *Variation on a Gavotte by Corelli* | Chappell & Co. |

Heiden	*Sonata*	Associated Music Pub., Inc.
Vivaldi-Marx	*Sonata No. 6 in G Minor*	McGinnis & Marx

Tenor Saxophone

Grade I

Glinka-Schuman	*Romance Melody*	Spratt Music Publishers
Handel-Rascher	*Largo*	Belwin-Mills
Vander Pals-Rascher	*Shepherd's Dance*	Belwin-Mills

Grade II

Bach-Rascher	*Musette*	Belwin-Mills
Lully-Felix	*Dances for the King*	Edition Musicus
Schubert-Rascher	*Andante*	Belwin-Mills

Grade III

Bach-Rascher	*Gavotte and Bourree*	Belwin-Mills
Mozart-Voxman	*Adagio and Menuetto*	Rubank, Inc.
Prokofiev-Hummel	*Romance and Troika*	Rubank, Inc.
Tschaikowsky	*Suite from "The Children's Album"*	Edition Musicus

Grade IV

Barat-Voxman	*Berceuse*	Rubank, Inc.
Corelli-Maganini	*Suite in B♭ Major*	Edition Musicus
Handel-Londeix	*Sonata No. 1*	LeDuc
Vivaldi-Maganini	*Suite in C Minor*	Edition Musicus

Grade V

Galliard-Rascher	*Sonata IV*	McGinnis & Marx
Handel-Voxman	*Concerto in G Minor*	Rubank, Inc.
Telemann-Voxman	*Sonata in C Minor*	Rubank, Inc.

Grade VI

Hartley	*Poem*	Theodore Presser Co.
Stein	*Sonata*	Southern Music Co.
Vivaldi-Rascher	*Sonata in G Minor*	McGinnis & Marx

Baritone Saxophone

Grade I

Mozart-Voxman	*Menuetto from Divertimento No. 1*	Rubank, Inc.

| Petrie-Buchtel | *Asleep in the Deep* | Neil A. Kjos Music Co. |

Grade II

| Beethoven-Rascher | *The Heavens Resound* | Belwin-Mills |
| Schumann-Rascher | *The Happy Farmer* | Belwin-Mills |

Grade III

| Corelli-Voxman | *Sarabande and Gigue* | Rubank, Inc. |
| Gliere-Hurrell | *Russian Sailor's Dance* | Rubank, Inc. |

Grade IV

| Bach-Rascher | *If Thou Be Near* | Belwin-Mills |
| Frangkiser | *Canzona* | Belwin-Mills |

Grade V

| Koepke | *Recitative and Rondino* | Rubank, Inc. |
| Long | *Undercurrent* | Rubank, Inc. |

Grade VI

| Bach-Kasprzyk | *Suite No. 4* | Southern Music Co. |
| Hoffmann | *Serenade Basque* | Belwin-Mills |

French Horn

Grade I

| Jones, M. | *First Solos for the Horn Player* | G. Schirmer, Inc. |
| Langrish (arr.) | *Eight Easy Pieces* | Oxford University Press |

Grade II

| Bakaleinikoff | *Cavatina* | Belwin-Mills |
| McKay | *Three Pastoral Scenes* | G. Schirmer, Inc. |

Grade III

Bach, J. S.-Gounod	*Ave Maria*	Carl Fischer
Handel-Ployhar	*Hornpipe*	Belwin-Mills
Koepke-Voxman	*La Chasse*	Rubank, Inc.

Grade IV

Brahms-Phillips	*Intermezzo in C*	Oxford University Press
Scarmolin	*Romanza and Allegro*	Cundy-Bettony Co.
Strauss, R.	*Andante*	Boosey-Hawkes, Inc.

Grade V

Adler	*Sonata*	Robert King
Busser	*Concert Piece in D*	Southern Music Co.
Handel-Reynolds	*Sonata No. 3*	Southern Music Co.
Mozart	*Concerto No. 1*	Cundy-Bettony Co.

Grade VI

Beethoven	*Horn Sonata, Opus 17*	Cundy-Bettony Co.
Haydn	*Concerto No. 1*	Cundy-Bettony Co.
Hindemith	*Sonata*	Schott & Co.
Mozart	*Concerto No. 4*	Carl Fischer
Strauss, R.	*Concerto, Op. 11*	Cundy-Bettony Co.

Cornet-Trumpet

Grade I

Fitzgerald (arr.)	*English Suite*	Theodore Presser Co.
Shelukov-Gower	*The Cavalier*	Rubank, Inc.

Grade II

Fitzgerald (arr.)	*Aria and Allegro*	Theodore Presser Co.
Shelukov-Gower	*Fanfare March*	Rubank, Inc.

Grade III

Anderson	*A Trumpeter's Lullaby*	Belwin-Mills
Corelli, A.	*Sonata en Fa*	Theodore Presser Co.
Purcell-Fitzgerald	*Purcell Suite*	Theodore Presser Co.

Grade IV

Bernstein	*Rondo for Lifey*	G. Schirmer, Inc.
Petit	*Etude de Concours*	Cundy-Bettony Co.
Ropartz	*Andante and Allegro*	Cundy-Bettony Co.

Grade V

Corelli-Fitzgerald	*Sonata VIII*	G. Ricardi & Co.
Handel-Fitzgerald	*Aria con Variazoni*	G. Ricardi & Co.
Hummel	*Concerto*	Robert King
Tuthill	*Sonata, Op. 29*	Warner Brothers 7-Arts Music

Grade VI

Haydn-Goeyens	*Concerto*	Carl Fischer

Hindemith	*Sonata for Trumpet and Piano*	International Music Co.
Kennon	*Sonata*	Warner Brothers
		7-Arts Music
Nelhybel	*Golden Concerto on a*	Edition Musicus
	Twelve Tone Row	

Trombone

Grade I

Concone-Gower	*Meditation*	Rubank, Inc.
McKay	*Ye Traveling Troubadour*	C. L. Barnhouse, Inc.

Grade II

Cimera	*Waltz Helen*	Belwin-Mills
Scarmolin	*Recitative and Romance*	Belwin-Mills

Grade III

Cowell	*Tom Binkley's Tune*	Mercury Music Corp.
Handel-Ostrander	*Honor and Arms*	Edition Musicus

Grade IV

Alary	*Contest Piece*	Cundy-Bettony Co.
McKay	*Concert Solo Sonatine*	Boston Music Co.
Ostransky	*Concertino*	Rubank, Inc.
Pergolesi-Barnes	*Canzona*	Spratt Music Publishers

Grade V

Corelli-Ostrander	*Sonata in F Major*	Edition Musicus
Galliard	*Sonata No. 1*	McGinnis & Marx
Nelhybel	*Suite for Trombone and Piano*	General Music
		Publishing Co.
Poot	*Etude de Concert*	M. Baron Co.

Grade VI

Barat	*Andante et Allegro*	Cundy-Bettony Co.
Blazhevich	*Concerto No. 2*	International Music Co.
Jacob	*Concerto for Trombone*	Jos. Williams Co.
		(Galaxy Music Co.)
Mozart-Ostrander	*Concerto for Trombone,*	Edition Musicus
	K. 191	
Niverd	*Legende*	Albert J. Andraud
Pfeiffer	*Solo de Trombone*	Albert J. Andraud

Baritone

Grade I

Smith-Falcone	*Song Without Words*	Belwin-Mills
Wagner-Smith	*Song to the Evening Star*	Belwin-Mills

Grade II

Bach-Smith	*Arioso*	Belwin-Mills
Niverd	*Six Petites Pieces De Style*	M. Baron Co.

Grade III

Nelhybel	*Concert Piece*	E. C. Kerby Ltd.
Rossini-Ostrander	*Lord Preserve Me*	Edition Musicus
Whitney	*Cortege*	Bourne, Inc.

Grade IV

Alary	*Contest Piece*	Cundy-Bettony Co.
Ostrander	*Concert Piece in Fugal Style*	Edition Musicus

Grade V

Barat	*Andante et Allegro*	Cundy-Bettony Co.
David	*Concertino*	Carl Fischer
Galliard	*Sonata 2*	McGinnis & Marx

Grade VI

Hindemith	*Sonata for Trombone and Piano*	Associated Music Pub., Inc.
Mozart-Ostrander	*Concerto for Trombone K. 191*	Edition Musicus
Savard	*Morceau de Concours*	Cundy-Bettony Co.

Tuba

Grade I

Bell	*Gavotte*	Carl Fischer
Peter-Bell	*The Jolly Coppersmith*	Belwin-Mills

Grade II

Bell	*Folksong Medley*	Belwin-Mills
Handel-Bell	*Honor and Arms*	Belwin-Mills

Grade III

Scarmolin	*Pomp and Dignity*	Pro-Art Publications

VanderCook	*Bombastoso*	Rubank, Inc.

Grade IV

Bach-Bell	*Air and Bouree*	Carl Fischer
Ostrander	*Concert Piece in Fugal Style*	Edition Musicus

Grade V

Frackenpohl	*Variations (The Cobbler's Bench)*	Shawnee Press Inc.
Hartley	*Aria for Tuba and Piano*	Elkan-Vogel Co.
Mueller	*Praeludium Chorale Variations and Gigue*	Edition Musicus

Grade VI

Beethoven-Bell	*Variations on the Theme of "Judas Maccabaeus"*	Carl Fischer
Hindemith	*Sonate*	Schott & Co.
Holmes	*Emmet's Lullaby*	Rubank, Inc.
Williams, E.	*Concerto No. 2*	Charles Colin

Snare Drum

Grade I

Brown	*Flim Flam*	Kendor Music Inc.
Hoey	*The Drummer Boy*	Belwin-Mills

Grade II

Goldenberg	*A Little Suite for Snare Drum*	Shapiro-Bernstein
Prentice	*Toyland Parade*	Belwin-Mills

Grade III

Pratt	*Here's to the Ratamaque*	Belwin-Mills
Weinberger	*The Peasant Drummer*	Associated Music Pub., Inc.

Grade IV

Buggert	*Rolling Accents*	Rubank, Inc.
Schinstine	*Festival Drummer*	Southern Music Co.

Grade V

Buggert	*Thundering Through*	Rubank, Inc.
Goldenberg	*6/8 Etude*	Plymouth Music Co., Inc.

Grade VI

Benson	*Three Dances for Solo Snare Drum*	Chappell & Co.
Schinstine	*Space Probe*	Southern Music Co.

Timpani

Grade I

Firth	*Sitting Bull*	Henry Adler

Grade II

Firth	*Lone Wolf*	Henry Adler
Noak	*Andante*	Plymouth Music Co., Inc.

Grade III

Firth	*Geronimo*	Henry Adler
Sosnik	*Concertino for Timpani and Band*	Bourne, Inc.

Grade IV

Firth	*Solo Impression for Two Timpani*	Carl Fischer
Schinstine	*Timpendium*	Southern Music Co.

Grade V

Beck	*Sonata for Timpani*	Boston Music Co.
Firth	*The Solo Timpanist,* (Nos. 1, 2 or 3)	Carl Fischer

Grade VI

Bergamo	*Four Pieces for Timpani*	Plymouth Music Co., Inc.
Firth	*Solo Impression for Three Timpani*	Carl Fischer

Xylophone or Marimba

Grades I and II

Handel-Feldstein	*Sonata No. 3*	Henry Adler
Ostling	*Bellistics*	Belwin-Mills

Grade III

Bartok-Harris	*Evening in the Country for Marimba and Piano*	Ludwig Music Pub.
Brown	*Marimba Bossa Nova*	Kendor Music Inc.

Grade IV

Beethoven-Nagy	*Turkish March for Marimba and Piano*	Ludwig Music Pub.
Haydn-Barnes	*Gypsy Rondo*	Ludwig Music Pub.
Lecuona-Peterson	*Malaguena*	Edward B. Marks Corp.

Grade V

DeGastyne	*Toccata*	Fereol Publications
Weber-Sifert	*Invitation to the Dance*	Belwin-Mills

Grade VI

Bach-Goldenberg	*Violin Concerto in A Minor* (from *Modern School of Xylophone, Marimba and Vibraphone*)	Chappell & Co.
Sifler	*Marimba Suite*	Western International Music

APPENDIX C

SELECTED SMALL ENSEMBLE MATERIALS

Flute Duets

Grades I and II

Blavet-Mann	*French Duets*	McGinnis & Marx
Kohler	*Forty Progressive Duets, Opus 55, Vol. I*	Carl Fischer
Kummer	*Three Duos, Op. 20*	Theodore Presser Co.
Moyse	*30 Easy Duets*	McGinnis & Marx

Grades III and IV

Berbiguier	*Six Easy Duets, Op. 59*	Edition Musicus
Gariboldi	*Six Little Duets, Op. 145B*	Cundy-Bettony Co.
Gariboldi	*Six Melodic Duets, Op. 145C*	Cundy-Bettony Co.
Kohler	*Forty Progressive Duets, Opus 55, Vol. II*	Carl Fischer
Kohler	*Six Sonatinas, Op. 96*	Southern Music Co.
Soussmann	*Twelve Light Pieces*	Edition Musicus
Taylor (ed.)	*The Flutist's Classic Duet Repertoire*	Witmark & Sons

Grades V and VI

Bach	*Fifteen Two-Part Inventions*	Cundy-Bettony Co.
Berbiguier	*Three Duo Concertants, Op. 11*	Edition Musicus
Kuhlau	*Three Duos Concertants, Op. 10*	Carl Fischer
Mozart	*Six Duets, Op. 75*	Cundy-Bettony Co.
Quantz	*Six Duets, Op. 2*	G. Schirmer Inc.
Telemann	*Six Sonatas* (2 vols.)	Mercury Music Corp.

Flute Trios

Grades I and II

———————	*Flute Sessions*	Shawnee Press Inc.

| Hudadoff | *24 Flute Trios* | Pro-Art Publications |
| Voxman | *Chamber Music for Three Flutes* | Rubank, Inc. |

Grades III and IV

Anderson, Leroy	*Penny-Whistle Song*	Belwin-Mills Publishing Co.
Hook-Voxman	*Six Trios, Op. 83*	Rubank, Inc.
Moyse	*Four Pieces*	G. Schirmer Inc.

Grades V and VI

Barrere	*Two Short Pieces*	Carl Fischer
Simeone	*Flute Cocktail*	Shawnee Press Inc.
Tchaikowsky	*Dance of the Mirlitons*	Southern Music Co.

Flute Quartets

Grades I and II

| Eck | *Quartet Album* | Belwin-Mills Publishing Co. |
| Holmes (arr.) | *Flute Symphony* | Rubank, Inc. |

Grades III and IV

Cohen	*Colonial Sketches*	Boosey-Hawkes, Inc.
McKay	*Christmas Morning Suite*	Southern Music Co.
Voxman (arr.)	*Quartet Repertoire*	Rubank, Inc.

Grades V and VI

Bennett, R. R.	*Rondo Capriccioso*	Chappell & Co.
Desportes	*Suite Italienne*	Southern Music Co.
Gabrielski	*Grand Quartet in A, Op. 53*	Edition Musicus
Kohler	*Grand Quartet, Op. 92*	Southern Music Co.

Oboe Duets

Grades I and II

| Rikko (arr.) | *9 French Dances* | McGinnis & Marx |
| Scarmolin | *Duet Collection* | Ludwig Music Pub. |

Grades III and IV

Freundlich (arr.)	*Four Old Dances*	G. Ricardi & Co.
Gearhart (arr.)	*Duet Sessions*	Shawnee Press Inc.
Kaplan (ed.)	*Gotham Collection of Duets, The*	Jack Spratt Music Co.

Grades V and VI

Devienne	*Six Sonatas*	Edition Musicus
Ferling-Andraud	*48 Famous Studies for Oboe or Saxophone* (3 Duos Concertants for 2 oboes or 2 saxophones)	Southern Music Co.
Luft	*Twenty-Four Etudes in Duet Form for Two Saxophones or Oboes*	Carl Fischer

Bassoon Duets

Grades I and II

————	*Bass Clef Sessions*	Shawnee Press Inc.
Porret	*12 Duos Facile, Op. 6, No. 48*	Henri Elkan Music Publishers

Grades III and IV

Blume	*12 Melodious Duets*	Carl Fischer
Mueller	*35 Duets for Two Bassoons*	Spratt Music Publishers

Grades V and VI

Ferling-Thornton	*3 Duos Concertantes, Op. 8*	Southern Music Co.
Mozart	*Sonata for 2 Bassoons, K. 292*	Southern Music Co.
Telemann	*Sonata No. 4*	McGinnis & Marx

Clarinet Duets

Grades I and II

Mozart-Bellison	*Twelve Duets* (3 Parts)	G. Ricardi & Co.
Rosenthal	*Clarinet Duos, 18th Century*	Marks Music Corporation
Rosenthal	*15 Easy Duets for Two Clarinets*	David Gornston (Sam Fox Publishing Co.)

Grades III and IV

Amsden	*Amsden's Celebrated Practice Duets*	C. L. Barnhouse Inc.
Bach-Simon	*Bach for the Clarinet*	G. Schirmer Inc.
Gearhart	*Duet Sessions*	Shawnee Press, Inc.
Kaplan (arr.)	*The Gotham Collection of Duets*	Spratt Music Publishers (Plymouth Music Company, Inc.)

Mozart-Rosenthal	*Clarinet Duet Arrangements*	Mercury Music Corp.
Scarlatti-Rosenthal	*Clarinet Duet Arrangements Vol. I*	Mercury Music Corp.

Grades V and VI

Kroepsch	*Five Duos for Two Clarinets*	Marks Music Corporation
Mozart-Langenus	*Three Duos for Two Clarinets*	Carl Fischer
Mozart-Magnani	*Six Duets* (2 Books)	Cundy-Bettony Co.

Clarinet Trios

Grades I and II

Rosenthal (arr.)	*Clarinet Trios, 18th Century*	Marks Music Corporation
Rosenthal (arr.)	*Clarinet Trios from Corelli to Beethoven*	Marks Music Corporation
Voxman	*Chamber Music for Three Clarinets* (2 Vols.)	Rubank, Inc.

Grades III and IV

Cassel-Gearhart	*Clarinet Sessions*	Shawnee Press, Inc.
Nelhybel	*9 Trios for Clarinet*	Franco Colombo, Inc. (Belwin-Mills Publishing Corp.)
Rosenthal (arr.)	*Clarinet Trios, Russian Composers*	Marks Music Corporation

Grades V and VI

Bach-Cochrane	*Fifteen Three-Part Inventions*	Cundy-Bettony Co.
Bouffil	*Three Trios, Op. 7*	Cundy-Bettony Co.

Clarinet Quartets

Grades I and II

Arnold	*Everybody's Favorite Clarinet Quartets*	Amsco Music Publishing Co.
Liegl (trans.)	*Collection of Clarinet Quartets*	Warner Brothers 7-Arts Music
Seay (ed.)	*The Gotham Collection of Clarinet Quartets*	Spratt Music Co.
Voxman	*Ensemble Classics, Book I*	Rubank, Inc.

Grades III and IV

Erickson-Waln	*Petite Suite*	Cundy-Bettony Co.

Grundman	*Bagatelle*	Boosey-Hawkes, Inc.
Holmes	*Clarinet Symphony Collection*	Rubank, Inc.
Rosenthal (arr.)	*Clarinet Quartets, 18th Century*	Marks Music Corporation
Simon (arr.)	*Three Minuets*	Marks Music Corporation
White	*Suite Spirituale*	Henri Elkan Music Publishers

Grades V and VI

Endresen	*Clarinet Quartet No. 1*	Belwin-Mills Publishing Corp.
Desportes	*French Suite*	Southern Music Company
Desportes	*Normandie*	Southern Music Company
Gabrielsky	*Grand Quartet*	Southern Music Company
Mendelssohn-Howland	*Rondo Capriccioso*	Schmitt, Hall & McCreary Co.
Waterson	*Grand Quartet*	Southern Music Company
Whitney	*Roulade*	Carl Fischer

Saxophone Duets

Grades I and II

Scarmolin	*Duet Time*	Ludwig Music Pub.
Voxman (ed.)	*Selected Duets, Vol. I*	Rubank, Inc.

Grades III and IV

Kaplan (ed.)	*Gotham Collection of Duets*	Spratt Music Co.
Voxman (ed.)	*Selected Duets, Vol. II*	Rubank, Inc.

Grades V and VI

Bach-Teal	*Fifteen Two-Part Inventions*	Theodore Presser Co.
Luft	*Twenty-Four Etudes in Duet Form*	Carl Fischer

Saxophone Trios

Grades I–III

Voxman (ed.)	*Chamber Music for 3 Saxophones* (2 altos, tenor)	Rubank, Inc.

Grades IV–VI

Hook-Voxman	*Six Trios*	Rubank, Inc.

Saxophone Quartets

Grades I–III

Patrick & Rascher (eds.)	*Five Centuries for Saxophone Quartet*	Bourne, Inc.
Patrick & Rascher (eds.)	*Masterpieces for Saxophone Quartet* SATB	Bourne, Inc.
Voxman & Hervig (eds.)	*Quartet Repertoire*	Rubank, Inc.

Grades IV–VI

Teal	*Ten Saxophone Quartets*	G. Schirmer Inc.

Woodwind Trios

Grades I–III

Voxman (ed.)	*Chamber Music Collection* (Flute, Clarinet and Bassoon)	Rubank, Inc.
Voxman (ed.)	*Chamber Music for Three Woodwinds, Vol. I* (Flute, Oboe and Clarinet)	Rubank, Inc.

Grade III

Mozart-Kauffman	*Two Trios* (Oboe, Clarinet & Bassoon)	McGinnis & Marx
Spratt	*Three Miniatures for Three Woodwinds* (Oboe, Clarinet and Bassoon)	Spratt Music Publishers

Grade IV

Bach-Cochrane	*Fifteen Three Part Inventions* (Flute, Oboe and Bassoon)	Cundy-Bettony Co.
Andraud (ed.)	*18 Trios* (Flute, Oboe and Clarinet)	Southern Music Company

Grades V–VI

Daniels	*Three Observations for Three Woodwinds* (Flute, Clarinet and Bassoon)	Carl Fischer
Kummer	*Trio in F* (Flute, Clarinet, and Bassoon)	Rubank, Inc.

| Washburn | *Three Pieces for Three Woodwinds* (Flute, Clarinet and Bassoon) | Oxford University Press |

Woodwind Quartets
(Flute, Oboe, Clarinet, and Bassoon)

Grades I–II

Brahms-Hunter	*Three Easy Quartets*	Belwin-Mills Publishing Corp.
Handel-Ostling	*Petite Fugue*	Belwin-Mills Publishing Corp.
Kabalevsky-Seay	*Children's Suite, Op. 27*	Spratt Music Publishers

Grades III–IV

| Beethoven-Hahn | *Contra Dance* | Carl Fischer |
| Fischer-Andraud | *Banquet Music* | Southern Music Company |

Grades V–VI

| Mozart-Kesnar | *Rondo* | Cundy-Bettony Co. |
| Stamitz | *Quartet in E♭* | Leuckart, Salomonstrasse, Leipzig, Germany |

Woodwind Quintets

Grades I–II

| Taylor (ed.) | *Music for the Young* | Western International Music |

Grades II–VI

| Andraud (ed.) | *Twenty-Two Woodwind Quintets* | Southern Music Company |
| Taylor (ed.) | *The Ross Taylor Woodwind Quintets* | Southern Music Company |

Grade III

Bach-Gordon	*Sarabande and Gavotte*	Cundy-Bettony Co.
McKay	*Bainbridge Island Sketches*	C. L. Barnhouse, Inc.
Rubank (pub.)	*Ensemble Repertoire for Woodwind Quintet*	Rubank, Inc.

Grade IV

Beethoven-DeBueris	*Country Dance No. 1*	Carl Fischer
Washburn	*Suite for Woodwind Quintet*	Elkan-Vogel Co.

Grade V

Beethoven-Holmes	*Allegretto from Sixth Symphony*	C. L. Barnhouse, Inc.
Bright	*Three Short Dances*	Shawnee Press Inc.
Frackenpohl	*Suite for Woodwind Quintet*	Theodore Presser Co.
McKay	*Three Sea Sketches*	C. L. Barnhouse, Inc.
Mozart-Cailliet	*Quintet in F Major*	Elkan-Vogel Co.

Grade VI

Arnold	*Three Shanties for Wind Quintet*	Carl Fischer
Beethoven	*Quintet in E-flat*	Theodore Presser Co.
Carter	*Woodwind Quintet*	Associated Music Pub., Inc.

French Horn Duets

Grades II–III

Pottag (ed.)	*Sixty French Horn Duets, Bk. I*	Belwin-Mills Publishing Corp.
Williams, Clifton	*Twenty-Four Duo Studies*	Southern Music Co.

Grades IV–V

Franz	*100 Duets, Bk. I & Bk. II*	Southern Music Co.
Mozart	*Duos, K. 487*	McGinnis & Marx
Pottag (ed.)	*Sixty French Horn Duets, Bk. II*	Belwin-Mills Publishing Corp.
Voxman (ed.)	*Selected Duets, Vol. I and II*	Rubank, Inc.
Williams, Clifton	*Twenty-Four Duo Studies*	Southern Music Co.

Grade VI

Schenk-Reynolds	*Six Sonatas for Two Horns*	MCA Music
Voxman (ed.)	*Selected Duets, Vol. II*	Rubank, Inc.

French Horn Quartets

Grades I–III

Holmes (arr.)	*Horn Symphony Collection*	Rubank, Inc.

| Howe (arr.) | *24 Horn Quartets* | Charles Colin |
| Muller | *29 Quartets* | Southern Music Co. |

Grade IV

McKay	*Suite for Four Horns*	C. L. Barnhouse, Inc.
Ostransky	*Aeolian Suite*	Rubank, Inc.
Pottag	*In the Country*	Carl Fischer
Weber-Pottag	*Hunting Chorus* (from *Der Freischutz*)	Belwin-Mills Publishing Corp.

Grades V–VI

Hindemith	*Sonata for Four Horns*	Schott and Co. (Belwin-Mills)
Nelhybel	*Quartet for Horns*	General Music Publishers Co.
Reynolds	*Short Suite for Horn Quartet*	Robert King
Wagner-Pottag	*Tannhauser Selections*	Belwin-Mills Publishing Corp.

Cornet Duets

Grades I–III

Carnaud	*Thirty Progressive Duets*	Boosey-Hawkes, Inc.
Hering	*Miniature Classics*	Carl Fischer
Hering	*More Miniature Classics*	Carl Fischer
Porret	*12 Duos Faciles*	Henri Elkan Music Publisher
Voxman	*Selected Duets, Vol. I*	Rubank, Inc.

Grade III

| Clarke (arr.) | *A Purcell and Handel Album* | Oxford University Press |
| Hering | *Trumpets for Two* | Carl Fischer |

Grades V–VI

Cox	*12 Concert Duets*	Rubank, Inc.
Porret	*12 Duos Progressifs*	Henri Elkan Music Publisher
Voxman	*Selected Duets, Vol. II*	Rubank, Inc.
Williams, E.	*Artistic Duets*	Charles Colin

Cornet Trios

Grades I–II

| McKay | *Three Amigos* | C. L. Barnhouse, Inc. |

| Nelhybel | *12 Concert Pieces for Three Trumpets* | Franco Colombo Inc. |
| Schaeffer | *Cornet Trio Album* | Pro-Art Publications |

Grades III–IV

Clarke	*Flirtations*	Carl Fischer
Nelhybel	*12 Concert Pieces for Three Trumpets*	Franco Colombo, Inc.
Ostrander	*Suite*	Edition Musicus
Ostransky	*The King's Heralds*	Rubank, Inc.

Grade V

| Anderson | *Bugler's Holiday* | Belwin-Mills Publishing Corp. |
| Williams | *Three Blue Jackets* | Charles Colin |

Grade VI

Gabrieli	*Sonata Con Tre Trombe*	Philharmusica Corp.
Handel-Hanson	*Sonata No. 2*	Ludwig Music Pub.
Simons	*La Spaniola*	Carl Fischer

Trumpet Quartets

Grades I–IV

(Collection)	*Quartet Repertoire*	Rubank, Inc.
(Collection)	*Trumpet Quartets*	Amsco Music Publishing Co.
(Collection)	*Trumpet Sessions*	Shawnee Press Inc.
(Collection)	*Trumpet Symphony*	Rubank, Inc.

Grade V

| Leidzen | *The Four Heralds* | Bourne, Inc. |
| Ostransky | *Dance Suite* | Rubank, Inc. |

Grade VI

| Dubensky | *Suite for Trumpets* | Charles Colin |
| Gillis | *Sonatine No. 2* | Boosey-Hawkes, Inc. |

Trombone Duets

Grades I–II

| Henning | *Twenty-Four Easy Duets* | Cundy-Bettony Co. |
| Tallmadge-Lillya | *56 Progressive Duets* | Belwin-Mills Publishing Corp. |

| Uber | Twentieth Century Duets for Two Trombones | Henry Adler |
| Voxman | Selected Duets, Vol. 1 | Rubank, Inc. |

Grades III–IV

Amsden	Practice Duets	C. L. Barnhouse, Inc.
Cornette	Six Concert Duets	Cundy-Bettony Co.
Uber	Ten Concert Duets for Two Trombones, Vol. 1	Edition Musicus
Voxman	Selected Duets, Vol. II	Rubank, Inc.

Grades V–VI

Bach-Miller	12 Two-Part Inventions	Ensemble Publications
Blume	12 Melodious Duets	Carl Fischer
(Collection)	Bass Clef Sessions	Shawnee Press Inc.
Dieppo-Ostrander	Virtuoso Studies for Two Trombones	Edition Musicus
Telemann	Six Sonatas	McGinnis & Marx
Voxman	Selected Duets, Vol. II	Rubank, Inc.

Trombone Trios

Grades I–II

| (Collection) | Bass Clef Sessions | Shawnee Press Inc. |
| Williams-Hudadoff | 24 Trombone Trios | Pro-Art Publications |

Grades III–IV

Frescobaldi-Fetter	Canzona I	Ensemble Publications
Mozart-Ostrander	Suite for Three Trombones	Edition Musicus
Simeone	Slide Kicks	Shawnee Press Inc.
Uber	Modern Trios	Edition Musicus

Grades V–VI

| Handel-Ostrander | Suite for Three Trombones | Edition Musicus |
| Uber | Manhattan Vignettes | Edition Musicus |

Trombone Quartets

Grades I–II

Arnold	Everybody's Favorite Trombone Quartets	Amsco Music Publishing Co.
Bowles	Four Folk Tunes for Four Trombones	H. T. FitzSimons Co.
(Collection)	Bass Clef Sessions	Shawnee Press Inc.

| (Collection) | *Quartet Repertoire* | Rubank, Inc. |
| (Collection) | *Trombone Symphony* | Rubank, Inc. |

Grades III–IV

Bach	*Sixteen Chorales*	Robert King
Beethoven	*Three Equali*	Robert King
Berlioz-Ostrander	*Excerpts from "Damnation of Faust"*	Edition Musicus
Muller	*Trombone Quartets*	Cundy-Bettony Co.

Grade V

Berlioz	*Rakoczy March*	Belwin-Mills Publishing Corp.
Laudenslager	*Preludes & Fugues for Trombone Quartet*	Cor Publishing Co.
Muller	*Twenty Quartettes*	Cundy-Bettony Co.

Grade VI

| Frackenpohl | *Trombone Quartet* | Ensemble Publications |
| Jacob | *Suite for Four Trombones* | Boosey-Hawkes, Inc. |

Tuba Duets

Grades III–IV

| Nelhybel | *Eleven Duets for Tuba* | General Music Publishing Co. |

Grades V–VI

| DeJong | *Music for Two Tubas* | Elkan-Vogel Co. |
| Goldman | *Duo for Tubas* | Theodore Presser Co. |

Brass Quintet

Grades I–II

(Collection)	*Festival Repertoire*	Rubank, Inc.
King (Ed.)	*Reformation Chorales*	Robert King
Schaeffer	*Five Brass Quintets*	Pro-Art Publications

Grade III

Bach-King	*Contrapunctus V*	Robert King
Gabrieli	*Canzona per Sonare No. 1*	Robert King
Pezel-King	*Sonata No. 22* and *Sonata No. 25*	Robert King

Grade IV

Couperin	*Two Pieces*	Robert King
Ewald-King	*Symphony in Brass*	Robert King
Purcell	*Two Trumpet Tunes and Ayre*	Robert King
Scheidt	*Suite for Brass Quintet*	Theodore Presser Co.

Grade V

Adler	*Five Movements for Brass Quintet*	Robert King
Ewald	*Quintet in B Minor*	Rubank, Inc.
Nelhybel	*Brass Quintet No. 2*	Galaxy Music Co.

Grade VI

Joplin-Frackenpohl	*Three Scott Joplin Rags*	Belwin, Inc.
Persichetti	*Parade for Brass Quintet*	Theodore Presser Co.
Washburn	*Quintet for Brass*	Oxford University Press

Brass Sextets

Grades I–II

(Collection)	*Brass Sextet Album*	Neil A. Kjos Music Co.
(Collection)	*Concert Repertoire*	Rubank, Inc.
(Collection)	*Festival Repertoire*	Rubank, Inc.

Grade III

Bach	*Contrapunctus No. 3*	Robert King
Franck	*Two Intradas*	Rubank, Inc.
Gabrielli-Shuman	*Ricercare Del 12 Tono*	Southern Music Co.
Pezel	*Three Pieces*	Robert King

Grade IV

Busch	*Prelude and Chorale*	Carl Fischer
Holmes	*Castilla*	C. L. Barnhouse, Inc.
McKay	*Prelude and Allegro*	C. L. Barnhouse, Inc.
Ostransky	*Suite for Brass Sextet*	Rubank, Inc.
Wagner-Gallagher	*Die Meistersinger (Prelude to Act Three)*	Boosey-Hawkes, Inc.

Grades V–VI

Dunham	*Sextet for Brass*	Boosey-Hawkes, Inc.
Ewald	*Symphony in Brass*	Robert King
Purcell	*Voluntary on 100 Psalm*	Robert King
Tschaikowsky-Tallmadge	*Capriccio Italien*	Belwin-Mills Publishing Corp.

Miscellaneous Sources for Brass Ensemble Music

King, Robert (ed.)	*Music for Brass* (Catalog)	Robert King Music Co.
Rasmussen, Mary	*A Teacher's Guide to the Literature of Brass Instruments* (Book)	The Cabinet Press, Milford, N. H. 1968

Snare Drum Duets

Grades I–II

Schinstine	*Drumming Together* (Collection)	Southern Music Co.
Schinstine	*Southern Special* (Collection)	Southern Music Co.

Grades III–IV

Bellson	*Six Solos and Four Duets* (Collection)	Sam Fox Publishing Co.
Firth	*The Solo Snare Drummer* (Collection)	Carl Fischer
Harris	*The Solo Drummer* (Collection)	G. Ricardi & Co.
Schinstine	*Drum Ensembles for All Occasions*	Southern Music Co.
Schinstine	*Four Hands A-Round* (Collection)	Southern Music Co.

Grades V–VI

Pratt	*Ancient Rudimental Snare and Bass Drum Solos*	Belwin-Mills Publishing Corp.
Schinstine	*Drumming Together*	Southern Music Co.

Percussion Ensembles

Grades I–II

Brown	*Percussion Studies Produce Ensembles*	Kendor Music Inc.
Feldstein	*Breeze Easy Percussion Ensembles*	Warner Brothers, 7 Arts Co.
Kinyon	*Percussion Ensembles for Young Performers*	Alfred Music Co., Inc.

Grades III–IV

Benson	*Three Pieces for Percussion Quartet*	G. Schirmer Inc.
Brown	*Percussion Studies Produce Ensembles*	Kendor Music Inc.

Feldstein (arr.)	*Mallets Go Latin*	Edward B. Marks Music Corp.
Ostling	*Suite for Percussion*	Belwin-Mills Publishing Corp.

Grades V–VI

Benson	*Trio*	Plymouth Music Company, Inc.
Brown	*Four Times Three*	Kendor Music Inc.
Delp	*Announcement for Percussion Quartet*	Kendor Music Inc.
Feldstein	*Variations on a Four Note Theme*	Belwin-Mills Publishing Corp.
Goodman	*Theme and Variations*	Belwin-Mills Publishing Corp.

APPENDIX D

SELECTED MUSIC FOR FULL BAND

Marches (Easy)

Bennett	*Activity*	Fillmore
Bennett	*Military Escort*	Fillmore
Buchtel	*Old Comrades*	Niel A. Kjos Music Co.
Finlayson	*Storm King*	Boosey & Hawkes
Goldman, Edwin Franko	*Parade March No. 1*	Edward B. Marks Music Corp.
Goldman, Edwin Franko	*Parade March No. 2*	Edward B. Marks Music Corp.
Huff	*Show Boy*	Fillmore
King	*University of North Dakota*	King
Kinyon	*Highland Park Festival*	Luverne Publications
Sousa-Buchtel	*Semper Fidelis*	Niel A. Kjos Music Co.
Sousa-Yoder	*Liberty Bell*	Carl Fischer

Marches (Medium)

Alfred	*Colonel Bogey*	Boosey & Hawkes
Chambers-Roberts	*March Religioso*	Carl Fischer
Farrar-Roberts	*Indiana State*	Carl Fischer
Fillmore	*Americans We*	Carl Fischer
Fillmore	*Footlifter*	Carl Fischer
Fillmore	*Lassus Trombone*	Fillmore
Fillmore	*Man of the Hour*	Carl Fischer
Fillmore	*Men of Ohio*	Carl Fischer
Fillmore	*Noble Men*	Fillmore
Goldman	*Jubilee*	Leo Feist
Goldman	*On the Alert*	Carl Fischer
Goldman-Lake	*On the Mall*	Carl Fischer
Hall	*The New Colonial March*	Presser
Hall	*Tenth Regiment*	Carl Fischer
Sousa	*El Capitan*	Church
Sousa	*Fairest of the Fair*	Church

369

Sousa	*The Gallant Seventh*	Sam Fox
Sousa	*King Cotton*	Church
Sousa	*Sabre and Spurs*	Sam Fox
Sousa	*The Thunderer*	Carl Fischer
Sousa	*Washington Post*	Carl Fischer

Marches (Difficult)

Bagley	*National Emblem*	Walter Jacobs, Inc.
Fillmore	*His Excellency*	Carl Fischer
Fillmore	*His Honor*	Fillmore
Fillmore	*The Klaxon*	Carl Fischer
Goldman	*Alouette*	Carl Fischer
Huffine	*Them Basses*	Fillmore
McCoy-Roth	*Lights Out*	Carl Fischer
Seitz	*Brook's Chicago Marine March*	Seitz
Sousa	*The Liberty Bell*	Presser
Sousa	*Semper Fidelis*	Carl Fischer
Sousa	*The Stars and Stripes Forever*	Church

Circus Marches

King	*Center Ring*	King
King	*The Trombone King*	King
Klohr	*Billboard*	Church

Spanish or Latin Marches

| Tarver | *El Charo* | Boosey & Hawkes |
| Tarver | *La Donna* | Boosey & Hawkes |

Valuable Football Band Materials

| Yoder (arr.) | *College Songs for School Bands* (Separate books for each instrument) | Edwin H. Morris & Company, Inc. |
| Smith | *Star-Spangled Banner* | Carl Fischer |

Composer	*Composition*	*Publisher*	*Difficulty*

Christmas

Anderson	*A Christmas Festival*	Mills	IV–V
Anderson	*Sleigh Ride*	Mills	III–IV
Anderson	*Suite of Carols for Brass Choir*	Mills	IV
Anderson	*Suite of Carols for Woodwind Ensemble*	Mills	IV

Bach-Richardson	*Sheep May Safely Graze*	Boosey & Hawkes	III
Beeler (arr.)	*Frosty the Snowman*	Hansen	II
Burden (arr.)	*Caribbean Christmas*	Charter Publications, Inc.	IV
Cacavas (arr.)	*Christmas Music for Winds*	Bourne	IV
Cacavas (arr.)	*Do You Hear What I Hear?; Snow Bells*	Pepper	III
Faith-Warrington	*Brazilian Sleigh Bells*	Cimino Publications, Inc.	IV
Frangkiser	*A Merry Christmas*	Belwin	IV
Giovannini-Robinson	*Silver Sleigh*	Southern Music Company	IV
Gould	*Adeste Fideles*	Chappell	III–IV
Gould	*Jingle Bells*	Chappell	IV
Grundman	*Three Songs for Christmas*	Boosey & Hawkes	III
Herbert-Cray	*March of the Toys*	Witmark	III
Kaempfarth-Mihon-Nowak	*Toy Parade*	Big Bells Inc.	III
Krance	*Prelude to Christmas*	Witmark	IV
Lang	*Yuletide Overture*	Mills	IV
Lillya	*A Christmas Fantasy*	ABC Standard Music Publ. Inc.	IV
Lowden (arr.)	*Great Songs of Christmas*	Big Bells Inc.	IV
Markham (arr.)	*Let It Snow; I'll Be Home for Christmas; Home for the Holidays*	Pepper	IV
Nestico	*Toboggan*	Kendor	III
Prokofieff-Walters	*Troika* (from *Lieutenant Kije Suite*)	Rubank	III
Reed	*Russian Christmas Music*	Sam Fox	V
Rossini-Respighi	*La Boutique Fantasque*	Chappell	V–VI
Schubert-Johnson	*Ave Maria*	Rubank	III
Walters	*Christmas Suite*	Rubank	III
Warrington (arr.)	*Winter Wonderland*	Bregman, Vocco, and Conn. Inc.	III

Concert Band

Akers	*Little Classic Suite*	Carl Fischer	I
Bennett, R. R.	*Suite of Old American Dances*	Chappell	VI
Bennett, R. R.	*Symphonic Songs for Band*	Chappell	VI
Bilik	*American Civil War Fantasy*	Southern Music Co.	V
Bilik	*Rhapsody on Russian Folk Songs*	Southern Music Co.	V
Bright	*Prelude and Fugue in F Minor*	Shawnee Press	VI

Cacavas	*Aria for Winds*	Bourne	III
Cacavas	*Ceremony for Winds*	Bourne	III
Cacavas	*Symphonic Prelude*	Carl Fischer	III
Carter	*Overture for Winds*	Bourne	IV
Carter	*Overture in E-flat*	Bourne	IV
Carter	*Proclamation*	Belwin-Mills	V
Carter	*Symphonic Overture*	Carl Fischer	IV
Chance	*Blue Lake*	Boosey & Hawkes	VI
Chance	*Variations on a Korean Folk Tune*	Boosey & Hawkes	V
Christiansen	*First Norwegian Rhapsody*	Witmark	IV
Davis	*Scotch Folk Suite*	Ludwig	III
Dedrick	*Design for Autumn*	Kendor	II
Del Borgo	*Chorale and Variant*	Alfred	VI
Dello Joio	*Scenes from the Louvre*	Edward B. Marks Music Corp.	V
Dello Joio	*Songs of Abelard*	Edward B. Marks Music Corp.	VI
Eberlin-Barnes	*Toccata and Fugue*	Pro Art	IV
Erickson	*Balladair*	Bourne	II
Erickson	*Earth Song*	G. Schirmer	V
Erickson	*Festival*	Belwin-Mills	I
Erickson	*Golden Gate Overture*	Bourne	V
Erickson	*Irish Folk Song Suite*	Bourne	III
Erickson	*Little Suite for Band*	Bourne	II
Erickson	*Overture for Billy*	Bourne	III
Erickson	*Rhythm of the Winds*	Belwin	III
Erickson	*Royal Armada*	Carl Fischer	V
Erickson	*Saturnalia*	G. Schirmer	V
Erickson	*Scherzo for Band*	Bourne	III
Erickson	*Second Symphony for Band–Finale*	Bourne	V
Erickson	*Tamerlane*	Bourne	IV
Erickson	*The Three B's*	Bourne	II
Erickson	*Toccata for Band*	Bourne	IV
Erickson	*Two Marches for Band*	Bourne	II
Farnon	*Portugal Em Festa*	Boosey & Hawkes	IV
Fote	*Niagara Overture*	Kendor	IV
Frackenpohl	*Allegro Giocoso*	Shawnee	VI
Frackenpohl	*Cantilena for Band*	Edward B. Marks Music Corp.	III
Frackenpohl	*Diversion in F*	Shawnee Press	V
Giovannini-Robinson	*Chorale and Capriccio*	Sam Fox	IV
Giovannini-Robinson	*Fanfare, Chorale and Fugue*	Southern Music Co.	IV

Giovannini-Robinson	*Overture in B-flat*	Sam Fox	IV
Gordon	*Andante for Band*	Bourne	I
Grainger	*Irish Tune from County Derry Shepherd's Hey*	Carl Fischer	V
Grainger	*Lincolnshire Posy*	G. Schirmer	VI
Gross	*Songs of the Sea*	Edward B. Marks Music Corp.	V
Grundman	*An American Folk Rhapsody*	Boosey & Hawkes	IV
Grundman	*An American Folk Rhapsody No. 2*	Boosey & Hawkes	IV
Grundman	*An American Scene*	Boosey & Hawkes	IV
Grundman	*The Black Knight*	Boosey & Hawkes	II
Grundman	*The Blue and the Gray (Civil War Suite)*	Boosey & Hawkes	IV
Grundman	*Fantasy on American Sailing Songs*	Boosey & Hawkes	IV
Grundman	*Irish Rhapsody*	Boosey & Hawkes	III
Grundman	*Kentucky 1800*	Boosey & Hawkes	III
Grundman	*Little Suite for Band*	Boosey & Hawkes	III
Grundman	*Spirit of '76*	Boosey & Hawkes	III
Grundman	*Three Sketches for Winds*	Boosey & Hawkes	V
Grundman	*Two American Songs*	Boosey & Hawkes	I
Grundman	*Two Moods*	Boosey & Hawkes	II
Grundman	*A Walking Tune*	Boosey & Hawkes	II
Grundman	*A Welsh Rhapsody*	Boosey & Hawkes	III
Grundman	*A Westchester Overture*	Boosey & Hawkes	III
Hanson	*Chorale and Alleluia*	Carl Fischer	V
Hermann	*Concord Overture*	Carl Fischer	IV
Hermann	*North Sea Overture*	Educational Music Service	VI
Holst	*First Suite for Military Band in E-flat*	Boosey & Hawkes	V
Holst	*Hammersmith*	Boosey & Hawkes	VI
Holst	*Second Suite for Military Band in F Major*	Boosey & Hawkes	VI
Hunsberger	*Folk Legend*	Sam Fox	V
Issac	*Russian Chorale and Overture*	Carl Fischer	III
Jackson	*Little English Suite*	Witmark	I
Jacob	*Concerto for Band*	Boosey & Hawkes	VI
Jacob	*Flag of Stars*	Boosey & Hawkes	VI
Jacob	*An Original Suite*	Boosey & Hawkes	VI
Jenkins	*American Overture for Band*	Presser	VI
Jenkins	*Charles County Overture*	Bourne	V

Johnson	*Golden Glow*	Boosey & Hawkes	II
Kinyon	*Appalachian Suite*	Bourne	II
Kinyon	*Songs of the Sea*	Alfred	I
Latham	*Court Festival*	Summy-Birchard	IV
Latham	*Serenade for Band*	Shawnee Press	IV
Leidzen	*Folksongs for Band Suite*	Summy-Birchard	IV
McBeth	*Chant and Jubilo*	Southern Music Co.	IV
McBeth	*Meadowlands*	Alfred	II
Meacham	*American Patrol*	Carl Fischer	IV
Morrissey	*An American Weekend*	Witmark	V
Morrissey	*Carnival Day in New Orleans*	Remick	V
Morrissey	*Four Episodes for Band*	Edward B. Marks Music Corp.	III
Morrissey	*Punch and Judy Overture*	Remick	II
Morrissey	*Songs for Band*	Edward B. Marks Music Corp.	III
Nelhybel	*Estampie*	Frank Music Co.	V
Nelhybel	*Festivo*	Franco Colombo Inc.	V
Nelhybel	*Russian Chant and Dance*	E.C. Kerby Ltd.	III
Nelhybel	*Tritico*	Franco Colombo Inc.	VI
Nelson	*Mayflower Overture*	Boosey & Hawkes	VI
Nestico	*Sleepy Village*	Kendor	I
Ostransky	*A Civil War Set*	Rubank	IV
Pearson	*Repercussion*	Volkwein Bros Inc.	VI
Persichetti	*Bagatelles for Band*	Elkan-Vogel Co.	VI
Persichetti	*Chorale Prelude: So Pure the Star*	Elkan-Vogel Co.	V
Persichetti	*Divertimento for Band, Op. 42*	Ditson-Presser	VI
Persichetti	*Pageant*	Carl Fischer	V
Persichetti	*Psalm for Band*	Elkan-Vogel Co.	VI
Persichetti	*Serenade for Band*	Elkan-Vogel Co.	V
Persichetti	*Symphony For Band*	Elkan-Vogel Co.	VI
Reed	*A Festival Prelude*	Edward B. Marks Music Corp.	V
Reed	*A Festive Overture*	Frank Music Corp.	V
Schuman	*Chester Overture for Band*	Theodore Presser Co.	VI
Schuman	*George Washington Bridge*	G. Schirmer	VI
Skornicka	*Overture Militaire*	Belwin	III
Skornicka	*Pastel Moods*	Belwin	II
Stainer-Righter	*Fughetta*	Schmitt	II

Vaughan Williams	*English Folk Song Suite*	Boosey & Hawkes	V
Vaughan Williams	*Toccata Marziale*	Boosey & Hawkes	VI
Walker	*Nineveh*	Kendor	IV
Walters	*Deep River Rhapsody*	Rubank	III
Washburn	*Burlesk for Band*	Boosey & Hawkes	IV
Washburn	*Ode for Band*	Shawnee Press	IV
Washburn	*Overture: Elkhart 1960*	Shawnee Press	VI
Whitney	*Bazaar*	Boosey & Hawkes	IV
Whitney	*A Foster Fantasy*	G. Schirmer	V
Whitney	*Holiday Tune*	Witmark	II
Whitney	*River Jordan* (Fantasy on Negro Spirituals)	G. Schirmer	IV
Williams, C.	*Fanfare and Allegro*	Summy-Birchard	V
Williams, C.	*Pastorale*	Summy-Birchard	IV
Williams, C.	*Symphonic Suite*	Summy-Birchard	VI
Williams, C.	*Variation Overture*	Ludwig	IV
Wood	*Mannin Veen*	Boosey & Hawkes	VI
Wood	*Manx Overture*	Boosey & Hawkes	VI
Wood	*The Seafarer*	Boosey & Hawkes	VI
Zdechlik	*Chorale and Shaker Dance*	Neil A. Kjos Music Co.	VI

Concert Marches

Antonini-Cacavas	*World's Fair March*	Bourne	IV
Barber	*Commando March*	Schirmer	V
Beethoven-Kinyon	*Turkish March*	Alfred	I
Berlioz-Erickson	*March of the Pilgrims*	Belwin-Mills	I
Berlioz-Lake	*Marche Hongroise (Damnation of Faust)*	Carl Fischer	IV
Cacavas	*Days of Glory*	Frank	III
Cacavas	*The Gallant Men*	Chappell	II
Cacavas	*The Sentry Boy*	Sam Fox	III
Coates-Yoder	*Knightsbridge March*	Chappell	IV
Goldmann R. F.	*Two Marches from Revolutionary America*	Music Press	IV
Handel-Strasser-Leidzen	*Slow March from Scipio*	Presser	III
Hanssen-Bainum	*Valdres-Marsi*	Boosey & Hawkes	V
Holst-Jacob	*Moorside March*	Boosey & Hawkes	IV
Kenny	*Coat of Arms*	Summy-Birchard	IV
Latham	*Brighton Beach*	Summy-Birchard	IV
Luthold	*March Onward*	Ludwig	IV
Mendelssohn-Lake	*War March of the Priests*	Carl Fischer	IV
Moore	*Marcho Poco*	Mills	III
Nelhybel	*Marcia Dorica*	Franco Colombo (Belwin-Mills)	IV

Nestico	*Vaquero*	Kendor	II
Olivadoti	*Hall of Fame*	Rubank	III
Olivadoti	*Our Glorious Land*	Rubank	III
Osterling	*Charter Oak*	Bourne	IV
Osterling	*Mustang March*	Chappell	IV
Osterling	*The Nutmeggers*	Bourne	IV
Pearson	*Minuteman*	Marks	IV
Riddle	*Profiles in Courage*	Shawnee Press	IV
Rimsky-Korsakoff- Leidzen	*Procession of the Nobles*	Carl Fischer	V
Rodgers-Leidzen	*Guadalcanal March*	Williamson	IV
Schubert- Laurendeau	*March Militaire I & II*	Carl Fischer	IV
Smetsky- Osterling	*March of the Spanish Soldiery*	Ludwig	IV
Sousa	*George Washington Bicentennial March*	Sam Fox Pub. Co.	IV–V
Sousa-Fennell	*The Black Horse Troop*	Sam Fox Pub. Co.	IV
Sousa-Fennell	*Golden Jubilee March*	Sam Fox Pub. Co.	IV
Tchaikowsky- Norman	*March from Tchaikowsky's 6th Symphony*	Staff	IV
Vaughan Williams	*Sea Songs*	Boosey & Hawkes	IV–V
Wagner-Lavalle	*Under the Double Eagle*	Stargen	IV
Washburn	*March and Chorale*	Shawnee Press	V
Williams, C.	*The Strategic Air Command*	Southern Music Co.	IV

Ensemble and Band

Anderson	*Bugler's Holiday* (Trumpet Trio)	Mills	IV
Bennett	*Tournament of Trumpets* (Quartet)	Carl Fischer	III
Burton	*Tropical Flutes*	Kendor	III
Cacavas	*Midnight Soliloquy* (Sax Trio)	(Pepper)	III
Christensen	*Beguine for Trombones*	Kendor	III
Dedrick	*Space Cadets* (Trumpet Trio)	Kendor	II
Del Borgo	*Canticle* (Flute Trio)	(Pepper)	V
Franceschini- Nagel	*Sonata for Two Trumpets*	(Pepper)	III
Robinson (arr.)	*The Flea* (Flute Section)	Sam Fox	IV
Simeone	*Flute Cocktail* (Trio)	Shawnee Press	V
Vivaldi-Lang	*Concerto in B-Flat* (Two Trumpets)	(Pepper)	V

Williams	*Three Bluejackets* (Trumpet Trio)	Morris	IV

Latin Rhythms

Anderson	*Blue Tango*	Mills	II
Anderson	*Serenata*	Mills	V
Benjamin-Lang	*Jamaican Rhumba*	Boosey & Hawkes	IV
Binge	*Red Sombrero*	Kendor	V
Bowles	*Rhumbah Numbah*	Belwin	II–III
Cacavas	*Matador*	Bourne	IV
Curzon	*Bravada*	Boosey & Hawkes	IV
Edmunds	*Lullaby in Latin*	Kendor	III
Faith	*Carmellita Tango*	Carl Fischer	III
Giacco-Osterling	*Latinette*	Belwin	III
Granados-Picket	*Danse Espagnole* (Jota)	Omega Mus. Ed.	IV
Haenschen-Cacavas	*La Rosita*	Sam Fox	III
Isaac	*Mexican Overture*	Carl Fischer	III–IV
Johnson	*Burrito*	Schmitt, Hall & McCreary	IV
Lecuona	*Bolero Espanole*	Marks	V
Lecuona-Beeler	*Malaguena*	Marks	IV
Mancini	*Tango Americano*	Leeds Mus. Corp.	III
Morrissey	*Martinique*	Remick	V
Nestico	*Montego Bay* (Samba)	Kendor	III
Osser	*Beguine Festival*	Leeds	III
Osser	*ChaCha for Band*	Leeds	III
Osser	*Tango for Band*	Leeds	III
Osterling	*Blue Mist Beguine*	Ludwig	III
Parera-Walters	*El Capeo* (march)	Rubank	III
Petersen	*Concert Rumba*	Luverne	IV
Porter-Krance	*Begin the Beguine*	Harms	IV
Reed	*La Fiesta Mexicana*	Belwin-Mills	VI
Schaefer	*Caribeguine*	Carl Fischer	IV
Tarver	*El Conquistador* (march)	Hal Leonard	V
Texidor	*Amparita Roca* (march)	Boosey & Hawkes	IV
Torroba-Beeler	*Gardens of Granada*	Marks	IV
Tucci-Hunsberger	*La Bamba De Vera Cruz*	Sam Fox	IV

Keyboard Transcription

Bach-Albert	*Chorale and Fugue in G Minor*	Schirmer	VI
Bach-Chiaffarelli	*Sleepers' Wake*	Carl Fischer	IV
Bach-Erickson	*Chaconne*	Bourne	VI

Bach-Leidzen	*Jesu, Joy of Man's Desiring*	Carl Fischer	IV
Bach-Leidzen	*Komm Sosser Tod*	Carl Fischer	II
Bach-Leidzen	*Toccata and Fugue*	Carl Fischer	VI
Bach-Lillya	*A Mighty Fortress Is Our God*	Carl Fischer	V
Bach-Moehlmann	*If Thou Be Near*	FitzSimons	III
Bach-Moehlmann	*Prelude and Fugue in B♭ Major*	Remick	IV
Bach-Moehlmann	*Prelude and Fugue in B♭ Major No. 2*	FitzSimons	IV
Bach-Moehlmann	*Prelude and Fugue in D Minor*	FitzSimons	V
Bach-Moehlmann	*Prelude and Fugue in F Minor*	FitzSimons	III
Bach-Moehlmann	*Prelude and Fugue in G Minor*	Remick	IV
Bach-Willhoite	*Gavotte*	Shawnee Press	V
Bartok-Gordon	*Children's Album*	Elkan-Vogel	II
Beethoven-Walters	*Adagio Cantabile from Sonata No. 8*	Rubank	III
Franck-Johnson	*Piece Heroique*	Carl Fischer	V
Frescobaldi-Gray	*Preludium and Canzona*	Mills	VI
Frescobaldi-Slocum	*Toccata*	Belwin-Mills	V
Holst (arr.)	*Bach's Fugue A La Gigue*	Boosey & Hawkes	VI
Jacob	*Giles Farnaby Suite*	Boosey & Hawkes	V
Jacob	*William Byrd Suite*	Boosey & Hawkes	VI
Palestrina-Gordon	*Three Hymns*	Bourne	II
Prokofiev-Leidzen	*Summer Day Suite*	Leeds	IV

Musical Comedy

Bart-Leyden	*Selections from Oliver*	Hollis Music Inc.	III
Bernstein-Duthoit	*Westside Story*	Chappell	V
Bock-Warrington	*Fiddler on the Roof Selections*	Valando Music Corp.	IV
Bricusse-Whitcomb	*Selections from Doctor Doolittle*	Hastings Music Corp.	III–IV
Cacavas (arr.)	*Selections from Applause*	Edwin H. Morris and Company, Inc.	IV
Coleman-Whitcomb	*Selections from Sweet Charity*	Robbins Music Corp.	IV–V
Edwards-Erickson	*Selections from 1776*	Schirmer	IV
Herman-Krance	*Mame (Highlights)*	Edwin H. Morris and Company Inc.	V

Kander-Leyden	*Cabaret Selections for Concert Band*	Valando Music Corp.	V
Kern-R. R. Bennett	*Show Boat*	Harms	IV
Leigh-Erickson	*Man of La Mancha Selections*	Sam Fox	IV
Lerner-Lane-R. R. Bennett	*On a Clear Day You Can See Forever*	Chappell	IV
Loewe-R. R. Bennett	*Gigi*	Chappell	IV–V
Loewe-R. R. Bennett	*My Fair Lady Selections*	Chappell	IV–V
Loewe-Leidzen	*Brigadoon*	Sam Fox	IV
Lowden (arr.)	*Selections from The Wiz*	Big Bells Inc.	IV
Porter-R. R. Bennett	*Can-Can*	Chappell	V
Rodgers-R. R. Bennett	*The King and I*	Williamson	IV
Rodgers-R. R. Bennett	*Sound of Music*	Williamson	IV
Rodgers-Cacavas	*Two by Two*	Williamson	IV
Rodgers-Lang	*Flower Drum Song*	Williamson	IV
Rodgers-Leidzen	*Carousel*	Williamson	IV
Rodgers-Leidzen	*Oklahoma*	Williamson	IV
Rodgers-Leidzen	*South Pacific*	Williamson	IV
Schwartz-Bullock	*Godspell Medley*	Valondo Music Inc.	IV
Sherman-Reed	*Mary Poppins*	Wonderland	IV
Styne-Merrill	*Funny Girl Overture*	Chappell	V
Sullivan-R. R. Bennett	*H.M.S. Pinafore*	Chappell	IV
Sullivan-R. R. Bennett	*The Mikado Highlights*	Chappell	IV
Webber-Lewis	*Selections from Jesus Christ Superstar*	Leeds	V
Whitcomb (arr.)	*Selections from Hair*	United Artists Mus. Co. Inc.	IV
Willson-Lang	*Selections from The Music Man*	Frank	IV
Woldin-Holcomb	*Raisin (Selections from)*	Big Bells Inc.	V

Novelty

Nestico	*Cable Car*	Kendor	III
Nestico	*Model-T*	Kendor	III
Velke	*Plaything*	Shawnee Press	IV

Walters	*Badinage for Brasses*	Rubank	III
Walters	*Waggery for Woodwinds*	Rubank	III
Yoder	*The Cricket and the Bull Frog* (piccolo and tuba with band)	Rubank	III

Orchestral Transcriptions

Bach-Frackenpohl	*Five Chorales*	Shawnee Press	IV
Bach-Gordon	*Grand Finale*	Bourne	II
Beethoven-Barnes	*Prometheus Overture*	Ludwig	VI
Beethoven-Cailliet	*King Stephen Overture*	Sam Fox	VI
Beethoven-Skornika	*Eroica Overture*	Belwin	III
Beethoven-Winterbottom	*Egmont Overture*	Boosey & Hawkes	VI
Berlioz-Safranek	*Roman Carnival Overture*	Carl Fischer	VI
Bernstein-Krance	*Danzon*	Harms	VI
Borodin-Leidzen	*First Movement from the Second Symphony*	Carl Fischer	VI
Copland	*Variation on a Shaker Melody* (from "Appalachian Spring")	Boosey & Hawkes	V
Corelli-Gordon	*Sarabande and Gavotte*	Bourne	III
Couperin-Milhaud-Walker	*Overture and Allegro from La Sultane*	Elkan-Vogel	VI
Debussy-Clay	*Golliwogg Cakewalk*	Elkan-Vogel	IV
Elgar-Slocum	*Enigma Variations*	Shawnee Press	VI
Frescobaldi-Johnson	*Galliard and Courante*	Rubank	III
Friedmann-Lake	*Slavonic Rhapsody No. 1*	Carl Fischer	VI
German-Laurendeau	*Three Dances from Henry VIII*	Carl Fischer	V
Gershwin-Krance	*An American in Paris*	Harms	V
Gershwin-R. R. Bennett	*Porgy and Bess Selections*	Chappell	V
Gillette	*Short Classics for Band*	Carl Fischer	III
Gluck-Barnes	*Paris and Helena Overture*	Ludwig	IV
Gluck-Cailliet	*Iphigenia in Aulis*	Sam Fox	IV
Gossec-Goldman	*Military Symphony in F*	Mercury	IV
Gould-Yoder	*Pavanne*	Mills	III
Gounod-Laurendeau	*Ballet Music from Faust*	Carl Fischer	V
Grainger-Bainum	*Spoon-River (An American Folk Dance)*	Schirmer	V

Handel-Anderson	*Song of Jupiter*	Mills	III
Handel-Gordon	*Fireworks Music*	Shapiro-Bernstein	II
Handel-Gordon	*Sarabande and Menuetto*	Edward B. Marks	II
Handel-Houseknecht	*Thanks Be to Thee*	Kjos	III
Handel-Osterling	*An Occasional Suite*	Ludwig	III
Handel-Osterling	*Sarabande and Bourree*	Ludwig	III
Hanson-Goldberg	*Symphony No. 2, 2nd Movement*	Carl Fischer	VI
Haydn-DeRubertis	*Orlando Palandrina*	Remick	V
Holst	*Mars (From The Planets)*	Boosey & Hawkes	VI
Humperdinck-Maddy	*Prayer and Dream Pantomine*	Remick	IV
Ippolitov Ivanov-DeLamater	*Procession of the Sardar*	Rubank	IV
Ives-Sinclair	*Country Band March*	Theodore Presser Co.	VI
Ives-Schumann-Rhoads	*Variations on America for Band*	Presser	VI
Liadov-Gordon	*Eight Russian Folk Songs*	Mills	V
Luigini-D. Bennett	*Ballet Egyptian*	Belwin-Mills	V
Lully-Beeler	*Sarabande and Gavotte*	Elkan-Vogel	IV
Massenet-Harding	*Meditation from Thais*	Kjos	IV
Massenet-Safranek	*Phedre Overture*	Carl Fischer	VI
Menotti-Lang	*Overture and Caccia*	Franco Columbo	VI
Milhaud	*Suite Francaise*	Leeds	VI
Mozart-Barnes	*Impressario Overture*	Ludwig	V
Mozart-Krance	*Overture to Titus*	Witmark	V
Mozart-Moehlmann	*Cosi Fan Tutti*	FitzSimons	VI
Mozart-Osterling	*Trauermusik*	Ludwig	V
Mozart-Slocum	*Marriage of Figaro Overture*	Belwin-Mills	VI
Nicolai-Laurendeau	*Merry Wives of Windsor*	Carl Fischer	VI
Offenbach-Issac	*Ballet Parisien*	Carl Fischer	V
Poulenc-Cailliet	*Les Biches*	Theodore Presser	VI
Prokofieff-Cailliet	*March and Scherzo (Love for Three Oranges)*	Carl Fischer	V
Puccini-Herfurth	*First Pucciniana Fantasy*	Ricordi	V
Purcell-Gordon	*Air and March*	Bourne	II
Ravel-Erickson	*Bolero*	Elkan-Vogel	VI

Rimsky-Korsakoff-Cacavas	*Cortege and Fanfare* (from *Snow Maiden*)	Satz	III
Rodgers-R. R. Bennet	*Victory at Sea*	Williamson	IV
Rossini-Cailliet	*Italian in Algiers Overture*	Sam Fox	VI
Rossini-Cailliet	*La Gazza Ladra Overture*	Sam Fox	VI
Rossini-Hansen	*Ballet Music from William Tell*	Ludwig	V
Rossini-Lake	*Barber of Seville Overture*	Carl Fischer	V
Saint Saens-DeRubertis	*Symphony in E♮ No. 1 (Finale)*	Witmark	V
Shostakovich-Hunsberger	*Festive Overture, Opus 96*	Leeds	VI
Shostakovich-Lang	*Polka from the Golden Age*	Mills	IV
Sibelius-Cailliet	*Finlandia*	Carl Fischer	VI
Strauss, J.-Nelson	*The Gypsy Baron Overture*	Forest R. Etling	III
Strauss, R.-Davis	*Allerseelen*	Ludwig	IV
Strauss, R.-Davis	*Die Nacht*	Ludwig	V
Tchaikovsky-Laurendeau	*Marche Slave*	Carl Fischer	VI
Tchaikovsky-Safranek	*Symphony Pathetique (mvts. 2 & 4)*	Carl Fischer	VI
Thompson-Erickson	*Fugue and Chorale on Yankee Doodle*	Schirmer	III
Wagner-Bainum	*Liebestod from Tristan and Isolde*	Kjos	V
Wagner-Cailliet	*Elsa's Procession to the Cathedral* (from *Lohengrin*)	Remick	V
Wagner-Fall	*Tannhauser*	Rubank	IV
Wagner-Leidzen	*Trauersinfonie*	Associated Music Publishers, Inc.	V
Wagner-Osterling	*Die Meistersinger*	Ludwig	IV
Wagner-Osterling	*Lohengrin* (excerpts)	Ludwig	III–IV
Wagner-Osterling	*Rienzi*	Ludwig	V
Wagner-Slocum	*Good Friday Spell*	Mills	V
Wagner-Winterbottom	*Tannhaeuser Overture*	Boosey & Hawkes	VI
Wagner-Whear	*Siegfried's Funeral Music*	C. L. Barnhouse	VI
Weinberger	*Polka and Fugue from Schwanda*	Associated Music Publishers, Inc.	VI

Parade and Ceremonial Music

Elgar-Lockhardt	*Land of Hope and Glory (Pomp and Circumstance No. I)*	Boosey & Hawkes	II
Ewell-Nelson	*Procession*	C. L. Barnhouse	IV
Erickson	*Ceremonial for Band*	Bourne	III
Frackenpohl	*Academic Processional March*	Shawnee Press	IV
Grundman	*March Processional*	Boosey & Hawkes	III
Handel-Goldman, R. F.	*March and Chorus (Judas Maccabaeus)*	Carl Fischer	IV
Meyerbeer-Eymann	*Coronation March*	Belwin	III–IV
Vaughan Williams-Rosenberg-Houseknecht	*Sine Nomine*	Carl Fischer	III
Verdi-Eymann	*Grand March from Aida*	Belwin	III–IV
Wagner-Eymann	*Processional March from Die Meistersinger*	Belwin	IV
Ward-Dragon	*America, the Beautiful*	Sam Fox	V
Washburn	*Pagentry*	Boosey & Hawkes	V
Williams	*Festival Prelude*	Southern	V

Piano and Band

Addinsell-Leidzen	*Warsaw Concerto*	Chappell	V
Grieg-Bain	*First Movement of Piano Concerto in A Minor*	Schirmer	V
Rodgers-Lang	*Slaughter on 10th Avenue*	Chappell	V

Popular

Alpert-Reynolds	*The Concert Band Sound of Herb Alpert & the Tijuana Brass*	Hansen	IV
Anderson	*The Penny-Whistle Song*	Mills	III
Anderson-Lang	*Jazz Pizzicato*	Mills	III
Anderson-Lang	*Syncopated Clock*	Mills	III
Bacharach-Cacavas	*Medley from Butch Cassidy and the Sundance Kid*	Blue Seas Music 20th Century Music Corp.	III–IV
Bacharach-Cacavas	*Popular Medley No. 1*	Blue Seas Music Hansen	III
Barry-Miller	*Born Free*	Screen-Gems Columbia Music, Inc.	II

Brubeck-Gearhart	*Natus: Drums*	Shawnee Press	IV
Cacavas (arr.)	*Great Themes from Great Italian Movies*	Marks	III
Cacavas (arr.)	*I Don't Know How to Love Him*	Leeds Music Corporation	II
Cacavas (arr.)	*Sounds of the Carpenters*	J. W. Pepper and Son. Inc.	III
Cacavas	*Theme and Rock Out*	Chappell	III
Ellington- D. Bennett	*Caravan Overture* (Caravan; Solitude; In a Sentimental Mood)	Mills	III
Ellington-Yoder	*Rhythm Moods* (Sophisticated Lady; Mood Indigo; Black and Tan Fantasy	Mills	III
Erickson (arr.)	*Walt Disney Overture*	Bourne	III
Giovannini	*Rondo Rococo* (Latin Rock)	Bourne	IV–V
Giovannini- Robinson	*Alla Barocco* (Folk-Rock)	Sam Fox	IV
Gold-Reed	*Exodus*	Chappell	IV
Green-Giovannini	*Black Magic Woman*	Bourne, Inc.	IV
Hawkins (arr.)	*How the West Was Won* (*A Western Fantasy)*	Robbins	V
Hayes-Lowden	*Selections from Shaft*	Big Bells, Inc.	IV
Hayes-Nowak	*Theme from The Men*	Big Bells, Inc.	IV
Holcombe (arr.)	*California Dreamin';* *Monday, Monday*	Pepper Sound Series	IV
Holcombe (arr.)	*The House of the Rising Sun*	Pepper Sound Series	IV
Holcombe (arr.)	*It's Not Unusual/Delilah*	Pepper Sound Series	IV
Holcombe (arr.)	*Lennon-McCartney Portrait*	Charter	IV
Holcombe (arr.)	*Sounds of Sonny & Cher*	Charter Sound Series	V
Jarre-Reed	*Lawrence of Arabia*	Gower	IV
Jarre-Whitcomb	*Themes from Dr. Zhivago*	Robbins Mus. Corp.	IV
Joplin-Cacavas	*Music from The Sting*	Mills	IV
Joplin-Nowak	*The Entertainer*	Big Bells, Inc.	IV
Karas-Cacavas	*The 3rd Man Theme*	Chappell	III
Ketelbey	*In a Persian Market*	Belwin	III
Krance (arr.)	*Broadway Curtain Time*	Pepper	IV
Lamm- Edmondson	*Chicago V*	Hansen	V
Leigh-Cacavas	*Hey, Look Me Over*	Morris	III

Lennon-McCartney-Schaefer	*Sgt. Pepper's Lonely Hearts Club Band Medley*	Charter Publications Inc.	IV
Lowden (arr.)	*Carly Simon* (You're So Vain; The Right Thing to Do)	Quackenbush Music Ltd.	IV
Lowden (arr.)	*Marching Up Broadway* (Cabaret; Hey Look Me Over; Consider Yourself)	Big Bells, Inc.	IV
Lowden (arr.)	*New Sounds of the Carpenters*	Big Bells Inc.	III
Lowden (arr.)	*Selections from Rocky*	United Artists	V
Lowden (arr.)	*Sounds of the Three Dog Night*	Big Bells Inc.	IV
Mancini-Reed	*Mancini*	Pennbeck	IV
Mancini-Warrington	*The Pink Panther*	United Artists	III
Nowak (arr.)	*The BBI Beginning Band Series*	Big Bells Inc.	I–II
Osser	*Italian Festival*	Leeds	III
Porter-R. R. Bennett	*Cole Porter Songs*	Chappell	V
Porter-Krance	*Night and Day*	Music Publishers Holding Corp.	IV
Porter-Robinson	*A Symphonic Portrait for Concert Band*	Chappell	V
Werle (arr.)	*An Ellington Portrait*	Belwin-Mills	V
Whitcomb (arr.)	*Chitty Chitty Bang Bang*	Unmart Music Corp.	II
Whitcomb (arr.)	*The Windmills of Your Mind*	United Artists Music	III
Williams-Burden	*Star Wars*	Fox Fanfare Music Inc.	V
Williams-Cacavas	*Jaws (Suite from)*	MCA Music	IV

Solo and Band

Anderson-Lang	*Trumpeter's Lullaby*	Mills	III
Barat-Marsteller	*Andante and Allegro* (Trombone)	(Pepper)	VI
Cavallini-Waln	*Adagio-Tarantella* (Clarinet)	Kjos	VI
Chaminade-Wilson-Wilkins	*Concertino* (Op. 107) (Flute)	(Pepper)	VI
Clarke	*Carnival of Venice* (Trumpet)	(Pepper)	VI
DeLamater	*Rocked in the Cradle of the Deep* (Tuba)	Rubank	II

Goldman	*Jupiter* (Cornet)	Carl Fischer	III
Handel-Nagel	*Baroque Trumpet Suite*	(Pepper)	III–IV
Kennon	*Night Soliloquy* (Flute)	Carl Fischer	VI
Llewellyn	*My Regards* (Trumpet/Trombone)	(Pepper)	III
Morrissey	*Interlude* (Clarinet)	Remick	IV
Morrissey	*Soliloquy for Trumpet*	Morris	III
Morrissey	*Swing Low, Sweet Chariot* (Trombone)	Mills	IV
Mozart-Fote	*Concerto in B♭, K. 191 (Rondo)* (Trombone)	(Pepper)	V
Pierne-Reed	*Serenade for Clarinet*	Shawnee	IV
Pryor	*Blue Bells of Scotland* (Trombone)	(Pepper)	V
Reed	*Serenade* (Clarinet)	Hansen	V
Staigers	*Carnival of Venice* (Cornet)	Carl Fischer	V
Vivaldi-Reed	*Concerto in C Major for Piccolo and Band*	Colombo	VI
Weber-Reed	*Concertino* (Clarinet)	Kendor	VI

APPENDIX E

SELECTED STAGE BAND CHARTS AND SOURCES

Grades I and II

Alfred's Convertibles Series		Alfred Music Co., Inc.
Alfred's Mini Jazz-Rock Ensembles for the Young Stage Band		Alfred Music Co., Inc.
Changeover, The	La Porta, J.	Berklee Press Pub.
Easy Jazz Ensemble Series	Nestico, S. (arr.)	Hal Leonard Music Inc.
Hangin' Out	Mancini-Lowden	Big Bells Inc.
Learnin' Stage Series		Theodore Presser Co.
Music for Young Jazz-Rock Ensembles		Studio P/R Inc.
New Music Reviews, Jazz/Stage Band (The Instrumentalist)		The Instrumentalist Co.
Sugar Beat	Fote, R.	Kendor Music, Inc.

Grades III and IV

Alfred's All-Pro Jazz-Rock Ensembles		Alfred Music Co., Inc.
Alfred's Jazz Rock Ensembles		Alfred Music Co., Inc.
Alfred's Stage Band Convertibles		Alfred Music Co., Inc.
Another Shade of Blue	Fenno, D.	C. L. Barnhouse, Inc.
Cast a Spell	Martino, R.	C. L. Barnhouse, Inc.
Chicago Hits		Columbia Pictures Publ.
Color Me Warm	Nestico, S.	Kendor Music, Inc.
Disco Lab Band Series		Columbia Pictures Publ.
Dixieland Series		Schmitt, Hall & McCreary Co.
From the Stan Kenton Library		Creative World
Front Burner	Nestico, S.	Hal Leonard Music Inc.
Funky Shuffle, The	Feldstein, S.	Alfred Music Co., Inc.

Getting Into It! Series		HSP Music (Belwin-Mills Publ. Corp.)
Intermediate Jazz Ensemble Series	Pemberton, R. (arr.)	Hal Leonard Music Inc.
Jazz Combo Series		Hal Leonard Music Inc.
Jazz Giants Series		Kendor Music, Inc.
Jazz Lab Band Series		Columbia Pictures Publ.
Jazz Rock in Our Times		Columbia Pictures Publ.
Kendor Specials for Jazz Ensembles		Kendor Music, Inc.
Lady in Lace	Fenno, D.	Hal Leonard Music Inc.
Lil Darlin'	Hefti, N.	Cimino Publications, Inc. (Vogue Music Co.)
Mancini Series, The		Kendor Music, Inc.
Midnight in Moscow	Lowden, R. (arr.)	Big Bells Inc.
Nestico Sound Series, The		Hal Leonard Music Inc.
New Dimensions Series		C. L. Barnhouse, Inc.
New Music Reviews, Jazz/Stage Band, The Instrumentalist		The Instrumentalist Co.
On Stage Series		Kendor Music, Inc.
Play-Easy Series		C. L. Barnhouse, Inc.
Pop Stage Band Series		Columbia Pictures Publ.
Prom Series, The		Kendor Music, Inc.
Queen Bee, The	Nestico, S.	Kendor Music, Inc.
Series 70		Hal Leonard Music Inc.
Sound of Rock, The		Alfred Music Co., Inc.
Steppin' in It	Hancock-Chattaway	Charles Hansen Music Corp.
Studio Jazz/Rock Series		Studio P/R Inc.
Studio Lab Band Series, The		Hal Leonard Music Inc.
Swingin' Stage Band Series		Hal Leonard Music Inc.
Take Care	Lowden, R.	C. L. Barnhouse, Inc.
That Warm Feeling	Nestico, S.	Kendor Music Inc.
Today's Pops		C. L. Barnhouse, Inc.
TSOP (The Sound of Philadelphia)	Gamble-Huff-Nowak	Big Bells Inc.
Warner's Jazz/Rock Ensembles		Warner Bros., Seven Arts Music Co.
You Are the Sunshine of My Life	Lowden, R.	C. L. Barnhouse, Inc.
You Turned the Tables on Me	Wright, R.	Sam Fox Publishing Co.

Grades V and VI

Back Bone	Jones, T.	Kendor Music, Inc.

Big Dipper	Jones, T.	Kendor Music, Inc.
Donald Byrd Jazz-Rock Series		Alfred Music Co., Inc.
Farewell, The	Jones, T.	Kendor Music, Inc.
(Part III of "Suite for		
Pops")		
Festival Series		Studio P/R Inc.
Love and Harmony	Bridgewater, C.	Kendor Music, Inc.
Meetin' Place	Jones, T.	Kendor Music, Inc.
"Name" Arranger Series		Studio P/R Inc.
New Music Reviews,		The Instrumentalist Co.
Jazz/Stage Band		
The Instrumentalist		
Old Devil Moon	Nestico, S. (arr.)	Kendor Music, Inc.
Primal Scream	Ferguson-Chattaway	Creative World
Thad Jones Series, The		Kendor Music, Inc.
That Old Black Magic	May, B.	Kendor Music, Inc.
Woody Herman Series, The		Hal Leonard Music Inc.

INDEX